S0-AZT-212

Prof. JAINI

(Home) 510- 524- 1438

THE CENTER FOR SOUTH AND SOUTHEAST ASIA STUDIES of the University of California is the coordinating center for research, teaching programs, and special projects relating to the South and Southeast Asia areas on the nine campuses of the University. The Center is the largest such research and teaching organization in the United States, with more than 150 related faculty representing all disciplines within the social sciences, languages, and humanities.

The Center publishes a Monograph Series, an Occasional Papers Series, and sponsors a series of books published by the University of California Press. Manuscripts for these publications have been selected with the highest standards of academic excellence, with emphasis on those studies and literary works that are pioneers in their fields, and that provide fresh insights into the life and culture of the great civilizations of South and Southeast Asia.

Recent Publications of the Center
for South and Southeast Asia Studies:

Kenneth E. Bryant
POEMS TO THE CHILD-GOD: STRUCTURES AND STRATEGIES IN THE POETRY OF SŪRDĀS

Frank F. Conlon
A CASTE IN A CHANGING WORLD: THE CHITRAPUR SARASWAT BRAHMANS

Karen I. Leonard
SOCIAL HISTORY OF AN INDIAN CASTE: THE KAYASTHS OF HYDERABAD

Leonard Nathan
THE TRANSPORT OF LOVE: THE MEGHADŪTA OF KĀLIDĀSA

M. N. Srinivas
THE REMEMBERED VILLAGE

The Jaina Path of Purification

This volume is sponsored by the
Center for South and Southeast Asia Studies,
University of California, Berkeley

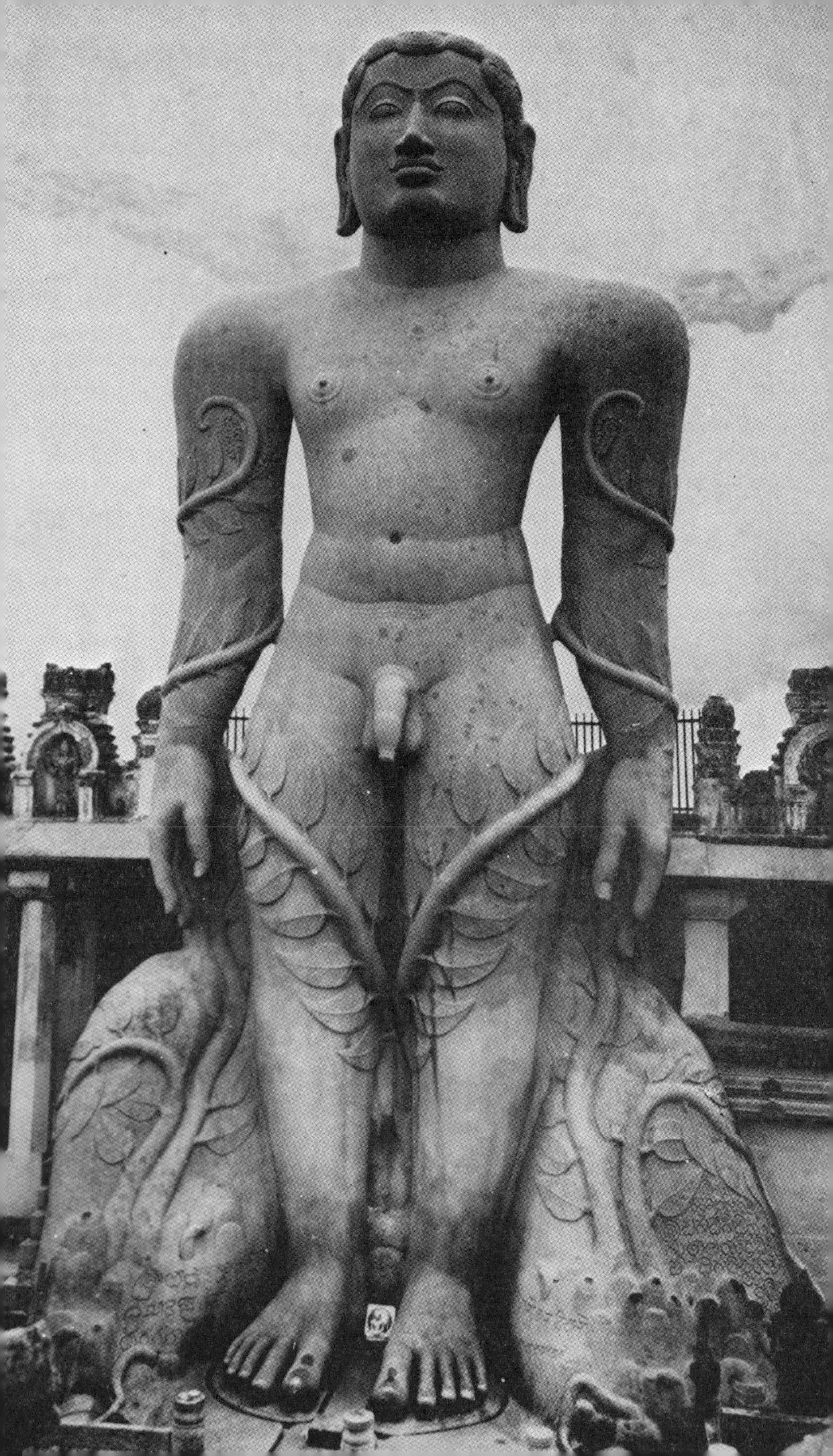

Padmanabh S. Jaini

The Jaina Path of Purification

University of California Press
BERKELEY · LOS ANGELES · LONDON

University of California Press
Berkeley and Los Angeles, California

University of California Press, Ltd.
London, England

Copyright © 1979 by
The Regents of the University of California

ISBN 0-520-03459-7
Library of Congress Catalog Card Number: 77-73496
Printed in the United States of America

1 2 3 4 5 6 7 8 9

to the Memory of My Parents

Contents

Illustrations

Preface

The great French scholar Louis Renou, in his 1953 lectures on the religions of India, observed that "the Jaina movement presents evidence that is of great interest, both for the historical and comparative study of religion in ancient India and for the history of religion in general. Based on profoundly Indian elements, it is at the same time a highly original creation, containing very ancient material, more ancient than that of Buddhism, and yet highly refined and elaborated."[1] These remarks are certainly well-founded; the Jaina tradition is not only very old, but continues to manifest a great number of those religious and philosophical elements which had already made it unique some 2,500 years ago. For various reasons, however, Western scholarship dealing with this tradition has never attained to a degree of development commensurate with the importance of its subject in the sphere of Indological studies.[2]

Among those works which have appeared on Jainism, the best-known are now unfortunately out of date. Jacobi's pioneering translations, for example, were first published in his two-volume *Jaina Sūtras* (1884 and 1895); these have recently been reprinted without any revision (1968). Another widely read book, Stevenson's *Heart of Jainism,* made its initial appearance in 1915; in spite of the clearly biased conclusions arrived at by its Christian missionary author, the work has been reprinted unchanged (1970).

1. Renou 1953: 133.
2. See my article "The Jainas and the Western Scholar" (1976a).

Two excellent German studies—Glasenapp's *Der Jainismus* (1925) and Schubring's *Die Lehre der Jainas* (1934, now available in a 1962 English translation entitled *The Doctrine of the Jainas*)—provide much useful information on various aspects of the Jaina religion; but these too have been largely superseded by recent research.

Only a few important studies focusing on Jaina materials have been published in the postwar era. Most notable among these are Tatia's *Studies in Jaina Philosophy* (1951) and Williams' *Jaina Yoga* (1963), both of which make original contributions to the knowledge of Jainism but deal with topics mainly suited to the advanced student. There remains, in other words, a definite need for a work that can introduce Jainism, not only as a religious tradition, but as a literary and sociohistorical one as well, to those with only a general knowledge of India and its major faiths. The present work is an attempt to fill this need.

Although doctrinal explanations have been kept as simple as possible, it has nevertheless been necessary to introduce a number of Sanskrit and Prakrit technical terms. Each of these is italicized and defined at the point of its initial appearance in the text; thereafter, the reader is referred to the Glossary of Sanskrit and Prakrit Words, wherein short definitions and page references for such terms are to be found. I have included a large amount of canonical and commentarial material, in the original languages, among the footnotes. This has been done to partially overcome the difficulty of finding such material in libraries outside of India. It is hoped that the passages thus made available will be of benefit to those specialists who wish to consult them.

It would perhaps have been impossible to write a book such as this without having had recourse to the great number of works on Jainism in Indian languages. In addition to such works, I have depended heavily upon information supplied by a number of esteemed Indian friends, most of whom are both scholars and followers of Jainism. Thanks are especially due to Brahmacāri Shri Manikchandra Chaware of the Mahāvīra Jaina Gurukula, Karanja, who was most gracious in helping me obtain large numbers of Jaina books and in providing learned elucidations of several obscure points of Jaina doctrine. I am also very grateful to Messrs. Kantilal D. Kora, Valchand D. Shah, Manikchandra J. Bhisikar, Prem Jain, Shashidhar M. Karnad, Thomas Peele, and Dr. Saryu Doshi for their assistance in obtaining suitable illustrations.

I wish to thank several of my colleagues, at Berkeley and elsewhere, for their encouragement and helpful criticism during the early stages of this work: notably, Professors Frederick Streng, Lewis Lancaster, and Stephen Beyer. I have also received valuable assistance from Mr. Joseph Clack, a graduate student in the Buddhist Studies program, both in organizing the material and in preparing the text. Without his enthusiastic cooperation the book would not have reached its present state.

Finally, I would like to thank Shashi, Aravind and Asha Jaini for their unflagging patience and support throughout the long period which was devoted to completion of this work.

P. S. J.

University of California, Berkeley
1977

Abbreviations

AdS	*Anuyogadvāra-sūtra* (*Suttāgame* edition)
AP	*Ādipurāṇa*
AS	*Ācārāṅga-sūtra* (*Suttāgame* edition)
BhS	*Bhagavatī-sūtra* (*Suttāgame* edition)
BJP	Bhāratīya Jñānapīṭha Publications (Varanasi)
JJG	Jivaraj Jaina Granthamālā (Sholapur)
JOI	*Journal of the Oriental Institute* (Baroda)
JP	*Jñānapīṭha-pūjāñjali*
JSK	Jinendra, *Jainendra Siddhānta Kośa*
JY	Williams, *Jaina Yoga*
k	kārikā (Sanskrit verse)
KS	*Kalpa-sūtra* (Suttāgame edition)
NNP	*Nityanaimittika-pāṭhāvalī*
NS-ADS	*Nandisuttaṃ Aṇuogaddārāiṃ ca*
RŚr	*Ratnakaraṇḍaśrāvakācāra*
SamS	*Samavāya-sūtra* (*Suttāgame* edition)
SD	*Sāgāradharmāmṛta*
SJP	Tatia, *Studies in Jaina Philosophy*
SM	*Syādvādamañjarī*
SMJVGJV	*Shrī Mahāvīra Jaina Vidyālaya Golden Jubilee Volume* (Bombay)
SS	*Sarvārthasiddhi*
SthS	*Sthānāṅga-sūtra* (*Suttāgame* edition)
TS	*Tattvārtha-sūtra*
TSPC	*Triśaṣṭiśalākāpuruṣacaritra*
UP	*Uttarapurāṇa*
UtS	*Uttarādhyayana-sūtra* (*Suttāgame* edition)

I

Mahāvīra and the Foundations of Jainism

It is August, 1955. On the holy mount of Kunthalagiri, in the state of Maharashtra in India, an old man called Śāntisāgara (Ocean of peace) is ritually fasting to death. He is the *ācārya* (spiritual leader) of the Digambara Jaina community; now, after thirty-five years as a mendicant, he is attaining his mortal end in the holy manner prescribed by the great saint Mahāvīra almost 2,500 years earlier. Śāntisāgara has owned nothing, not even a loincloth, since 1920. He has wandered on foot over the length and breadth of India, receiving food offerings but once a day, and then with only his bare hands for a bowl; he has spoken little during daylight hours and not at all after sunset. From August 14 until September 7 he takes only water; then, unable to drink without help, he ceases even that. At last, fully conscious and chanting the Jaina litany, he dies in the early morning of September 18.[1] The holiness and propriety of his life and of the manner of his death are widely known and admired by Jainas throughout India.

Who Are the Jainas?

The designation Jaina, applied to the approximately four million members of one of India's most ancient *śramaṇa* or non-Vedic religious traditions,[2] literally means "follower

1. For a detailed description of ācārya Śāntisāgara's last days, see *Sanmati* (Marathi monthly), Oct. 1972, Bahubali, Kolhapur.

2. Jainas have always claimed for themselves a degree of antiquity greater than that of Buddhism, the other important religion of this type. Their claim

of a *Jina*."[3] The Jinas are "spiritual victors," human teachers said to have attained *kevalajñāna* (infinite knowledge) and to have preached the doctrine of *mokṣa* (salvation). Such figures are also called *Tīrthaṅkaras* (Builders of the ford [which leads across the ocean of suffering]).[4] It is believed that twenty-four of them appear in each half of a time cycle,[5] have done so from beginningless time, and will continue to do so forever.

Hence a Jina or Tīrthaṅkara is not the founder of a religion; he is rather the propagator of a truth and a path which have been taught in the same manner by all teachers of his everpresent, imperishable tradition. Each Jina reanimates this tradition for the benefit of succeeding genera-

rests mainly upon an appeal to legendary materials; those few sources which do lend themselves to historical verification might allow us to push the date of Jainism to the ninth century B.C., but certainly no further. (For a more detailed discussion of the evidence available here, see nn. 16–19.) In any case, at this point the fundamental attitudes characterizing any group to which the rubric "non-Vedic" has been applied should be clarified. They are three in number: rejection of the scriptural authority of the Vedas, Brāhmaṇas, Upaniṣads, *Mahābhārata*, *Rāmāyaṇa*, and Dharmaśātras; denial of the efficacy of sacrifice; and refusal to accord any "divine" status to Brahmā, Viṣṇu, Śiva, or the great avatars depicted in the eighteen traditional Purāṇas. While ancient India abounded with various heterodox mendicant sects, only those which displayed this sort of pronounced antagonism towards brahmanical tradition received the appellation *śramaṇa*. For a discussion of the conflict between the śramaṇas and brahmanical society, see P. S. Jaini 1970.

3. In ancient times the epithet Jina was applied by various groups of śramaṇas to their respective teachers. Mendicant followers of what eventually became known as the Jaina tradition were originally known as Nigaṇṭha (Sanskrit Nirgrantha), meaning "the unattached ones." It was only after other śramaṇa sects using the term Jina (e.g., the Ājīvikas) either died out or simply abandoned this term in favor of another (as in the case of the Buddhists) that the derived form *Jaina* (Jina-disciple) came to refer exclusively to the Nigaṇṭhas. This seems to have occurred by around the ninth century, from which time inscriptions have been found containing the word "vardhatāṃ Jainaśāsanam" (may the Jaina teaching prosper). See Upadhye 1939. For Buddhist references to Nigaṇṭhas, see Malalasekera 1938: II, 61–65; C. J. Shah 1932: 5–7; P. S. Jaini 1976b; and n. 17 below.

4. Early Buddhist texts employ this term (*titthiya* in Pali) as the general (and derogatory) label for teachers of non-Buddhist schools; Jainas have themselves used it exclusively for the teacher-propagators of their own faith. Here the traditional Jaina definition is followed—in terms of which "Jina" and "Tīrthaṅkara" are equivalent. (Modern usage sometimes applies the former designation to any *kevalin*—any person who has attained kevalajñāna—whether he goes on to fulfill the role of exalted teacher or not.)

5. For a description of these cycles, see *SS*: §418.

tions. The teachings are neither received through divine revelation nor manifested through some inherent magical power (as, for instance, the Vedas are alleged to be). It is the individual human soul itself which, aided by the earlier teachings, comes to know the truth. Strictly speaking, then, worshipping or following the teachings of a *particular* Jina has no special significance; nothing new is taught, and the path remains always the same. Even so, it is natural that those teachers who most immediately precede the present age would be remembered more readily. Thus we find that the last few Jinas—Nemi, Pārśva, and especially Mahāvīra, final teacher of the current time cycle—are often regarded as *the* teachers and taken as the objects of a certain veneration. Recent activities in the Jaina community celebrating the 2,500th anniversary of Mahāvīra's *nirvāṇa* (final death) attest to this phenomenon.

Although the scriptures assert time and again that the Jina is a human being, born of human parents in the usual way, the Jaina laity is usually raised to regard him more as a superhuman personage. Certain fantastic attributes are popularly held to characterize the Jina-to-be. He is born with a special body, its frame having an adamantine (*vajra*) quality; such a body is considered necessary if he is to withstand the terrible rigors of meditation intense enough to bring salvation in the present life. As a psychic corollary to this physical aspect, he possesses supermundane cognition—*avadhijñāna*—by means of which he may perceive objects and events at enormous distances. Similarly, a fixed and rather stylized set of supernatural occurrences is said to mark his career. Although he has practiced the virtues requisite to Jinahood during several previous lives, he is not spontaneously aware of his impending attainment in the present one. Hence the gods, appearing miraculously at the appropriate moment, urge him to awaken to his real vocation and thus to renounce the household life. And whereas ordinary men require a *guru* for initiation into the spiritual life of a mendicant (*muni*), the Jina-to-be needs no teacher or preceptor. He renounces the world on his own, becoming the first monk of a new order. Upon attainment of Jinahood, he enters the state of kevalajñāna, from which there can be no falling away. At this point all normal bodily activities—eating, sleeping, talking, and so on—come to an end; the Jina sits, absolutely unmoving, in his omniscient state. And yet, as he sits there, a miraculous sound (*divyadhvani*) will be heard emanating from his body. Several *gaṇadharas* (supporters of the order) will then appear. Each will possess the ability to interpret the divyadhvani and thus to convey the Jina's teachings to others, answering accurately all questions pertaining to his path and doctrine. Finally, at the end of his life, the Jina sheds his mortal body and ascends to his permanent resting place at the very apex of the universe.

This, then, is the Jina ordinarily envisioned by the Jaina layperson. But in the sacred literature of the tradition we find a picture that conforms much more closely to the usual image of a saintly human teacher. With reference to the career of Mahāvīra, for example, there are numerous details of his daily life prior to the enlightenment: his family, his personality, the travails of the quest. Rainy seasons spent in different cities, encounters with heretical contemporaries, and various discourses to disciples, all following his attainment of omniscience, are likewise described. On the basis of such descriptions it is possible to construct a brief biography of Mahāvīra, most recent of the historical Jinas and of greatest importance to the shape of the present order. This account of the Jaina religion most appropriately begins with the great saint's life; for in considering what may at first glance seem the bare facts of an individual existence, the reader will discover ties with the prehistoric past, a fantastically complex cosmological system, and the seeds of controversies that have split the Jaina community for 2,000 years.

The Digambara and Śvetāmbara Schism

In recounting the story of Mahāvīra we are actually dealing with two stories, or rather with divergent narratives each purporting to accurately describe a single set of events. These conflicting versions reflect the positions of two distinct and virtually irreconcilable traditions within Jainism: that of the Digambaras (Sky-clad) and that of the Śvetāmbaras (White [cotton]-clad). This split among the followers of the Jina may have originated with the southward flight of one portion of the previously unified Jaina community in the face of a disastrous famine, circa 360 B.C.

Some sources suggest that a large group of migrants was led by the famous ācārya Bhadrabāhu into what is now Karnataka State (Mysore), where they resided for some twelve years. It is further held that Bhadrabāhu himself passed away before any return was possible, but that his followers did make their way back to Pāṭaliputra (modern Patna in Bihar State), only to discover that an "official" recension of the sacred texts had been prepared in their absence. Many points of this recension, codified under the leadership of Sthūlabhadra, were unacceptable to the recently returned monks; even more significantly, the "northerners" had taken up certain habits, especially the use of clothing, which the southern group found intolerable. Unable to effect any alterations either with regard to the contested doctrinal issues or to the "lax" conduct of Sthūlabhadra's followers, this group (later called Digambaras) not only declared the entire canon heretical and invalid, but proclaimed themselves the only "true" Jainas. Eventually they wrote their own *purāṇas* (legends), giving a history of Mahāvīra which often contradicted that found in the texts possessed by the other faction, the Śvetāmbaras.[6] Our story will attempt to reflect both versions, and to bring into focus the points of contention from which

6. The account given here of the Pāṭaliputra council and the subsequent schism follows main elements of the Digambara and Śvetāmbara description of these events. It should be noted that Śvetāmbaras do not completely accept the Digambara version of the migration incident, contending that Bhadrabāhu was at that time not in the south but in Nepal. They also maintain that the schism actually began in the 609th year after the nirvāṇa of Mahāvīra (A.D. 82), when an order of naked (*boḍiya*) monks was established by one Śivakoṭi in Rathavīrapura; members of this order supposedly became the

such important religious and social ramifications have developed.

Vardhamāna Mahāvīra: Legends Connected with His Birth

The word Mahāvīra, great hero, is an epithet, not the given name of the man to whom it is applied; but the universality of its application has rendered it functionally equivalent to a personal name. Tradition has it that this Jina-to-be was born in 599 B.C. at Kuṇḍagrāma, a large city in the kingdom of Vaiśāli (near modern Patna).[7] His father was one Siddhārtha, a warrior (*kṣatriya*) chieftain of the Jñātṛ clan; his mother, Triśalā, was the sister of the Vaiśāli ruler Ceṭaka.

Before a description of the birth itself, several important events said to have preceded it must be considered. According to Śvetāmbara sources, conception of the child was accompanied by Triśalā's witnessing of fourteen dreams (see pl. 4): (1) A white elephant; (2) a white bull; (3) a lion; (4) Śrī, the goddess of beauty; (5) garlands of mandāra flowers; (6) the full moon; (7) the rising sun; (8) a large and beautiful flag; (9) a vase of costly metal, filled with water; (10) a lake adorned with lotuses; (11) an

---

first of the "sky-clad" sect. (See Stevenson 1915: 70–80; C. J. Shah 1932: 67–74; Schubring 1962. §26–27.) Digambaras, for their part, claim that Bhadrabāhu migrated to Mysore together with Candragupta Maurya, first king of the Maurya dynasty, who had become a Jaina mendicant. It is believed that they both ended their lives in the holy manner on the site of modern Shravanabelgola. Numerous inscriptions in that area, dating from the fifth century A.D., lend some credibility to the account of a southward migration, though not necessarily to the fact that either Candragupta or Bhadrabāhu took part therein. (See B. L. Rice 1909: intro. 3–10; Saletore 1938: 4, n. 1.)

Certain Jaina sources (e.g., the Kannada *Vaḍḍārādhane* of Śivakoṭi, circa A.D. 1000) place the great schism not in Pāṭaliputra but in Ujjeni. They also indicate that final separation between the two sects occurred in Valabhi, when those monks wearing a single loincloth (*ardha-phālaka*) were required by King Lokapāla to become fully clothed in white garments; this group thus came to be known as Śvetapaṭa or Śvetāmbaras.

7. For the Svetāmbara accounts of Mahāvīra's life, see Jacobi 1884; *TSPC*: X (tr. Johnson); Boolchand 1948; Schubring 1962: §17–22. For the Digambara version, see *UP*: lxxiv–lxxvi; and *Mahāpurāṇu*: lxv–cii. For a complete bibliography, see H. Jain 1974: 41–45.

ocean of milk; (12) a celestial abode (a glorious house in the sky); (13) an enormous heap of jewels; (14) a blazing fire. To this list the Digambaras add: (15) a lofty throne; and (16) a pair of fish playing in a lake.

Jainas recall and re-enact these dreams even today when they celebrate the five auspicious moments (*kalyāṇakas*) of Mahāvīra's life: conception (*garbha*), birth (*janma*), renunciation (*vairāgya*), enlightenment (kevalajñāna) and final death (nirvāṇa). The dreams are also depicted in the sculptures and paintings which adorn the interiors of Jaina temples. They seem to allegorically portray the descent of Mahāvīra's soul into the womb from an exalted and heavenly abode. Such symbols indicate that he was destined to become either a universal monarch (*cakravartin*) or a great saint, a Tīrthaṅkara.

In the Śvetāmbara texts there is also an unusual prebirth episode, unknown to the Digambaras: a change of womb during the early embryonic period. This story maintains that the child was originally conceived by a brahman couple, Ṛṣabhadatta and Devānandā. But Śakra, king of the gods, found this situation unacceptable and transferred the embryonic Jina-to-be to the womb of the kṣatriya woman Triśalā; the baby she had been carrying was placed within Devānandā.[8] It is well known in the Jaina tradition, as well as in the Buddhist, that only a member of the warrior caste can become a "monarch," whether spiritual or temporal.[9] But this tenet itself reflects the underlying conviction that, contrary to the ordinary caste hierarchy

8. The actual transference was carried out by Harinegamesi, commander of Śakra's celestial armies. The antiquity of this legend is attested to by its representation in certain sculptures found at Mathura; these, depicting Harinegamesi as a goat-headed demigod, probably date from around A.D. 200. See Smith 1901. Also, see below, pl. 5.

9. . . . na eyaṃ bhūyaṃ na eyaṃ bhavvaṃ, na eyaṃ bhavissaṃ, jaṃ naṃ arahaṃtā vā cakkavaṭṭī vā . . . bhikkhāyakulesu vā māhaṇakulesu vā āyāyiṃsu. *KS*: §21. Compare: tato kulam olokayanto "Buddhā nāma vessakule vā suddakule vā na nibbattanti, lokasammute pana khattiyakule vā brāhmaṇakule vā dvīsu yeva kulesu nibbattanti, idāni ca khattiyakulaṃ lokasammataṃ, tattha nibbattissāmī" ti kulaṃ passi. *Jātaka*: I, 40.

which places *brahmans* at the apex, it is in fact the kṣatriyas who are highest. The rationale here is that a brahman must depend for his subsistence upon the gifts of others; he is thus placed in a lower position than the kṣatriya, who not only gets what he wants or needs in the world by his own power, but also supports the brahman out of his goodness and generosity. The brahmanical tradition, of course, rejects any such notion, and it is to the proponents of this tradition that the story seems addressed. Not only does it suggest that the great saint was born as a kṣatriya, but also that the opportunity for birth as a brahman was available and yet was rejected.

While this tale has been treated here as a pointed metaphor, the Śvetāmbaras consider it true; indeed, they sometimes list the time of embryo transfer as a sixth auspicious moment in Mahāvīra's life. One scholar has suggested that Devānandā was in fact a brahman wife of Siddhārtha, and that her child by him was foisted upon the kṣatriya queen to give it greater status.[10] This explanation seems dubious, however, in light of the strict rules that have always prevailed forbidding the marriage of a brahman woman and a kṣatriya man. Certain modern Jaina scholars have dealt with the problem by proposing that Devānandā was perhaps a wet nurse to the baby.[11] This view is given some credence by a famous scene in the *Bhagavatī-sūtra*, in which Devānandā, now an old woman, meets the fully-grown Mahāvīra. Milk flows from her breast at that moment, while he is heard to say, "This is my mother."[12]

A final important prebirth episode relates how, even in Triśalā's womb, the baby Mahāvīra displayed a highly developed sense of *ahiṃsā*, nonharming, the primary moral precept for all Jainas. He lay completely still, lest his kicks should cause his mother pain. Only when he

10. Jacobi 1884: intro. xxxi, n. 2.

11. Boolchand 1948: 23.

12. Devāṇaṃdā māhaṇī mama ammagā, ahaṃ ṇaṃ Devāṇaṃdāe māhaṇīe attae. *BhS*: ix, 33 (§380).

perceived with his supernatural knowledge that Triśalā feared him dead did he stir slightly to reassure her. Further, his awareness at this time of the ease with which parental concern is converted into mental anguish moved him to vow that he would not renounce the household life until both his parents had passed away.[13] This last point is not accepted by the Digambaras, who believe that Mahāvīra became a mendicant while his parents still lived, although he solicited and received their permission to do so. Both versions stand in sharp contrast to the description of Gautama's renunciation in the Buddhist Pāli literature, where great emphasis is placed upon the need to abandon the worldly life no matter how strong familial pressures to the contrary.

The birth was attended by numerous marvels: gods and humans celebrated, music filled the air, a general amnesty was proclaimed throughout the land. The prenaming rites were performed on Mount Meru, where the baby had been taken immediately after birth by the power of Śakra. Following the ritual bath and various auspicious rites, the child was named Vardhamāna, he who brings prosperity, apparently because his parents' wealth had increased markedly during the pregnancy. The name Vardhamāna was of course only the first of many to be given him: Vīra (Hero); Mahāvīra (Great hero);[14] Sanmati (Of excellent wisdom); Kāśyapa, his lineage name; Jñātṛputra,[15] his clan

13. tae ṇaṃ samaṇe bhagavaṃ Mahāvīre gabbhatthe ceva imevārūvaṃ abhiggahaṃ abhigaṇhai: no khalu me kappai ammāpiūhiṃ jīvaṃtehiṃ . . . agārāo anagāriyaṃ pavvaittae. *KS*: §91.

14. According to the canonical tradition, the name Mahāvīra was given to Vardhamāna by the gods in recognition of the fortitude and steadfastness with which he performed austerities: bhīmabhayabheravaṃ urālaṃ acelayaṃ parisahaṃ sahai tti kaṭṭu devehiṃ se ṇāmaṃ kayaṃ samaṇe bhagavaṃ Mahāvīre. *AS*: §998. A later tradition suggests that they gave him this name when, as a baby, he caused Mount Meru to tremble by pressing it with his toe: ākampio va jeṇaṃ Merū aṃguṭṭhaeṇa līlāe/ teṇeha Mahāvīro nāmaṃ si kayaṃ surindehiṃ// *Paumacariya*: ii, 26.

15. Prakrit Ṇāyaputta (or Ṇātaputta): teṇaṃ kāleṇaṃ . . . samaṇe bhagavaṃ Mahāvīre Ṇāyaputte Ṇāyakulaṇivvatte . . . *AS*: §1002. It is identical with the Pali Nātaputta. See Malalasekera 1938: II, 61–65.

name; and śramaṇa *bhagavān* [venerable] Mahāvīra (the Venerable Ascetic Mahāvīra).

Mahāvīra's Early Life

It should be noted that both Siddhārtha and Triśalā are described in the *Ācārāṅga-sūtra* as followers of Pārśva,[16] the penultimate Jina of the time cycle that Mahāvīra was to complete. The historicity of this Pārśva, who is said to have flourished in Banaras circa 850 B.C., seems definite. Buddhist texts refer to the existence of large numbers of Nigaṇṭhas (Unattached ones) who followed the *cātuyāma-saṃvara,*[17] the fourfold restraint that Jacobi and others have convincingly identified with the teachings of Pārśva.[18] Such references, moreover, suggest a Jaina community older than that of the Buddhists, hence predating Mahāvīra as well. This conclusion is based upon the fact that sectarian writings of the period were not ordinarily willing to grant "established" status to rival groups only then developing (witness the failure of Jaina texts to provide any mention whatsoever of the Buddha or his followers). The Nigaṇṭhas of the Pali literature, therefore, must have been members of a very ancient religious order.[19]

Little information is available pertaining to Mahāvīra's childhood. There is one story of how he subdued a terrify-

16. samaṇassa bhagavao Mahāvīrassa ammāpiyaro Pāsāvaccijjā samaṇovāsagā yāvi hotthā. *AS*: §1002. For an account of the legends surrounding Pārśva, see Jacobi 1884: 271–275; Bloomfield 1919; B. D. Jain 1925; Zimmer 1951: 181–204.

17. idha, mahārāja, Nigaṇṭho Nātaputto cātuyāmasaṃvarasaṃvuto hoti. *Dīghanikāya*: I, 57 (Sāmaññaphala-sutta).

18. See Jacobi 1880; also n. 32 below.

19. Jacobi seems to have been the first scholar to recognize this fact: "The Nirgranthas are frequently mentioned by the Buddhists, even in the oldest part of the *Piṭakas.* But I have not yet met with a distinct mention of the Buddhas in any of the old Jaina *Sūtras,* though they contain lengthy legends about Jamāli, Gosāla and other heterodox teachers. As this is just the reverse position to that which both sects mutually occupy in all aftertimes, and as it is inconsistent with our assumption of a contemporaneous origin of both creeds, we are driven to the conclusion that the Nirgranthas were not a newly founded sect of Buddha's time. This seems to have been the opinion of the *Piṭakas* too; for we find no indication of the contrary in them." Jacobi 1880: 161.

ing snake by means of his great courage and peaceful aura; beyond this, we know virtually nothing. It can be assumed that as a member of a royal household the child must have spent his time in mastering the arts suitable to the vocation of a prince: writing, mathematics, archery, and the like.

With regard to Mahāvīra's family life after coming of age, both traditions provide commentaries; these diverge along lines generally corresponding to those laid down in the controversy over the saint's vows *in utero*. Śvetāmbaras contend that the young man fulfilled all duties of the householder: that he married the princess Yaśodā, fathered one daughter called Priyadarśanā,[20] and, as mentioned above, continued in this role until both his parents had died. The Digambaras, on the other hand, believe that Mahāvīra remained a bachelor throughout his life (although they do not hold that this is a prerequisite to the attainment of Jinahood). In general, their version stresses his disinclination for worldly affairs from an early age.

Both traditions agree that when Mahāvīra was thirty years of age certain gods appeared and urged him to renounce the world; only thus could he fully develop the predispositions towards becoming a Tīrthaṅkara that had been fostered during so many previous lives. This encouragement of the Jina-to-be is customarily performed by a particular type of god called Laukāntika, world-ender; the designation refers to the fact that such beings are in their last birth but one (that is, that they will take human form and achieve *mokṣa*, release, in the very next lifetime).[21] Their words to Mahāvīra:

> Victory, victory to thee, gladdener of the world! Victory, victory to thee, fortunate one! Luck to thee, bull of the best kṣatriyas! Awake, reverend lord of the world! Establish the

20. samaṇassa bhagavao Mahāvīrassa bhajjā Jasoyā gotteṇaṃ Koḍiṇṇā, dhūyā Kāsāvagotteṇaṃ, tīse ṇaṃ do nāmadhejjā evaṃ āhijjaṃti: Aṇojjā i vā Piyadaṃsaṇā i vā. *AS*: §1001.

21. lokānte bhavāḥ laukāntikāḥ. te sarve parītasaṃsārāḥ, tataścyutā ekaṃ garbhāvāsaṃ prāpya parinirvāsyanti. SS: §489.

dharma-tīrtha (teaching of the holy path) for the sake of every living being in the entire universe; it will bring supreme benefit to all![22]

The Great Renunciation

Mahāvīra's renunciation is made much of in the texts; indeed, such an act engenders widespread glorification of the renunciant in Jaina communities even today. One reads that he was adorned with garlands by the gods, then carried on a palanquin in magnificent procession through the city and beyond it to a large park. There, accompanied by a great retinue, he descended from his seat and, beneath a holy aśoka tree, renounced all possessions. According to the Digambaras he removed his clothing and garland-ornaments and then, following the ancient tradition, pulled out his hair by hand; this final act indicates both an end of concern for the body and willingness to face pain for the sake of the goal. Having thus become "sky-clad" (totally nude), he abandoned the household life.[23]

The Śvetāmbara version of this event states that after arriving at the park Mahāvīra isolated himself and sat, fasting, for two-and-a-half days. Then still completely alone, he put on a *deva-dūṣya* (divine cloth) given to him by Śakra, tore out his hair as above, and set forth upon the mendicant's path.[24] It is further said that he continued to wear the deva-dūṣya for thirteen months thereafter;[25] at that point, the garment was accidentally caught on a

22. jaya jaya naṃdā! jaya jaya bhaddā! bhaddaṃ te jaya jaya khattiya-varavasahā! bujjhāhi bhagavaṃ loganāhā! pavattehi dhammatitthaṃ . . . *KS*: §110.

23. vastrābharaṇamālyāni svayaṃ śakraḥ samādade/ muktāny etāni pūtāni matvā māhātmyam īdṛśam// *UP*: xlvii, 305.

24. . . . āharaṇamallālaṃkāraṃ omuittā sayameva paṃcamuṭṭhiyaṃ loyaṃ karei . . . chaṭṭheṇaṃ bhatteṇaṃ apāṇaeṇaṃ . . . egaṃ devadūsaṃ ādāya ege abīe muṇḍe bhavittā āgārāo aṇagāriyaṃ pavvaie. *KS*: §114. The deva-dūṣya would appear to be a finely woven piece of cloth thrown over the shoulders: komalaṃ dhavalaṃ sūkṣmaṃ syūtaṃ candrakarair iva/ devadūṣyaṃ devarājaḥ skandhadeśe nyadhād vibhoḥ// *TSPC*: I, iii, 64.

25. saṃvaccharaṃ sāhiyaṃ māsaṃ jaṃ ṇa rikkāsi vatthagaṃ bhagavaṃ/ acelao tato cāī taṃ vosirijja vattham aṇagāre// *AS*: §465.

thorn bush and pulled off. Either Mahāvīra neglected to pick it up or he remained unaware of the loss until later, when the cloth had already been carried off by a brahman.[26]

The latter narrative brings to attention what is doubtless the single most important point of contention between the two traditions: *is a man who wears clothing truly a monk*? The Digambaras believe that Mahāvīra and the other Jinas were sky-clad at all times after their respective renunciations, and that anyone who claims to be a true follower of the Jina's path, a Jaina mendicant, must adopt the practice of nudity. The fact that Mahāvīra eventually became sky-clad even in the Śvetāmbara story does not alter the basic difference of *intent* in the two recensions. Whereas the Digambaras clearly show the renunciant purposely casting aside all garments, the Śvetāmbaras not only suggest that he wore clothes for a time but even that he may not have given them up voluntarily. Of course, they do not assert that the great saint was *attached* to clothing; after all, he never bothered to obtain a second garment. Indeed, one passage in the Śvetāmbara canon goes so far as to show Mahāvīra saying "I uphold the practice of nudity."[27] Nevertheless, the Śvetāmbaras maintain that he did not require his mendicant disciples to go naked. All of this is nothing less than anathema to the Digambaras, for whom the retention of clothing indicates the retention of shame; hence it constitutes a falling away from the strict renunciation of all possessions, internal as well as external, that is required of a Jaina monk. Of course a man who goes naked may still harbor a sense of shame; nudity alone does not make one a monk. But for the Digambara the use of any clothing whatsoever is an *absolute* indicator of residual shame and thus negates all pretensions to monkhood.

26. This narrative is found only in the commentaries and such later works as Hemacandra's *TSPC*. See Johnson 1962: 40ff.

27. mae samaṇāṇaṃ ṇiggaṃthāṇaṃ paṃcamahavvaie sapaḍikkamaṇe acelae dhamme paṇṇatte. *SthS*: §916.

The controversy is deepened by Śvetāmbara doctrine concerning the practices of Jinas other than Mahāvīra. Not only do they maintain that Ṛṣabha, first Tīrthaṅkara of the present cycle, went naked in the same rather haphazard or optional manner that Mahāvīra did (see pl. 1), but they hold further that the twenty-two remaining Jinas never abandoned the clad state. (It is even suggested that some of them wore decorative clothes of variegated colors.)[28] In the context of such a belief, Mahāvīra's practice of nudity can be depicted as a departure from the tradition of his predecessor, Pārśva. This theory is based mainly upon the Keśi-Gautama-saṃvāda,[29] a dialogue in the Śvetāmbara text *Uttarādhyayana-sūtra.* Here Keśi, a fully-clad mendicant-disciple of Pārśva, is discussing doctrinal issues with the naked monk Indrabhūti Gautama, chief disciple of Mahāvīra. The two consider certain differences in doctrine between their respective sects, especially those pertaining to the use of clothing. They eventually arrive at a compromise, concluding that external signs are of little consequence and function merely to help identify various groups engaging in particular practices.[30] The underlying implication of the dialogue is, of course, that since Pārśva is more ancient than Mahāvīra his teachings are in some sense superior; thus it is better to remain clad, or at most to have nudity as an optional practice. The Digambaras reject the

28. Devendra (KS: app. I, nn. 7–10) quotes the following in support of these beliefs: "acelatvaṃ" śrī Ādinātha-Mahāvīra-sādhūnāṃ vastraṃ mānapramāṇasahitaṃ jīrṇaprāyaṃ dhavalaṃ ca kalpate. śrī Ajitādiviṃśatitīrthaṅkarasādhūnāṃ tu pañcavarṇam. (*Kalpa-sūtrakalpalatā*); ācelukko dhammo purimassa ya pacchimassa ya jiṇassa/ majjhimagāṇa jiṇāṇaṃ hoi sacelo acelo ya// (*Kalpasamarthana*).

29. Jacobi 1895: 119–129.

30. acelago ya jo dhammo, jo dhammo saṃtaruttaro/ desiyo Vaddhamāṇeṇa Pāseṇa ya mahājasā// ekakajjapavannāṇaṃ visese kiṃ nu kāraṇaṃ/ liṃge duvihe mehāvī kahaṃ vippaccao na te// Kesim evaṃ buvāṇaṃ tu Goyamo iṇamabbavī/ vinnāṇeṇa samāgamma dhammasāhaṇamicchiyaṃ// paccayatthaṃ ca logassa nāṇāvihavigappaṇaṃ/ jattatthaṃ gahaṇatthaṃ ca loge liṃgapaoyaṇaṃ// aha bhave painnā u, mokkhasabbhūyasāhaṇā/ nāṇaṃ ca daṃsaṇaṃ ceva carittaṃ ceva nicchae// sāhu Goyama! pannā te, chinno me saṃsao imo// *UtS*: xxiii, 29–34.

authenticity of this dialogue, as well as the sort of compromise it explicitly suggests.

Indeed, the history of Jainism is rather remarkable for the almost total lack of doctrinal accommodation between sects that has taken place over the centuries, especially regarding the issue of nudity. There was only one apparent "compromise" movement, now long extinct, that probably flourished in South India circa A.D. 500. Literary evidence indicates that monks of this sect, known as Yāpanīyas, went naked in the forest but wore a single piece of clothing (*eka-phālaka*) when in populated areas.[31] They recognized the authenticity of the Śvetāmbara scriptures, and they propounded two doctrines traditionally acceptable only to Śvetāmbaras: that women can attain salvation and that the omniscient being partakes of food. The Yāpanīyas seem to have eventually merged into the larger Digambara community by which they were surrounded; their tendencies toward a more ecumenical Jainism died with them.

The Tradition of Pārśva: Cāturyāma-dharma

A second issue raised by the discussion between Keśi and Gautama has to do with the apparent difference between the "law of the four restraints" (*cāturyāma-dharma*) preached by Pārśva and the five great vows (*pañca mahāvrata*) taken by mendicant followers of Mahāvīra.[32] The affiliation of Mahāvīra's own parents with the tradition of Pārśva has already been noted, as has the existence of Buddhist materials which specifically identify cāturyāma

31. For various traditions concerning the origin of the Yāpanīyas, see Upadhye 1933; Premi 1956: 56–73; and n. 92 below.

32. cāujjāmo ya jo dhammo, jo imo paṃcasikkhio/ desio Vaddhamāṇena, Pāseṇa ya mahāmuṇī// egakajjapavannāṇaṃ, visese kiṃ nu kāraṇaṃ/ dhamme duvihe mehāvī, kahaṃ vippaccao na te// tao Kesiṃ buvaṃtaṃ tu, Goyamo iṇam abbavī/ pannā samikkhae dhammaṃ, tattaṃ tattaviṇicchayaṃ// . . . purimāṇaṃ duvisojjho u, carimāṇaṃ duraṇupālao/ kappo majjhimagāṇaṃ tu, suvisojjho supālao// sāhu Goyama pannā te, chinno me saṃsao imo/ . . . *UtS*: xxiii, 23–27. For a translation of this section, see Jacobi 1895: 119–129. For further details on the four vows and five vows, see Jacobi 1880; Schubring 1962: §16.

with this tradition. Whereas the Digambaras may reject the authenticity of the Keśi-Gautama dialogue, particularly with regard to its position on nudity, the Buddhist reference to cāturyāma forces them to confront the "discrepancy" between the teachings of Pārśva and Mahāvīra which this dialogue seems to express. The problem is rendered even more crucial by the Śvetāmbaras' use of this discrepancy to support their view that not all Jinas propound identical doctrines; once such variation is admitted, it is only a small step to suggesting that Pārśva need not have required nudity even if Mahāvīra did.[33]

Although Buddhists employ the term *cāturyāma-saṃvara* (Pali: cātuyāma-saṃvara) to describe the teachings of Pārśva, they fail to make clear exactly what the term entails.[34] The Śvetāmbara canon gives the first comprehensive definition. Here, the cāturyāma is said to involve restraint from four sorts of activities: injury, nontruthfulness, taking what is not given, and possession.[35] This list agrees with that of Mahāvīra except that it omits the fourth of his five vows, which specifically prohibits sexual activity.[36] But even the Śvetāmbaras have not been willing to suggest that Pārśva allowed his monks to engage in such activity; their later eleventh-century commentators Abhayadeva and Śāntyācārya interpreted the vow of nonpos-

33. . . . purimapacchimavajjā majjhimagā bāvīsaṃ arahaṃtā bhagavaṃtā cāujjāmaṃ dhammaṃ pannaviṃti. *SthS*: §329.

34. idha, mahārāja, Nigaṇṭho cātuyāmasaṃvarasaṃvuto hoti. kathaṃ ca . . . hoti? idha, mahārāja, Nigaṇṭho sabbavārivārito ca hoti, sabbavāriyutto ca hoti, sabbavāridhuto ca, sabbavāriphuṭo ca. *Dīghanikāya*: I, 57. The Pali commentaries suggest that the word *vāri* in this passage refers to water and thus explain the cātuyāma-saṃvara as restraint from the use of water (by a Nigaṇṭha mendicant). See Malalasekera 1938: II, 61. The Buddha is said to have also taught a kind of cātuyāma-saṃvara, in this case involving the four precepts against injury, stealing, lying, and unchastity. See *Dīghanikāya*: III, 48.

35. . . . cāujjāmaṃ dhammaṃ . . . taṃ jahā: savvāo pāṇāivāyāo veramaṇaṃ, evaṃ musāvāyāo, adinnādāṇāo, savvāo bahiddhādāṇāo veramaṇam. *SthS*: §329.

36. paṃca mahavvayā pannattā taṃ jahā: savvāo pāṇāivāyāo veramaṇaṃ, savvāo musāvāyāo veramaṇaṃ, savvāo adinnādāṇāo veramaṇaṃ, savvāo mehuṇāo veramaṇaṃ, savvāo pariggahāo veramaṇaṃ. *SthS*: §48.

session as including celibacy.[37] Even so, they imply that the slight difference in emphasis between the two sets of rules does leave open the possibility of variation from one Jina to the next.

Western scholars, following Jacobi, have generally accepted the Śvetāmbara interpretation and understood the cāturyāma as above, prohibiting four specific kinds of action.[38] The recent research of P. K. Modi, however, shows that this interpretation is subject to serious difficulties.[39] First, we should expect Mahāvīra, as a follower of the tradition of Pārśva, to have initially taken the same vows as his predecessor. Yet even the *Ācārāṅga-sūtra* of the Śvetāmbaras has him pledging only to follow a single great restraint called *sāmāyika-cāritra,* which entails avoiding all evil actions whatsoever.[40] Moreover, the term cāturyāma never appears in Digambara literature; Mahāvīra is invariably said therein to have undertaken the *sāmāyika-saṃyama,* which in the *Bhagavatī-sūtra* is shown to be identical to the sāmāyika-cāritra.[41] In light of

37. "cāturyāma . . . sa eva maithunaviramaṇātmakaḥ pañcavratasahitaḥ . . ." Quoted from Modi in *Pāsaṇāhacariu*: intro. 47 (from Śāntyācārya's commentary on the *UtS.*).

38. For example, Renou (1953: 115): "Mahāvīra seems to have developed the ethical aspect of Jainism by introducing a fifth axiom which brought a modification in the import of the fourth . . . Finally, it was he who required his monks to dispense with clothing, setting an example himself, whereas Pārśva's monks were clothed." Jacobi's rather pro-Śvetāmbara views on both the cāturyāma and the issue of nudity generated a good deal of heated discussion between followers of the two Jaina sects. The Śvetāmbara and Digambara positions in this interesting dispute have been set forth, respectively, by P. C. Nahar 1929, 1930, and K. P. Jain 1930.

39. Modi's ed. (1965) of the *Pāsaṇāhacariu*: intro. 46–53.

40. tao ṇaṃ samaṇe bhagavaṃ Mahāvīre . . . paṃcamuṭṭhiyaṃ loyaṃ karettā siddhāṇaṃ namokkāraṃ karei, karettā savvaṃ me akaraṇijjaṃ pāvakammaṃ ti kaṭṭu sāmāyiaṃ carittaṃ paḍivajjai. *AS*: §1013. Jacobi (1884: 198) seems to have gone wrong here by translating sāmāyika simply as "holy"; failing to understand the technical meaning of the term, he was unable to see its wider implications. See P. S. Jaini 1976a.

41. Modi quotes the following passages from the Digambara text *Mūlācāra*: virado savvasāvajjaṃ tigutto pihitiṃdiyo/ jīvo sāmāiyaṃ ṇāma saṃjamaṭṭhāṇam uttamaṃ// vii, 23. Compare: sāmāiyammi u kae cāujjāmaṃ aṇuttaraṃ dhammaṃ/ tivaheṇa phāsayaṃto sāmāiyasaṃjao sa khalu// *BhS*: xxv, 7, 1 (§785).

these facts, Modi has suggested that cāturyāma did not imply four *vows* at all, but rather the four *modalities* (mind, body, speech, and the senses) through which evil could be expressed.[42] Thus, he concludes, both Pārśva and Mahāvīra practiced and taught the same, single, all-encompassing sāmāyika restraint, while the five vows that Mahāvīra set forth are no more than a specification of the main areas of conduct to which this restraint applied. Whether or not any variation of doctrine between Jinas is possible remains an open question; in any case, the "cāturyāma evidence" so often used in support of such a possibility can no longer be considered particularly significant.

Addressing the issue of nudity more directly, the Śvetāmbaras have cited passages from the Buddhist Pali texts that talk of certain "*eka-śāṭaka*" (one-cloth) Nigaṇṭhas;[43] this is taken as testimony to the clothed state of at least some Jaina monks in Mahāvīra's time. The Digambaras interpret this admittedly unbiased evidence as referring simply to certain laymen who progressively renounce their possessions while continuing in the household life.[44] This sort of renunciation involves eleven stages (*pratimā*); in the final stage, called *ailaka* (perhaps Prakrit for *acelaka*, unclothed), the aspirant retains only one piece of clothing.[45] Such "progressive renunciants" are found in the Digambara community even today. They take no "great" vows (mahāvrata) and thus technically remain householders until such time as these vows, which go hand in hand with complete nudity, are taken. Digambaras further cite a passage from the Śvetāmbaras' own *Ācārāṅga-sūtra* in support of their position. This passage states that weak men, who cannot tolerate going sky-clad but wish to practice fasting and other virtuous activities, should do so

42. Compare: cauvvihe saṃjame paṇṇatte taṃ jahā: maṇasaṃjame, vaisaṃjame, kāyasaṃjame, uvagaraṇasaṃjame. *SthS*: §385.
43. *Aṅguttaranikāya*: III, 384.
44. K. P. Jain quotes *SD*: vii, 38, 48.
45. See below, ch. VI n. 54.

while continuing to wear clothing.[46] The Digambaras wish to identify the "clothed Nigaṇṭhas" of the Buddhist sources with these "weak" practitioners—whom they regard as engaged in beneficial but not mokṣa-producing activities.[47] Even some of their own books, such as *Mūlācāra*, seem to support such modified practices in certain unusual cases.[48] But to suggest that these practices are legitimate for *all* monks, as well as for a Tīrthaṅkara, is of course unacceptable to them.

Modern scholars tend to favor the Śvetāmbara contention that followers of Pārśva did wear clothes while those of Mahāvīra did not.[49] Some have suggested that Mahāvīra instituted the practices of nudity as a result of meeting with and being influenced by the naked ascetic Makkhali Gosāla, eventually leader of the Ājīvika school. There is an apparent correspondence in time between their meeting and Mahāvīra's "loss" of his garment. It has been held that this is too great a coincidence to ignore;[50] but this contention is somewhat weakened by the fact that the Ājīvikas were far from being the only mendicant sect of that period given to nudity. Furthermore, the canonical description of the first encounter between the two men shows Gosāla as a clothed householder who threw away his garments and

46. je bhikkhū acele parivusie tassa ṇaṃ evaṃ bhavai: cāemi ahaṃ taṇaphāsaṃ . . . siyaphāsaṃ . . . teuphāsaṃ . . . ahiyāsaettae . . . hiripaḍicchādaṇaṃ ca'haṃ no saṃcāemi ahiyāsettae. evaṃ se kappai kaḍibaṃdhaṇaṃ dhārittae. *AS*: §433.

47. K. P. Jain 1928: 61ff.

48. Compare: āryikāṇām āgame anujñātaṃ vastraṃ, kāraṇāpekṣayā bhikṣūṇām. hrīmān ayogyaśarīrāvayavo duścarmābhilambamānabījo vā parīṣahasahane vā akṣamaḥ sa gṛhṇāti. *Mūlācāra* [*Vijayodayā-ṭīkā*] 427. Premi (1956: 63) is of the opinion that the *Mūlācāra* was originally a text of the Yāpanīya sect.

49. For example, see Weber (1958: 196): "The severity of the flight from the world appears to have varied. According to the tradition, it must have increased; originally it entailed neither absolute lack of possessions nor unconditional chastity. It is controversial which of the two forms was introduced at a later time as an absolute commandment. As this supplementary introduction is ascribed to Mahāvīra, in contrast to the milder commandments of the penultimate tīrthankara, it is identical with the formation of the order of monks itself."

50. Ghatge, quoted by Deo (1956: 75): ". . . some significance must be attached to the coincidence of Mahāvīra giving up his garment in the year of his meeting with Gosāla."

begged Mahāvīra to take him as a disciple.[51] The whole problem of this and other contacts between these teachers is of great interest to the study of both doctrine and practice in Jainism; we shall have reason to return to it shortly.

In the final analysis, Digambaras have shown very little interest in such academic discussions. Śvetāmbaras have traditionally recognized two sorts of monks, the *jinakalpin* (who follows Mahāvīra's example and lives alone, naked, in the forest) and the *sthavirakalpin* (who lives clothed and in an ecclesiastical community), and have considered both practices equally valid paths to salvation; but all such distinctions are heretical and even blasphemous to the Digambaras.[52] For them, nudity remains *the* necessary condition for mokṣa; hence they denounce Śvetāmbara mendicants as false Jainas (*Jainābhāsa*).

On this level, the level of faith and practice, matters of textual criticism and scholarly research have had negligible impact. Thus the two sects have remained generally indifferent to one another through the ages; there have been no joint councils and few cordial meetings of monks. Encounters between the two laities have been purely for the purpose of disputation; indeed, it is only recently that leaders of the long-estranged communities have begun to suggest that, in light of the Jainas' extreme minority position in India, certain joint activities might be valuable. Thus far these have been restricted to shared celebration of the auspicious moments in Mahāvīra's career. It remains to be seen whether such efforts will be fruitful in healing a rift of two millennia. When such factors are considered as the continuing Digambara claim that the Śvetāmbara scriptures are totally inauthentic, or the still prevalent Śvetām-

51. sāḍiyāo ya pāḍiyāo ya kuṇḍiyāo ya pahāṇāo ya cittaphalagaṃ ya māhaṇe āyāmettā . . . *BhS*: xv, §540. See Basham 1951: 40.

52. The Digambaras recognize these two categories of monks but maintain that both must adhere to the vow of nudity: "jinā iva viharantīti jinakalpikā eka evety atiśayo jinakalpikānām. itaro liṅgādir ācāraḥ prāyeṇa vyāvarṇitarūpa eva." Quoted in *JSK*: II, 329. For the Śvetāmbara view, see Caillat 1968: 94–95, n. 22–23.

bara practice of marking the lips, eyes, and torsos of naked Jina-images (even those of Mahāvīra) in their temples, thus "clothing" them and making it impossible for Digambaras to worship there, it must be admitted that a full-fledged reconciliation may not be forthcoming in the near future.

Mahāvīra's Encounters with Makkhali Gosāla

To return to Mahāvīra's postrenunciation career, both traditions have him wandering from place to place for twelve years, engaging with grim determination in severe penances. The most important of these voluntary mortifications involved complete fasting—abstaining from water as well as food, sometimes for as long as a week. The epithet *dīgha-tapassī* (he who engages in extended penances), which is applied to Nigaṇṭhas in the Buddhist texts, probably alludes to this sort of fasting.[53] The practice has made an indelible impression upon the Jaina psyche; even today many of the Jina's followers, from children to the elderly, occasionally undertake long waterless fasts as a major expression of the holy life. This emphasis upon fasting, more than any other single factor, distinguishes the religious practice of the Jaina layperson from that of the Hindu communities which surround him. Jaina monks undergo such fasts as a common and regular aspect of their daily existence.

The Digambaras have a tradition that Mahāvīra observed a vow of silence during these twelve years as a wanderer. Since silence is not a prerequisite to the saintly life even for Digambaras, we may well be justified in regarding this notion as a sectarian device aimed at denying certain episodes found in the Śvetāmbara version of the same period. Of greatest import here are several stories, to which we have alluded earlier, involving Mahāvīra and the Ājīvika Makkhali Gosāla. Gosāla was by profession a

53. tena kho pana samayena Nigaṇṭho Nātaputto Nāḷandāyaṃ paṭivasati mahatiyā Nigaṇṭhaparisāya saddhiṃ. atha kho Dīghatapassī Nigaṇṭho . . . yena bhagavā ten' upasaṅkami . . . *Majjhimanikāya*: I, 371 (Upāli-sutta).

bard, spinning tales and showing pictures for the entertainment of local audiences. He was the follower of an old, established Ājīvika sect; eventually he came to be regarded as the leader of this sect and as the chief spokesman of the "fatalist" doctrines to which it adhered.

According to the *Vyākhyāprajñapti* (also known as the *Bhagavatī-sūtra*),[54] a prominent Śvetāmbara scripture, Gosāla heard tales of Mahāvīra's miraculous powers, particularly his uncanny accuracy in prognostication; wishing to come into contact with such powers himself, the Ājīvika came to the future Jina and asked to become a disciple. It is further related that the two spent six years together. On one occasion Mahāvīra displayed his yogic prowess to his companion, when they came across a heretical brahman ascetic named Vesiyāyana, who was doing penance by fasting and sitting with hands upraised to the sun for several days. He was covered with lice but was too compassionate to hurt them. Gosāla taunted him, saying, "Are you a muni (sage), or a host for lice?" When this insult was uttered a second time, Vesiyāyana became enraged; stepping back eight paces, he released in Gosāla's direction the magical heat which he had accumulated through long yogic practice. But Mahāvīra quickly neutralized the effects of this deadly heat with a cooling emanation of his own. The brahman recognized that he was no match for Mahāvīra.

Gosāla begged to be given the secret of such power. Granting his request, Mahāvīra described the six-month penance required for accomplishment of the goal. Gosāla then left his teacher and pursued his own career; eventually, through the practices that Mahāvīra had taught him, he attained great yogic powers and proclaimed himself a Jina. It is said that he made his headquarters in Śrāvastī at the workshop of the potter woman Hālāhalā, with whom he lived under compromising circumstances. There he spent his time codifying the Ājīvika scriptures

54. *BhS*: xv. For a complete account, see Basham 1951: 39–79.

and mounting polemics against all rivals, even his former companion and instructor.

Makkhali Gosāla has one other important part to play in the life of Mahāvīra. To observe this we must go ahead of the story for a moment to a time long after Mahāvīra's enlightenment, when the Jina felt it necessary to make public the history of his relation with the Ājīvika leader and to show the latter's claim to Jinahood for the sham it was. Gosāla reacted to this "slander" with verbal threats against Mahāvīra's life. When this produced no effect beyond the refusal of Jainas to associate with Ājīvikas, he sought out and reviled Mahāvīra, even using his magic powers to incinerate two of the Jina's disciples when they tried to oppose him. Finally he turned his power on Mahāvīra himself, accompanying it with a curse: "You are now pervaded by my magic forces, and within six months you will die of a fever."[55] But Mahāvīra's superiority and purity protected him; although he did become ill, he was able to cure himself.[56] As for Gosāla, it is said that the evil

55. tumaṃ ṇaṃ āuso Kāsavā, mamaṃ taveṇaṃ teeṇaṃ annāiṭṭhe samāṇe anto chaṇhaṃ māsāṇaṃ pittajjaraparigayasarīre dāhāvakkaṃtīe chaumatthe ceva kālaṃ karessasi. *BhS*: xv, §552.

Even Śvetāmbaras have difficulty in dealing with this particular episode. They have traditionally shared with Digambaras a belief that the area surrounding a Tīrthaṅkara is pervaded by peace and good feeling; to accommodate this belief with an acceptance of the kind of malice and death manifested in the story is no easy task. Hence they classify the whole occurrence as an extraordinary thing (*āścarya*), an unheard of calamity (*upasarga*), an event so astonishing that it could happen only once in billions of years. In fact the Śvetāmbaras have noted altogether ten such events described in their scriptures. Of the remaining nine, two are points of great controversy with the Digambaras, who of course reject them completely: the transfer of embryo episode (see above, n. 8) and the attainment of Tīrthaṅkara status by a woman (see below, n. 93). A list of all ten āścaryas is given in the *SthS*: §777.

It should be noted here that the Digambaras have a similar belief, subsumed under the doctrine of *huṇḍāvasarpiṇī*. This designates a period during which there may occur certain extraordinary events, for example, a calamity befalling a Tīrthaṅkara. The *Tiloyopaṇṇatti* (k 1615–1623), in which this topic is discussed, informs us that the current avasarpiṇī falls into the *huṇḍa* category, but the text remains silent on whether or not any untoward events actually affected Mahāvīra himself. See *JSK*: II, 91–92.

56. The circumstances surrounding this cure are controversial. First of all, even Śvetāmbaras would never suggest that the Jina was so attached to life as to personally desire such a cure. The text relates, however, that one mendicant

power of his attack returned to its source; he became delirious and died soon afterwards in the workshop of Hālāhalā.

Both of these tales, found in the *Bhagavatī-sūtra*, are unknown to, and thus rejected by, the tradition of the Digambaras. While they would clearly suppress, on the basis of doctrinal considerations, any notion of a perfected Jina engaging in worldly dispute, their nearly total lack of awareness of the significant place held by Makkhali Gosāla in Mahāvīra's pre-enlightenment career is less easily explained.[57] Perhaps the idea of a Jina-to-be associating so intimately with a heretic was repugnant to them. Other

---

disciple, called Sīha, was distraught over the possibility that his master's illness would prove fatal. To assuage Sīha's anguish, Mahāvīra sent him to procure a particular medicinal substance which would undo the harmful effects of Gosāla's attack. The substance in question is called *kukkuṭa-māṃsa*, which ordinarily refers to the flesh of a chicken. But no Jaina can accept the idea of even an ordinary mendicant consuming meat, regardless of circumstances; to suggest that a Jina might have done so is nothing less than blasphemous. The Śvetāmbara commentators have therefore gone to great pains to show that the term kukkuṭa-māṃsa here refers not to meat at all but to the flesh of a certain seed-filled fruit (called *bījapūraka-kaṭāha*, perhaps Aegle Marmelos, or *bel-phal* in Hindi) commonly used for medical purposes (to treat dehydration;) such "animal" terminology for an herbal substance is often found, for example, in the *Āyurveda*. The fact that this term was not suppressed or eliminated from the literature long ago supports their interpretation; those commentators closest in time to the original text must have assumed that there would be no danger of misunderstanding. Indeed, it was not until the 1941 publication of Dharmananda Kosambi's *Bhagavān Buddha* (in Marathi) that anyone (in India) even suggested the possibility of taking kukkuṭa-māṃsa as actual flesh. The controversy raised among Jainas by Kosambi's remarks was of course restricted to the Śvetāmbara community; Digambaras, who deny that a kevalin eats anything at all (see below, n. 83), found the entire issue irrelevant.

The controversial passage appears as follows in the *BhS*: xv (Vaidya ed., p. 34.): taṃ no khalu ahaṃ Sīhā . . . kālaṃ karessaṃ; ahaṃ ṇaṃ annāiṃ soḷasavassāiṃ jiṇe suhatthī viharissāmi. taṃ gacchaha ṇaṃ tumaṃ Sīhā, Meṇḍhiyagāmaṃ nayaraṃ, Revaīe gāhāvaiṇīe gihe. tattha ṇaṃ Revaīe . . . mamaṃ aṭṭhāe duve kavoyasarīrā uvakkhaḍiyā, tehiṃ no aṭṭho. atthi se anne pāriyāsie majjārakaḍae kukkuḍamaṃsae, tamāharāhi, eeṇaṃ aṭṭho. ("mārjāro" virālābhidhānako vanaspativiśeṣas tena "kṛtaṃ" bhāvitaṃ yat tat tathā, kiṃ tat? ity āha "kukkuṭamāṃsakaṃ" bījapūrakaṃ kaṭāhaṃ, "āharāhitti" niravadyatvād iti.") *Abhayadevasūri-vṛtti* (quoted in Vaidya ed., p. 66).

57. Digambaras do admit an encounter between the two men shortly after Mahāvīra's attainment of kevalajñāna, but they describe Makkhali Gosāla (called Makkaḍi or Masayari) as a mendicant in the tradition of Pārśva who wished to become one of Mahāvīra's gaṇadharas. Failing to be chosen, he established his own school—for which heresy he is said to have suffered rebirth in the dismal state of the *nigodas* (see Ch. IV, n. 7): Masayari-pūraṇa-risiṇo

possibilities have been suggested by Hoernle and Basham. The former makes the rather sweeping statement that the Ājīvikas were in fact themselves the earliest form of the Digambara movement; this idea seems to be based on certain similarities in the dietary practices of the two sects (for example, the lack of a begging bowl), as well as on the rather unconvincing premise (noted above) that nudity was introduced by the Ājīvikas.[58] Basham's theory is more reasonable, suggesting that many Ājīvikas were absorbed into the Digambara community in medieval times.[59]

In either case, it might follow that the Digambaras would thus have quashed all reference to the "heretical" background of part of their community in order to ensure homogeneity and orthodoxy in the present; this phenomenon is common enough in cases of conversion and assimilation. It would seem however, that we can understand the Digambaras' glaring omission of so important a figure as Gosāla without resorting to such speculations. In their displeasure over certain portions of the codified canonical recension of Pāṭaliputra, they probably rejected so much material as to leave themselves with virtually no canon whatsoever. This explanation also fits well with the Digambaras' extreme emphasis upon aspects of practice (especially nudity) rather than literature, for in the absence of ancient scripture it was finally only the code of conduct of their sect which could define it as a unique and individual entity.

Mahāvīra's Austerities

If any single event can be labeled the most significant of Mahāvīra's life, it must be his attainment of kevalajñāna,

---

uppaṇṇo Pāsaṇāhatitthammi/ siriVīrasamavasaraṇe agahiyajhuṇinā ṇiyatteṇa// . . . ṇa muṇai jiṇakahiyasuyaṃ sampai dikkhāya gahiya Goyamao/ vippo veyabbhāsī tamhā mokkhaṃ ṇa ṇāṇāo// *Bhāvasaṅgraha*: k 76–78. See also: siriVīraṇāhatitthe bahussudo Pāsasaṃghagaṇisīso/ Makkaḍapūraṇasāhū aṇṇāṇaṃ bhāsaye loe// Jiṇamaggabāhiraṃ jaṃ taccaṃ saṃdarisiūṇa pāvamaṇo/ ṇiccaṇigoye patto satto majjesu vivihesu// *Darśanasāra*: k 20–23. See Upadhye 1933: K. P. Jain 1928: 20; Premi 1956: 202; P. S. Jaini 1976a.

58. *Encyclopaedia of Religion and Ethics*: I. 259–269.

59. Basham 1951: 277.

for it was upon this experience that his entire career as a Tīrthaṅkara was based. He is said to have pursued the austerities leading up to this event with unswerving dedication, never once deviating from their practice. The *Ācārāṅga-sūtra* has many passages describing such austerities:

> Ceasing to inflict injury on living beings, abandoning concern for the body, and having perceived the true nature of the self, the Venerable One, houseless, endured the thorns of the villages [that is, the abusive language of the peasants].
>
> Like an elephant at the head of battle, so was Mahāvīra there victorious. Sometimes, in the country of Lāḍha, he could not even enter a village [to stay overnight].
>
> At other times, when he approached a village the inhabitants met him outside and attacked him, saying, "Get away from here."
>
> He was struck with sticks, fists, and lances; he was hit with fruit, clods, and potsherds. Beating him again and again, they raised a huge din.
>
> Once when he [sat in meditation], his body unmoving, they cut his flesh, tore his hair, and covered him with dirt. They picked him up and then dropped him, disturbing his meditational postures. Abandoning concern for his body, free from desire, the Venerable One humbled himself and bore the pain. Just as a hero at the head of a battle is surrounded on all sides, so was Mahāvīra there. Undisturbed, bearing all hardships, the Venerable One proceeded [on the path of salvation].[60]

Or again:

> Being averse to the impressions of the senses, he wandered about, speaking little. Sometimes in the cold season the Venerable One meditated in the shade.

60. nihāya daṇḍaṃ pāṇehiṃ taṃ vosajja kāyam aṇagāre/ aha gāmakaṃṭae bhagavaṃ te ahiyāse abhisameccā// nāo saṃgāmasīse va pārae tattha se Mahāvīre/ evaṃ pi tattha Lāḍhehiṃ aladdapuvvo vi egadā gāmo// uvasaṃkamaṃtaṃ apaḍinnaṃ gāmaṃtiyaṃ pi appattaṃ/ paḍinikkhamittu lūsiṃsu etāo paraṃ palehi tti// hayapuvvo tattha daṃḍeṇa aha vā muṭṭhiṇā aha phaleṇaṃ/ aha leḷunā kavāḷeṇaṃ haṃtā haṃtā bahave kaṃdiṃsu// maṃsūṇi chinnapuvvāiṃ oṭṭhabhiyāe egadā kāyaṃ/ parissahāiṃ luṃciṃsu ahavā paṃsuṇā uvakariṃsu// uccāliya nihiṇiṃsu aha vā āsaṇāo khalaiṃsu/ vosaṭṭhakāe paṇatāsī dukkhasahe bhagavaṃ apaḍinne// sūro saṃgāmasīse va saṃvuḍe tattha se Mahāvīre/ paḍisevamāṇe pharusāiṃ acale bhagavaṃ rīitthā// *AS*: §502–507.

> In summer he exposed himself to the heat, squatting beneath the blazing sun. He lived on rough foods: rice, pounded jujube, and beans. Taking only these three, the Venerable One sustained himself for eight months. Sometimes he drank nothing for two weeks or even for a month. And sometimes he did not drink for more than two months, or even for six months; day and night he was without desire [for food and water]. Even when he did eat, his food was always of a tasteless kind. Sometimes he ate only every sixth day, or every eighth, or every tenth, or every twelfth; free of desires, he remained engrossed in meditation. He meditated free from aversion or desire, attached neither to sounds nor to colors; though still in bondage (*chadmastha*), he never behaved carelessly during his wanderings.[61]

Thus:

> With supreme knowledge, with supreme intuition, with supreme conduct, with supreme uprightness, with supreme valor, with supreme dexterity, with supreme patience . . . with supreme contentment, with supreme insight, on the supreme path to that final liberation which is the fruit of truthfulness, restraint, and good conduct, the Venerable One meditated for twelve years on the nature of the self.[62]

Jainas point with pride to the fact that Gautama Buddha, unlike his Nigaṇṭha counterpart, gave up extreme austerities and followed the "middle path"; they suggest that this model of less than single-minded purpose led the Buddhist order (*saṃgha*) to fall eventually into various sorts of laxity from which the Jaina community, based upon the example of Mahāvīra, remained free.

The Enlightenment

Mahāvīra's actual attainment of kevalajñāna took place precisely twelve years, six months, and fifteen days after he set out upon the mendicant's path:

61. *AS*: §512–521. According to Śvetāmbara commentators, during the more than twelve years that Mahāvīra wandered prior to his enlightenment, he took food on only 349 days. At other times he fasted completely. See Devendra's *Kalpa-sūtra*: 185.

62. tassa ṇaṃ bhagavaṃtassa . . . appāṇaṃ bhāvemāṇassa duvālasasaṃvaccharāiṃ vikkaṃtāiṃ. *KS*: §120.

> During the thirteenth year, in Vaiśākha, in the second month of summer (May/June), on the tenth day of the waxing moon, when the shadow had turned towards the east . . . outside the town of Jṛmbhikagrāma, on the bank of the river Ṛjupālikā, not far from an old temple, in the field of the householder Samaga, when the moon was in conjunction with the constellation Uttaraphālguṇi, (the Venerable One) sat with joined heels, exposing himself to the heat of the sun. After fasting for two-and-a-half days, taking not even water, engaged in deep meditation, he reached the highest *jñāna* (knowledge) and *darśana* (intuition), called kevala, which is infinite, supreme, unobstructed, unimpeded, complete, and full.[63]

> When the Venerable Ascetic Mahāvīra had become a Jina and an *arhat* (worthy of worship), he was a kevalin, Omniscient, comprehending all objects. He saw and knew whence they had come, where they would go, and whether they would be reborn as men, animals, gods, or hell beings. He knew the ideas and thoughts, the food, doings, desires, and deeds of all the living beings in the world.[64]

Upon attaining the omniscient state Mahāvīra became, as we have noted earlier, the twenty-fourth and final Jina of the present cycle. In order to understand exactly what this means, it is necessary to digress once more from the

63. terasamassa saṃvaccharassa aṃtarā vaṭṭamāṇassa je se gimhāṇaṃ māse cautthe pakkhe vaisāhasuddhe tassa ṇaṃ . . . dasamīe . . . Jambhiyagāmassa nagarassa bahiyā Ujuvāliyāye naīe tīre viyāvattassa ceīyassa adūrasāmaṃte Sāmāgassa gāhāvaissa kaṭṭakaraṇaṃsi sālāpāyavassa ahe godohiyāe ukkuḍuyanisijjāe āyāvaṇāe āyāvemāṇassa chaṭṭheṇaṃ bhatteṇaṃ hatthuttharāhiṃ nakkhatteṇaṃ jogaṃ uvāgaeṇaṃ jhāṇaṃtariyāe vaṭṭamāṇassa aṇaṃte aṇuttare nivvāghāe nirāvaraṇe kasiṇe paḍipuṇṇe kevalavaranāṇadaṃsaṇe samuppanne. *KS*: §120. See also: bhagavān Vardhamāno 'pi nītvā dvādaśavatsarān/ chādmasthyena jagadbandhur Jṛmbhikāgrāmasannidhau// Ṛjukūlānadītīre manoharavanāntare/ mahāratnaśilāpaṭṭe pratimāyogam āvasan// sthitvā ṣaṣṭhopavāsena so 'dhastāt sālabhūruhaḥ/ vaiśākhe māsi sajyotsnādaśamyām aparāhnake// . . . paramātmapadaṃ prāpat parameṣṭhī sa Sanmatiḥ// *UP*: lxxiv, 348–355.

64. tae ṇaṃ se bhagavaṃ arahā jāe jiṇe kevalī savvannū savvadarisī sadevamaṇuyāsurassa logassa pariyāyaṃ jāṇai pāsai, savvaloe savvajīvāṇaṃ āgaiṃ gaiṃ ṭhiiṃ cavaṇaṃ uvavāyaṃ takkaṃ maṇo māṇasiyaṃ bhuttaṃ kaḍaṃ padiseviyaṃ āvikammaṃ rahokammaṃ arahā arahassabhāgī taṃ taṃ kālaṃ maṇavayaṇakāyajoge vaṭṭamāṇāṇaṃ savvajīvāṇaṃ savvabhāve jāṇamāṇe pāsamāṇe viharai. *KS*: §121.

life of Mahāvīra, this time to explore the larger cosmological system of which that life is a part.

The Jaina Universe and the Role of the Tīrthaṅkaras

Jainas envision the universe as a vast but finite three-dimensional structure, somewhat resembling a man with arms akimbo and legs apart. Within this structure are three main tiers, ordered vertically. The middle tier, called Madhya-loka, is of primary concern to us, for here exist the "worlds" in which all human activity takes place. These worlds are arranged in countless (*asaṃkhyāta*) concentric rings of land surrounding a central island (*dvīpa*); each ring is separated by water, much in the manner of coral reefs. The land of the second ring from the center of this system is divided into inner and outer halves by a range of huge mountains. It is usually believed that human beings cannot be born anywhere beyond this range;[65] outlying regions are hence the domain solely of the animals and the vegetable kingdom.

The central island is called Jambūdvīpa, after the jambū tree which stands, atop Mount Meru, at its very center. Jambūdvīpa comprises seven *varṣa* or "continents": Bharata, Haimavata, Ramyaka, Videha, Hari, Hairaṇyaka, and Airāvata.[66] These continents are separated from one another by six great mountains. Of the seven continents, only Bharata, Airāvata, and half of Videha are *karma-bhūmi*, or realms of action, that is, places in which mokṣa can be attained. Actions which bring about rebirth in the highest heaven or the lowest hell are also limited to these karma-bhūmis. The remaining four-and-a-half continents are *bhoga-bhūmi*, realms of enjoyment, where there occurs

65. The upper and lower tiers are for the most part occupied by gods and hell beings, respectively. For details, see below, Ch. IV, the sketch of loka-ākāśa.

66. prāṅ Mānuṣottarān manuṣyāḥ/ *TS*: iii, 35. Puṣkaravaradvīpabahumadhyadeśabhāgī valayavṛtto Mānuṣottaro nāma śailaḥ. tasmāt prāg eva manuṣyā na bahir iti. *SS*: §434.

nothing but the experiencing of sense pleasures; such places are not, of course, conducive to renunciation.[67]

The first ring surrounding Jambūdvīpa is called Dhātakī-khaṇḍa; its land mass is twice that of Jambū, and it has an identical arrangement of continents and bhūmis. Next is Puṣkaravara, which is in turn double the size of Dhātakī-khaṇḍa; it too has an analogous internal structure. (As we have seen, however, only the interior half of this ring is inhabitable by human beings. Questions of action [karma] versus enjoyment [bhoga] thus become irrelevant beyond this point.) Given the fact that Jinahood can only be attained in a karma-bhūmi area, we are now in a position to tentatively calculate how many continents are "available," as it were, to the appearance of a Tīrthaṅkara. Jainas perform this calculation by taking the continent-size of Jambūdvīpa as the standard of measurement.

Thus we have:

Jambūdvīpa
2½ karma-bhūmi continents

Dhātakī-khaṇḍa
5 karma-bhūmi continents (2½ x 2, since each continent is twice the size of its Jambūdvīpa counterpart)

Puṣkaravara
5 karma-bhūmi continents (2½ x 4 = 10 x ½ = 5, since each continent is four times the size of its Jambūdvīpa counterpart, but only half the land is inhabitable by human beings)

This gives a total of twelve-and-a-half continents conceivably suitable for the arising of a Jina. The situation is complicated further, however, by the Jainas' belief that karma-bhūmi areas are subject to an endless temporal cycle, half progressive and half regressive. These half-cycles, called *utsarpiṇī* and *avasarpiṇī*, respectively, are themselves each divided into six time stages (*kāla*) as follows.

67. . . . kṛṣyādilakṣaṇasya . . . tatraivārambhāt karmabhūmivyapadeśo veditavyaḥ. itarās tu . . . kalpavṛkṣakalpitabhogānubhavanād bhogabhūmayaḥ . . . *SS*: §437.

utsarpiṇī (progressive half-cycle):
1) *duṣamā-duṣamā* (extremely unhappy)
2) *duṣamā* (unhappy)
3) *duṣamā-suṣamā* (more unhappy than happy)
4) *suṣamā-duṣamā* (more happy than unhappy)
5) *suṣamā* (happy)
6) *suṣamā-suṣamā* (extremely happy)

avasarpiṇī (regressive half-cycle):
1) suṣamā-suṣamā (extremely happy)
2) suṣamā (happy)
3) suṣamā-duṣamā (more happy than unhappy)
4) duṣamā-suṣamā (more unhappy than happy)
5) duṣamā (unhappy)
6) duṣamā-duṣamā (extremely unhappy)[68]

The utsarpiṇī and avasarpiṇī follow directly upon one another in unbroken succession; there is no period of *pralaya* (demanifestation) during which the karma-bhūmis are not in one of the above stages. These half-cycles each last for a vast but finite number of years. The life expectancy of human beings dwelling in the karma-bhūmis increases with each stage of the utsarpiṇī, and correspondingly decreases with each stage of the avasarpiṇī. It is believed that only during the third and fourth stages of a half-cycle, when there is neither an extremity of happiness nor of unhappiness, can anyone possibly attain mokṣa. The point is that only at such a time are human beings sufficiently short-lived and unhappy to understand impermanence and suffering, yet free enough from misery to conceive of and pursue mokṣa. Jainas claim that there will be precisely twenty-four Jinas during each half-cycle;[69] this is true for every karma-bhūmi continent except the Videhas (that is, the "half-in-karma-bhūmi" areas of each

68. *SS*: §418.

69. Some of the Jina's followers may also attain to kevalajñāna, hence mokṣa, during this period. But they are known as kevalin or arhat, not Jina. The distinction here derives not only from the fact that they do not become teacher-propagators, as Jinas do, but also that without the Jina's assistance they would not have reached so exalted a state in the first place. For a discussion on the status of an arhat in Jainism and Buddhism, see Ch. VIII, n. 31.

dvīpa), which are said to be *always* in a condition equivalent to the end of the third stage. This latter claim underlies the further contention that at every moment there is a living Jina *somewhere.* In other words the path of salvation is open at any time; one need only be born into one of the Videhas in order to have an immediate chance for mokṣa.[70]

At the present time our earth (Bharata-kṣetra) is in a descending or regressive half-cycle, an avasarpiṇī. The first Tīrthaṅkara of this avasarpiṇī was Ṛṣabha, who is said to have introduced agriculture, the caste system, law, monarchy, and the spiritual path of the mendicant. Thus he was, in the Jaina view, not only the first to undertake the holy life in this era, but also responsible for laying the groundwork of our entire civilization. After living for an extremely long period, approximately 600,000 years, he obtained mokṣa on the summit of Mount Kailāsa. The cult of Ṛṣabha has long been extremely popular among Jainas; indeed, during the medieval period, this cult was so well known in India that the Hindu text *Bhāgavata Purāṇa* included Ṛṣabha as an *aṃśāvatāra* (minor incarnation of Viṣṇu).[71]

We may thus assume that the first Tīrthaṅkara has been the object of more worship than even Mahāvīra; but it is probably not correct to infer that he was ever considered *the* teacher of our era; this role has belonged to Mahāvīra alone. One interesting tale, found in the later Purāṇas, links these two Jinas by suggesting that Ṛṣabha's grandson, Marīci, was later born as Mahāvīra.[72] It is further related how this Marīci became full of vanity and conceit upon hearing a prophecy of his future Jinahood; such excessive pride necessitated that he become the last (shortest-lived) Jina of the cycle. Scholars like Hiralal Jain have tried to

70. Such ācāryas as the famous Kundakunda are reputed to have traveled to these "continents" by yogic methods, obtaining first-hand clarification on doctrinal matters from the Tīrthaṅkaras living there. See *Pravacanasāra*: intro. 6.

71. *Śrīmad Bhāgavata*: V, iii–vii. See P. S. Jaini 1977a.

72. See *Viśeṣāvaśyaka-bhāṣya*: k 1781–1812; *AP*: xviii, 61–65; *TSPC*: I, vi, 1–52.

bring the first Jina, and thus the beginnings of Jainism, into historical times, maintaining that the name Ṛṣabha (having the sense of "bull") appears as an honorific term in the *Ṛgveda* and could there refer to the Jaina lawgiver.[73] More convincing theories, taking note of the yogic, śramaṇic, and anti-Vedic underpinnings of Jaina tradition, have sought to discover the roots of this tradition in pre-Āryan Indic civilizations. Nude standing images found in the Indus Valley ruins bear a striking resemblance to the oldest Jaina sculptures;[74] further, there may be a link between the Indus bull-seals and the bull-insignia of Ṛṣabha.

Of the remaining Tīrthaṅkaras, only three can in any way be connected with historical evidence. The twenty-second, Nemi, seems to have flourished in Saurashtra, near the famous Girnar mounts (site of the Aśokan inscriptions), and to have been a contemporary of Kṛṣṇa.[75] Pārśva, as we have seen, lived and taught in Banaras; he was of course followed in the same area some 250 years later by Mahāvīra.[76] Thus, while Jainism may very well be pre-Vedic, the geographical location of at least its two most recent teachers does not suggest an origin in the Indus valley. A. N. Upadhye has proposed that in light of the other śramaṇa sects (Ājīvika, Buddhism, the antiritualistic Upaniṣadic tradition, and so on) which flourished in the Magadha region along with Jainism, we can reasonably postulate a distinct Magadhan religious complex, devel-

73. H. Jain 1962: 11–18.

74. "Another familiar motif is that of a nude man represented as a repeat motif in rigidly upright posture, his legs slightly apart, arms held parallel with the sides of his body, which recurs later as the Jain Tīrthāṅkara, repeated row upon row. The hieratic style favoured by that religious community . . . its rigid conformism, and its utilitarian outlook, so resemble the Harappan culture that it appears more than likely that the prehistoric traits were handed down over many centuries." Lannoy 1974: 10.

75. "Even more remarkable is the traditional contemporaneousness of Nemi and the divine hero Kṛṣṇa . . . Kṛṣṇaism seems to have left its mark on Jaina legend, a Kṛṣṇaism which we must assume . . . to be an earlier form than that described in the Brahmanical texts." Renou 1953: 114. See Jacobi 1884: 276–279; and Ch. IX, no. 54.

76. Pārśveśatīrthasantāne pañcāśad dviśatābdake/ tad abhyantaravartyāyur Mahāvīro 'tra jātavān// *UP*: lxxiv, 279.

oped at the foot of the Himalayas where Āryans from the Punjab encountered the non-Vedic cultures of the Ganges Valley.[77]

Mahāvīra's Career as a Tīrthaṅkara

All these questions remain open to debate. Our aim here is not to solve such problems, but to gain some feeling for the position of Mahāvīra in the overall Jaina scheme of universal cycles and Tīrthaṅkara lineages. It is said that Mahāvīra was born when seventy-five years, eight-and-a-half months were left in the fourth stage of the current avasarpiṇī, and that he remained in the world for exactly seventy-two years. Thus the fifth stage began less than three years after his death; no more Jinas will appear in our world until it enters the third stage of the upcoming utsarpiṇī. As the fifth and sixth stages last 21,000 years each, it will be a long time before the next half-cycle even begins, and far longer before it reaches its third phase. Hence, despite the fact that there has been an infinite number of Jinas and that somewhere in the universe a Jina is at this very moment preaching the path of salvation, the accomplishment of Mahāvīra nevertheless assumes majestic proportions when considered from the limited perspective of the average person. By attaining the omniscient state, he reached a position so rare and exalted that we can hardly be surpsied to find that most Jainas view him as something more than human.

As we have seen, the Digambaras adopt this "more than human" position doctrinally as well as on the level of conventional belief. They describe Mahāvīra after his enlightenment as totally free from the eighteen defects of human existence—hunger, thirst, sleep, sweat, fear, disease, aging, and so on.[78] He is said to have engaged, at that time, in no mundane activities whatsoever, since omniscient

77. See Upadhye, intro. to *Pravacanasāra.*

78. For eighteen imperfections (*doṣa*) from which a kevalin is forever freed, see *Upāsakādhyayana*: k 52–56.

cognition and sensory cognition are held to be mutually antithetical. Thus he sat in the lotus posture, maintaining constant omniscient trance, housed in an assembly hall which had been miraculously created by the gods. His body, free from all impurities, shone like a crystal on all sides.[79] Above his head was hoisted the royal insignia of a white umbrella, signifying that nothing could be higher or holier than he. A divine sound (divyadhvani) emanated from his person for the benefit of the audience. As this audience consisted of gods, demi-gods, human beings, and animals, the entire assembly was called *samavasaraṇa*, a place of resort for all.[80] Although the perfected Jina initiated no acts of organization, a Jaina community was nevertheless formed through the efforts of the gaṇadharas attracted by his Tīrthaṅkara nature. In this sense the Jina is conventionally said to have "established" the four-fold *tīrtha*: monks, nuns, laymen, and laywomen.

Specifically, according to Digambaras, sixty-six days after the enlightenment there appeared on the scene a brahman called Indrabhūti Gautama; although well-versed in the Vedas and proud of his knowledge, he could not comprehend the Jaina teachings when they were conveyed to him by Indra, king of gods (disguised as a brahman). Thus he went to the assembly hall where Mahāvīra dwelt in all his splendor. At the mere sight of the pillar standing before this hall, all of Gautama's pride and vanity disappeared; he instantly understood the teachings and became the first of the gaṇadharas.[81] His brothers, Agnibhūti and Vāyubhūti, followed his lead. Soon the three of them were

79. It is said that even the blood which flowed through his veins became transparent or milky in color (gokkhīrapaṇḍure maṃsa-soṇie, *SamS*: §111). Zimmer (1951: 209) suggests that the use of alabaster in making Jina images, as well as the practice of pouring milk over these images during the *abhiṣeka*, can be traced to this belief.

80. For a description of the samavasaraṇa, see *AP*: xxii, 76–312; *TSPC*: I, iii, 452–477. See below, pl. 10.

81. Pillars which stand before Digambara temples are thus called *mānastambha* (that which brings an end to pride); these typically include at their apex a four-faced Jina in samavasaraṇa. For further details, see Fergusson 1891: 276–278, U. P. Shah 1955: 60ff. See below, pl. 23.

joined by eight other brahmans. These eleven gaṇadharas formed the nucleus of the new order; having mastered the Jina's doctrine upon hearing his divine sound, they in turn composed all the Jaina litanies, rules of conduct, and so on.

According to the Śvetāmbaras, Mahāvīra's first audience after his enlightenment consisted only of gods, to whom he preached his doctrine for a short time. After a while he approached a ceremonial enclosure, where a Vedic sacrifice was in progress. There he delivered a sermon on the virtue of nonharming and was subsequently able to convert three of the brahman priests, Indrabhūti Gautama and his two brothers. These three, along with their 1,500 disciples, were immediately received into the new mendicant order. Soon thereafter, eight other brahmans were converted, completing the "inner circle" of eleven chief disciples, the gaṇadharas.[82] The addition of their many followers to the Jaina order swelled its ranks to over 4,000.

Countering the Digambara belief that a person endowed with kevalajñāna does not partake of ordinary human food (*kavala-āhāra*, literally "food made into morsels") but subsists merely on the (involuntary) intake of some subtle food, such as that partaken by the gods,[83] Śvetāmbaras maintain that existence in the state of embodiment requires even the most exalted one to obey bodily laws. Hence they suggest that the Jina must eat and perform other mundane activities; but these activities are said to in no way interfere with his omniscient cognition.[84]

Consistent with their belief in the relatively "human" characteristics of the Jina, the Śvetāmbaras have preserved a meticulous record of Mahāvīra's travels during and after

82. See Solomon 1966; *Viśeṣāvaśyaka-bhāṣya*: k 1993–2080.

83. For the Digambara position on this as well as on *strīmukti* see *Pravacanasāra* [*Tātparyavṛtti*]: i,20; iii,25. For a refutation of the Digambara views (by Yāpanīyācārya Śākaṭāyana) see *Strīnirvāṇa-Kevalibhuktiprakaraṇe*.

84. Śvetāmbara commentators have sought to "refine" these activities in the case of the Jina by adding that he did not beg; food was brought to him by the disciple Lohārya. It is held, moreover, that no one ever saw him eat or engage in other bodily functions; these were carried out in absolute privacy: pacchanne āhāranīhāre adisse maṃsacakkhuṇā/ *SamS*: §111.

his enlightenment. The following passage, for example, lists the various places in which he resided during the forty rainy seasons of his teaching career:

> At that time, the Venerable Ascetic Mahāvīra stayed the first rainy season in Asthikagrāma, three rainy seasons in Campā and Pṛṣṭicampā, twelve in Vaiśāli and Vāṇijagrāma, fourteen in Rājagṛha and the suburb of Nālandā, six in Mithilā, two in Bhadrikā, one in Śrāvastī, and one in the town of Pāpā in King Hastipāla's office of the scribes; that was his very last rainy season.[85]

Regardless of their dispute over the location and method of his preaching, both Digambaras and Śvetāmbaras agree that during Mahāvīra's career as a Tīrthaṅkara the Jaina congregation grew to a large number: ostensibly, 14,000 monks, 36,000 nuns (under the supervision of the chief nun Candanā), 159,000 laymen, and 318,000 laywomen.[86] The preponderence of female followers probably resulted from the fact that many men had more than one wife, and that these wives became nuns when their husbands took the vows of a monk.[87]

Mahāvīra's Death

It is agreed by both traditions that at the age of seventy-two the Venerable Ascetic Mahāvīra passed into nirvāṇa; he thus became a *siddha*, one who is fully liberated, forever free of embodiment. Śvetāmbara records tell us that this event took place at the office of scribes maintained by King Hastipāla in the town of Pāpā, identified with modern Pāvāpurī, near Patna. The traditional date of Mahāvīra's death is fixed near the end of the rainy season in 527 B.C.; it is from this date that Jainas count the Vīranirvāṇa period, the longest continuous "era" in Indian

85. *KS*: §122.
86. Ibid.: §133–135.
87. This step seems to have been preferable to functional widowhood. The Jainas were probably the first religious sect in India to open their ranks in this manner to the female relatives of initiates. See Ch. VIII n. 8.

history.[88] At the time of Mahāvīra's departure from this earth, only two of the eleven gaṇadharas—Indrabhūti Gautama and Sudharman—still lived.[89] It is believed that Indrabhūti Gautama attained omniscience in a matter of hours after his teacher had passed away. These two nearly simultaneous events are celebrated by the Jainas in their Dīpāvalī (Festival of lights), following a tradition supposedly begun by the local kings on that very day so many years ago. As the *Kalpa-sūtra* says:

> On that night during which the Venerable Ascetic Mahāvīra died . . . cut asunder the ties of birth, old age, and death, became a siddha, finally liberated . . . his oldest disciple, the monk Indrabhūti of the Gautama gotra, obtained the highest knowledge and intuition, called kevala, which is infinite, supreme . . . and full.[90]

> And on that night during which the Venerable Ascetic Mahāvīra died . . . the eighteen confederate kings of Kāśi and Kośala, the nine Mallikas and nine Licchavis instituted an illumination on the day of the new moon, which was a fasting day; for they said: "Since the internal (*bhāva*) light (of intelligence) is gone, let us make an illumination with the external (*dravya*) light (of matter)."[91]

Points of Controversy between the Two Major Sects

In the account above many examples of conflict have been noted between the Digambara and Śvetāmbara traditions

88. One Jaina source (Hemacandra's *Pariśiṣṭaparva*: viii, 341) places this event at 427 B.C.; this is somewhat closer to the approximate date of 477 B.C. put forth by Jacobi (1932: intro. vii). See Basham 1951: 77ff. H. Jain (1974: 50–52) refutes these views in favor of the traditional date.

89. For details concerning the gaṇadharas, see Ch. II.

90. *KS*: §126.

91. jaṃ rayaṇiṃ ca ṇaṃ samaṇe bhagavaṃ Mahāvīre . . . jāva dukkhappahīṇe taṃ rayaṇiṃ ca ṇaṃ nava Mallī nava Licchavī Kāsī-Kosalagā aṭṭhārasa vi gaṇarāyāṇo amāvāse pārābhoyaṃ posahovavāsaṃ paṭṭhavaiṃsu, gate se bhāvujjoe davvujjoyaṃ karissāmo. *KS*: §127. Compare: tatas tu lokaḥ prativarṣam ādarāt, prasiddha-dīpālikayātra bhārate/ samudyataḥ pūjayituṃ jineśvaraṃ, jinendranirvāṇavibhūtibhaktibhāk// *Harivaṃśapurāṇa*: lxvi, 21.

of Jainism. It might now be helpful to categorize these points of controversy in a general way.[92] Three issues seem paramount:

1. *The nature of the omniscient Jina.* For Digambaras, such a being engages in no worldly activity and no bodily functions (eating meals, for example), since these are considered antithetical to omniscient cognition. He "preaches" by means of a magical "divine sound." Śvetāmbaras see the Jina as engaging in normal human activities and functions while *simultaneously* enjoying omniscient cognition.

2. *The role of nudity in the holy life.* Digambaras, as their name implies, stress the practice of nudity as an absolute prerequisite to the mendicant's path—the only mode of conduct through which one can become truly free of shame and sexuality and thus hope to attain mokṣa. Śvetāmbaras emphasize the optional nature of this practice; while they decry *attachment* to clothing, they do not admit that clothing per se is an obstacle to salvation. The Digambaras hold that retaining *any* possession is functionally equivalent to retaining *all* possessions, that is, to remaining a householder. Hence they deny that Śvetāmbara monks are monks at all.

3. *The position of women.* Digambaras believe that a woman lacks the adamantine body necessary to attain mokṣa; hence, she must be reborn as a man before such an attainment is possible. Śvetāmbaras take the opposite position, stating that women can be born with such bodies and thus are capable, in the present lifetime, of the same spiritual accomplishments as men. Indeed, they claim that the

92. Guṇaratnasūri, a Śvetāmbara writer (circa 1400), summarizes the main features of the various Jaina sects as follows: Jaināḥ dvividhāḥ Śvetāmbarā Digambarāś ca. tatra Śvetāmbarāṇāṃ rajoharaṇa-mukhavastrikālocādi liṅgaṃ, colapaṭṭakalpādiko veśaḥ . . . Digambarā punar nāgnyaliṅgāḥ pāṇipātrāś ca. te caturdhā Kāṣṭhāsaṃgha-Mūlasaṃgha-Māthurasaṃgha-Gopyasaṃgha-bhedena. Ādyās trayo 'pi saṃghāḥ . . . strīṇāṃ muktiṃ kevalināṃ bhuktiṃ sadvratasyāpi sacīvarasya muktiṃ ca na manvate, Gopyās tu . . . strīṇāṃ muktiṃ kevalināṃ bhuktiṃ ca manyante. Gopyā Yāpanīyā ity apy ucyante . . . śeṣam ācāre gurau ca deve ca sarvaṃ Śvetāmbarais tulyaṃ, nāsti teṣāṃ mithaḥ śāstreṣu tarkeṣv aparo bhedaḥ. *Ṣaḍdarśanasamuccaya*: iv, 1. For a history of the three saṃghas mentioned in this passage, see Johrapurkar 1958.

nineteenth Tīrthaṅkara, Malli, was a woman.[93] These conflicting doctrines seem to grow mainly out of the social implications of the nudity issue. The idea of a woman appearing naked in public, particularly while subject to the menstrual cycle, is unacceptable to Indian society at large; neither of the Jaina traditions allows its nuns to go about sky-clad.[94] For the Śvetāmbaras, of course, this poses no doctrinal difficulty with regard to salvation, but for the Digambaras it is an automatic disqualification.

Other important differences in practice between the two traditions which should be noted here concern begging and eating habits. Śvetāmbara monks carry small pots and beg food door-to-door. They may not enter a house to eat; all food and water must be collected in bowls, taken back to the monastery, and there entirely consumed. A Digambara monk, on the other hand, has no pot or bowl; he receives

93. In addition to its unique claim that Tīrthaṅkarahood is available to women, the Śvetāmbara legend of Malli provides useful insight into Jaina ideas on the factors leading to a female birth. It is said that the soul which later became Malli was in a former life a male, specifically, a king named Mahābala. This king, together with seven friends, renounced the world and became a Jaina mendicant. All eight made a solemn agreement to undertake an identical number of fasts as part of their austerities. Mahābala, however, constantly found excuses (ill health, and so on) to skip meals; he thus abrogated the agreement by deviously accumulating a larger number of fasts than his friends. His conduct being in all other ways quite faultless, and including the several virtues prerequisite to Tīrthaṅkarahood, he attained in the second subsequent birth to the destiny of a teacher-savior. The prior misdeed of "cheating" on a pact, however, could not go without retribution. Thus the soul of this being, although ready for the exalted status of a Tīrthaṅkara, was born as a female, Malli. During her youth she was sought after by numerous lustful suitors, some of whom went to war over her. Disgusted both by being regarded as a sexual object and by being the cause of violence, she renounced the world, became a nun, attained to kevalajñāna, and propagated the Jaina doctrine. Both Digambaras and Śvetāmbaras, while disagreeing over the verity of this particular story, share the notion that such vices as cheating, capriciousness, greed, and cunning are the fundamental causes of rebirth as a woman. For the Śvetāmbara account of Malli, see *Jñātṛdharmakathā-sūtra*: viii; *TSPC*: VI, vi, 19–213. For the Digambara version, see *UP*: lxvi, 1–65. For a sculptural representation of the female Malli, see U. P. Shah 1956. See below, pl. 9.

94. Āśādhara, a Digambara writer of the thirteenth century, approved of administering vows of nudity to a woman on her deathbed; he appears to have been the only authority to adopt such a position, however: yad autsargikam anyad vā liṅgam uktaṃ jinaiḥ striyāḥ/ puṃvat tad iṣyate mṛtyukāle svalpīkṛtopadheḥ// *SD*: viii, 38.

offerings in his upturned palms, called *pāṇi-pātra* (hand-bowl). He may enter a house and eat if he has gone there only to beg, without any prior invitation.[95] Even inside, however, he must use no plate or utensils. Finally, the Śvetāmbara monks beg and take food two or three times daily; Digambaras are restricted to a single meal.

Thus concludes this brief introduction to the foundations of the Jaina faith, and to the two traditions through which this faith has manifested itself. We have seen the ways in which these traditions differ: one a bit more conservative, with a doctrine that rests heavily upon faith; the other tending to be more liberal, relaxed, pragmatic, and oriented toward scriptural and historical evidence. But in the remainder of this book we shall discover that on many levels, from the layperson's daily practice to the logical intricacies of the philosopher-monk's most abstruse formulations, it is in fact a combination of essential contributions from both traditions that has sustained the vital flow of the Jina's teachings through so many centuries.

95. For details on the rituals pertaining to this practice, see Ch. VII.

II

The First Disciples and the Jaina Scriptures

The "Divine Sound" of the Tīrthaṅkara

Earlier, the Jaina belief that the sermons of a Jina take the form known as divyadhvani, the divine sound, was alluded to. It is said, moreover, that this sound manifests *artha,* the meaning or import of a Jina's teachings. Artha is in turn translated into *sūtra,* the canonical scriptures, by the several gaṇadharas or chief disciples;[1] these gaṇadharas must have taken their mendicant vows in the presence of the Jina and must be endowed with such purity as to attain nirvāṇa in that very life.[2] All Jainas accept the fact that their scriptures originated in this way. There is sectarian disagreement, however, over the precise nature of the events involved. Whereas Digambaras imagine the divyadhvani as a monotone—like the sound of oṃ—which only the gaṇadharas are able to comprehend, Śvetāmbaras suggest that the Jina speaks in a human language that is divine in the sense that men of all regions, and animals, can benefit from hearing it.[3] In the latter interpretation, the role

1. "atthaṃ bhāsai arahā suttaṃ gaṃthaṃti gaṇaharā niunạm/ sāsaṇassa hiyaṭṭhāe tao suttaṃ pavattai//" Quoted in *NS-ADS*: intro. 11 (from *Āvaśyaka-niryukti*: k 92). Compare: arahaṃtabhāsiyatthaṃ gaṇaharadevehiṃ gaṃthiyaṃ savvaṃ/ paṇamāmi bhattijutto sudaṇāṇamahovayaṃ sirasā// *JP*: 465..

2. "sagapādamūlammi paḍivaṇṇamahavvayaṃ mottūṇa aṇṇaṃ uddissiya divvajjhuṇī kiṇṇa pavaṭṭade? sāhāviyādo." *JSK*: II, 430 (quoted from *Dhavalā*).

3. The Śvetāmbara scriptures maintain that Mahāvīra spoke Ardhamāgadhī, a Prakrit dialect of Magadha: bhagavā ca ṇaṃ Addhamāgahīe bhāsāe āikkhai, sā vi ya ṇaṃ Addhamāgahī bhāsijjamāṇī tesiṃ savvesiṃ āriyamaṇāriyāṇaṃ appaṇo hiyasivasuhayabhāsattāe pariṇamai . . . *SamS*: §111. The Digambaras

of the gaṇadharas would be less one of translation than simply of compiling and organizing the Jina's words into a comprehensive and systematic body of teachings.

The Gaṇadharas: the Chief Disciples of Mahāvīra

Tradition has preserved the names and brief accounts of the lives of Mahāvīra's gaṇadharas.[4] These men belonged without exception to the brahman caste, a fact which might seem unusual in light of the pro-kṣatriya bias among śramaṇa sects noted above in discussing Mahāvīra's birth. Even so, the pattern of a kṣatriya monarch surrounded by brahman ministers was typical in India at the time, and thus may well have been an acceptable norm even for Jainas. These gaṇadharas came from the neighborhood of modern Patna and were new converts to the Jaina faith. Rather than graduating from the lay state to mendicancy, the normal procedure under Jaina law, they took all monastic vows on the same day, at the very moment of their conversion, and adopted the practice of nudity as prescribed by Mahāvīra. At this time, five of the eleven

---

seem to have similar views on the nature of this "language": "yojanāntaradūrasamīpasthāṣṭādaśabhāṣāsaptaśatakubhāṣāyutatiryagdevamanuṣyabhāṣākāra. . . vāgatiśayasampannaḥ . . . Mahāvīro 'rthakartā." *JSK*: II, 431 (quoted from *Dhavalā*).

4. paḍhamettha Iṃdabhūī bīo puṇa hoi Aggibhūi tti/ taie ya Vāyubhūī tao Viyatte Suhamme ya// Maṃḍiya-Moriyaputte Akaṃpie ceva Ayalabhāyā ya/ Meyajje ya Pabhāse ya gaṇaharā huṃti Vīrassa// *NS-ADS*: k 20–21. Compare: Indrabhūtir iti proktaḥ prathamo gaṇadhāriṇām/ Agnibhūtir dvitīyaś ca Vāyubhūtis tṛtīyakaḥ// Śucidattas turīyas tu Sudharmaḥ pañcamas tataḥ/ ṣaṣṭo Māṇḍavya ity ukto Mauryaputras tu saptamaḥ// aṣṭamo 'kampanākhyātir Acalo navamo mataḥ/ Medāryo daśamo 'ntyas tu Prabhāsaḥ sarva eva te// *Harivaṃśapurāṇa*: iii, 41–43. For further biographical information on these gaṇadharas, see Solomon 1966: 22–32. Both traditions depict the gaṇadharas as endowed with great yogic powers and adamantine bodies. The following description of Indrabhūti Gautama seems to have been taken as a model for the others: samaṇassa bhagavao Mahāvīrassa jeṭṭhe antevāsī Indabhūī nāmaṃ aṇagāre Goyamasagotteṇaṃ sattussehe samacauraṃsasaṃṭhāṇasaṃṭhie vajjarisahanārāyasaṃghayaṇe kaṇapulagaṇibhasapamhagore uggatave dittatave tattatave mahātave orāle ghore ghoraguṇe ghoratavassī ghorabambhaceravāsī ucchūḍhasarīre saṃkhittaviulateyalese coddasapuvvī caunāṇovagae savvakkharasannivāī samaṇassa bhagavao Mahāvīrassa adūrasāmante uḍḍhaṃjāṇū ahosire jhāṇakoṭṭhovagae saṃjameṇaṃ tavasā appāṇaṃ bhāvamāṇe viharai. *BhS*: i, 7 (§7).

(namely, Indrabhūti Gautama, Ārya Vyakta, Sudharman, Maṇḍika, and Mauryaputra) were in their early fifties and four (Agnibhūti, Vāyubhūti, Akampita, and Acalabhrātā) were in their forties; Metārya was thirty and Prabhāsa, the youngest, was only sixteen.

With the exceptions of Indrabhūti Gautama and Sudharman, all attained to omniscience (kevalajñāna) after approximately twelve years of mendicancy. The youthful Prabhāsa became a *kevalin* at the remarkable age of twenty-four and died, that is, went to nirvāṇa, in his fortieth year. This life-span of sixteen years after the attainment of kevalajñāna was fairly typical for the other gaṇadharas as well. These kevalin disciples had reached a level of perfection equivalent to that of their master; they were the Jina's equals in every respect, but did not preach the doctrine and were not surrounded by the miraculous phenomena that attend a Tīrthaṅkara.[5] With the attainment of omniscience their clerical activities came to an end; thereafter they were gaṇadharas in name only. Thus it would seem that whatever "transmission" of the Jina's teachings these gaṇadharas had performed must have taken place during their "pre-omniscience" careers as ordinary mendicants. Digambaras and Śvetāmbaras are in basic agreement on this point, although the former take a more strict position, maintaining that the gaṇadharas, like anyone who has become a kevalin, ceased to partake of any food after reaching that state. Śvetāmbaras believe that the disciples continued to take food until one month before death, eventually laying down their bodies in Rājagṛha at a park named Guṇaśīla.

Agnibhūti, Vāyubhūti, Ārya Vyakta, and Metārya died a few years before Mahāvīra; Maṇḍika, Mauryaputra,

5. A Tīrthaṅkara is said to be distinguished from an ordinary kevalin by the presence of the following eight *prātihāryas* (miraculous phenomena):aśokavṛkṣaḥ surapuṣpavṛṣṭir divyadhvaniś cāmaram āsanañ ca/ bhāmaṇḍalaṃ dundubhir ātapatraṃ satprātihāryāṇi jineśvarāṇām// *JP*: 85. For a more elaborate list, comprising some thirty-four items, see *SamS*: §111; *JSK*: I, 141.

Akampita, and Acalabhrātā passed away in the same year as did their master. The effective leaders of the saṃgha during the kevalin period of these chief disciples were the two gaṇadharas, Indrabhūti Gautama and Sudharman, who had not yet attained to kevalajñāna and were thus still "available" to lead the community after the death of Mahāvīra. It is likely, therefore, that the extant Jaina canon comprises the recensions of only these two gaṇadharas, who must have previously absorbed the recensions of the others (if there were any), and who therefore figure in the canon as the major interlocutors to whom Mahāvīra's answers are directed. Indrabhūti Gautama, like his contemporary Ānanda,[6] chief attendant of Gautama the Buddha, was unable to attain arhatship due to his deep attachment to his master. Even the practice of severe austerities, which earned him the title *ghoratavassi*, could not overcome the bonds of this devotion. The tenth lecture of *Uttarādhyayana*, a subsidiary canonical text, is said to have been delivered by Mahāvīra on the last day of his life with the specific aim of curing his chief disciple of this weakness. In words which move the hearts of Jainas to this day, Mahāvīra exhorted Indrabhūti Gautama not to linger on the path and not to miss the moment (*samaya*) of self-realization:

> As the fallow leaf of the tree falls to the
> ground when its days are gone, even so the life
> of men [will come to its end];
> Gautama, be careful all the while!
> As a dewdrop clinging to the top of a blade
> of Kuśa-grass lasts but a short time,
> even so the life of men;
> Gautama, be careful all the while!
> You have crossed the great ocean; why do
> you halt so near the shore? Make haste

6. See Malalasekera 1938: I, 264.

to attain the other side;
Gautama, be careful all the while![7]

Tradition is unanimous in asserting that Mahāvīra died soon after giving this sermon, and that Indrabhūti Gautama, "cutting off love and hatred," attained the noble goal of omniscience on that same day, making it a doubly memorable one for followers of the Jina. He lived on as a kevalin for twelve years, finally entering nirvāṇa in Rājagṛha at the age of 92.

Since the kevalin neither administers nor preaches, Sudharman must have assumed the leadership of the Jaina order upon Indrabhūti Gautama's attainment of omniscience. He also remained sole custodian of the scripture, which now contained, in addition to his own version, the recension handed down in the tradition of Indrabhūti Gautama. This body of sacred material he taught to his disciple Jambū. Most sermons of the extant canon thus begin with Sudharman saying to Jambū: "Oh long-lived One! Thus have I heard the following discourse from the Venerable [Mahāvīra]" (*suyaṃ me āvusaṃ! teṇaṃ bhagavayā evaṃ akkhāyaṃ*). Sudharman taught the scriptures for some twelve years after Mahāvīra's nirvāṇa; in the thirteenth year he himself reached omniscience.

With Sudharman's death in that year (his hundredth), the first generation of the disciples of Mahāvīra came to an end. Jambū then succeeded to leadership of the order and taught for eight years. Upon attaining kevalajñāna and entering nirvāṇa in the sixty-fourth year after Mahāvīra's death, he became the last person in this time cycle to reach mokṣa. The tradition of oral transmission was carried on for a century and a half by his successors in the line of Prabhava, Śayyambhava, Yaśobhadra, and finally Bha-

7. dumapattae paṃḍuyae jahā nivaḍai rāigaṇāṇa accae/ evaṃ maṇuyāṇa jīviyaṃ, samayaṃ Goyama mā pamāyae//1// kusagge jaha osabiṃdue, thovaṃ ciṭṭhai laṃbamāṇae/ evaṃ maṇuyāṇa jīviyaṃ, samayaṃ Goyama mā pamāyae//2// tiṇṇo hu si aṇṇavaṃ mahaṃ, kiṃ puṇa ciṭṭhasi tīramāgao/ abhitura pāraṃ gamittae, samayaṃ Goyama mā pamāyae//35// *UtS*: x, 1–2, 35.

drabāhu, in whose time, as we have seen, the Jaina community was scattered by famine and suffered a major loss of its canon.[8]

The Literature

The canonical literature (*āgama*) of the Jainas is known variously as *Nigaṇṭha-pāvayāṇa* (sermons of the Nirgrantha), *gaṇi-piḍaga* (basket of the gaṇadharas), *suya-ñāṇa* (scriptural knowledge), or merely *siddhānta* (doctrine).[9] It consists of some sixty texts divided into three groups of works known as *pūrva*, *aṅga*, and *aṅgabāhya*, all handed down in an ancient Magadhan language called Ardhamāgadhī:[10]

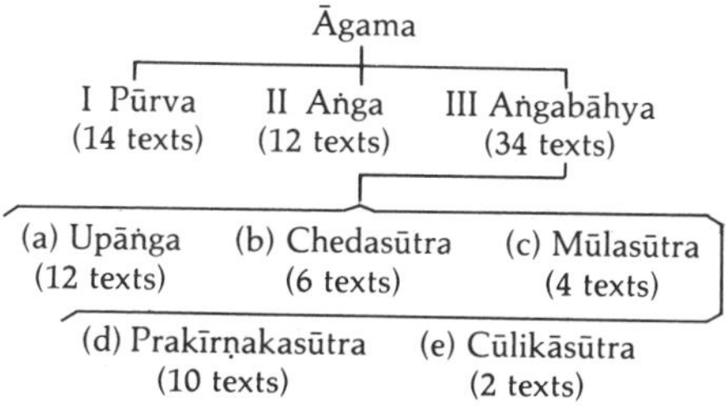

I. The fourteen Pūrvas (all extinct)[11]
(1) *Utpāda (Uppāda)*; (2) *Agrāyaṇī (Aggāṇiya)*; (3) *Vīrya (Viriya)*; (4) *Astināstipravāda (Atthinatthi-pavāya)*; (5) *Jñānapravāda (Nāṇa-p.)*; (6) *Satyapravāda (Sacca-p.)*; (7) *Ātmapravāda (Āya-p.)*; (8) *Karmapravāda*

8. For a Jaina history of the patriarchate from Jambū to Bhadrabāhu, see Jacobi 1932: intro, xxxviff.

9. For histories of Jaina literature, see Winternitz 1933: II, 424–595; Kapadia 1941; Schubring 1962: §37–50; Folkert 1976.

10. Ardhamāgadhī was employed only in the most ancient times; the language of extant Śvetāmbara texts is very close to Mahārāṣṭrī Prakrit and is often referred to as Jaina Mahārāṣṭrī by modern scholars. Digambaras adopted another dialect called Śauraseni Prakrit, the language of the *Ṣaṭkhaṇḍāgama* and other works. See *NS-ADS*: intro, 19.

11. The original Prakrit titles are given in parentheses. I have used Sanskrit equivalents throughout, following the practice adopted by the Jainas.

(Kamma-p.); (9) *Pratyākhyānapravāda (Paccakkhāṇa-p.)*; (10) *Vidyānuvāda (Vijjā-p.)*; (11) *Kalyāṇavāda (Kallāṇavāda*—also known as *Avanjha)*; (12) *Prāṇavāda (Pāṇavāda)*; (13) *Kriyāviśāla (Kiriyavisāla)*; (14) *Lokabindusāra (Logabindusāra)*.

II. The twelve Aṅgas

(1) *Ācārāṅga-sūtra (Āyāraṃga-sutta)*; (2) *Sūtrakṛtāṅga (Sūyagaḍaṃga)*; (3) *Sthānāṅga (Ṭhāṇaṃga)*; (4) *Samavāyāṅga (Samavāyaṃga)*; (5) *Bhagavatī Vyākhyāprajñapti (Bhagavaī Viyāhapannatti)*; (6) *Jñātṛdharmakathā (Nāyādhammakahāo)*; (7) *Upāsakadaśāḥ (Uvāsagadasāo)*; (8) *Antakṛddaśāḥ (Aṃtagaḍadasāo)*; (9) *Anuttaraupapātikadaśāḥ (Aṇuttarovavāiyadasāo)*; (10) *Praśnavyākaraṇa (Paṇhāvāgaraṇāiṃ)*; (11) *Vipākaśruta (Vivāgasuyaṃ)*; (12) *Dṛṣṭivāda (Diṭṭhivāya)*, extinct.

III. a. The twelve Upāṅgas

(1) *Aupapātika (Uvavāiya)*; (2) *Rājapraśnīya (Rāyapaseṇaijja)*; (3) *Jīvājīvābhigama (Jīvājīvābhigama)*; (4) *Prajñāpanā (Pannavaṇā)*; (5) *Sūryaprajñapti (Sūriyapannatti)*; (6) *Jambūdvīpaprajñapti (Jambuddīvapannatti)*; (7) *Candraprajñapti (Caṃdapannatti)*; (8) *Nirayāvalī (Nirayāvalī)*; (9) *Kalpāvataṃsikāḥ (Kappāvaḍaṃsiāo)*; (10) *Puṣpikāḥ (Pupphiāo)*; (11) *Puṣpacūlikāḥ (Pupphacūliāo)*; (12) *Vṛṣṇidaśāḥ (Vaṇhidasāo)*.

b. The six Chedasūtras

(1) *Ācāradaśāḥ (Āyāradasāo)*; (2) *Bṛhatkalpa (Bihākappa)*; (3) *Vyavahāra (Vavahāra)*; (4) *Niśītha (Nisīha)*; (5) *Mahāniśītha (Mahānisīha)*; (6) *Jītakalpa (Jīyakappa)*.

c. The four Mūlasūtras

(1) *Daśavaikālika (Dasaveyāliya)*; (2) *Uttarādhyayana (Uttarajjhayaṇa)*; (3) *Āvaśyaka (Āvassaya)*; (4) *Piṇḍaniryukti (Piṃḍanijjutti)*.

d. The ten Prakīrṇakasūtras

(1) *Catuḥśaraṇa (Causaraṇa)*; (2) *Āturapratyākhyāna (Āurapaccakkhāṇa)*; (3) *Bhaktaparijñā (Bhattaparinnā)*; (4) *Saṃstāraka (Saṃthāra)*; (5) *Taṇḍulavaicārika (Taṃdulaveyāliya)*; (6) *Candravedhyaka (Caṃdāvijjhaya)*; (7) *Devendrastava (Deviṃdatthaya)*; (8) *Gaṇividyā*

(Gaṇivijjā); (9) *Mahāpratyākhyāna (Mahāpaccakkhāṇa)*; (10) *Vīrastava (Vīratthaya)*.

e. The two Cūlikāsūtras

(1) *Nandī-sūtra (Ṇaṃdī-sutta)*; (2) *Anuyogadvāra-sūtra (Aṇuogaddārāiṃ)*.[12]

I. THE PŪRVAS (OLD TEXTS)

The Pūrvas include fourteen works of great antiquity, claimed by the Jainas to go back to the time of Pārśva. These texts are no longer extant, but brief descriptions of their contents have survived in the later literature. They seem to have included the most ancient Jaina speculations on the nature of the cosmos, doctrines pertaining to the bondage of the soul by matter, and polemics against contemporary philosophical schools. They also contained a great deal of Jaina astrology and astronomy, as well as esoteric methods of attaining yogic and occult powers. The Pūrvas were transmitted in an oral tradition (*śruta*) and are said to have been preached anew by Mahāvīra and systematized by the gaṇadharas. Eventually, much of this material was probably integrated into the Aṅga texts, which originated with Mahāvīra himself. Indeed, Jainas believe that the twelfth Aṅga, called *Dṛṣṭivāda*, contained the main Pūrva teachings.[13]

Partly because it was thus incorporated into the Aṅgas, and perhaps due to the esoteric nature of its subject matter, this branch of the canon appears to have been mastered by

12. All forty-five extant texts referred to here are accepted as canonical by the Śvetāmbaras. Members of the Sthānakavāsi sect (see Ch. IX), however, recognize only thirty-one of these as authentic: the eleven Aṅgas, twelve Upāṅgas, six Chedasūtras, and four texts from various categories (*Daśavaikālika*, *Nandī-sūtra*, and *Anuyogadvāra-sūtra*). They also include in this category one work known as *Āvaśyaka-sūtra*, which seems to be a collection of material culled from various Prakīrṇakasūtras. Digambaras, while retaining identical names for the Pūrva and Aṅga texts, do not admit that any of these have survived in authentic form. Among all the remaining works, they recognize only a few of the Prakīrṇakasūtras as valid scripture.

It should be noted here that in the Śvetāmbara tradition, several extra-canonical texts have gained a status functionally equivalent to that of the scriptures themselves; notable among these are *Ṛṣibhāṣitāni (Isibhāsiyāiṃ)* and *Aṅgavidyā (Aṃgavijjā)*. For details, see Schubring 1962: §56.

13. On the possible contents of the *Dṛṣṭivāda*, see Alsdorf 1973.

very few. The Jaina tradition is unanimous in affirming that the great pontiff Bhadrabāhu (circa 360 B.C.) was the last person who knew all fourteen Pūrvas by heart. After him, knowledge of the Pūrvas was lost; most of those mendicants who had memorized portions thereof perished in the great Magadha famine. Thus no more than a small part of the *Dṛṣṭivāda* seems to have been recited at the first Jaina council, held under the leadership of Sthūlabhadra.

Even this incomplete *Dṛṣṭivāda* was totally lost from the Śvetāmbara tradition in a subsequent period. But the Digambaras were able to preserve a few sections dealing with karma theory from the third book, called *Pūrvagata* (That which belongs to the Pūrva). These were transmitted by the Digambara mendicant Dharasena (circa A.D. 156) to his disciples Puṣpadanta and Bhūtabali, who in turn committed the teaching to writing. The resulting work, known as *Ṣaṭkhaṇḍāgama* (Scripture in six parts), was probably the first written scripture of the Jainas. Soon thereafter another Digambara mendicant named Guṇabhadra, drawing upon the same sources as had Dharasena, compiled a second work called *Kaṣāyaprābhṛta.* Both of these early texts deal with Jaina theories of bondage of the soul, and were probably comprehensible only to the most advanced mendicant scholars of the day. Voluminous commentaries are reported to have been written on them, most notably Vīrasena's *Dhavalā* (The luminous) on the *Ṣaṭkhaṇḍāgama* (A.D. 800) and Jinasena's *Jayadhavalā* (The victoriously luminous) on the *Kaṣāyaprābhṛta* (A.D. 820).[14] The texts and their commentaries run altogether to some 120,000 verses; preserved on palm-leaf manuscripts (perhaps the oldest of their kind to have been found in India), they have only recently been critically edited and published.

14. This entire literature consists of some thirty-eight volumes (16 volumes of the *Dhavalā*, 7 of the *Mahādhavalā*, and 15 of the *Jayadhavalā*). It compares well with the Śvetāmbara literature on the doctrine of karma, known as the *Karmagrantha* of Devendrasūri (fourteenth century), vols. I–VI. See Glasenapp 1942: xii–xx.

The *Ṣaṭkhaṇḍāgama* and *Kaṣāyaprābhṛta* are the only canonical works that the Digambaras possess;[15] followers of this tradition have consistently maintained that the Aṅga and Aṅgabāhya texts were "totally lost" as early as the second century A.D.

Fortunately, however, the loss was not really "total." The Digambaras perhaps first adopted this expression in order to reject, for reasons discussed earlier, the authenticity of scriptures retained by their Śvetāmbara rivals. It is also likely that the former sect actually did lose whatever canonical materials they may have possessed during their migration to the south and subsequent isolation from the bulk of the Jaina mendicant community. Whatever the case, the Śvetāmbaras who had inherited the scriptures that had been approved at the Pāṭaliputra council were able to preserve large portions of the Aṅga and the Aṅgabāhya materials, even though they had lost the Pūrvas and the *Dṛṣṭivāda* Aṅga. We do not know the earliest date at which they began to put the canon into written form; this must have taken place prior to the second council, which was held at Mathura in the fourth century A.D. under the guidance of Pontiff Skandila (A.D. 300–343).

The Śvetāmbara tradition that speaks of this council also alludes to another synod held concurrently at Valabhi (in Saurashtra) under the supervision of one ācārya Nāgārjuna. It is said that the two leaders could not meet in order to resolve the differences in their recensions at that time; such a resolution was accomplished, however, by a third and last council, again in Valabhi, which took place either 980 or 993 years after Mahāvīra's nirvāṇa (that is, either in A.D. 453 or 466).[16] The leader of this meeting, Devardhi-

15. In medieval times this literature was known as siddhānta, and one who mastered it was honored by the title *siddhānta-cakravarti.* The famous author Nemicandra (A.D. 950) was a scholar of this type; his *Gommaṭasāra* was considered the most sacred of available Digambara texts until the recent discovery of the works noted above. For an analysis of the *Gommaṭasāra,* see Jindal 1958: 94–186.

16. See Kapadia 1941: 63.

gaṇi Kṣamāśramaṇa, compiled the final redaction of the extant canon and had it committed to writing in its entirety.[17]

II. THE AṄGAS (LIMBS)

The Aṅgas, so called because they were seen as components of the body of scripture, include twelve texts; of these only the twelfth, the aforementioned *Dṛṣṭivāda*, is no longer extant. There is also a subsidiary canon, the Aṅgabāhya (Outside the limbs), which is a collection of miscellaneous texts that in some cases originate not from Mahāvīra directly but from certain Elders (*sthaviras*) of a later date. The overall canon in its present form cannot be claimed to go back to the times of Mahāvīra. Hermann Jacobi, who prepared the first critical edition and translation of the *Ācārāṅga* (the first Aṅga),[18] has established that the canon was recited neither in a single period nor by a single individual. The appearance of different spellings for the same word indicate Prakrit recitations from various periods. It is also possible to find long, archaic chapters side by side with relatively modern ones in a single work; this strongly suggests the attempt to fill in a previously incomplete version.[19] There are even entire texts (for example, the tenth Aṅga, called *Praśnavyākaraṇa*) the contents of which are at variance with the descriptions applied to them in older sources, indicating that later substitutions were made for materials lost in the process of oral transmission. In spite of all such omissions, additions, and

17. "śrīDevarddhigaṇikṣamāśramaṇena śrīVīrād aśītyadhikanavaśata (980) varṣe jātena dvādaśavarṣīyadurbhikṣavaśād bahutarasādhuvyāpattau bahuśrutavicchittau ca jātāyāṃ . . . bhaviṣyadbhavyalokopakārāya śrutabhaktaye ca śrīsaṅghāgrahād mṛtāvaśiṣṭatadākālīnasarvasādhūn Valabhyām ākārya tanmukhād avicchinnāvaśiṣṭān nyūnādhikān truṭitānutruṭitān āgamālāpakān anukrameṇa svamatyā saṅkalayya pustakārūḍhāḥ kṛtāḥ. tato mūlato gaṇadharabhāṣitānām api āgamānāṃ kartā śrīDevarddhigaṇikṣamāśramaṇa eva jātaḥ." Quoted in Kapadia 1941: 63, n. 1 (from the *Sāmācārīśataka* of Samayasundara).

18. *The Āyāraṃga Suttạ of the Śvetāmbara Jains*, London, 1882, tr. Jacobi 1884.

19. Compare, e.g., the eighth lecture of *AS* (§462–522), bk. I, with the obviously older materials of lectures 1–7 (§1–461).

modifications, a considerable portion of the extant canon must be considered authentic, reflecting (at least in those discussions where sectarian conflict is absent) the earliest and most basic teachings of Mahāvīra.

The eleven Aṅga texts can be broadly categorized into four areas: ecclesiastical law; the examination of false views; doctrine; and finally, narratives for the edification of the laity. The first Aṅga, appropriately called *Ācāra* (Conduct), forms the law book for Jaina monks and nuns. It regulates their conduct by delineating the obligatory vows (such as the vow to avoid injuring even the most minute forms of life), and also by giving specific instructions pertaining to permissible methods for obtaining such requisites as food, clothing, lodging, and medicine. The *Ācārāṅga* is accorded great reverence, not only because its explication of the law forms the very foundation of mendicant conduct, but also because it contains what is certainly our most authoritative account of the life of Mahāvīra. The work has been judged on linguistic and metrical grounds to comprise the oldest portion of the extant canon, and it may well have preserved Mahāvīra's own words on the cardinal doctrine of ahiṃsā (noninjury).

A person may enter monastic life with the noblest of motives and yet be led into "wrong" paths by advocates of "false," that is, heretical, doctrines. A critical examination of teachings opposed to that of the Jina is therefore undertaken in the *Sūtrakṛta*, the second Aṅga.[20] *Niyativāda* (fatalism), *ajñānavāda* (agnosticism), and several types of *akriyāvāda* (nonaction)—Sāṃkhya eternalism, Cārvāka annihilationism, and others—are discussed in this Aṅga; all are rejected as being one-sided (*ekāntavāda*) and thus inferior to the comprehensive (*anekānta*) Jaina view of reality.

The third Aṅga volume, entitled *Sthāna* (Cases), is a kind of encyclopedia; it considers an almost bewilderingly

20. Translated by Jacobi 1895: 235–435.

detailed variety of doctrinal issues in a schematic way, calculated to aid in their memorization and comprehension.

The fourth Aṅga, *Samavāya* (Putting together), is a continuation of the third. It preserves what is probably the earliest record of the contents of the twelve Aṅgas, and is therefore of great importance in determining the authenticity of the extant canon.

The fifth, *Vyākhyāprajñapti* (Proclamation of explanations) is by far the most voluminous work of the entire canon.[21] Countless questions, asked by Indrabhūti Gautama, fill the text. Mahāvīra's answers demonstrate his unique method of responding to each question with a statement "subject to qualifications" (*syādvāda*).[22] This practice was to have a profound effect upon the development of Jaina philosophy; thus we find the *Vākhyāprajñapti* held in high esteem and referred to as *Bhagavatī*, the venerable. The *Bhagavatī* is also of great historical importance, containing the controversial episodes of Mahāvīra's encounters with the Ājīvika teacher Makkhali Gosāla and the events that culminated in the latter's tragic death.

The remaining Aṅgas, with the exception of the tenth, can be grouped under the genre of *kathā*, narratives intended for the edification of the laity. The sixth, *Jñātṛdharmakathāḥ*,[23] sets the tone for such religious tales (*dharma-kathā*), which came to be a favorite genre among Jainas of the medieval period.[24] Of special importance in this text is the narrative concerning Malli, the female Tīrthaṅkara of the Śvetāmbara sect. The next (seventh) Aṅga,

21. For a study and analysis of this work, see Sikdar 1964; Deleu 1970: intro. 17–50.

22. The following provides a good example of such a dialogue: jīvā ṇaṃ bhaṃte! kiṃ sāsayā, asāsayā? Goyamā! jīvā siya sāsayā, siya asāsayā. se kiṇaṭṭheṇaṃ bhaṃte! evaṃ vuccai "jīvā siya sāsayā, siya asāsayā"? Goyamā! davvaṭṭhayāe sāsayā, bhāvaṭṭhayāe asāsayā; se teṇaṭṭheṇaṃ Goyamā! evaṃ vuccai ". . . jāva siya asāsayā." *BhS*: vii, 2 (§273).

23. See Schubring 1962: §46.

24. For a survey of the Jaina narrative literature (*kathā*), see Upadhye's intro. to the *Bṛhatkathākośa*; Ghatge 1934.

Upāsaka-daśāh,[25] sets forth the lives of ten exemplary laymen; we will have occasion to look more closely at one of these, the tale of Ānanda, in a later chapter.

The *Antakṛddaśāḥ* (eight) and the *Anuttaraupapātika-daśāḥ*[26] (nine) recount legends of monks undergoing extreme austerities. The former describes individuals whose practice leads them to nirvāṇa, while the latter deals with those who attain rebirth in the highest heavens. The *Antakṛddaśāḥ* contains several stories set in the time of Nemi, the twenty-second Tīrthaṅkara. The famous Hindu *avatāra* Kṛṣṇa is here integrated into Jaina mythology by being described as the nephew of Nemi; several stories deal with his exploits.

The tenth Aṅga, called *Praśnavyākaraṇa*, delineates the mahāvratas. As above, the content of the extant text does not agree with that ascribed to it in the *Samavāya*. The style too betrays a later hand, and it seems likely that the version which has come down to us was not composed until after the last Valabhi council (A.D. 450).[27]

The eleventh and last Aṅga is the *Vipākaśruta*. This work deals with the irrevocable law of karma; the sorts of results (*vipāka*) that follow from good and bad deeds performed in previous lives are vividly described. The tale of Miyaputta, born with a terribly deformed body due to previous sinful conduct, dominates the collection. These stories, which depict ten good and ten evil "outcomes," must have acted both as powerful deterrents to wrongdoing and as inducements to undertaking the holy life of a mendicant.

III. THE AṄGABĀHYA

The Aṅgabāhya (Subsidiary canon) originates not with the gaṇadharas but with the sthaviras, mendicant authors

25. Translated by A. F. R. Hoernle 1890.
26. Translated by L. D. Barnett 1907.
27. See *NS-ADS*: intro. 28.

of a subsequent period.[28] In ancient times this collection was also known as *Prakīrṇaka* (The miscellaneous)[29] and contained some eighteen texts, mostly employed in confessional rites; a large number of these have survived.[30] This group formed the nucleus of the extant Śvetāmbara Aṅgabāhya, which probably reached its present form at or around the time of the Valabhi council and comprises thirty-four texts arranged in five groups: Upāṅga, Chedasūtra, Mūlasūtra, Prakīrṇakasūtra, and Cūlikāsūtra.

a. The Upāṅgas.—The Upāṅga (Subsidiary to the Aṅga) consists of twelve texts, mostly narratives addressed to the laity. The first, *Aupapātika,* opens with a beautiful description of the grand reception accorded Mahāvīra by King Kūṇika and his subjects when the Jina arrived in a park outside the city of Campā. This section is called samavasaraṇa (The coming together), a term that figured significantly in later ideas of the "holy assembly" of the Tīrthaṅkara; representation of such an assembly, moreover, became an important feature of Jaina art and temple architecture.

The main story of the *Aupapātika* concerns the extraordinary behavior of a group of non-Jaina mendicants (*parivrājakas*). Finding themselves in a forest with no access to any laypersons (the only acceptable source of alms), they bravely chose to face death by fasting rather

28. gaṇadharakayamaṃgagayaṃ, jaṃ kata therehi bāhiraṃ taṃ tu/ niyataṃ vaṃgapaviṭṭhaṃ, aṇiyayasuyabāhiraṃ bhaṇiyaṃ// Quoted in *Nandisūtra* [Haribhadra's *Vṛtti*]: §79.

29. See *NS-ADS*: intro. 23.

30. Two ancient lists have survived: (1) Umāsvāti's *Tattvārthabhāṣya* (i, 20) accepted only by the Śvetāmbara tradition as an authentic work of this author) enumerates the following texts under the category of Aṅgabāhya: *Sāmāyika, Caturviṃśatistava, Vandana, Pratikramaṇa, Kāyavyutsarga, Pratyākhyāna, Daśavaikālika, Uttarādhyayana, Daśā, Kalpa-vyavahāra, Niśītha, Ṛṣibhāṣita,* and so on. (2) Vīrasena's *Dhavalāṭīkā,* accepted by the Digambara tradition, gives a somewhat different version: tattha Aṅgabāhirassa coddasa atthāhiyārā, taṃ jahā *Sāmāiyaṃ, Cauvīsatthao, Vaṃdaṇā, Paḍikammaṃ, Veṇaiyaṃ, Kidiyammaṃ, Dasaveyāliyaṃ, Uttarajjhayaṇaṃ, Kappavavahāro, Kappākappiyaṃ, Mahākappiyaṃ, Puṇḍarīyaṃ, Mahāpuṇḍarīyaṃ, Ṇisīhiyaṃ* cedi. *Dhavalāṭīkā*: I, 96. For a concordance of these two lists, see *NS-ADS*: intro. 21ff.

than breaking their vow of *adattādāna-virati* (not taking what is not given).[31] Although these mendicants belonged to a brahmanical order, they had at one time been disciples of a Jaina layman named Ammaḍa; thus they now decided to take refuge in Mahāvīra (becoming his disciples by invoking his name) and to fast to death.[32] This holy conduct brought about their rebirth (*upapāta*) in heavenly abodes.

It should be noted here that Jainas admit the possibility of any mendicant, regardless of sectarian affiliation, attaining to the heavens, so long as he keeps his vows; the *Aupapātika* even provides specific information about the kinds of heavens that are open to members of various heretic orders.[33] This story, moreover, goes beyond a mere generalized emphasis upon adherence to vows; by depicting even death as preferable to improper conduct, it underlines the belief of Mahāvīra's followers that no other mendicants are as strongly committed as they to the rules of the holy life.

The second Upāṅga, called *Rājapraśnīya*, is a dialogue between a Jaina mendicant named Keśi and one King Pāesi (Prasenajit) of Seyaviyā concerning the existence of the soul. This work is of great historical importance for two reasons: it resembles, in both form and content, the Pāyāsirājaññasutta of the Buddhist canon (*Dīghanikāya*: II.x.), and it employs a disciple of Pārśva as a proponent of Jaina doctrine. The story begins with a description of the king, who is a ruler bereft of righteousness. Harsh and cruel, the destroyer of many animals, he shows no respect to brahmans or ascetics and scourges his subjects with unbearable

31. iha ṇaṃ devāṇuppiyā! udagadātāro ṇatthi taṃ ṇo khalu kappai ahme adiṇṇaṃ giṇhittae adiṇṇaṃ sāijjittae, taṃ seyaṃ khalu amhaṃ . . . vāluyāsaṃthārae saṃtharittā saṃlehaṇājhosiyāṇaṃ bhattapāṇapaḍiyāikkhiyāṇaṃ pāovagayāṇaṃ kālaṃ aṇavakaṃkhamāṇāṇaṃ viharittae . . . *Aupapātika-sūtra*: §38.

32. On this holy practice, called *sallekhanā*, see Ch. VII.

33. Ājivika mendicants, for example, are said to attain an exalted heavenly abode called *Acyuta-kalpa*: se je ime gāmāgāra jāva saṃnivesesu Ājīvikā bhavaṃti . . . teṇaṃ eyārūveṇaṃ vihāreṇaṃ viharamāṇā bahūiṃ vāsāiṃ pariyāyaṃ pāuṇittā kālamāse kālaṃ kiccā ukkoseṇaṃ Accue Kappe devattāe uvavattāro bhavaṃti . . . *Aupapātika-sūtra*: §40.

taxation. At one time, this king sent his charioteer Citta to the neighboring city of Śrāvasti, where it happened that Keśi, a lifelong celibate (*kumāra-śramaṇa*) ordained in the discipline of Pārśva (*Pāsāvaccijja*), was also in temporary residence.[34] Upon listening to the mendicant's sermon on the four-fold restraint, Citta became Keśi's disciple;[35] returning to Seyaviyā, he persuaded the king to visit his new teacher.

The subsequent exchange between Keśi and the skeptical Pāesi is valuable in that it brings to light various popular notions regarding the soul, as well as the Jaina theories that were put forth to counter those of the materialists and of the brahmanical schools.[36] The *Rājapraśnīya* presents an important Jaina concept regarding the "dimensions" of the soul, stated in what is probably its most ancient form. Almost every soul-affirming Indian system holds that the soul, being nonmaterial, is totally free from limits and therefore all-pervasive (*vibhu*). Only the Jainas have posited a soul which is nonmaterial and yet subject to contraction and expansion when in its mundane state; such a soul is therefore of the same dimension as its body (*svadeha-parimāṇa*). King Pāesi asks, pertinently, whether such a soul would not lose weight when reincarnating from a large body into a small one, and if this process would not eventually result in its destruction. Keśi responds by introducing an important Jaina technical term, *agurulaghutva*, which designates a quality (*guṇa*) whereby there is neither gain (*guru*) nor loss (*laghu*) in the *innate* extent of a soul

34. teṇaṃ kāleṇaṃ teṇaṃ samaeṇaṃ Pāsāvaccijje Kesī nāmaṃ kumārasamaṇe jāisaṃpanne kulasaṃpanne . . . caudasapuvvī caunāṇovagae paṃcahiṃ aṇagārasaehiṃ saddhiṃ saṃparivuḍe . . . Sāvatthīe nayarīe bahiyā koṭṭhae ujjāṇe . . . saṃjameṇaṃ tavasā appāṇaṃ bhāvemāṇe viharai. *Rājapraśnīya-sūtra*: §48.

35. tae ṇaṃ se Kesī kumāṛasamaṇe Cittassa sārahissa tīse mahaimahāliyāe mahaccaparisāe cāujjāmaṃ dhammaṃ parikahei. taṃ jahā: savvāo pāṇāivāyāo veramaṇaṃ, savvāo musāvāyāo veramaṇaṃ, savvāo adinnādāṇāo veramaṇaṃ, savvāo bahiddhādāṇāo veramaṇaṃ. Ibid.: §50.

36. "Paesī, amhaṃ samaṇāṇaṃ Nigganthāṇaṃ esā sannā . . . jahā anno jīvo annaṃ sarīraṃ no taṃ jīvo taṃ sarīraṃ." Ibid.: §61.

even when it undergoes fluctuations to "fit" one particular body or another.[37] Such a process is illustrated by the example of a piece of cloth, which retains its original mass whether it is folded or spread out.

The notion of agurulaghutva became especially significant in later literature, when Jaina scholastics began grappling with the fundamental problem of change. The fact that this doctrine of "no *essential* change in the soul, even under conditions of defilement" is here enunciated not by Mahāvīra, but by a member of the older school, seems calculated to lend it greater authority by virtue of increased antiquity. The *Rājapraśnīya* goes on to tell us that King Pāesi was converted and became a Jaina layman (*upāsaka*). His queen, who like her husband had for many years been dedicated to the hedonistic life, could not bear the king's new austerity and poisoned him. But Pāesi had changed so completely that he went immediately to the public hall of fasting (*posaha-sālā*) where, taking the vows of a mendicant, he peacefully laid down his body; not a single thought of ill will towards his wife had entered his mind, and he was instantly reborn in a heavenly abode.[38] The story ends with the prophecy that Pāesi will eventually become a mendicant and attain nirvāṇa.

The third Upāṅga, *Jīvājīvābhigama* (Understanding the sentient and the insentient), is devoted to a discussion of these two modes of being, which together describe the totality of existents set forth in Jaina ontology. The work opens with a salutation to the twenty-four Tīrthaṅkaras,[39]

37. evāmeva Paesī, jīvassa agurulahuyattaṃ paḍucca jīvaṃtassa vā tuliyassa muyassa vā tuliyassa natthi kei āṇatte vā jāva lahuyatte vā . . . Ibid.: §67.

38. tae ṇaṃ se Paesī rāyā Sūriyakaṃtāe devīe attāṇaṃ saṃpaladdhaṃ jāṇittā Sūriyakaṃtāe devīe maṇasā vi appadussamāṇe jeṇeva posahasālā teṇeva uvāgacchi . . . dabbhasaṃthāragaṃ saṃtharei . . . samāhipatte kālamāse kālaṃ kiccā . . . Ibid.: §76.

39. ṇamo Usabhāiyāṇaṃ titthayarāṇaṃ. iha khalu jiṇamayaṃ . . . jiṇadesiyaṃ . . . aṇuvīiya taṃ . . . roemāṇā therā bhagavaṃto Jīvājīvābhigamaṇāmaṃ ajjhayaṇaṃ paṇṇaviṃsu. *Jīvājīvābhigama-sūtra*: §1. For the names of the Tīrthaṅkaras, as well as a description of their iconographic representations, see Ch. VI n. 19.

indicating that widespread belief in these exalted figures goes back to a very early period. The *Jīvājīvābhigama* is a virtual compendium of Jainism presented in dialogue form; the chief interlocutor, just as in the *Vyākhyāprajñapti* Aṅga, is Indrabhūti Gautama.

The fourth Upāṅga, called *Prajñāpanā* (Explanations), claims to present the essence of the long-lost *Dṛṣṭivāda* or twelfth Aṅga. Being the sole representative of the extinct Pūrva traditions, as well as of the *Dṛṣṭivāda*, the *Prajñāpanā* is viewed with great reverence by Śvetāmbaras, who refer to it as *Bhagavatī* (a title normally applied only to the Aṅga text *Vyākhyāprajñapti*). In both style and content the *Prajñāpanā* resembles the *Ṣaṭkhaṇḍāgama* of the Digambaras, indicating that both derive from similar, if not identical, traditions.[40] The work is rather voluminous, consisting of some thirty-six chapters in which the author considers the *jīva* (soul) in its manifold aspects: births (*gati*), sense organs (*indriya*), bodies (*śarīra*), language (*bhāṣā*), sexual feelings (*veda*), passions (*kaṣāya*), karma, the spiritual path (*saṃvara*), and so on. It is further distinguished by the fact that its authorship is known; the writer was apparently a monk called Ārya Śyāma, who flourished circa 79 B.C.[41]

The next three Upāṅgas, *Jambūdvīpaprajñapti, Sūryaprajñapti* and *Candraprajñapti,* deal respectively with cosmology, movements of the sun, and movements of the moon. Jambūdvīpa, as we have seen earlier, is the center of the universe (*loka-ākāśa*); it is of primary interest to the Jainas in that it contains the "continent" of Bharata (Bharata-kṣetra), one of the few areas of habitation where Tīrthaṅkaras are born and where other human beings may obtain mokṣa by following their teachings. The *Jambūd-*

40. For a comparison of the two texts, see Malvania 1969.

41. suyasāgarā viṇeūṇa jeṇa suyarayaṇamuttamaṃ dinnaṃ/ sīsagaṇassa bhagavao tassa namo Ajjasāmassa// ajjihayaṇamiṇaṃ cittaṃ suyarayaṇaṃ Diṭṭhivāyaṇīsaṃdaṃ/ jaha vanniyaṃ bhagavayā ahamavi taha vannaissāmi// *Prajñāpanā-sūtra*: §i, 4–5. On the date of Ārya Śyāma, see Malvania 1969: 43ff.

vīpaprajñapti furnishes a great mass of information on the progressive (utsarpiṇī) and regressive (avasarpiṇī) time cycles; it also discusses the dawn of current human civilization, when Ṛṣabha, first Tīrthaṅkara of our period, established the new tīrtha. The legends of Ṛṣabha are of great significance, expressing the Jaina attempt to show that the first Jina was also the first lawgiver, the individual who set up secular as well as spiritual laws for mankind. At a later time, Jaina teachers proclaimed Ṛṣabha to be the originator of even the caste system; this idea, as we shall see in a subsequent chapter (IX, nn. 24–28), was promulgated with the aim of protecting the Jaina laity from total absorption by brahmanical institutions.

Of still greater importance is the legend pertaining to Ṛṣabha's eldest son, Bharata, the first cakravartin (Universal monarch), after whom the Jainas' "Bharata-kṣetra" (probably identical with the Indian subcontinent) is named. Although he had conquered the entire realm, Bharata is said to have been an ideal Jaina king, adhering to the layman's vow of nonviolence and unattached to his wealth and domain. So pure was his heart, so perfect his conduct, and so firm his faith in Jaina doctrine that the seemingly trivial event of seeing a ring fall accidentally from his finger made him realize the futility and vanity of worldly wealth; then and there, even without formally renouncing the household life, he attained to kevalajñāna. The story of Bharata is unique in that the canon nowhere else suggests the possibility of achieving omniscience without first taking the mendicant vows.[42]

Digambaras totally reject this particular episode as contrary to the Law, but they do consider Bharata a man of great purity who attained to kevalajñāna as soon as he had actually become a monk. He reigns supreme in their

42. See *Jambūdvīpaprajñapti-sūtra*: §70. Later Śvetāmbara literature does refer to other instances of such an achievement; see, e.g., the story of Marudevī, below, Ch. VII n. 25.

purāṇas and romances as a sage among kings, an ideal layman whose true vision (*samyak-darśana*) was never flawed by the vicissitudes of worldly existence.[43]

The remaining five Upāṅgas (*Nirayāvalī, Kalpāvataṃsikāḥ, Puṣpikāḥ, Puṣpacūlikāḥ* and *Vṛṣṇidaśāḥ*)[44] may have originally formed the nucleus of the entire collection; they are mainly narratives describing various laymen and laywomen who engage in good and evil actions and then reap the fruits appropriate thereto. The last text, *Vṛṣṇidaśāḥ*, is of particular interest in that it contains legends pertaining to Nemi; like the eighth Aṅga (*Antakṛddaśāḥ*), it incorporates many stories about members of the Vṛṣṇi clan, especially Kṛṣṇa and Balarāma.

b. The Chedasūtras.—Another important group of works is that of the Chedasūtras, which could collectively be called a Jaina "book of discipline" (Vinaya Piṭaka). This group originally consisted of seven texts, *Ācāradaśāḥ, Bṛhatkalpa, Vyavahāra, Niśītha, Mahāniśītha, Pañcakalpa*, and *Jītakalpa*, of which all but the sixth are extant. The *Bṛhatkalpa, Vyavahāra*, and *Niśītha* are known to be the works of Bhadrabāhu (circa 360 B.C.).

Cheda is a technical term in Jaina ecclesiastical law; it refers to a reduction in a monk's seniority, accompanied by appropriate expiation (usually fasting), for offences committed. The first text, *Ācāradaśāḥ*[45] (also dalled *Daśāśrutaskandha*), is a compendium of such rules. It lists, for example, twenty-one offences (*śabala*) against the vows of monkhood, thirty-three kinds of disrespects (*āśātanā*) to the elders (particularly those shown by a student to his preceptor), eight qualifications (*sampadā*) of a leader (*gaṇin*) of the order, and twelve kinds of progressively more difficult austerities (*bhikṣu-pratimā*). There is also a fairly

43. Especially noteworthy is a Kannada romance by Ratnākara Varṇī (circa 1500) entitled *Bharateśavaibhava*, which seeks to synthesize the paths of renunciation and lay discipline.

44. See Deleu 1969.

45. See Caillat 1965, 1968; and Schubring 1966.

detailed account of the eleven stages of laymanship (*upāsaka-pratimā*). These stages together make up a course of increasingly more comprehensive renunciation of worldly activities, eventually bringing the layman to the brink of mendicancy.[46]

The eighth chapter of *Ācāradaśāḥ*, entitled *Paryuṣaṇa-kalpa* or *Sāmācārī*, gives rules for monastic life during the rainy season. Since monks and nuns are obliged to remain in a particular place while the monsoon continues, they must at that time undergo an unusual amount of contact with lay society. The spiritual hazards of such extended contact are well-known; hence the strictures laid down by the *Sāmācārī* serve a useful and highly regarded function in the life of the mendicant. The chapter has in fact been made into a separate book, to which are appended both a collective biography of the Jinas (*Jinacarita*) and a lineage of successors to the gaṇadharas (*Sthavirāvalī*). These three short works together comprise the so-called *Kalpa-sūtra*,[47] which is recited even today during the annual ceremony of public confession and forgiveness known as *saṃvatsarī*.[48]

The remaining portions of the Chedasūtras are devoted to further codification of monastic law.[49] They furnish details on what constitutes transgressions, as well as setting forth appropriate proceedings (*vyavahāra*) to be brought against offenders. Although of little interest to the general reader, these texts are tremendously useful to anyone studying the growth of the monastic community. They

46. See Ch. VI.

47. Translated by Jacobi 1884: 217–311.

48. On saṃvatsarī, see Ch. VII.

Tradition holds that the *Kalpa-sūtra* has been used in public recitation for over 1,500 years, ever since Devarddhigaṇi chanted it before King Dhruvasena of Valabhi to relieve the latter's grief over the death of his son. Indeed, no other text has achieved such popularity among Jainas; the many ornate and beautifully illustrated manuscripts of the work that have come down to us attest to this esteem. See Brown 1934. (See pl. 12.)

49. For details on the *Vyavahāra* and *Niśītha*, see Schubring (with Caillat) 1966; for *Mahāniśītha*, see Hamm (with Schubring) 1951 and Deleu (with Schubring) 1963.

also provide valuable insight into the numerous restrictions imposed upon itself by that community, mainly in order to preserve its integrity in the face of increasing dependence upon the laity.

c. The Mūlasūtras.—Of the four Mūlasūtras, three have been preserved. One, the *Daśavaikālika,*[50] contains ten lectures (*adhyayana*) and two appendices (*cūlikā*) which together formed the material for study "beyond the prescribed hours" (*vaikālika*). The work is ascribed to Ārya Śayyambhava (circa 429 B.C.), who is said to have compiled it for his son Maṇaka. It begins with a declaration that dharma, the Law, consists of ahiṃsā, *saṃyama* (restraint), and *tapas* (austerity), and that even the gods bow down to one who abides by this Law.[51]

The lectures are mostly in verse and cover a variety of topics pertaining to the monastic life. The first, called Druma-puṣpika (Trees and flowers), compares the begging habits of a mendicant to the activity of a bee, who gathers honey by moving gently from flower to flower without ever becoming a burden. The second warns that a monk should guard his senses, for "How will he remain an ascetic if he does not shun sense-pleasure? Sinking at each step, he will fall under the control of lustful thoughts."[52] It goes on to tell a famous story concerning Rājimati, bride of Prince Nemi. When Nemi abandoned her to follow the mendicant path (for he was to become the twenty-second Tīrthaṅkara in that very life), Rājimati took the vows of a nun. At some later time she was caught in a sudden rainstorm and retired to a cave to dry her clothing. There she was faced with amorous advances by Nemi's younger brother, himself a monk; rather than give in to the man's

50. Translated by K. C. Lalwani 1973.

51. dhammo maṃgalam ukkiṭṭhaṃ, ahiṃsā saṃjamo tavo/ devā vi taṃ namaṃsaṃti, jassa dhamme siyā maṇo// *Daśavaikālika-sūtra*: §i, 1.

52. kahaṃ nu kujjā sāmaṇṇaṃ, jo kāme na nivārae/ pae pae visīyaṃto, saṃkappassa vasaṃ gao// Ibid.: §ii, 1.

desires, she admonished him in terms that well illustrate the Jaina attitude towards those who fall away from their vows:

> Shame on you, who seek defeat! Shame, that you should crave for that which has been once abandoned. It would be better for you to die keeping your vows than to live in disgrace! And if you continue to feel desire whenever you see a woman, surely, oh unfortunate one, you will lose stability and will be destroyed like a boat assailed by strong winds![53]

This legend has formed the basis of several popular dramas and narratives, still widely read and told among Jainas today.

The third lecture, entitled Kṣudrakācāra-kathā, enumerates fifty-two kinds of conduct that are not permitted to members of the mendicant community.[54] A Jaina renunciant must not, for example, receive food from the palace of a king, or food which is specially cooked or bought for him; neither may he store it nor eat it after sunset. He must neither bathe nor brush his teeth, nor sponge his body; he may not fan himself, or wear sandals, or use an umbrella. He must not live with a householder, or serve him, or assist him in his profession. Jaina ascetics are praised for their austerity and commended for "suffering heat in the summer, remaining uncovered in the winter, and remaining within shelters, fully restricted, during the rainy season."[55]

In the fourth lecture we read of the six kinds of living beings (*ṣaṭ-jīva-nikāya*) and of the duty of a mendicant to refrain from hurting them. This lecture also contains several highly inspiring verses which admonish the monk to

53. dhiratthu te 'jasokāmī, jo taṃ jīviyakāraṇā/ vaṃtaṃ icchasi āveuṃ, seyaṃ te maraṇaṃ bhave// jai taṃ kāhisi bhāvaṃ, jā jā icchasi nārio/ vāyāviddhovva haḍo, aṭṭhiappā bhavissasi// Ibid.: §ii, 8–10.

54. Ibid.: §iii, 1–10.

55. āyāvayaṃti gimhesu, hemaṃtesu avāvuḍā/ vāsāsu paḍisaṃlīṇā, dhuyamohā jiyiṃdiyā// Ibid.: §iii, 12.

"walk mindfully, stand mindfully, sit and sleep mindfully."[56] He must know the nature of the self and of others: "First knowledge, then compassion; thus does one remain in full control. How can an ignorant person be compassionate, when he does not know good from evil?"[57]

Knowledge leads to compassion; compassion is manifested in behavior:

> Whatever beings there are, whether moving or non-moving, thou shall not hurt, whether knowingly or unknowingly . . . All beings desire to live; no one wants to die. Therefore a nirgrantha refrains from all acts of injury.[58]

The remaining lectures continue in a similar vein, eulogizing the ascetic life while warning of its rigors: "It is terrible, it is not easy to undertake . . . nowhere but in Mahāvīra's order is there such pure conduct, nor shall there ever be another Discipline like this one."[59]

Another *Mūlasūtra*, the *Uttarādhyayana*[60] (Book of later instructions) is claimed to be the last sermon of Mahāvīra. Probably the best-known Jaina anthology, it seems to include the works of numerous authors, compiled over an extended period. The *Uttarādhyayana* is a mixture of dialogues, parables, and catechisms, mostly in verse. There are thirty-six lectures (adhyayanas), and except for the last few of these the text can be considered

56. kahaṃ care? kahaṃ ciṭṭhe? kahamāse? kahaṃ sae?/ kahaṃ bhuṃjaṃto bhāsaṃto, pāvakammaṃ na baṃdhaī?// jayaṃ care, jayaṃ ciṭṭhe, jayamāse, jayaṃ sae/ jayaṃ bhuṃjaṃto bhāsaṃto pāvakammaṃ na baṃdhaī// savvabhūyappabhūyassa sammaṃ bhūyāi pāsao/ pihiyāsavassa daṃtassa pāvaṃ kammaṃ na baṃdhāı// Ibid.: §iv, 7.

57. paḍhamaṃ nāṇaṃ tao dayā, evaṃ ciṭṭhai savvasaṃjae/ aṇṇāṇī kiṃ kāhī, kiṃ vā nāhii seyapāvagaṃ// Ibid.: §iv, 10.

58. tatthimaṃ paḍhamaṃ ṭhāṇaṃ, Mahāvīreṇa desiyaṃ/ ahiṃsā niuṇā diṭṭhā, savvabhūesu saṃjamo// jāvaṃti loe pāṇā, tasā aduva thāvarā/ te jāṇamajāṇaṃ vā, na haṇe no vi ghāyae// savve jīvā vi icchaṃti, jīviuṃ na marijjiuṃ/ tamhā pāṇivahaṃ ghoraṃ, niggaṃthā vajjayaṃti ṇaṃ// Ibid.: §iv, 11.

59. haṃdi dhammatthakāmāṇaṃ, niggaṃthāṇaṃ suṇeha me/ āyāragoyaraṃ bhīmaṃ sayalaṃ durahiṭṭhiyaṃ// nannattha erisaṃ vuttaṃ jaṃ loe paramaduccaraṃ/ viulaṭṭhāṇabhāissa na bhūyaṃ na bhavissaī// Ibid.: §vi, 4–5.

60. Translated by Jacobi 1895: 1–232.

fairly ancient. It is of historical importance in that it contains the controversial dialogue between Keśi and Gautama discussed in Chapter I. Portions of the work are also valuable for their descriptions of the milieu in which the monastic order developed, as well as of the social influence exerted by the order.

It has earlier been noted that all eleven of the original disciples of Mahāvīra were of the brahman caste, also that they entered his order together with hundreds of their students. This kind of large-scale movement of young people into the monastic life must have had a tremendous effect upon the society of the time; several lectures of the *Uttarādhyayana* (for example, x, *Nemi-pravrajyā*; xiv, *Iśukārīyam*; xx, *Mahānirgranthīyam*; xxi, *Samudrapālīyam*; xxii, *Rathanemīyam*) attest to the presence of a widely felt uneasiness among householders in the face of such a phenomenon. Renunciation of the world was ordinarily not considered appropriate until an individual had fulfilled his social duties and reached a fairly advanced age; those who violated this norm to follow Mahāvīra must have done so despite tremendous familial and societal pressures to "enjoy worldly pleasures first."

Ancient Indian society was also structured around a fairly rigid system of castes, in terms of which one was born as either a priest (brahman), a warrior (kṣatriya), a merchant (*vaiśya*), or a wage-earner (*śūdra*). The breaking of caste rules was a very serious transgression, directly defying the value system enforced by the Vedic priesthood. This system held that caste distinctions were permanent, and that only the male members of the upper three castes (called twice-born (*dvija*) because they had received the Vedic initiations) were entitled to enter the mendicant life; in fact, many considered this vocation almost an exclusive privilege of the brahmans. The Jainas of Mahāvīra's time undoubtedly believed in some kind of caste hierarchy

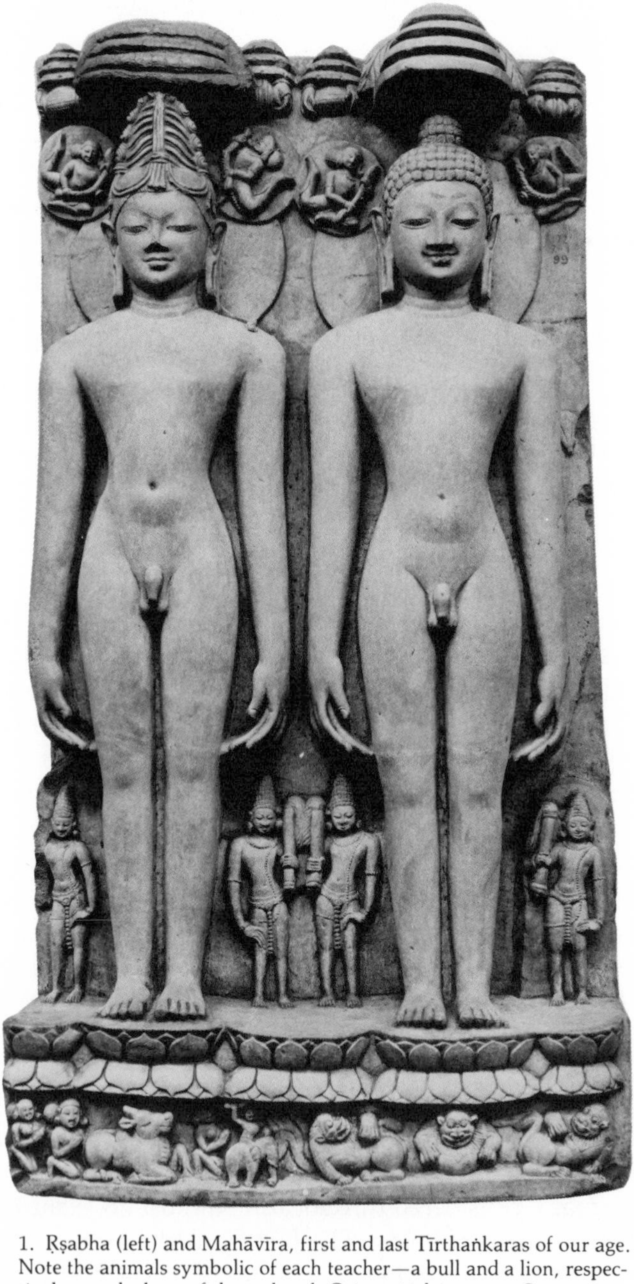

1. Ṛṣabha (left) and Mahāvīra, first and last Tīrthaṅkaras of our age. Note the animals symbolic of each teacher—a bull and a lion, respectively—at the base of the pedestal. Orissa. 13th century. Courtesy of the Trustees of the British Museum, London (see p. 14).

'ārśva, seated beneath the raised
d of a cobra (detail of āyāga-
from Mathura, circa A.D. 200).
know Museum. Courtesy of
y Tartakov (see p. 10).

'he fourteen dreams of Triśalā,
her of Mahāvīra (miniature from
-century illuminated manuscript
ie *Kalpa-sūtra*). Courtesy of the
hsonian Institution, Freer
ery of Art, Washington D.C.
p. 6).

3. Śvetāmbara image of Ṛṣabha, the first Tīrthaṅkara. White marble, South Rajasthan, 12th century. The von der Heydt collection, Rietberg Museum, Zurich. Photo by Ernst Hahn.

J.626
महावीरकेभ्रूणको देवनन्दाकेगर्भसेहटाकर त्रिशलाकेगर्भमेंस्थापितकरते हुए हरिनेगमेशी
ल. प्रथम शती ई.
प्राप्ति – मथुरा.

5. Relief fragment depicting Mahāvīra's change of embryo (see p. 7). Mathura, circa A.D. 100. Lucknow Museum. Courtesy of American Institute of Indian Studies, Varanasi.

6. Mahāvīra being led in procession to the site of his renunciation. From Helmuth von Glasenapp's *Der Jainismus*. Berlin: Alf Hager Verlag, 1925.

7. Mahāvīra preaching. From illustrated manuscript of the *Kalpasūtra*. Courtesy of the Smithsonian Institution, Freer Gallery of Art, Washington, D.C.

8. Śāntinātha, the sixteenth Tīrthaṅkara, attended by yakṣas. Courtesy of Victoria and Albert Museum, London.

9. Stone image of a female ascetic, probably depicting the Śvetāmbara Tīrthaṅkara Malli (see p. 40). Courtesy of Lucknow Museum.

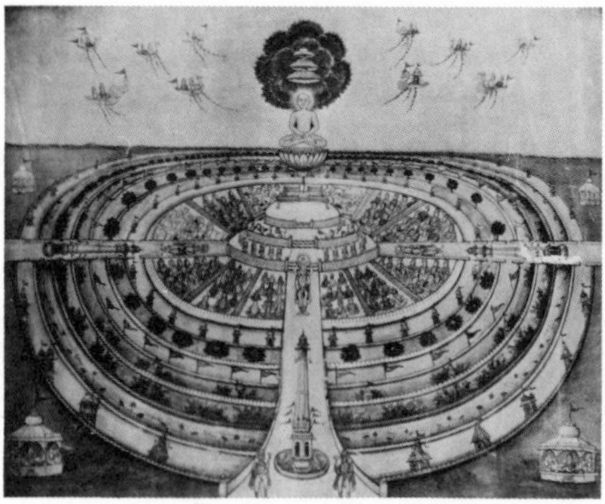

10. Pictorial representation of the samavasaraṇa as envisioned by Digambaras (see p. 56).

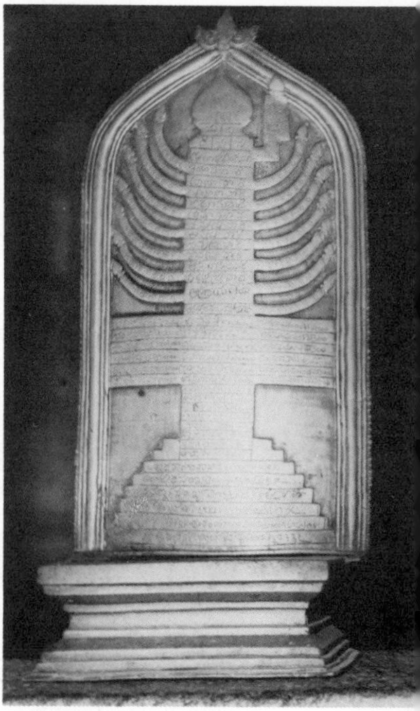

11. The Gaṇadharavalaya-yantra (see p. 254n20), a diagrammatic representation of the Pūrvas and Aṅgas, found in a Digambara temple, Mudbidre, South Kanara. Courtesy of Cārukīrti Bhaṭṭāraka Paṭṭācārya, of Mudbidre Jaina Maṭha.

12. Page from an illustrated manuscript of the *Kalpa-sūtra*. From Helmuth von Glasenapp's *Der Janismus*. Berlin: Alf Hager Verlag, 1925 (see p. 63).

13. Candraprabha, the eighth Tīrthaṅkara (18th century, reddish stone). Courtesy of Victoria and Albert Museum, London. The seven heads, unique in Jaina art, probably represent the sapta-bhaṅgi of Jaina philosophy (see p. 95).

(*varṇa*); otherwise they would not have suggested the superiority of the warrior caste over all others (as demonstrated in the "transfer of embryo" myth related earlier). Nevertheless, they made no doctrinal claim of a divine origin for the castes, as did the brahmans, nor did they hesitate to admit members of any caste into their order; even the outcastes, or "untouchables," were welcomed.[61]

Two lectures in the *Uttarādhyayana* give a good idea of the situation created by violation of caste duties and distinctions. Each describes the encounter of a Jaina mendicant with brahman householders performing a Vedic sacrifice. The first narrative (xxv, *Yajñīya*) concerns the monk Jayaghoṣa, who had been a brahman prior to entering the order (and thus losing his caste identity). Wandering from place to place, he came at one time to Banaras and took residence in a park outside the city. He had fasted for an entire month; now, begging for alms, he happened to approach the house of a brahman named Vijayaghoṣa, who was offering a sacrifice in which brahman householders were given food as part of the ceremony. Jayaghoṣa, however, was given nothing; rather, he was turned away by the host with the words:

> I shall not give you alms, mendicant; beg somewhere else. This food is meant only for brahmans, who are well versed in the Vedas and well grounded in the sacrificial science; they are the ones who deserve charity, because they save themselves and others.[62]

The Jaina monk became neither angry nor disheartened; instead he calmly stated the qualities of the "true brah-

61. For later modifications, especially among the Digambaras, see Ch. IX n. 32.

62. aha se tattha aṇagāre, māsakkhamaṇapāraṇe/ Vijayaghosassa jannaṃmi, bhikkhamaṭṭhā uvaṭṭhie// samuvaṭṭhiyaṃ tahiṃ saṃtaṃ, jāyago paḍisehae/ na hu dāhāmi te bhikkhaṃ, bhikkhū, jāyāhi annao// je ya veyaviū vippā, jannaṭṭhā ya je diyā/ . . . je samatthā samuddhattuṃ, paramappāṇameva ya/ tesiṃ annamiṇaṃ deyaṃ, bho bhikkhū savvakāmiyaṃ// *UtS*: xxv, 5–8.

man," adding that only a Jaina monk, such as Mahāvīra, was worthy of that designation:

> He who is exempt from love, hatred and fear, and who shines forth like burnished gold, purified in fire, him we call a brahman. He who thoroughly knows living beings, those which move about (*trasa*) and those which do not (*sthāvara*), and does not injure them, him we call a brahman.
> He who does not take anything that is not given him, be it small or large, him we call a brahman. He who is not defiled by pleasures (of the senses), just as a lotus grows on the water and yet is not immersed in it, him we call a brahman.[63]

The redefinition of the term brahman coupled with the claim that the Jaina mendicant's vows constituted the essence of brahmanhood was an important milestone in the development of Jaina society; it made conduct (*cāritra*), rather than birth (*jāti*), the basis for determining the superiority of one person or group over another. It is for this reason that Mahāvīra, although a kṣatriya, is often called a *māhaṇa* (Prakrit for Sanskrit *brāhmaṇa*).[64]

The importance of conduct is further emphasized in the second tale, called Harikeśīya (lecture xii). This account centers around one Harikeśa, who had been a *śvapāka* prior to becoming a monk. Śvapākas, also known as *caṇḍālas*, make up the lowest community in the Indian social hierarchy; they are called "untouchables," and any contact with them is considered ritually polluting by the rest of the society. Harikeśa was given to great austerities; like Jayaghoṣa, he had just completed a long fast when, in search of alms, he came to the enclosure of a brahmanical

63. jāyarūvaṃ jahā maṭṭhaṃ, niddhaṃtamalapāvagaṃ/ rāgadosabhayāīyaṃ, taṃ vayaṃ būma māhaṇaṃ//22// tasapāṇe viyāṇettā, saṃgaheṇa ya thāvare/ jo na hiṃsai tiviheṇa, taṃ vayaṃ būma māhaṇaṃ//23// jahā pomaṃ jale jāyaṃ, novalippai vāriṇā/ evaṃ alittaṃ kāmehiṃ, taṃ vayaṃ būma māhaṇaṃ//28// Ibid.: §xxxv, 22–28.

64. kammuṇā baṃbhaṇo hoi, kammuṇā hoi khattiyo/ vaisso kammuṇā hoi, suddo havai kammuṇā// ee pāukare buddhe, jehiṃ hoi siṇāyao/ savvakammaviṇimmukkaṃ, taṃ vayaṃ būma māhaṇaṃ// Ibid.: §xxv, 33–34.

sacrifice. Recognizing an untouchable at the holy place, the brahmans—referred to by the text as "killers of animals, rigid with the pride of birth"—reviled the sage, adding: "Better this food and drink should rot, than that we should give it to you."[65]

When the Jaina monk did not leave, but stated in a firm and yet peaceful manner that their behavior was improper, they "rushed forward and beat the sage with sticks, canes and whips."[66] Bloodshed was prevented by the intervention of a demigod (*yakṣa*) on the monk's behalf. Seeing this supernatural being, the brahmans begged Harikeśa for forgiveness. He pardoned them and proceeded to preach his views on the true meaning of sacrifice. Sacrifice was said to mean not bathing in holy waters or kindling the fire or offering animals to the gods, but rather guarding one's purity by means of the saṃvaras, the restraints of a Jaina monk.[67]

Such internalization of the sacrifice was not unknown to the Vedic brahmans; it is nevertheless true that external rituals, including the sacrifice of animals, formed an essential part of their religion. Jainas seldom missed an opportunity to condemn this practice as unethical; their constant attacks on so important an aspect of Vedic religion earned them the undying hostility of the brahmanical community.

d. The Prakīrṇakasūtras.—The Prakīrṇaka (The miscellaneous) is a collection of ten short texts containing both ceremonial hymns and descriptions of the rituals to be used in preparation for a holy death.[68] The subject matter of each text is clearly indicated by its title: (1) *Catuḥśaraṇa*

65. jāimayapaḍitthaddhā, hiṃsagā ajiyiṃdiyā/ abaṃbhacāriṇo bālā, imaṃ vayaṇamabbavī//5// . . . ajjhāvayāṇaṃ paḍikūlabhāsī, pabhāsase kiṃ nu sagāsi amhaṃ/ avi eyaṃ viṇassau annapāṇaṃ, na ya ṇaṃ dāhāmu, tuvaṃ nigaṃṭhā//16// Ibid.: §xii, 5–6.

66. ajjhāvayāṇaṃ vayaṇaṃ suṇettā, uddhāiyā tattha bahū kumārā/ daṃḍehiṃ vettehiṃ kasehiṃ ceva, samāgayā taṃ isi tālayaṃti// Ibid.: §xii, 19.

67. susaṃvuḍā paṃcahiṃ saṃvarehiṃ, iha jīviyaṃ aṇavakaṃkhamāṇā/ vosaṭṭhakāyā suicattadehā, mahājayaṃ jayai jannasiṭṭhaṃ// Ibid.: §xi, 42.

68. For details on the Prakīrṇakas, see Winternitz 1933: 459–461.

(Taking the four refuges); (2) *Āturapratyākhyāna* (Renunciation by the sick); (3) *Bhaktaparijña* (Renunciation of food); (4) *Saṃstāraka* (Preparing the deathbed); (5) *Taṇḍulavaicārika* (Contemplation on rice, that is, on food and the conditions of a living being); (6) *Candravedhyaka* (Hitting the mark, that is, retaining consciousness at the last moment of life); (7) *Devendrastava* (Praise of the Jinas by the king of gods); (8) *Gaṇividyā* (Knowledge of propitious times for monastic activities); (9) *Mahāpratyākhyāna* (Renunciation at the time of death); (10) *Vīrastava* (In praise of Mahāvīra).

e. The Cūlikāsūtras.—The final portion of the Aṅgabāhya is entitled Cūlikā, Appendix. It contains two works: the *Nandī-sūtra,* ascribed to Devavācaka, and the *Anuyoga-dvāra-sūtra,* by an Elder named Ārya Rakṣita.[69] Both include valuable section-by-section summaries of the material found in most of the other canonical texts.

Thus concludes the list of works that constitute the basic Jaina canon. This canon was extensively studied by the monks, who produced scores of commentaries and subcommentaries thereon during the seven centuries after its compilation at Valabhi. The earliest forms of such commentarial literature were the Niryuktis and Bhāṣyas, composed in Prakrit verse; these were followed by the Cūrṇis in Prakrit prose and finally by the Ṭīkās in Sanskrit prose.[70] Most famous among the commentators were Bhadrabāhu (author of the *Ācārāṅga-niryukti,* fifth century A.D.) and Jinabhadra (author of the *Viśeṣāvaśyaka-bhāṣya,* sixth century A.D.). Other important figures were Jinadāsa (seventh century), Haribhadra (seventh century), Śīlāṅka (ninth century), Abhayadeva (eleventh century), Maladhāri Hemacandra (twelfth century), and finally Malayagiri (thirteenth century).

69. For a critical study of the *Anuyogadvāra,* see Hanaki 1970.
70. On the exegetical literature, see Kapadia 1941: 171–205.

The Anuyogas ("Expositions")

As noted earlier, the Digambaras preserved only a small portion of the original canon, the portion dealing mainly with the doctrine of karma; most of their scriptures (āgama) are thus the postcanonical compositions of various learned ācāryas. Most of these monk-scholars came from the south of India, principal region of Digambara strength since the time of Bhadrabāhu. Their literary output was enormous, resulting in the body of works called Anuyoga (The expositions), which have long enjoyed canonical status in the Digambara tradition.

Śvetāmbara monks produced a comparable secondary canon, also called Anuyoga, to supplement the older materials already in their possession. Taken together, these "expositions" of the two schools constitute one of the greatest collections of non-Vedic Indian literature. The collection is divided into four categories, sometimes styled "the four Vedas" of the Jainas.

THE PRATHAMĀNUYOGA

The first of these Anuyogas is called Prathamānuyoga, the primary exposition. It contains biographies of the Jinas and of certain famous mythological figures; these biographies, as the title suggests, form the basis of religious teaching for the layperson. Most notable of the Digambara writings in this category are the *Ādipurāṇa* of Jinasena (eighth century) and the *Uttarapurāṇa* of Guṇabhadra (ninth century); among the Śvetāmbara texts, the *Triṣaṣṭiśalākāpuruṣacaritra*[71] of Hemacandra (twelfth century) is best known. Such works were highly influential in popularizing and spreading the Jaina faith among the masses.

THE KARAṆĀNUYOGA

The second of the four categories, Karaṇānuyoga (exposition on technical matters), contains treatises on such

71. Translated by Helen M. Johnson 1931–1962 (6 vols.).

ancient sciences as cosmology and astronomy. This group is represented by the *Trilokaprajñapti* (seventh century), *Trilokasāra* (eleventh century), *Jambūdvīpaprajñapti* (thirteenth century), and similar works.

THE CARAṆĀNUYOGA

Third is the Caraṇānuyoga, exposition on discipline. The discipline referred to is twofold; one set of rules applies to the mendicant, the other to the layperson. The most important Digambara work on mendicant discipline (*anagāra-dharma*) is the *Mūlācāra* of Vaṭṭakera. A collection of 1,243 verses arranged in twelve chapters, it has often been called the "Digambara *Ācārāṅga.*" Another influential Digambara text on ecclesiastical law is the *Bhagavatī Ārādhanā* of Śivārya, which contains 2,116 verses. Both works are fairly ancient (circa second century A.D.), and both contain materials not strictly in keeping with the Digambara rules on nudity; this may indicate some connection with the Yāpanīya sect.[72]

Orthodox Digambara tradition is best represented in the works of Kundakunda, who lived sometime in the second or third century A.D. He is credited with the authorship of several Prakrit texts which together form the most authoritative source for the study of the Digambara faith. Most important of these are *Niyamasāra* and *Pravacanasāra*, which deal at great length with the *āvaśyakas* (essential duties) of a monk. Also well known are the eight short *prābhṛta* ("gifts") texts, respectively called *Darśana* (Right view), *Cāritra* (Conduct), *Sūtra* (Scripture), *Bodha* (Knowledge), *Bhāva* (Internal practice), *Mokṣa* (Liberation), *Liṅga* (The emblem), and *Śīla* (Purity); these emphasize the essential aspects of inner development.[73]

While they paid great attention to monastic law, Jaina ācāryas did not fail to provide rules and regulations for the conduct of the laity as well. This fact is demonstrated

72. See Premi 1956: 56–86.
73. See Upadhye, intro. to the *Pravacanasāra*.

by the large number of *śrāvakācāras* (books of the layman's discipline) that have come to light.[74] Earliest of these in the Digambara tradition is probably the *Ratnakaraṇḍa* of Samantabhadra (fifth century), followed by such works as the *Śrāvakācāra* of Amitagati (eleventh century) and the *Puruṣārthasiddhyupāya* of Amṛtacandra (twelfth century).[75] One discipline text worthy of special notice is the *Sāgāradharmāmṛta* of Āśādhara (thirteenth century), the only such work known to have been written by a layman. The same author also produced a manual on mendicant law entitled *Anagāradharmāmṛta*. Among Śvetāmbara texts we may mention the *Dharmabindu* of Haribhadra (eighth century), as well as Hemacandra's *Yogaśāstra*[76] (twelfth century).

The Jaina discipline (*ācāra*) is heavily oriented towards tapas (austerities) and ritualized confession (*pratikramaṇa*, and so on). Such activities aim mainly at bringing the aspirant to a state of pacification, but lay little stress upon the spiritually more important aspect of insight. One expects to find, therefore, a set of works relating more directly to meditation and similar practices. In this area the foremost writer is again Kundakunda, who espouses a *niścaya-naya* (nonconventional point of view) that concentrates on the "innate" purity of the soul rather than on the "conditioned" state of its bondage. His *Samayasāra*,[77] along with Amṛtacandra's celebrated *Ātmakhyāti* commentary thereon, emphasizes this nonconventional viewpoint more than any other Jaina text; it must certainly be considered the pioneer work on Jaina yoga. The *Anuprekṣā* of Kārtikeya, *Samādhiśataka* of Pūjyapāda, and *Paramātmaprakāśa* of Yogindu, all from the sixth century, carried on the tradition of Kundakunda.

74. For a complete bibliography, see *JY*: intro. xxvii–xxx.

75. Translated by Ajit Prasada 1933.

76. Translated by Windisch 1874. For a brief survey of the main śrāvakācāra works of both the Śvetāmbara and Digambara sects, see *JY*: 1–31.

77. Translated by Chakravarti 1971. On the vyavahāra and niścaya-naya in Kundakunda's works, see Bhatt 1972.

As for the Śvetāmbara approach to yogic discipline, it found its ultimate expression in the works of Haribhadra (eighth century). His *Yogaśataka*, *Yogabindu*, and *Yoga-dṛṣṭisamuccaya* not only set forth the tenets and practices of Jaina yoga, but also represent the only attempt to compare these with other yogic systems prevalent in the India of Haribhadra's day.[78]

DRAVYĀNUYOGA

The fourth and final group of texts making up the secondary canon is that called Dravyānuyoga. Dravya is a technical term meaning "substance" or "existent." Jainas enumerate six kinds of such existents, namely, souls (jīva), material atoms (*pudgala*), the principle of motion (*dharma-dravya*), the principle of rest (*adharma-dravya*), space (*ākāśa*), and time (kāla). The Dravyānuyoga literature, in considering these factors, touches upon almost every essential aspect of Jaina philosophy: ontology, epistemology, psychology, and so on.

Although Kundakunda's works probably have as much bearing on the existents (dravya) as on practice (*caraṇa*), the honor of systematizing Jaina canonical teachings into an integrated darśana (philosophical school) belongs to the ācārya Umāsvāti (second century A.D.). His *Tattvārtha-sūtra*[79] is the first Jaina text written in Sanskrit, the language of the brahmanical scriptures. Umāsvāti's choice of this language indicates that the Jainas had by that time begun to write their texts not simply for the benefit of their own community, but also in order to dispute with proponents of rival darśanas. The *Tattvārtha-sūtra* is also the first Jaina work to use the terse, aphoristic mode of presentation known as sūtra style; its place in Jaina philosophy is comparable to that of Patañjali's *Yoga-sūtras* and Bādarāyaṇa's *Vedānta-sūtras* in the Yoga and Vedānta

78. For Haribhadra's comparative studies on yoga, see Sanghavi 1963; *SJP*: 293–304.

79. Translated by Jacobi 1906.

traditions, respectively. Umāsvāti manages to synthesize virtually the entire Jaina doctrinal system into a mere 350 sūtras, arranged in ten chapters as follows: (1) the path of salvation (*mokṣa-mārga*); (2) the states of the soul (*bhāva*); (3) the lower worlds and the human abodes (*naraka* and dvīpa); (4) the celestial abodes (*deva*); (5) the insentient existents (*ajīva-dravya*); (6) karmic influx (*āsrava*); (7) wholesome and unwholesome karmas (*śubha-aśubha karma*); (8) karmic bondage (*bandha*); (9) stoppage of karmic influx and disassociation from karmic bondage (saṃvara and *nirjarā*); (10) liberation of the soul from the bondage of embodiment (mokṣa).

The *Tattvārtha-sūtra* also has the distinction of being the one text recognized as authoritative by Digambaras and Śvetāmbaras alike. Both sects claim Umāsvāti as one of their own, and their respective versions of his work show predictable disagreement on such controversial matters as the nudity of the mendicant and the partaking of food by the kevalin. Each tradition has produced its own commentaries on the text; although these developed independently, they nevertheless present almost identical explications of Jaina doctrine.

Umāsvāti is credited by the Śvetāmbaras with having written an autocommentary, the *Svopajña-bhāṣya.*[80] Two major subcommentaries (*vṛtti*) on this *bhāṣya* (commentary) appear among Śvetāmbara writings, one by Siddhasena (also called Gandhahastin, eighth century) and another by Haribhadra Gaṇi (ninth century). Digambaras have disputed the authenticity of the *Svopajña-bhāṣya,* since it contains certain sections not in accord with their views. The earliest extant Digambara commentary on the *Tattvārtha-sūtra* is the *Sarvārthasiddhi,*[81] an encyclopedic

80. See *Tattvārtha-sūtra,* Hindi exposition, by Sanghavi 1952: intro. 33–83. For a Digambara refutation of the Śvetāmbara claim, see *Sarvārthasiddhi,* Hindi tr. by Phoolchandra 1971: intro.

81. Translated by S. A. Jain 1958.

work produced in the sixth century by the grammarian Devanandi (known popularly as Pūjyapāda). It was followed by two other commentaries, Akalaṅka's *Rājavārttika* (A.D. 780) and the *Ślokavārttika* of Vidyānanda (ninth century). These three works even today comprise the basic textual materials used by advanced students in Digambara monasteries.

One other important writer is claimed equally by both Jaina schools; this is Siddhasena Divākara (fifth century), who actually seems to have been a member of the Yāpanīya sect.[82] Divākara authored two pioneering works in the field of Jaina logic: the *Nyāyāvatāra* and the *Sanmatisūtra*. The latter is a short Prakrit treatise which seeks to establish the validity of the various viewpoints (*naya*) when approached in the spirit of syādvāda (qualified assertion), as well as their nonvalidity when put forth in the absolutist (*ekānta*) manner of non-Jaina systems. Jainas were probably drawn into the field of formal logic by the challenge of the Mīmāṃsakas, who staunchly supported the "infallible authority" of the Vedas, taking great exception to the Jaina claim that human Jinas are omniscient and able to show the path to heaven or salvation.

The first Jaina work to specifically take up this challenge seems to have been the *Āptamīmāṃsā*, composed in the fifth century by the Digambara ācārya Samantabhadra. The *Āptamīmāṃsā* (An examination of the perfect teacher) is a brief work of 114 verses written in *stotra* style, a sort of philosophical hymn; thus it was also known as the *Devāgamastotra*. Here Samantabhadra critically examines the nature of a Jina, pointing out that the true test of Jinahood consists not in the miracles that attend him (for example, *devāgama*, the arrival of gods at a holy gathering), but rather in his conduct and his teachings. He must be perfectly free from attachment and aversion (*vītarāga*),

82. For a bibliographic review, see *Nyāyāvatāra*, Upadhye intro.

and the tenets of his system must be uniquely capable of withstanding the critical application of logic (*yukti-śāstra-avirodhi-vāk*).[83] This position leads Samantabhadra to formulate an appropriate syllogism to "establish the omniscience" of the Jina, as well as to examine the validity of similar claims made by Buddhists for the Buddha and by theists for their God.

By dealing directly with the problem of how a given teacher could be legitimately claimed as final authority, the *Āptamīmāṃsā* introduced a major point of controversy into Indian philosophical dispute. This controversy inspired several Jaina logicians to produce extensive commentaries on Samantabhadra's work; most notable were the *Aṣṭaśatī* of Akalaṅka (eighth century) and the *Aṣṭasahasrī* of Vidyānanda (ninth century). These commentators were not content merely to expand upon the writings of their predecessors; each later produced several independent works of high quality. Akalaṅka, through such concise and closely reasoned texts as the *Laghīyastraya*, *Nyāyaviniścaya*, *Siddhiviniścaya*, and *Pramāṇasaṅgraha*, established a reputation as the outstanding critic of the Buddhist logician Dharmakīrti of Nālandā.[84] Vidyānanda wrote four "Examinations," entitled *Āptaparīkṣā*, *Pramāṇaparīkṣā*, *Patraparīkṣā*, and *Satyaśāsanaparīkṣā*, in which he developed a sophisticated refutation of the doctrines espoused by contemporary philosophical schools, especially with reference to their theories on epistemology.

Subsequent Digambara scholastic activity was devoted mainly to clarifying the material of these texts and assimilating the results into two manuals on Jaina logic. Important works of the latter type were the *Parīkṣāmukha* of Māṇikyanandi (eleventh century); Prabhācandra's com-

83. devāgamanabhoyānacāmarādivibhūtayaḥ/ māyāviṣv api dṛṣyante nātas tvam asi no mahān//1// tīrthakṛtsamayānāṃ ca parasparavirodhataḥ/ sarveṣām āptatā nāsti kaścid eva bhaved guruḥ//3// sa tvam evāsi nirdoṣo yukti-śāstrāvirodhivāk/ avirodho yad iṣṭaṃ te prasiddhena na bādhyate//6// *Āptamīmāṃsā*: k 1–6.

84. For Akalaṅka's critique of Dharmakīrti, see N. J. Shah 1967.

mentary thereon, entitled *Prameyakamalamārtaṇḍa* (eleventh century); and the same author's substantial *Nyāyakumudacandra* commentary on Akalaṅka's *Laghīyastraya.*[85]

The Śvetāmbaras also became involved in rigorous philosophical writing, particularly after the appearance of Siddhasena's *Sanmatitarka.*[86] This work inspired a 2,500 verse *ṭīkā* (commentary) by Abhayadeva (eighth century). Of those Śvetāmbara writers who produced independent works, the best known are Mallavādin (author of *Nayacakra*) and of course the celebrated Haribhadra; the latter's originality and level of erudition are especially evident in his *Ṣaḍdarśanasamuccaya.*[87] Haribhadra also has the distinction of being one of the few Jaina scholars to have written a commentary on a non-Jaina text, the *Nyāyapraveśa* of the Buddhist logician Dignāga (fifth century). The Śvetāmbara tradition produced numerous logicians; foremost among them was Hemacandra (twelfth century). His *Pramāṇamīmāṃsā*[88] and *Anyayogavyavacchedikā*, the latter made famous by Malliṣeṇa's *Syādvādamañjarī* commentary,[89] have been widely studied as the outstanding Jaina contributions to the "old" Nyāya tradition. The Navya, or "new" school of logic is represented by Yaśovijaya, an eighteenth-century philosopher-monk whose *Jainatarkabhāṣā,*[90] *Jñānabindu, Nyāyāloka,* and other works show that even at this late date the level of Jaina scholarship remained high.

Stotras.—The final body of literature to be included under the Dravyānuyoga is the stotra, poetical hymns in praise

85. For a detailed study of the major Jaina logical works, see Kailashchandra 1966.
86. Translated by Sanghavi (with Doshi) 1939.
87. For a critical evaluation of this work, see Malvania's intro. to *Ṣaḍdarśanasamuccaya* (ed. M. K. Jain 1969).
88. Text and tr. Mookerjee (and Tatia) 1970.
89. Translated by Thomas 1960. Text ed. J. C. Jain 1970 (1st ed. 1935).
90. Text and tr. Bhargava 1973.

of one or more Jinas (addressed either individually or collectively).[91] Strictly speaking, the only praiseworthy thing about a Jina is his preaching of the doctrine; hence the stotra assumes the nature of a philosophical poem, glorifying the Jina's doctrines (for example, ahiṃsā, *anekānta* [manifold aspects], syādvāda, *aparigraha* [nonpossession], and so on) and criticizing those of the *ekāntavādins* (who hold an absolutist doctrine). One expects to find the sort of flowery embellishments called for by standard Indian works on poetics in a romantic drama, or perhaps in an ode to nature. For the Jainas, who produced virtually no such secular literature, the finest ornamentations (*alaṅkāra*) of the poets found expression purely in texts that strove to refute rival philosophies. Canonical materials were, in practice if not in theory, accessible only to the mendicants, while the various scholarly works, although available to the laity, were by and large beyond the comprehension of ordinary people. The stotras thus became an excellent means not only of popularizing the cultic worship of the Jinas, but also of introducing members of the lay community to abstruse philosophical doctrines.

Samantabhadra's *Svayambhūstotra* provides a fine example of such a work. He praises the twenty-four Jinas individually (with an average of five verses apiece), each time taking up some new aspect of doctrine and expanding it in a scholarly manner. The clarity of his presentation is matched throughout by its poetical beauty. Other outstanding works of this type are Siddhasena Divākara's *Dvātriṃśikā* (thirty-two hymns of thirty-two verses each), Amṛtacandra's *Laghutattvasphoṭa* (A brief exposition of reality), containing twenty-five hymns of twenty-five verses each),[92] Hemacandra's *Anyayogavyavacchedikā* (Rescinder of other systems, in thirty-two verses),[93] and

91. For a list of approximately twenty-five Jaina hymns in Prakrit, Sanskrit, and Apabhraṃśa, see H. Jain 1962: 122–127.

92. Text and tr. P. S. Jaini 1978.

93. Translated by Thomas 1960.

the more popular *Upasargahara, Bhaktāmara, Akalaṅka,* and *Viṣāpahāra* stotras associated with certain miraculous events in the lives of their respective authors.[94] All of these fall under the Dravyānuyoga because they deal with the existents as taught by the Jina. They form, moreover, the basic recitations performed by a devout Jaina, thus sustaining his interest in both the cultic and intellectual aspects of his religion. The stotras also serve to maintain the literacy of the community at a high level, thereby assuring an unbroken tradition of canonical scholarship.

Even so incomplete a sketch of the Jaina literary tradition as presented here gives some idea of the immense vitality which has pervaded this tradition throughout its history. This phenomenon is due in part to the strong intellectual influence of brahmans, traditionally oriented towards scholarly pursuits, within the Jaina order, beginning with the eleven gaṇadharas and continuing through such great ācāryas as Bhadrabāhu, Siddhasena Divākara, Pūjyapāda, Haribhadra, and Jinasena. We must be careful, however, not to overemphasize this influence, since to do so would invite acceptance of the traditional Indian prejudice that only brahmans are fully suited for religious scholarship. Such outstanding Jaina writers as Samantabhadra, Akalaṅka, Somadeva, and Hemacandra, none of whom came from brahman families, make it very clear that the vigor of Jaina literature was by no means purely a matter of caste. Perhaps even more important than the scholarly interest of the ācāryas was their highly developed sense of missionary zeal, which caused them to focus careful attention on the spiritual needs of their laity; thus they were led to produce great popular narratives which competed successfully with the Hindu epics and Purāṇas.[95]

94. For the texts of these and several other popular hymns in daily use among the Jaina laity, see *JP*.

95. For an exhaustive survey of the Jaina Purāṇa literature, see H. Jain 1962: 127–180.

The Unity of Jaina Doctrine

We have seen the longstanding and perhaps irreconcilable differences that separate the two sects of Jainism. These sects have been very alike, however, in their remarkable unwillingness to depart from their basic doctrines and practices. No movement towards a more catholic viewpoint or liberalized discipline, no "Jaina Mahāyāna," was ever allowed to develop among either the Digambaras or the Śvetāmbaras. One does find canonical reports of certain disagreements over doctrine, but they failed to generate the rise of new sects; such heterodox views were simply labeled *nihnava* (falsehoods) and quickly died out.[96] As for arguments between ācāryas over minor philosophical issues, these have traditionally been accommodated within the spirit of syādvāda.

The basic Jaina doctrines thus show an extraordinary uniformity through the centuries; indeed it is possible to consider them as a coherent whole, with little reference to questions of interpretation or chronology. Students of such internally diverse traditions as Vedānta or Buddhism will be particularly struck by the degree to which Jainism lacks such diversity.

We have had a brief look at the literature through which the core teachings of Jainism have found expression.[97] Let us now examine the teachings themselves, keeping in mind their universal acceptance by, and hence profound influence upon, members of the Jaina community.

96. The *SthS* lists the following seven schisms: samaṇassa ṇaṃ bhagavao Mahāvīrassa titthaṃsi satta pavayaṇaniṇhagā pannattā, taṃ jahā: Bahurayā Jīvapaesiyā Avattiyā Sāmuccheyiyā Dokiriyā Terāsiyā Abaddhiyā. eesi ṇaṃ sattaṇṇaṃ pavayaṇaniṇhagāṇaṃ satta-adhammāyariyā hotthā taṃ hajā: Jamālī Tīsagutte Āsāḍhe Āsamitte Gaṃge Chalue Goṭṭhāmāhile. eesi ṇaṃ sattaṇṇaṃ pavayaṇaniṇhagāṇaṃ satta uppattinagarā hotthā, taṃ jahā: Sāvatthī Usabhapuraṃ Seyaviyā Mihila-Mullagātīraṃ/ Purimaṃtaraṃji Dasapura niṇhaga-uppattinagarāiṃ// *SthS*: §744. For further details, see Sen 1931: 44; P. R. Jain 1956: 61–73.

97. Mention should be made here of the considerable contribution of Jainas to Indian narrative literature (particularly in Tamil and Kannada), as well as to their work in such scientific fields as astronomy, mathematics, rhetoric, and grammar. (See Chakravarti 1974; E. P. Rice 1921; Saletore 1938: 111. Jaina themes also dominate the surviving Apabhraṃśa materials. (See H. Jain 1962: 153–164, 181–200.)

III

The Nature of Reality

The Theory of Being (*Sat*)

The religious experience of one who follows the Jaina tradition cannot be properly understood without first grasping the theory of "existents" developed by that tradition. Not being a theist, the Jaina is unable to support himself through faith in "divine grace"; he is forced to rely a great deal on his own initiative and effort, both for his worldly requirements and for his salvation.[1] He is therefore in need of a philosophical system that neither demands too much unquestioning faith nor is at variance with everyday experience.

The authority of the Jaina teachings rests ultimately on the fact that they were preached by an omniscient being; thus they are every bit as unverifiable and dogmatic as those accepted by an orthodox Hindu or Christian. Nevertheless, Jaina teachers claim that only the teachings of the Jina can stand the scrutiny of reason; they further contend that in comparison with other religions (for example, Vaiṣṇavism or Śaivism) Jaina doctrines are most consistent with the actual conduct demanded of the faithful.[2] Almost all the works mentioned in Chapter II, particularly those included under Dravyānuyoga, make a

1. Jaina arguments against the theory of a world-creating God are basically twofold. (1) Creation is not possible without a desire to create, and this implies imperfection on the part of the alleged creator. (2) If karma is relevant in the destinies of human beings, then God is irrelevant; if he rules regardless of the karma of beings, then he is cruel and capricious. See Thomas 1960: 29–36.

2. For the Jaina rejection of the "divinity" of Hindu gods and the "asceticism" of Śaiva and Vaiṣṇava mendicants, see Handiqui 1949: 326–376.

point of critically examining the doctrines of other philosophical schools. While these doctrines are invariably described as "wrong" on account of their one-sidedness, it is nevertheless held that from the proper perspective (that of syādvāda, discussed below), they can be well integrated into the Jaina system.

The Doctrine of Anekānta (Manifold Aspects)

The Jaina term for "existent" is sat (literally, being). This term designates an entity comprised of three aspects: substance (dravya), quality (guṇa), and mode (*paryāya*). By substance the Jaina understands a support or substratum (*āśraya*) for manifold qualities (guṇas). The qualities are free from qualities of their own (otherwise they would themselves become substances), but invariably they undergo modifications (*pariṇāma*) in the form of acquiring (*utpāda*) new modes (paryāya or bhāva) and losing (*vyaya*) old modes at each moment.[3] Thus, any existent must be seen on three levels: the modes, which last only a moment and belong to the qualities; the qualities, which undergo changes and yet inhere forever in their substances; and the substance, which remains the abiding common ground of support for the qualities and their modes.

A material atom (*pudgala-paramāṇu*), for example, is considered by the Jaina as a substance. It possesses at all times four qualities, namely, a color (*varṇa*), a taste (*rasa*), a smell (*gandha*), and a certain kind of palpability (*sparśa*, touch). These qualities will vary from one moment to another—for example, a red color being replaced by blue, or a sweet taste by bitter—but an atom will never be found without these qualities or without some mode of each one of them. The same rule applies to an animate entity like a soul (jīva). A soul is designated as substance (dravya) in that it is the locus of innumerable qualities such as knowl-

3. sad dravyalakṣaṇam/ utpādavyayadhrauvyayuktaṃ sat/ guṇaparyayavad dravyam/ *TS*: v, 29, 30, 38. For a discussion of the Jaina theory of substance, see Padmarajiah 1963; Matilal 1976.

edge (jñāna), bliss (*sukha*), energy (*vīrya*). The knowledge-quality, for example, will increase and decrease, but there is never a time when the soul is without knowledge; otherwise it would become by definition a nonsoul, a material atom. The states of imperfection and perfection, expressed by such terms as *matijñāna* (mind-based knowledge) and kevalajñāna (omniscience), are in turn modes of this quality.[4] The other qualities of the soul similarly undergo constant change. These changes do not take place merely on a surface level; rather, their cumulative effect so transforms the soul that we can distinguish various states—bound and free, pure and impure, and so on—and yet relate them to one and the same soul.

Because the qualities are innumerable and their modes are infinite, stretching from the beginningless past to the endless future, it is not possible for an ordinary (non-omniscient) person to perceive the existent in its entirety. At a single moment he can be aware either of the persisting unity (*ekatva*) of the substance or the transient multiplicity (*anekatva*) of its modes. This complexity of the existent—its simultaneous unity and multiplicity, eternity and transience—finds expression in the Jaina term anekānta, manifold aspects, which purports to fully describe the existent's nature.[5]

Criticism of Non-Jaina Systems

Jainas claim that non-Jaina systems (darśanas) are defective in that they view Being (sat) in only a single aspect (ekānta), either as eternal (*nitya*) or noneternal (*anitya*),

4. dravyaṃ dravyāntarād yena viśiṣyate sa guṇaḥ. tad yathā—jīvaḥ pudgalādibhyo jñānādibhir guṇair viśiṣyate, pudgalādayaś ca rūpādibhiḥ. teṣāṃ vikārā viśeṣātmanā bhidyamānāḥ paryāyāḥ. ghaṭajñānaṃ paṭajñānaṃ krodho māno . . . ity evam ādayaḥ. tebhyo 'nyatvaṃ kathaṃcid āpadyamānaḥ samudāyo dravyavyapadeśabhāk. *SS*: §600.

5. tattvaṃ paramārthabhūtaṃ vastu jīvājīvalakṣaṇam anantadharmātmakam eva. anantās trikālaviṣayatvād aparimitā ye dharmāḥ sahabhāvinaḥ kramabhāvinaś ca paryāyāḥ. ta evātmā svarūpaṃ yasya tad anantadharmātmakam. yad anantadharmātmakaṃ na bhavati tat sad api na bhavati. *SM*: k 20. For a critical study of the anekānta-vāda, see Mookerjee 1944.

unchanging (*apariṇāmin*) or changing (*pariṇāmin*). The monistic (Advaita) school of the Vedānta system maintains, for example, that Being is unitary (*eka*) and that this Being, called *Brahman,* is eternal and absolutely unchanging. It denies the existence of the phenomenal world, that is, multiplicity and change, relegating it to the realm of illusion (*vivarta*). Another school of the Vedic tradition, the Sāṃkhya, on the other hand, is a dualist who postulates two kinds of Being: one an eternal but constantly changing (*pariṇāmi-nitya*) mind-matter complex (*prakṛti*), the other a multiplicity of eternal and totally incorruptible, unchangeable (*kūṭastha-nitya*) souls (*puruṣas*). Here prakṛti is conceived in a manner very similar to the Jaina view of the total range of Being, but puruṣa resembles the Brahman of Advaita. Consequently, the Sāṃkhya too ends up by saying that "bondage" of puruṣas by the prakṛti is illusory and not to be taken as real.[6]

The Jaina maintains that both these schools can be categorized as "extremist" (ekāntavāda), propounding a one-sided dogma of eternalism (*nityavāda*). They are said by the Jaina to perceive only the substance aspect of the existent, denying its modal aspect; thus they cannot explain the true nature of bondage and are unable to teach the path of salvation.

The Buddhist—particularly the Ābhidharmika, who upholds a doctrine of discrete (*niranvaya*) and momentary (*kṣaṇika*) elements (*dharmas*)—is considered an ekāntavādin of the other type, one who follows the dogma of noneternalism (anityavāda). He denies the reality of an abiding substance (the dravya, or the *ātman*), accepting the existence only of what would in Jaina doctrine be called modes. This denial of substance, according to the Jaina critique, makes it impossible for Buddhists to explain logically either bondage by karma (*saṃsāra*) or the release

6. tasmān na badhyate 'ddhā na mucyate nāpi saṃsarati kaścit/ saṃsarati badhyate mucyate ca nānāśrayā prakṛtiḥ// *Sāṃkhyakārikā*: k 62.

from this bondage (nirvāṇa). Such a doctrine, being annihilationist (*ucchedavādin*), must be rejected.[7]

Partial Truths (Nayas)

In condemning the Vedāntin, Sāṃkhya, and Buddhist as extremists, the Jaina is not saying that their views are totally wrong. In fact he will admit that these views *are* valid when seen as nayas, or *partial* expressions of truth; they become false only when considered to possess an absolute and exclusive validity.[8]

The eternalist takes what the Jaina calls a synthetic view (*saṅgraha-naya*) of reality;[9] the noneternalist adopts an analytical standpoint (*ṛjusūtra-naya*—"straight thread," or pinpoint view).[10] For the Jaina, both positions are partially valid and must be accorded an equal place in describing the existent. Jainism maintains that an existent may simultaneously be both eternal (as substance) and non-eternal (as modes), but that it can be fully described only in a

7. naikāntavāde sukhaduḥkhabhogau, na puṇyapāpe na ca bandhamokṣau/ durnītivādavyasanāsinaivaṃ parair viluptaṃ jagad apy aśeṣam// *Anyayoga-vyavacchedikā*: k 27. ekāntavāde nityānityaikāntapakṣābhyupagame na sukhaduḥkhabhogau ghaṭete. na ca puṇyapāpe ghaṭete. na ca bandhamokṣau ghaṭete . . . tathāhi—ekāntanitye ātmani tāvat sukhaduḥkhabhogau nopapadyete . . . kiṃca, sukhaduḥkhabhogau puṇyapāpanirvartyau. tan nirvartanaṃ cārthakriyā. sā ca kūṭashtanityasya krameṇa akrameṇa vā nopapadyate . . . evam anityaikāntavāde 'pi sukhaduḥkhādy anupapattiḥ. anityaṃ hi atyantocchedadharmakam. tathābhūte cātmani puṇyopādānakriyākāriṇo niranvayaṃ vinaṣṭatvāt kasya nāma tatphalabhūtasukhānubhavaḥ? . . . evaṃ bandhamokṣayor apy asambhavaḥ . . . niranvayanāśābhyupagame caikādhikaraṇābhāvāt santānasya cāvāstavatvāt kutas tayoḥ sambhāvanāmātram api? . . . *SM*: k 27.

8. nīyate paricchidyate ekadeśaviśiṣṭo 'rtha ābhir iti nītayo nayāḥ . . . sad iti nayaḥ. sad eveti durnayaḥ . . . tathāhi—durnayas tāvat sad eveti bravīti . . . ayaṃ vastuni ekāntāstitvam evābhyupagacchan itaradharmāṇāṃ tiraskāreṇa svābhipretam eva dharmaṃ vyavasthāpayati . . . mithyārūpatvaṃ tatra dharmāntarāṇāṃ satām api nihnavāt. Ibid.: k 28.

9. svajātyavirodhena aikadhyam upānīya paryāyān ākrāntabhedān aviśeṣeṇa samastagrahaṇāt saṅgrahaḥ. sat, dravyaṃ, ghaṭa ity ādi. *SS*: §243.

10. ṛjuṃ praguṇaṃ sūtrayati tantrayatī ti ṛjusūtraḥ. pūrvāparāṃs trikālaviṣayān atiśayya vartamānakālaviṣayān ādatte atītānāgatayor vinaṣṭānutpannatvena vyavahārābhāvāt. tac ca vartamānaṃ samayamātram. tadviṣayaparyāyamātragrāhyam ṛjusūtraḥ. Ibid.: §245.

sequential order; the emphasis of the speaker (*vivakṣā*) will then determine which particular aspect receives precedence.[11] To describe the multidimensional existent solely as eternal or noneternal would be to deny the other aspects not expressly stated by the speaker. The Jaina recognizes this unavoidable limitation of language and seeks to overcome it by a device known as syādvāda, according to which a statement is correct only when it is qualified by the indeclinable *syāt*, reinforced by another indeclinable, *eva*. Syāt ordinarily has the optative sense of "might be" but in the Jaina usage is best rendered as "in some respect."[12] The further addition of eva (in fact) to an assertion qualified by syāt gives that assertion a certain necessary emphasis: that is, it is *this* particular perspective on reality (of the several which syāt implies) that the speaker has chosen to adopt.

Thus the statement "the soul is eternal," when read with syāt and eva, would mean: "In some respect—namely, that of substance and not of modes—the soul is in fact eternal." By qualifying the statement in this manner, the Jaina not only makes a meaningful assertion, but leaves room for other possible statements (for example, "it is not eternal") that can be made about the soul. This "balancing act" between two (or many) alternatives (nayas) in order to get at the truth is pictured as analogous to churning curds in order to obtain butter: the Indian milkmaid, rope in hand, draws one end taut as she slackens the other.

The Sevenfold Application of Syādvāda (Conditional Assertion)

The endeavor to be precise in making statements that do not violate the anekānta-vada has led to a system known

11. tadyathā—ekasya Devadattasya pitā putro bhrātā bhāgineya ity evamādayaḥ sambandhā janakajanyatādinimittā na virudhyante; arpaṇābhedāt. putrāpekṣayā pitā, pitrapekṣayā putra ity evam ādiḥ. tathā dravyam api sāmānyārpaṇayā nityam, viśeṣārpaṇayā 'nityam iti nāsti virodhaḥ. Ibid.: §588.

12. vākyeṣv anekāntadyotī gamyaṃ prati viśeṣaṇam/ syān nipāto 'rthayogitvāt tava kevalinām api// *Āptamīmāṃsā*: k 103.

as *sapta-bhaṅgi-naya,* the sevenfold application of syāt.[13] The Jaina maintains that every assertion, whether positive or negative, is made within the framework of a certain situation defined by four factors: the specific being (*sva-dravya*), the specific location (*sva-kṣetra*), the specific time (*sva-kāla*) and the specific state (*sva-bhāva*) of the referent. When one says, for example, "the book exists," it is understood that existence is not being asserted for all books in all places, times, and states, but only for a *particular* book (at a particular place, and so on). The term syāt indicates this complex set of conditions, which must be referred to if the predication "exists" is to be valid. At the same time, eva precludes other conditions in terms of which the book may be called nonexisting: the being, location, time, or state of other objects (*para-dravya/ -kṣetra/ -kāla/ -bhāva*).

Thus we may have the two statements "in some respect the book in fact exists" (*syād asti eva*) and "in some respect the book in fact does not exist" (*syād nāsti eva*). A third statement, combining the two but expressed in a sequential order (*krama*), is also possible: "In some respect the book in fact exists, and in some further respect in fact does not exist" (*syād asti-nāsti eva*). If the speaker wants to express both aspects simultaneously (*yugapat*), he encounters the difficulty imposed by the law of contradiction; thus, rather than saying "in some respect the book in fact both exists and does not exist," one can assert only that "in some respect the (ontological situation of the) book is in fact

13. atha ke 'mī saptabhaṅgāḥ . . .? ucyate. ekatra jīvādau vastuni ekaika-sattvādidharmaviṣayapraśnavaśād avirodhena pratyakṣādibādhāparihāreṇa pṛthagbhūtayoḥ samuditayoś ca vidhiniṣedhayoḥ paryālocanayā kṛtvā syāc chabdalāñchito saptabhiḥ prakārair vacanavinyāsaḥ saptabhaṅgīti gīyate. tadyathā—(1) syād asty eva sarvam iti vidhikalpanayā prathamo bhaṅgah. (2) syān nāsty eva sarvam iti niṣedhakalpanayā dvitīyaḥ. (3) syād asty eva syān nāsty eveti kramato vidhiniṣedhakalpanayā tṛtīyaḥ. (4) syād avaktavyam eveti yugapad vidhiniṣedhakalpanayā caturthaḥ. (5) syād asty eva syād avaktavyam eveti vidhikalpanayā yugapad vidhiniṣedhakalpanayā ca pañcamaḥ. (6) syān nāsty eva syād avaktavyam eveti niṣedhakalpanayā yugapad vidhiniṣedhakalpanayā ca ṣaṣṭhaḥ. (7) syād asty eva syān nāsty eva syād avaktavyam eveti kramato vidhiniṣedhakalpanayā yugapad vidhiniṣedhakalpanayā ca saptamaḥ. *SM*: k 23.

inexpressible" (*syād avaktavyaḥ eva*). A further combination of the fourth statement with each of the first three yields the fifth, sixth, and seventh nayas, thereby completing all possible ways in which an object can be described on the "existence" dimension.[14]

The sapta-bhaṅgi is admittedly a rather cumbersome method of characterizing the existent, and is employed by the Jaina only in philosophical discourse. The spirit of this approach, however, guards him at all times from extreme viewpoints, especially illusionism (*māyāvāda*, the basis of many Hindu sects), determinism (*niyativāda*, in which the Jaina includes all forms of theism), and annihilationism (ucchedavāda, best represented by modern notions of materialism). Jainas are encouraged to read extensively in the treatises of other schools—a practice that probably accounts for the richly varied libraries of Jaina monasteries—in order to identify extreme views and to apply the proper corrections.[15] This practice probably does not really increase tolerance of others' views; nevertheless it has generated a very well-informed (if not always valid) sort of criticism. It also seems likely that the failure of any significant doctrinal heresy to appear during nearly 3,000 years of Jaina tradition can be largely attributed to this highly developed tendency towards critical analysis and partial accommodation of extremes.

In terms of conduct, any doctrine which preaches the unreality of either bondage, the universe, or the self cannot consistently attach importance to worldly behavior; it

14. For illustrations of these combinations, see H. Bhattacharya 1953. On the concept of avaktavya, see Tripathi 1968.

15. The following verses demonstrate the spirit of accommodation, generated by the doctrines of anekāntavāda and syādvāda, through which Jaina teachers sought to integrate different schools of Indian philosophy into their own system: "Bauddhānām ṛjusūtrato matam abhūd Vedāntinām saṅgrahāt/ Sāṃkhyānāṃ tata eva naigamanayād Yaugaś ca Vaiśeṣikaḥ// Śabdabrahmavido'pi śabdanayataḥ sarvair nayair gumphitāḥ/ Jainī dṛṣṭir itīha sāratarată pratyakṣam udvīkṣyate// . . . yasya sarvatra samatā nayeṣu tanayeṣv iva/ tasyānekāntavādasya kva nyūnādhikaśemuṣī// tena syādvādam ālambya sarvadarśanatulyatām/ mokṣoddeśāviśeṣeṇa yaḥ paśyati sa śāstravit//" *SM*: intro. 31–32 (quoted from *Adhyātmasāra*).

must make salvation contingent solely upon insight (jñāna) into this unreality. At the other extreme, we may find total reliance upon the efficacy of action (karma), taking such forms as the Mīmāṃsā performance of Vedic sacrifices or the great faith and devotion shown by theists hoping for divine grace. The Jaina with his teaching of anekānta and its corollaries, nayavāda and syādvāda, escapes the doctrinal necessity of having to follow a single restricted path. All paths can be seen as valid in some respect; thus a Jaina is able to coordinate (*samuccaya*) various methods into his path of purification (mokṣa-mārga), which is defined as a combination of insight (darśana) into the nature of reality (along with faith in this view), critical knowledge (jñāna) as outlined in the scripture, and pure conduct (cāritra). This, for the Jaina, is the comprehensively valid path of salvation:

samyag-darśana-jñāna-cāritrāṇi mokṣa-mārgaḥ/[16]

Categories of Being

The Jainas divide all existents into three main categories: (1) those which are sentient; (2) those which are material; (3) those which are neither sentient nor material. "Sentient" here refers to the jīva or soul, which is characterized by consciousness. "Material" designates atoms (pudgala) possessing form/color, taste, smell, and palpability. The third category, called *arūpi-ajīva,* is understood to include four insentient, formless, yet existent substances (drayvas): space (ākāśa), the principle of motion (dharma-dravya), the principle of rest (adharma-dravya), and time (kāla).

Although "soul" is unquestionably the most important of these categories for the Jaina, our discussion of the

16. *TS*: i, 1. bhāvānāṃ yāthātmyapratipattiviṣayaśraddhānasaṅgrahārthaṃ darśanasya samyagviśeṣaṇam. yena yena prakāreṇa jīvādayaḥ padārthā vyavasthitās tenevāvagamaḥ samyagjñānam . . . jñānavataḥ karmādānanimittakriyoparamaḥ samyakcāritram. ajñānapūrvakācāranivṛttyarthaṃ samyagviśeṣaṇam . . . ity etat tritayaṃ samuditaṃ mokṣasya sākṣān mārgo veditavyaḥ. *SS*: §5.

existents cannot begin there; we must first understand the context of temporal, spatial, and material factors in which the soul finds itself, the very fabric of bondage from which it strives to escape.

The Nonsentient and Nonmaterial

Space, although fundamentally unitary, is often described in terms of two categories: that which is occupied by other substances and that which is not. These are designated as "space having worlds" (loka-ākāśa) and "space without worlds" (*aloka-ākāśa*), respectively. The loka-ākāśa, which is equivalent to the manifest universe, has the outline of a man standing with arms akimbo and legs apart.[17] All cases of jīva, pudgala, dharma, adharma, and kāla are said to occur within, or rather define the limits of, this three-dimensional shape. Unoccupied space, on the other hand, is infinite and totally empty. These "types" of space are of course continuous; the division between them indicates only the finite range of the other existents.[18] The distinguishing quality of space is its ability to provide a locus for such existents; this is true whether it actually does so (as in the case of loka-ākāśa) or not (as in the case of aloka-ākāśa). Hence there is only one "space"; its extent is infinite. Ākāśa is further described as divisible into infinitesimally small "space-points" (*pradeśa*);[19] these units have some dimension and yet cannot be subdivided.[20] In such

17. For a diagramatic sketch, see Ch. IV.

18. loka ity ucyate. ko lokaḥ? dharmādharmādīni dravyāṇi yatra lokyante sa loka iti . . . ākāśaṃ dvidhā vibhaktaṃ lokākāśam alokākāśaṃ ceti. loka uktaḥ. sa yatra tal lokākāśam. tato bahiḥ sarvato 'nantam alokākāśam. lokālokavibhāgaś ca dharmādharmāstikāyasadbhāvād vijñeyaḥ. *SS*: §549.

19. pradiśyanta iti pradeśāḥ . . . paramāṇuḥ . . . yāvati kṣetre vyavatiṣṭhate sa pradeśa iti vyavahriyate. Ibid.: §541.

20. Basham's note on pradeśa: "The *pradeśa*, though it roughly corresponds to the point in Euclidean geometry, is not quite the same concept. The Euclidean point has no dimension; the *pradeśa* has dimensions but they are infinitesimally small. It is a sort of atom of space, perhaps comparable to the point in the Gaussian system of geometry used by Einstein. The paradoxical 'dimensional point' is perhaps as good a translation of this difficult term as any other." Basham 1958: 77, n. 3. Souls, dharma, adharma, and the loka-ākāśa are said to possess uncountable (asaṃkhyāta) pradeśas and hence are called *asti-kāya* (having a body, i.e., an extension).

terms, occupied space may be said to have a finite (though uncountable [asaṃkhyāta]) number of space-points, while unoccupied space has an infinity thereof. Again, the distinction is a conventional one: the unity of space taken as a whole must of course possess an infinite number of pradeśas.

The principles of motion (dharma-dravya) and rest (adharma-dravya) seem to be unique to Jaina philosophy. Certain scholars have made the reasonable suggestion that these principles are traceable to an ancient notion of fluids flowing through the universe (compare Vedic *ṛta* and *dharma*).[21] Others relate dharma and adharma respectively to the *rajas* and *tamas* principles of Sāṃkhya. The latter theory fails to note that none of the four "insentient and immaterial" substances of the Jainas undergo the sorts of *defiled* modifications (*vikṛti*) which characterize the Sāṃkhya prakṛti (and, for that matter, the souls and material atoms posited by Jainas themselves). These four are said, rather, to remain always in their "pure state"; thus it seems clear that the modal alterations attributed by Jainas to these four substances in fact comprise a kind of "undefiled change" (*svabhāva-pariṇāma*).

This sort of change is totally free of contact with, hence defilement by, any other substance. Such a phenomenon is said to be possible because of the special nature of these third-category existents. The principle of movement (dharma-dravya), for example, does not itself set the souls and material atoms in motion; rather it provides the medium, the external efficient cause (*nimitta-kāraṇa*), through which movement can occur. The jīva and pudgala are described as analogous to fish moving through the water of dharma-dravya; they possess by nature the capacity to move (the material cause [*upādāna-kāraṇa*]), and yet cannot realize this potential unless dharma-dravya is present. Similarly, the principle of rest (adharma-dravya) is compared to the shade of a tree, which provides an appropriate

21. See Schubring 1962: §10.

situation or environment (and efficient cause) for someone to stop and relax. Both dharma-dravya and adharma-dravya are unitary substances which extend (again in terms of "an uncountable but finite number of space-points") throughout occupied space. They themselves undergo neither movement nor rest, "functioning" only insofar as other substances either move through space or come to a stop there.[22]

Jaina philosophers have not unanimously accorded the status of "independent substance" to time (kāla). While Digambaras definitely place it in this category, Śvetāmbaras remain divided on whether or not to do so. Like ākāśa, dharma-dravya, and adharma-dravya, kāla is a kind of efficient or instrumental cause. It is seen as necessary for the occurrence of change in all other substances, and yet it in no way either generates these changes or is "touched" by them.[23] Now, if kāla is itself a substance, a logical problem arises, for substances by definition go through constant change. Thus it seems that another kāla would be necessary to make possible the occurrence of this change in the first one, and so forth into an infinite regress.

A further problem is posed by the Jaina notion that each "point" of time, one for every space-point (pradeśa) of the loka-ākāśa, is unable to combine with other time-points (*kālāṇu*).[24] These points are seen as forever sep-

22. gatipariṇāmināṃ jīvapudgalānāṃ gatyupagrahe kartavye dharmāstikāyaḥ sādhāraṇāśrayo jalavan matsyagamane. tathā sthitipariṇāmināṃ . . . adharmāstikāyaḥ sādhāraṇāśrayaḥ pṛthivīdhātur ivāśvādisthitāv iti. *SS*: §559.

23. dharmādīnāṃ dravyāṇāṃ svaparyāyanirvṛttiṃ prati svātmanaiva vartamānānāṃ bāhyopagrahād vinā tadvṛttyabhāvāt pravartnopalakṣitaḥ kāla iti kṛtvā vartanā kālasyopakāraḥ. Ibid.: §569. A question could be raised concerning the possibility of change in modes on the part of the substance "space," since time units are not present beyond the loka-ākāśa. But if it is recalled that there is really only one continuous body of space, the problem disappears, for the existence of the time substance in any part of the whole is then "in contact," as it were, with any other part. The presence of time in each pradeśa of the loka-ākāśa is only necessary to make change possible for the *other* substances existing there, substances which are not unified in the way that space is.

24. lokākāśasya yāvantaḥ pradeśās tāvantaḥ kālāṇavo niṣkriyā ekaikākāśapradeśe ekaikavṛttyā lokaṃ vyāpya vyavasthitāḥ. Ibid.: §602.

arate, like a heap of unjoined pearls. Hence time cannot have extension in the ordinary sense; that is, it is not a vast unity (*asti-kāya*) like space, but has an uncountable (asaṃkhyāta) number of discreet, dimensionless units. Under such conditons it is hard to imagine the time-continuum implicit in such notions as past-present-future. Because of these difficulties with the idea of "time as substance," some ācāryas have asserted that kāla is only a convention (*vyavahāra*) or designation, rather than a separate dravya.[25] But most Jainas adhere to the "substance" view and tend to ignore the logical questions it entails.

MATTER (PUDGALA)

The Jaina term pudgala is traditionally said to be derived from *puṃ-* (joining) plus *-gala* (breaking). This gives an idea of how Jainas envision the formation and destruction of matter: through atomic aggregation (*saṃghāta*) and disjunction (*bheda*), respectively. Atoms (paramāṇu) are indivisible and infinite in number; being, furthermore, without extension, they are invisible and do not fill up even a single space-point of the loka-ākāśa. Each atom has the four material qualities noted above—form/color, taste, smell, and palpability (defined in terms of moist versus dry and heavy versus light). These qualities, moreover, undergo constant changes of modes along their respective continua.

Although atoms do not have extension, they are said to be capable of combining with other atoms to form aggregates that do. This process of combination can occur because of palpability differences between various atoms, specifically those along the moisture-dryness dimension (*snigdha-rukṣatva*). Hence atoms that are equally moist cannot be joined together, while one that is very dry will forge a strong bond with one that is very moist. In this way material aggregates (*pudgala-skandha*) are

25. For further details on this controversy, see N. J. Shah 1968.

formed.[26] These aggregates are capable of producing the effects (that is, the visible formations) of earth, water, fire, and air, as well as sound, darkness, shade, light, heat, and various shapes.[27] Most significantly, they provide the body, speech, mental organ, and vital breath which house the soul in the state of embodiment.[28] They also form the generalized karmic matter which, after being defiled in various ways by the force of volitions, constitutes the physical basis (*kārmaṇa-śarīra*)[29] of bondage itself.

THE SENTIENTS (JĪVA)

Occupied space (loka-ākāśa) contains an infinite number of immaterial souls (jīva). Unlike atoms (pudgala), these souls do not lack dimension; each has an uncountable (asaṃkhyāta) number of space-points (pradeśa) and exists within the physical limits of its current corporeal shape, just as a lamp illuminates only the room in which it stands. This adaptation to a particular body's dimensions, however, is said to involve no change in the nature of the soul; whether a given body is as large as the entire loka-ākāśa or as small as the tiniest object imaginable, the number of the soul's space-points remains the same.[30] As noted earlier, this phenomenon is compared to the case of a cloth, which can be folded into various shapes without any alteration of its mass.

26. dvayoḥ snigdharukṣayor aṇvoḥ parasparaśleṣalakṣaṇabandhe sati dvyaṇukaskandho bhavati. evaṃ saṃkhyeyāsaṃkhyeyānantapradeśaḥ skandho yojyaḥ. *SS*: §590.

27. sparśarasagandhavarṇavantaḥ pudgalāḥ/ śabdabandhasaukṣmyasthaulyasaṃsthānabhedatamaśchāyātapodyotavantaś ca/ *TS*: v, 23–24.

28. śarīravāṅmanaḥprāṇāpānāḥ pudgalānām/ sukhaduḥkhajīvitamaraṇopagrahāś ca/ Ibid.: v, 19–20.

29. See Ch. IV n. 55.

30. pradeśasaṃhāravisarpābhyāṃ pradīpavat/ *TS*: v, 16. amūrtasvabhāvasyātmano'nādibandhaṃ pratyekatvāt kathaṃcin mūrtatāṃ bibhrataḥ kārmaṇaśarīravaśān mahad aṇu ca śarīram adhitiṣṭhatas tadvaśāt pradeśasaṃharaṇavisarpaṇasvabhāvasya tāvatpramāṇatāyāṃ satyām asaṃkhyeyabhāgādiṣu vṛttir upapadyate, pradīpavat. *SS*: §557. For a Jaina critique of the Vaiśeṣika views about the size of the soul, see Thomas 1960: 52–56.

Orthodox Indian systems (darśanas) have generally described the soul either as omnipresent (vibhu) or as atomic (*aṇu*); but both descriptions stress the *absolute* unchangeability of this most important of all existents. While Jaina soul-theory per se does not fall easily into a general "heterodox" category (it accepts, for example, the kind of karmically generated retribution and bondage rejected by the Cārvāka materialists and also contradicts Buddhist views by postulating a real substance beyond momentary modes), it is nevertheless true that the Jaina suggestion—indeed requirement—of some form of change in the soul-substance constitutes a unique and significant departure from the mainstream of Indian thought. The sort of dimensional change described above is only one example of the ramifications of this position, as closer examination of Jaina statements about the jīva will show.[31]

First of all, a Jaina regards the existence of a bound and changeable soul as self-evident; such a soul is the reality without which his entire world-view and quest for salvation would be meaningless. External demonstrations or proofs for this reality are considered redundant and superfluous; the simple experience of self-awareness (*ahaṃpratyaya*) is proof enough. Even doubt—for example, "is there really a self here?"—supports this view when one asks the further question, "who is it that has the doubt?" The answer given, of course, is jīva, the basic "I" that stands behind all human actions.[32]

31. The following verse enumerates eight characteristics of jīva: jīvo uvaogamao amutti kattā sadehaparimāṇo/ bhottā saṃsārattho siddho so vissasoḍḍhagaī// *Dravyasaṅgraha*: k 2. Each of these is said to refute one of the "false" views held by various Indian schools: "jīvasiddhiḥ Cārvākaṃ prati; jñānadarśanopayogalakṣaṇaṃ Naiyāyikaṃ prati; amūrtajīvasthāpanaṃ Bhaṭṭa-Cārvākadvayaṃ prati; karmakartṛtvasthāpanaṃ Sāṃkhyaṃ prati; svadehapramitisthāpanaṃ Naiyāyika-Mīmāṃsaka-Sāṃkhyatrayaṃ prati; karmabhoktṛtvavyākhyānaṃ Bauddhaṃ prati; saṃsārasya vyākhyānaṃ Sadāśivaṃ prati; siddhatvavyākhyānaṃ Bhaṭṭa-Cārvākadvayaṃ prati; ūrdhvagatisvabhāvakathanaṃ Māṇḍalikagranthakāraṃ prati, iti matārtho jñātavyaḥ." *SM*: 201 (quoted in the notes from the *Dravyasaṅgrahavṛtti*).

32. On the problem of the existence of the soul, see *Gaṇadharavāda*: k 1549–1605 (Solomon 1966: 35–46).

Consciousness.—A soul is said to have three main qualities (guṇa) or functional aspects: consciousness (*caitanya*), bliss (sukha), and energy (vīrya). Of these, consciousness is central, representing what is in effect the distinguishing characteristic of the soul. It is through operation of this quality that a soul can be the knower (*pramātṛ*), that which illuminates both objects and itself. The application of consciousness is referred to as cognition (*upayoga*), which is twofold: perception (darśana), that is, first contact, indistinct awareness, or what might be called pure apprehension; and knowledge (jñāna), that is, comprehending the details of what has been perceived.[33] Since in the mundane state darśana and jñāna invariably operate in sequence, and are affected by different types of karmas, they are generally considered to be two distinct qualities (guṇas) of the soul rather than aspects of a single quality. In spite of certain controversies over this distinction, it will hereafter be employed with reference to the soul's cognitive functions.[34] .That is, reference will be made to both "perception" and "knowledge," rather than simply to "consciousness."

Bliss.—The next important quality of the soul is bliss (sukha), which can be experienced by the jīva through self-knowledge. This quality is said to be fully manifest only when the soul attains perfect purity; the extent to which it is experienced corresponds directly to the degree of that purity. Strictly speaking, "pure bliss" is simply a label for the perfected, self-contained (*svabhāva-sthita*) state of the soul;[35] bliss is impure or defiled (*vibhāva*), on the other hand, when the soul harbors a desire to reflect external

33. upayogo lakṣaṇam/ *TS*: ii, 8. ubhayanimittavaśād utpadyamānaś caitanyānuvidhāyī pariṇāma upayogaḥ . . . sa upayogo dvividhaḥ, jñanopayogo darśanopayogaś ceti . . . tayoḥ kathaṃ bhedaḥ? sākārānākārabhedāt. sākāraṃ jñānam anākāraṃ darśanam iti. tat chadmastheṣu krameṇa vartate, nirāvaraṇeṣu yugapat. pūrvakālabhāvino 'pi darśanāj jñānasya prāg upanyāsaḥ, abhyarhitatvāt. *SS*: §271–274.

34. For details on these controversies, see *SJP*: 70–80.

35. For a study of the contrast between the quality of bliss (sukha) and the ordinary "feeling of happiness" (*sukhā vedanā*), see P. S. Jaini 1977b.

objects. Although such desire is described as antithetical to bliss, it must be understood that these two are not mutually opposed entities; they are, rather, two ends of the same continuum, the defiled (vibhāva) and purified (svabhāva) states of the same quality. This is considered analogous to the case of water, which is cool by nature but becomes hot in the presence of fire. Taking coolness as the normal or "pure" state of water, hotness becomes an unnatural or "defiled" condition, reached in the presence of an outside agent. Similarly, the soul is by nature self-contained (uninterested in external things) and totally blissful; it becomes "desirous" through association with certain external factors called defiling karmas.

It is important to note here that bliss is the only quality of the soul which can truly be defiled, that is, transformed into something of a different nature; other qualities can only be "obscured" or "blocked" (*āvṛta*) by so-called obscuring (*āvaraṇīya*) karmas. (As will be seen below, a direct relation obtains between the degrees of obscuration and defilement.) Hence the expression "defiled soul" really refers specifically to change along the dimension of the bliss-quality.

Energy.—Another significant quality of the soul is that called energy (vīrya). This functions as a sort of meta-quality, an abstract force which energizes, as it were, the very operation of the knowledge and perception qualities. Thus it will be said that both forms of cognition are manifested, at a given moment, in exact proportion to whatever percentage of the soul's infinite energy is present at that moment. Limitations are imposed on the amount of available vīrya by the condition of embodiment itself. This karmically produced mundane state also channels or "perverts" the direct expression of energy, causing it to generate a certain movement or vibration (*yoga*) of the soul; such vibration draws new karmic matter into association with the soul substance. But vīrya is also the efficient cause by which the soul brings about modifications in the functions of the karmic matter drawn towards the soul.[36] Finally, vīrya is conventionally understood as the soul's capacity to engage in so-called giving (*dāna*), obtaining (*lābha*), enjoyment (*bhoga*), and repeated enjoyment (*upabhoga*) of worldly objects. A limited ability to take part in these activities during daily life is thought to be due to obstruction of vīrya by particular karmas.[37]

Jainas speak of the "innumerable qualities" of the soul. Nevertheless, it can legitimately be said that the presence of those qualities which have been briefly discussed above —perception, knowledge, bliss, and energy—are sufficient to define the soul as a totally distinct and unique entity, an existent separate from all others.

Thus concludes this introduction to the basic units of the Jaina universe, the living and nonliving factors in terms of which all experience must be analyzed and all religious meaning found. To approach the integrated concept of reality into which the Jaina has molded these factors, we must now begin from the same starting point that he does: the fact of the soul's long and painful entrapment in the chains of bondage, chains forged as much by the soul's own potential for defilement as by the effects of material "karma."

36. For details, see *SJP*: 252–254.
37. dānalābhabhogopabhogavīryāṇām/ *TS*: viii, 13.

IV

The Mechanism of Bondage

Saṃsāra: The Cycle of Transmigration

Jaina thinkers have invested a great deal of energy in describing the precise mechanism of bondage; no other Indian school has been nearly so concerned with the details thereof. This phenomenon perhaps reflects an attempt to lessen the heavy emotional burden which the Jaina's view of bondage places upon him. He envisions his soul's tormented involvement with the material universe on a vast scale; this involvement has had no beginning, and it is likely to continue almost indefinitely.[1] He further believes it incorrect to imagine that the soul was once pure but later became defiled. It has always been impure, just as a seam of gold has "always" been imbedded in the rock where it is found. (This analogy to gold ore is taken one step further: "Absolute purification may be achieved if the proper refining method is applied.")

Speaking in a general way, the Jaina will say that the defiled condition of the soul leads to its continuous rebirth in various states of embodiment. Existence in such states, characterized by desire, involves activities which draw karmic matter; this matter in turn contributes to the soul's further defilement, hence to further embodiment. Thus we have the basic process through which one is held in the cycle of transmigration (saṃsāra).[2]

1. saṃtāṇo'ṇātīo paropparaṃ hetuhetubhāvāto/ dehassa ya kammassa ya Maṃḍiya! bīyaṃkurāṇaṃ va// *Viśeṣāvaśyaka-bhāṣya*: k 1813.

2. karmavipākavaśād ātmano bhavāntarāvāptiḥ saṃsāraḥ. *SS*: §801.

The Four Stages of Birth

The saṃsāric cycle involves an infinity of possible birth-states, from the crudest forms of life to the most exalted and complex heavenly existences. It is not only said that a given soul *can* be born into uncountable states of every type, but that indeed it already *has* done so and will carry on in virtually endless repetition of these experiences. Four main birth categories or destinies (gati) are set forth: those of gods (*deva*), humans (*manuṣya*), hell beings (*nāraki*), and animals and plants (*tiryañca*).[3] These are often indicated by the stylized wheel of life called *svastika* (*su-asti-ka*, well-being), a symbol used thus by Jainas from the earliest times and found on nearly all their iconography even today.[4]

Three of the four gatis are said to have a corresponding realm or "habitation level" in the vertically-tiered Jaina universe; thus gods, humans and hell beings occupy the higher (heavenly), middle (earthly), and lower (hellish) realms, respectively.[5] This correspondence is not absolutely fixed; gods may often "leave home" to appear on earth, for example, and a whole class of demigods (for example, the Bhavanavāsi and Vyantara devas, namely spirits, demons, celestial musicians (*gandharvas*), yakṣas, goblins) is said to dwell not in heaven but in the space between hell and earth.[6] Even so, each of these three higher births is generally to be identified with its particular realm.

But the animal and plant (tiryañca) category constitutes a special case. It is first of all the lowest of possible destinies, characterized by extremely gross sensory activity and pervasive ignorance. Among the tiryañca are several subgroups, distinguished on the basis of sense faculties, that

3. gatiś caturbhedā, narakagatis tiryaggatir manuṣyagatir devagatir iti. tatra narakagatināmakarmodayān nārako bhāvo bhavatīti narakagatir audayikī. SS: §265.

4. For the use of this symbol in the Jaina ritual of worship, see Glasenapp 1925: 383. See below, Ch. VII (in discussion of *devapūjā*).

5. See a diagrammatic sketch of the Jaina universe at the end of this chapter.

6. See below, n. 60.

is, the number of modalities through which members of each group are able to experience the world. At the very bottom of this scale, hence comprising the lowest form of life, are the so-called *nigoda.* These creatures are submicroscopic and possess only one sense, that of touch. They are so tiny and undifferentiated that they lack even individual bodies; large clusters of them are born together as colonies which die a fraction of a second later.[7] These colonies are said to pervade every corner of the universe; in the earthly realms, they inhabit even the tissues of plant, animal, and human hosts. Just above the nigoda is another group of single-sense organisms whose members take the very elements—the subtlest possible units of matter—as their bodies; hence they are called the earth bodies (*pṛthvī-kāyika*), water bodies (*āpo-kāyika*), fire bodies (*tejo-kāyika*), and air-bodies (*vāyu-kāyika*), respectively.[8] These too are found throughout occupied space, but they do not permeate the bodies of other beings as the nigoda may do.

The remaining tiryañca are classified either as plants or animals proper; both groups exist only in the earthly realms.[9] Plant beings (*vanaspati-kāya*) may take individual (*pratyeka*) embodiment, but more commonly they assume

7. sāhāraṇodayeṇa ṇigodasarīrā havanti sāmaṇṇā/ te puṇa duvihā jīvā bādarasukumātti viṇṇeyā// sāhāraṇamāhāro sāhāraṇamāṇapāṇagahaṇaṃ ca/ sāhāraṇajīvāṇaṃ sāhāraṇalakkhaṇaṃ bhaṇiyaṃ// jatthekka marai jīvo tattha du maraṇaṃ have aṇaṃtāṇaṃ/ bakkamai jattha ekko bakkamaṇaṃ tattha'ṇaṃtāṇaṃ// *Gommaṭasāra–Jīvakāṇḍa*, k 191–193. For further details on the nigodas, see *SM*: k 29; and *JY*: 110–116.

8. pṛthivyaptejovāyuvanaspatayaḥ sthāvarāḥ/ *TS*: ii, 13. pṛthivīkāyo 'syāstīti pṛthivīkāyikaḥ. tatkāyasaṃbandhavaśīkṛta ātmā. *SS*: §286. Malliṣeṇa gives several reasons for considering these as animate entities: pṛthivyādīnāṃ punarjīvatvam itthaṃ sādhanīyam. yathā sātmikā vidrumaśilādirūpā pṛthivī, chede samānadhātūtthānād, arśo'ṅkuravat. bhaumam ambho'pi sātmakam, kṣatabhūsajātīyasya svabhāvasya sambhavāt, śālūravat . . . tejo'pi sātmakam, āhāropādānena vṛddhyādivikāropalambhāt, puruṣāṅgavat. vāyur api sātmakaḥ, aparapreritatve tiryaggatimatvād govat. vanaspatir api sātmakaḥ, chedādibhir mlānyādidarśanāt, puruṣāṅgavat. *SM*: k 29. For Jaina speculations on biology, see Sikdar 1974.

9. "Plants" and "animals" found in the heavens or the underworld are thought to actually be gods or hell beings who have deliberately assumed such forms.

collective (*sādhāraṇa*) forms; a tree, for example, is said to be comprised of many souls. While plants resemble the lower tiryañca in that they too possess only the sense of touch, they are distinguished by having a longer life-span and a more complex physical structure. Animals, for their part, possess from two to five senses.[10] Those with all five sensory capacities are further characterized as either totally instinctive (*asaṃjñī/amanaska*, literally, without mind) or able to reason (*saṃjñī/samanaska*).[11]

Gods and hell beings, although they occupy widely separate worlds, share many characteristics. They are born spontaneously (*aupapādika*), that is, they simply appear, with no need for parents, and can alter the appearance of their physical bodies at will. In addition to possessing the five senses and reasoning powers seen in many earthly creatures, they are naturally endowed with special "super-knowledges" (avadhijñāna) such as clairvoyance, memory of prior incarnations, and the ability to see objects at great distances.[12] The real difference between a birth in heaven and one in hell revolves around the effect produced by these special powers; whereas they increase the pleasure of a god's existence (he may remember, for example, his good deeds in a former life), they bring nothing but greater suffering to the hell being (for he will recall only the evil of his actions, the hatred of his enemies, and so on).

This brief description gives some idea of the great range of possible states in which the bound soul can find itself.

10. kṛmipipīlikābhramaramanuṣyādīnām ekaikavṛddhāni/ *TS*: ii, 23. "The worm and similar creatures possess the sense of taste in addition to the sense of touch. The ant and similar creatures possess the sense of smell in addition to the senses of touch and taste. The bee and creatures of that class possess the sense of sight in addition to the senses of touch, taste and smell. Man and the beings similar to him possess the sense of hearing in addition to the former four." S. A. Jain 1958: 67.

11. saṃjñinaḥ samanaskāḥ/ *TS*: ii, 24. hitāhitaprāptiparihāraparīkṣā . . . saṃjñā . . . *SS*: §301. It is believed that saṃjñī animals are capable of receiving religious instruction. See below, Ch. V n. 17.

12. bhavapratyayo'vadhir devanārakāṇām/ *TS*: i, 21. yathā patatriṇo gamanam ākāśe bhavanimittam, na śikṣāguṇaviśeṣaḥ, tathā devanārakāṇāṃ vrataniyamādyabhāve 'pi jāyata iti bhavapratyayaḥ. *SS*: §213.

Jainas believe that in every such state, no matter how low or simple, there will always be some residue of qualities that define the soul: perception, knowledge, energy, bliss, and so on.[13] Thus, even the huge mass of karmic matter which oppresses the very lowest being will not keep its soul at such a level forever; the potential for spiritual growth (progress to higher states) is never eliminated completely. It should be noted, however, that this is not a theory of necessary evolution; the Jaina also accepts the possibility of retrogression, and thus of eternal bondage.

The Idea of Karma

For most souls, then, there is the likely prospect of a virtually endless journey through the cycle of destinies; the number of existences which one has already been through, and must yet experience, are beyond imagining. In such a context it is not difficult to understand why Jainas have concentrated their attention on the karmic mechanism that "runs" this process, for only through accurate analysis of the causes of the soul's defilement will the proper means of purification be made clear. This analysis is centered, moreover, upon the interaction of soul and karma during the state of *human* existence; man's need to feel that his own actions in the present are efficacious, and thus meaningful, is doctrinally justified by the tenet that only in the human state can one finally cut the bonds that imprison his soul.[14] Let us examine the Jaina view of how these bonds are formed and how they are manifested in human experience.

Most Indian systems employ the term karma to designate certain traces (*vāsanā*) or seeds (*bīja*) left behind, as

13. "iha kevalajñānāvaraṇasya svāvāryaḥ kevalajñānalakṣaṇo guṇaḥ, sa ca yadyapi sarvātmanā "vriyate tathāpi sarvajīvānaṃ kevalajñānasyā 'nantabhāgo 'nāvṛta evāvatiṣṭhate . . . so 'pi cāvaśiṣṭo 'nantabhāgo . . . mati-śrutā-'vadhi-manaḥparyāyajñānāvaraṇair āvriyate, tathāpi kācid nigodāvasthāyām api jñā-namātrā 'vatiṣṭhate." *SJP*: 240 (quoted from the *Karmagrantha*).

14. . . . kasmin kṣetre siddhyanti? . . . janma prati pañcadaśasu karma-bhūmiṣu, saṃharaṇaṃ prati mānuṣakṣetre siddhiḥ . . . gatyā kasyāṃ gatau siddhih? . . . manuṣyagatau . . . *SS*: §937.

it were, by one's deeds. These residual factors will someday bear fruit in the sense of generating or conditioning experience; thus it is said: "Every action must eventuate in an appropriate reward or retribution to the performer of that action: this is karma."[15] Jainas adhere to the general outlines of this view; but they stand alone in asserting unequivocally that karma is itself actual *matter*, rather than the sort of quasi-physical or psychological elements envisioned by other schools.

Karmic matter is said to be found "floating free" in every part of occupied space. At this stage it is undifferentiated; various types (prakṛti) of karma, classifiable by function, are molded from these simpler forms only after interaction with a given soul has begun.[16] We have already seen that such interaction takes place because of the soul's impure state, a state which has prevailed since beginningless time. The energy quality, "perverted" by this impurity, produces vibrations (yoga), which bring about the influx (āsrava) of different kinds of material karma.[17] The vibrations referred to here actually denote the volitional activities of the individual. Such activities can be manifested through either body, speech, or mind; hence the soul's vibrations are said to be of three types, each corresponding to one of these modalities.

Vibrations alone, however, do not produce bondage. The karmic "dust" which they draw to the soul would simply fall away were the soul not "moistened," as it were, by its harboring of the passions (kaṣāyas): desire (*rāga*) and hatred (*dveṣa*). Karmas can stick to or bind (bandha)[18]

15. Compare: kleśamūlaḥ karmāśayo dṛṣṭādṛṣṭajanmavedanīyaḥ/ satimūle tadvipāko jātyāyurbhogāḥ/ Patañjali's *Yoga-sūtra*: ii, 12–13.

16. nāmapratyayāḥ sarvato yogaviśeṣāt sūkṣmaikakṣetrāvasthitāḥ sarvātmapradeśeṣv anantānantapradeśāḥ/ *TS*: viii, 24.

17. kāyavāṅmanaḥkarma yogaḥ/ sa āsravaḥ/ Ibid.: vi, 1–2. ātmapradeśaparispando yogaḥ. sa nimittabhedāt tridhā bhidyate, kāyayogo vāgyogo manoyoga iti . . . yogapraṇālikayā ātmanaḥ karma āsravatīti āsrava iti vyapadeśam arhati. *SS*: §610–611.

18. sakaṣāyatvāj jīvaḥ karmaṇo yogyān pudgalān ādatte sa bandhaḥ. *TS*: viii, 2. mithyādarśanādyāveśād ārdrīkṛtasyātmanaḥ . . . pudgalānāṃ karmabhāvayogyānām avibhāgenopaśleṣo bandha ity ākhyāyate. *SS*: §734.

a soul that is thus "moistened" but will have no effect upon one that is "dry" or passion-free (vītarāga). The latter situation occurs only in an omniscient being (kevalin); for all other souls, each intentional act leads inevitably to further defilement. The precise amount (pradeśa) of karma that engulfs the soul after a given activity is said to depend upon the *degree of volition* with which that activity was carried out.[19] The type of activity, moreover, determines the specific nature (prakṛti)[20] assumed by the theretofore undifferentiated karmic matter. One's attempt to withhold knowledge from another out of jealousy, for example, develops karmas which will at a later time function to obscure one's own knowledge.

As for the duration (*sthiti*) and result (*anubhava*) of given karmas—how long they will cling to the soul and what precise momentary effect they will eventually have upon it—these are fixed by the degree to which such passions (kaṣāya) as anger and lust colored the original activity.[21] Once a karma has given its result, it falls away (nirjarā) from the soul "like ripe fruit," returning to the undifferentiated state and thus to the infinite pool of "free" karmic matter;[22] eventually it will again become associated with the same or some other unliberated soul. Indeed: "The soul has successively taken in and cast off every particle of [karmic] matter in the universe."[23]

It should be made clear that Jainas view the soul's involvement with karma as merely an "association" (*ekakṣetrāvagāha,* literally, occupying the same locus); there is said to be no actual *contact* between them, since this

19. tīvramandajñātājñātabhāvādhikaraṇavīryaviśeṣebhyas tad viśeṣaḥ/ *TS*: vi, 6.

20. prakṛtiḥ svabhāvaḥ . . . jñānāvaraṇasya kā prakṛtiḥ? arthānavagamaḥ. darśanāvaraṇasya . . . arthānālokanam. darśanamohasya tattvārthāśraddhānam. cāritramohasyāsaṃyamaḥ . . . tad evaṃ lakṣaṇaṃ kāryaṃ prakriyate prabhavaty asyā iti prakṛtiḥ. *SS*: §736.

21. kaṣāyanimittau sthityanubhavau. Ibid.: §736.

22. pīḍānugrahāv ātmane pradāya . . . avasthānābhāvād karmaṇo nivṛttir nirjarā. Ibid.: §778.

23. uktaṃ ca—"savve vi puggalā khalu kamaso bhuttujjhiyā ya jīveṇa/ asaiṃ aṇaṃtakhutto puggalapariyaṭṭasaṃsāre//" Ibid.: §275.

would imply a soul which was, like karma, material by nature. Just how a nonmaterial thing can in any way interact with a material one is not well clarified. The texts simply suggest that we can *infer* such an association from our own "experience" of bondage, just as we infer the association of an immaterial consciousness and a material object from the experience of perception.[24]

The weakness of this explanation points up the formidable nature of the problem, which has vexed thinkers of virtually every Indian system. Jainas themselves are in fact not absolutely rigid in maintaining the immateriality of the soul.[25] They admit, for example, that a defiled soul can actually be "stained" by karmas; it is said to take a particular shade (*leśyā*) indicative of its spiritual level.[26] Thus, souls in the hellish existences are said to be black (*kṛṣṇa*), blue (*nīla*), or gray (*kāpota*), colors associated with the heavy karmic burden of a sinful nature. Lower tiryañcas, along with certain demigods of inferior type (those located somewhere between earth and hell), may possess souls of the above colors or of a yellow (*pīta*) hue. Dwellers in the heavenly regions have the yellow (pīta), lotus-pink (*padma*), or luminous white (*śukla*) tones characteristic of wholesome karmas. Human souls, as well as those of certain animals with five senses, show a very wide range of variation in moral development; they may evidence any one of the six colors, white (śukla-leśyā) being

24. amūrtasyāpy ātmano bandho bhavatīti siddhāntayati—rūpādikai rahitaḥ paśyati jānāti rūpādīni/ dravyāṇi guṇāṃś ca yathā tathā bandhas tena jānīhi// . . . tathā kilātmano nīrūpatvena sparśaśūnyatvān na karmapudgalaiḥ sahāsti sambandhaḥ, ekāvagāhabhāvāvasthitakarmapudgalanimittopayogādhirūḍharāgadveṣādibhāvasambandhaḥ karmapudgalabandhavyavahārasādhakastv asty eva. *Pravacanasāra* [*Tattvadīpikāṭīkā*]: ii, 82.

25. na ca bandhāprasiddhiḥ syān mūrttaiḥ karmabhir ātmanaḥ/ amūrter ity anekāntāt tasya mūrtitvasiddhitaḥ// anādinityasambandhāt saha karmabhir ātmanaḥ/ amūrtasyāpi satyaikye mūrtatvam avasīyate// *Tattvārthasāra*: v, 16–17.

26. leśyā kaṣāyodayarañjitā yogapravṛttiḥ. *SS*: §265. The notion of several soul-types, each with an identifying color, was also propounded by the Ājīvika sect; this may have been a common belief among various śramaṇa groups in ancient times. See Basham 1951: 245; Zimmer 1951: 229ff.

characteristic of those on the highest rungs of the spiritual ladder.

The Karmic Types

We have said that the soul's activities transform simple karmic matter into appropriate "specific-function karmas," which then interact with the soul in their characteristic ways. These karmas fall into two broad categories: (1) *ghātiyā*, those which have a directly negative effect upon the qualities of the soul; and (2) *aghātiyā*, those which bring about the state and particular conditions of embodiment. Each category includes karmas of several types. The ghātiyās are divided into four groups on the basis of which soul-quality they affect; thus we have perception-obscuring (*darśanāvaraṇīya*), knowledge-obscuring (*jñānāvaraṇīya*), energy-obstructing (*vīryāntarāya*), and bliss-defiling (*mohanīya*) karmas. Aghātiyās are also of four types: those pertaining to the pleasure (*sātā*) and pain (*asātā*) of mundane experiences (*vedanīya*), those determining destinies and body types (*nāma*), those determining longevity (*āyu*), and those determining environmental circumstances (*gotra*).

For most Jainas, these distinctions are important mainly on the level of conventional morality. It is thought that an individual's actions, reflecting the vibrations in his soul, will generate consequences specifically related to the mode (body, speech, or mind) and nature (wholesome or unwholesome) of the actions. Causing misery to others by speaking badly of them, for example, will result in one's own name being slandered at a later time. Selfless effort towards the welfare of strangers, on the other hand, will bring one unsolicited aid in the future. Such results are said to come "with interest;" just as a great tree will rise from a tiny seed, so will the scope and magnitude of a karmic effect far exceed those of the act which produced it.

The link between deed and consequence is not always so apparent as in the cases above, particularly with reference to the determination of one's future destiny. We are told that rebirth in hell, for example, results from ferocious, unrestrained efforts to obtain power and possessions, while the heavens may be attained through zealous performance of penances, charity, and similar wholesome activities. As for those who fall among the tiryañcas, it is thought that they must have displayed great cowardice or dishonesty in former existences. Finally, future incarnation as a human being appears to depend less upon *what* one does than upon *how* he does it; whereas all other destinies are reached by one or another form of excessive behavior, the key to attaining human state is moderation in all things.[27]

It may well be said that the connections between action and result which Jainas set forth often have a rather arbitrary feeling about them; this is particularly true in their explanations of the structure of human society. Lower-caste status, for example, is said to be the result of having indulged in self-aggrandizement during a former life, while birth in a highly-placed family is seen as the outcome of having praised the virtues of others.[28] Such teachings perhaps go beyond a strict system of "exactly appropriate" reward or retribution. Even so, their intention is clear: to foster socially desirable behavior by placing all human actions within a context of understandable and inevitable consequences.

For the philosopher-monks, seeking to comprehend every aspect of bondage, the conventional understanding of karma was not nearly sufficient. Thus they produced a highly sophisticated analysis of the various types of material karmas, noteworthy not only for its coherent systematization of the complex factors involved but also for the deep psychological insight which it reveals.[29]

27. bahvārambhaparigrahatvaṃ nārakasyāuṣaḥ/ māyā tairyagyonasya/ alpārambhaparigrahatvaṃ mānuṣasya/ svabhāvamārdavaṃ ca/ *TS*: vi, 15–18.

28. parātmanindāpraśaṃse sadasadguṇodbhāvane ca nīcair gotraysya/ tadviparyayo nīcair vṛttyanutseko cottarasya/ Ibid.: vi, 25–26.

29. See the schematic representation of this analysis at the end of this chapter.

THE GHĀTIYĀ (DESTRUCTIVE) KARMAS

It should be made clear at this point that for the Jaina karmas do not *impose* anything upon the soul. Although it may be said that a certain karma produces a certain effect, this must be understood in the context that a soul *is itself capable* of undergoing the change referred to; the karma's presence simply triggers this change. From the Jaina standpoint then, a karma can never be more than an efficient cause (nimitta); the soul itself is the material cause (upādāna) of whatever "happens to it."[30]

We have noted earlier that most karmas—those which affect perception, knowledge, and energy—act only to *obstruct* these qualities of the soul, to prevent their full manifestation in the way that dust may obscure the reflective power of a mirror. The bliss quality alone undergoes actual defilement, transformation into an impure state or mode, as the result of association with karmas. Jaina commentators have seen this process as analogous to the effect of wine on the body, in that drunkenness involves an actual alteration of one's internal chemistry. Defilement of the bliss quality, moreover, lies at the very heart of the bondage mechanism; in fact, the "obstructive" varieties of karmic matter can exert their respective influences *only* when such defilement obtains in the soul. Any discussion of karmas must therefore begin with an examination of those which generate this defilement: the mohanīyas or "producers of delusion."

Mohanīya karma.—Speaking in general terms, it can be said that mohanīya karmas cause the soul to become confused and desirous. It is the combined presence of confusion and desire which uniquely characterizes the defiled state of the soul's bliss-quality.[31] Bliss which is thus defiled, however, can no longer be properly called bliss; it has

30. rāgapariṇāma evātmanaḥ karma, sa eva puṇyapāpadvaitam. rāgādipariṇāmasyaivātmā kartā tasyaivopādātā hātā cety eṣa śuddhadravyanirūpaṇātmako niścayanayaḥ. *Pravacanasāra* [*Tattvadīpikāṭika*]: ii, 97.

31. mohayati muhyate 'neneti vā mohanīyam. *SS*: §738.

attained a state that requires a separate designation altogether. The particular state attained depends on the kind of mohanīya karmas present. These karmas are basically of two types: insight-deluding (*darśana-mohanīya*) and conduct-deluding (*cāritra-mohanīya*).

Darśana-mohanīya: The darśana-mohanīya karmas function to prevent a soul's insight into its own nature; hence they engender the state called *mithyātva*, or having a false view.[32] A soul in the state of mithyātva is born with a fundamental tendency to see things other than as they really are. This tendency is said to be developed by an individual's worldly experience into five major varieties of erroneous views: (1) Extremism (*ekānta*): taking a one-sided (eternalist or annihilationist) position about the nature of existents; (2) imputing to a thing certain characteristics which are actually contradictory to that thing's nature (*viparīta*), for example, imagining that God punishes or that sacrificing animals leads one to heaven; (3) doubt (*saṃśaya*)—skepticism or lack of conviction about the truths one has learned; (4) indiscriminate open-mindedness (*vainayika*), that is, accepting all religious paths as equally correct when in fact they are not; (5) basic ignorance (*ajñāna*) of what is and is not good for the soul (lack of awareness that one should take up "proper conduct," the Jaina path of purification). Thus we see that a soul in the state of mithyātva is not able to make even a start in the direction of conduct leading to salvation.

Cāritra-mohanīya: This problem is further compounded by the presence of the so-called "conduct-deluding karmas;" such karmas generate the various passions (kaṣāya)[33] that constitute the "desire" side of the defilement coin.

32. yasyodayāt sarvajñapraṇītamārgaparāṅmukhas tattvārthaśraddhāna-nirutsuko hitāhitavicārāsamartho mithyādṛṣṭir bhavati tan mithyātvam. Ibid.: §749.

33. kaṣāya iva kaṣāyaḥ. kaḥ upamārthaḥ? yathā kaṣāyo naiyagrodhādiḥ śleṣahetus tathā krodhādir apy ātmanaḥ karmaśleṣahetutvāt kaṣāya iva kaṣāya ity ucyate. Ibid.: §616.

While the passions are basically of two kinds, aversion (dveṣa) and attachment (rāga), the former is always divided into anger (*krodha*) and pride (*māna*), and the latter into deceitful manipulation (*māyā*) and greed (*lobha*). Each of these four is itself said to be of four types, arranged along a scale from gross to subtle. Passions of the most gross type are called "pursuers from the limitless past" (*anantānubandhī*);[34] they are manifested through the extreme forms of grasping and aggression that characterize most of human behavior. They operate, moreover, in conjunction with mithyātva to produce a condition of spiritual stupefaction. The individual, basing his strongly volitional activities upon false notions of reality, develops ever-increasing tendencies to think and behave in destructive ways. Mithyātva and the anantānubandhī passions invariably function together; any attempt to suppress or destroy one must involve simultaneous suppression or destruction of the other.

Even when one is able to overcome these very gross forms of passions, as well as the false views which accompany them, his spiritual progress is still hampered by the three more subtle types of passions that remain. Two of the types are said to prevent the abandonment of evil actions by rendering a person incapable of taking the vows that would eliminate such actions; they are called obstructors of partial renunciation (*apratyākhyānāvaraṇa*) and obstructors of complete renunciation (*pratyākhyānāvaraṇa*). The former group is the more gross and prevents one from undertaking even the *deśa-virati*, the set of restraints prescribed for a Jaina layperson.[35] Passions of the latter type are not antithetical to *partial* abstention from harmful activities (such as the deśa-virati requires). But

34. anantasaṃsārakāraṇatvān mithyādarśanam anantam. tad anubandhino 'nantānubandhinaḥ krodhamānamāyālobhāḥ. Ibid.: §751.

35. yad udayād deśaviratiṃ . . . kartuṃ na śaknoti . . . te 'pratyākhyānāvaraṇāḥ. Ibid.: §751.

their presence effectively blocks an individual from the *total* renunciation of evil demanded of a monk.[36]

The subtlest forms of the passions are called "the smoldering" (*saṃjvalana*).[37] These are not sufficiently strong to prevent one from entering the mendicant's path, but they induce an insidious state of apathy or inertia (*pramāda*), a lack of drive with regard to the actual purificatory practices entailed by that path. It is believed, moreover, that greed of the "smoldering" type generates an unconscious attachment to life itself. This attachment, combined with the sort of apathy mentioned above, constitutes the final and perhaps the most difficult obstacle which the mendicant must overcome.

Jainas also set forth a group of "subsidiary" passions (*no-kaṣāya*),[38] said to be present until every trace of the major ones is rooted out. This group comprises nine "everyday" passion-tinged experiences: laughter (*hāsya*), pleasure in sense activity (*rati*), displeasure in sense activity (*arati*), sorrow (*śoka*), fear (*bhaya*), disgust (*jugupsā*), and sexual cravings for the male, female, and hermaphrodite (*strīveda, puṃveda,* and *napuṃsakaveda*). The degree to which these no-kaṣāyas are manifest decreases with spiritual advancement; hence a monk is likely to laugh or weep or feel revulsion much less than ordinary people do, while for the kevalin there are no such activities or feelings whatsoever.

We now have some idea of the effects directly produced by deluding karmas: false views on the one hand, destructive passions on the other. But it is essential to understand that the ramifications of a soul's association with such karmas do not end here; in the defiled state that this association entails, the soul becomes a suitable ground for the

36. yad udayād viratiṃ kṛtsnāṃ saṃyamākhyāṃ na śaknoti kartuṃ te . . . pratyākhyānāvaraṇāḥ krodhmānamāyālobhāḥ. Ibid.: §751.

37. saṃyamena sahāvasthānād ekībhūya jvalanti . . . iti saṃjvalanāḥ. Ibid.: §751.

38. īṣadarthe nañaḥ prayogād īṣat kaṣāyo 'kaṣāya iti . . . navavidham . . . hāsyādibhedāt. Ibid.: §750.

continuing influence of *other types* of karmas, karmas that not only affect all its remaining qualities but that generate the very state of embodiment. In a beginningless cycle like that of bondage, it cannot be claimed that "the mohanīya karmas came first and all other followed"; even so, it *is* true that no other karmic influences can ever be eliminated as long as these deluding factors remain. Hence, although the other karmas are said to be materially and operationally independent, they do show an oblique sort of reliance upon the "foundation" of defilement; this relation must be kept in mind during our discussion of their nature and function.

The Āvaraṇīya (Obstructing) Karmas.—The close connection between the qualities of perception and knowledge has been noted above; the karmas which affect each of these qualities are related in a parallel manner and should be considered together. Their operation is categorized basically in terms of the various types of consciousness which living beings may possess. These types are said to be five in number.

1. *Mati*: possessing the use of one or more sense capacities, up to and including a sixth sense called "mind."[39] (This last faculty is not to be confused with consciousness; it is simply an integrator of input from the five senses.) Since some portion of the soul's awareness must remain forever free of obscuration, every living being possesses at least a rudimentary form of mati.

2. *Śruta*: the ability to use words or reasoning, hence to engage in inference and similar processes.[40]

3. *Avadhi*: a limited ability to become aware of things which lie beyond the normal range of the senses, as in clairvoyance, the "divine ear," and so on.[41] Gods and hell

39. indriyair manasā ca yathāsvam artho manyate anayā manute, mananamātraṃ vā matiḥ. Ibid.: §164. matiḥ smṛtiḥ saṃjñā cintā 'bhinibodha ity anarthāntaram/ *TS*: i, 13.

40. matipūrvaṃ śrutaṃ proktaṃ avispaṣṭārthatarkaṇam/ *Tattvārthasāra*: i, 24.

41. parāpekṣāṃ vinā jñānaṃ rūpiṇāṃ bhaṇito 'vadhiḥ/ *Tattvārthasāra*: i, 25.

beings are said to be born with this ability; humans can acquire it through yogic practices. Beginning with this level of consciousness, the six sense faculties are no longer employed; the soul's awareness has here gone beyond the limited channels provided by the senses.

4. *Manaḥparyaya*: awareness of the thought-forms of others.[42] This is a power available only to beings who have overcome all insight-deluding karmas.

5. *Kevala*: absolute, isolated omniscience, involving awareness of every existent in all its qualities and modes.[43]

For each type of consciousness, there is a corresponding knowledge (jñāna) derived thereby; thus we have matijñāna, śrutajñāna, avadhijñāna, manaḥparyayajñāna, and kevalajñāna. Each kind of knowledge is subject to obstruction by a particular *āvaraṇakarma*, named for the knowledge which it affects.

The situation with regard to perception (darśana)[44] is a bit more complicated. First of all, two kinds of perceptual activity are said to operate on both the mati and śruta levels of consciousness: the *cakṣurdarśana* (visual perception) and *acakṣurdarśana* (perception by means of the other senses, including the integrating "mind" discussed above). On the avadhi level, however, we should expect no perception whatsoever, since the sensory functions which this term implies have been transcended by the di-

42. parakīyamanogato 'rtho mana ity ucyate . . . tasya paryayaṇaṃ parigamanaṃ manaḥparyayaḥ. *SS*: §164.

43. asahāyaṃ svarūpotthaṃ nirāvaraṇam akramam// ghātikarmakṣayotpannaṃ kevalaṃ sarvabhāvagam/ *Tattvārthasāra*: i, 30–31.

44. Jainas originally referred to the process of omniscient cognition, wherein all knowables were effortlessly reflected in the soul, as *pratyakṣa*, direct perception; this was contrasted with *parokṣa*, indirect perception, i.e., any awareness gained through sensory activity, inference, etc. Later, however, they came into contact with the works of certain Indian logicians who employed the term pratyakṣa for the concept of "ordinary, sense-mediated perception." Seeing the utility of such a concept, but wishing to retain the supramundane sense of their own notion of pratyakṣa, Jaina teachers coined for the former the new technical expression *sāṃvyavahārika-pratyakṣa*. See *SJP*: 27; Kailashchandra 1966: 131.

rect cognitive activity of the soul. There is some question, then, about how to understand the *avadhidarśana* mentioned in the texts. Probably we should take darśana in this case not as "perception," but as a sort of "indistinct awareness" which precedes the more complete awareness that is avadhijñāna. Darśana is again employed in a special sense with reference to the omniscient soul. A soul in this state is said to simultaneously cognize both itself and others; these "two directions" of the basically unitary cognitive function are labeled *kevaladarśana* and kevalajñāna, respectively.[45] Thus we have four types of darśanas, each obstructed by a corresponding variety of āvaraṇakarma.

The Antarāya-Karma.—The final category of obstructing karmas is called *antarāya* (hindrance); members of this group function directly to limit the energy (vīrya) of the soul. The partial energy which results is manifested through vibrations; these attract new karmic matter, as we have seen. If the vīrya quality is understood as that which energizes all others, moreover, then antarāya-karmas can in a sense be said to weaken every aspect of the soul. Popular convention also considers certain worldly frustrations to be effects of the antarāyas.[46] These are: (a) hindrance to giving something away (*dāna-antarāya*), as when one's estate does not go to the intended recipient because of an error in the will; (b) hindrance to obtaining something (*lābha-antarāya*), as when one is prevented from getting a desired job by intervention of a rival; (c) hindrance to enjoyment (*bhoga-antarāya*), as when illness prevents giving free reign to a particular sensual impulse; (d) hindrance to repeated enjoyment (*upabhoga-antarāya*), as when one loses a favorite book that he takes pleasure in reading again and again.

45. Compare: eka evapayogas te sākāretarabhedataḥ/ jñanadarśanarūpeṇa dvitayīṃ gāhate bhuvam// *Laghutattvasphoṭa*: k 259. For details on this controversy, see *SJP*: 70–80.

46. yad udayād dātukāmo 'pi na prayacchati, labdhukāmo 'pi na labhate, bhoktum icchann api na bhuṅkte, upabhoktum abhivāñchann api nopabhuṅkte, utsahitukāmo 'pi notsahate ta ete pañcāntarāyasya bhedāḥ. *SS*: §759.

AGHĀTIYĀ KARMAS AND THE PROCESS OF EMBODIMENT

Jainas often group the karmas discussed above, mohanīya, jñānāvaraṇa, darśanāvaraṇa, and antarāya, into a general category called ghātiyā, the destroyers. It is held that the defiled and obstructed states which these produce in the soul engender the influx of still another set of karmas, referred to as aghātiyā (those which do not destroy). The distinction between these two groups actually has little to do with destruction or the lack thereof; such terminology is employed mainly to contrast the primary role played by members of the former category with the subsidiary function of those belonging to the latter.

Aghātiyā karmas function to generate embodiment; even so, this function is wholly dependent upon the presence of ghātiyā factors in the soul, and indeed is hardly more than a reflection of the defiled or obstructed states to which these factors have given rise.[47] Four categories of "nondestroyers" are set forth, each of which must be considered in some detail.

1. Most comprehensive of the aghātiyā categories is that designated by the label nāma-karma. These karmas are "responsible" for numerous aspects of the new incarnation.[48] Most important of such aspects are the following: (a) destiny (gati), whether one is to be reborn as a god, human, hell being, or tiryañca; (b) birth (*jāti*), "species" within a gati, such as lion or tiger, high or low class of gods (it is significant that Jainas recognize no subdivisions of the human destiny, thereby denying any cosmological basis for the caste system); (c) body (śarīra), such characteristics as size, shape, sex, mobility, birth in an egg or

47. It is true, of course, that embodiment may continue after destruction of all ghātiyā karmas, as in the case of the Jina or arhat. The body in question, however, is to be understood as nothing more than an irrevocable *effect* of aghātiyās which "acted" just prior to the time of birth; no new body will arise when this effect has run its course.

48. Forty-two such factors are listed: gati-jāti-śarīra-aṅgopāṅga-nirmāṇa-bandhana-saṃghāta-saṃsthāna-saṃhanana . . . tīrthākaratvaṃ ca/ *TS*: viii, 11. The last, *tīrthakaratva*, refers to such special faculties as the divyadhvani, which a Tīrthaṅkara is said to obtain automatically upon reaching the state of a kevalin. See below, Ch. VIII n. 26.

womb. Nāma-karmas pertaining to śarīra are also said to generate two subtle bodies underlying the manifest physical one. These are the *taijasa-śarīra*, heat body, which maintains the vital temperature of the organism, and the kārmaṇa-śarīra,[49] the karmic body, constituting the sum total of karmic material present in the soul at a given time. The conception that such bodies exist is important to the Jaina theory of rebirth, since they constitute the "vehicle" whereby a soul moves (albeit under its own power) from one incarnation to the next.

2. The second aghātiyā karma is called gotra, literally, family or lineage.[50] There has been some disagreement on the precise meaning of this term; for Jainas, it appears to be concerned not simply with mundane aspects of the birth environment, but rather with whether that environment is more or less conducive to the pursuit of the spiritual life. (It is in this sense that śramaṇa traditions describe a person who takes the mendicant vows as having "entered upon a new gotra."[51])

3. Next we have vedanīya, those karmas pertaining to feelings, which produce the ever-changing experiences of happiness (sātā) and unhappiness (asātā) that characterize mental life.[52] For Jainas, no external object or event "makes" one happy or unhappy; it has no inherent pleasantness or unpleasantness, but serves simply as a prop which reinforces whatever feeling is being karmically produced at that moment.

49. sarvaśarīraprarohaṇabhūtaṃ kārmaṇaṃ śarīram . . . *SS*: §310.

50. gotraṃ dvividhaṃ uccair gotraṃ nīcair gotram iti. yasyodayāl lokapūjiteṣu kuleṣu janma tad uccairgotram. yadudayād garhiteṣu kuleṣu janma tan nīcairgotram. Ibid.: §757. Compare: "uccairgotrasya kva vyāpāraḥ? na tāvad rājyādilakṣaṇāyāṃ sampadi, tasyāḥ sadvedyataḥ samutpatteḥ . . . nekṣvākukulādyutpattau, kālpanikānāṃ teṣāṃ paramārthato 'sattvāt, viḍbrāhmaṇasādhuṣv api uccairgotrasyodayadarśanāt . . . dīkṣāyogyasādhvācārāṇām sādhvācāraiḥ kṛtasambandhānāṃ . . . santānaḥ uccair gotram . . . tadviparītaṃ nīcairgotram." Quoted in Phoolchandra 1963: 327 (from *Dhavalāṭīkā*: 136).

51. See Ruegg 1969.

52. yad udayād devādigatiṣu śārīramānasasukhaprāptis tat sadvedyam. yatphalaṃ duḥkham anekavidhaṃ tad asadvedyam. *SS*: §746. For a comparison between the quality of bliss (sukha) and the sātā vedanīya, see P. S. Jaini 1977b.

4. Finally, Jainas postulate the so-called āyu (longevity) karma, which determines the precise duration of the coming existence.[53] The characteristics attributed to this karma render it in a sense paramount among the aghātiyās, for it is said that with the fixing of the coming life-span, all the other factors of embodiment "fall into place," as it were, in an appropriate manner. Āyu does not *precisely determine* the effects of nāma, gotra, and vedanīya, but it establishes a framework or set of limitations within which these can operate. The fixing of one's next term of existence at seventy years, for example, means that he is most likely to be born as a human being, since gods live for a much longer period, animals generally for a much shorter one, and so forth. Perhaps even more importantly, āyu is said to differ from other karmas in that it is not at every moment being bound to the soul. We are told, rather, that a person's āyu-karma is fixed or bound *only once* in a given lifetime, that this event takes place sometime during the last third of that lifetime, and that the individual in question is never aware of its occurrence.[54] The implications of such a doctrine on the level of religious practice are evident; by earnestly adhering to the path of proper conduct, a Jaina can hope, during the latter portion of his life, to greatly influence the determination of his āyu-karma and thus the character of his entire next existence.

At the moment of death, the aghātiyā karmas have preprogramed, as it were, the particular conditions of the coming embodiment. This information is carried in the kārmāṇa-śarīra, which, together with the taijasa-śarīra, houses the soul as it leaves its physical body. A soul is said to be inherently possessed of great motive force; set free of the state of gross embodiment, it flies at incredible speed and in a straight line to the destination which its

53. narakeṣu tīvraśītoṣṇavedaneṣu yannimittaṃ dīrghajīvanaṃ tannārakam āyuḥ. evaṃ śeṣeṣv api. *SS*: §753.

54. For details on the operation of the āyu-karma, see *JSK*: I, 270–274; P. S. Jaini, forthcoming (b).

accompanying karma has deemed appropriate. This movement is called *vigraha-gati;*[55] it is said to require, as noted above, only a single moment in time, regardless of the distance to be traversed.[56]

Thus the Jainas, unlike certain other Indian schools, set forth no theories of long-term transmigration, "searching" for new parents, and so on.[57] Under the influence of the aghātiyā karmas, the soul moves to its new state of embodiment in a straightforward and virtually instantaneous manner. The particular form and realm thus attained to may be any of those discussed earlier; the "map" (below, p. 128) of the Jaina universe will perhaps help the reader to recall these states and their respective locations.

It is perhaps appropriate that this study of the karmas has ended with a discussion of those which bring about the state of embodiment; for it is this very state which the Jaina mendicant strives ultimately to escape. We have looked at the process which he believes has brought him to a condition of such suffering; let us now turn to the path by which he hopes to break free of that condition forever.

The Jaina universe (loka or loka-ākāśa) is conceived as a three-dimensional structure. Just beyond the boundaries of this structure are three atmospheric layers (*valaya*), those of humid air (*ghana-ambu*), dense air (*ghana-vāta*), and rarefied air (*tanu-vāta*).[58] Finally there is the aloka-ākāśa, the empty space in which no world, atmosphere, motion, or anything else is to be found. Because this realm

55. vigrahagatau karmayogaḥ/ ekasamayā 'vigrahā/ *TS*: ii, 25, 29.

56. In special cases, e.g., rebirth from the human realm to that occupied only by the ekendriyas ([E] in the chart of the loka-ākāśa—pl. 14) several "turns" may be necessary due to the three-dimensional structure of the universe; under such circumstances, the vigraha-gati may take two or even three moments for completion. See S. A. Jain 1958: 70.

57. For example, the Buddhist *antarā-bhava.* See Ch. VII n. 54.

58. . . . sarvā etā bhūmayo ghanodadhivalayapratiṣṭhāḥ . . . ghanavātavalayapratiṣṭhaṃ . . . tanuvātavalayapratiṣṭhaṃ . . . ākāśapratiṣṭham. ākāśam ātmapratiṣṭham, tasyaivādhārādheyatvāt. *SS*: §148.

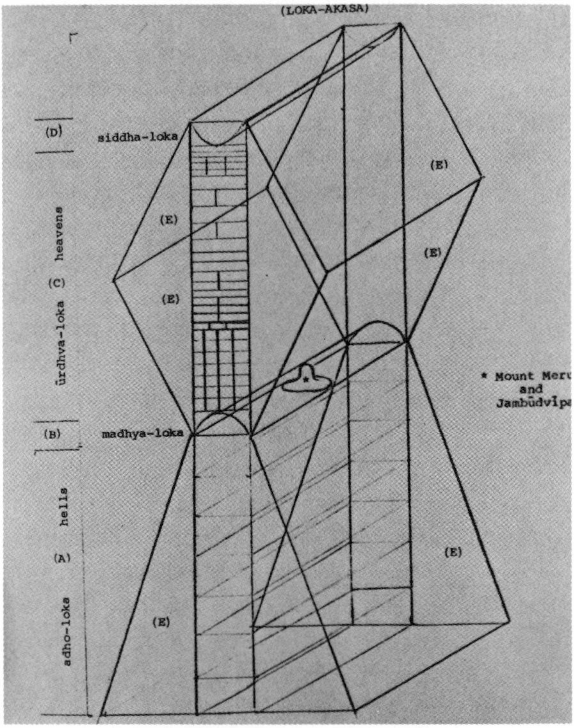

14. Loka-ākāśa, the Jaina universe: a diagrammatic representation, based on *JSK* 3:455. Sketch by Marilyn Leese.

encompasses the "occupied" universe, it is said to constitute the abode or support thereof.

As for the loka-ākāśa itself, Jainas have divided it into five parts, as follows.

A. The lower world (*adho-loka*) is the home of infernal beings (nāraki), as well as of certain demi-gods (demons, titans, and so on). This region consists of seven tiers (bhūmi), each darker than the one above: (1) *Ratna-prabhā* (having the color of jewels); (2) *Śarkarā-prabhā* (having the color of pebbles);

(3) *Vālukā-prabhā* (having the color of sand);
(4) *Paṅka-prabhā* (having the color of mud);
(5) *Dhūma-prabhā* (having the color of smoke);
(6) *Tamaḥ-prabhā* (having the color of darkness);
(7) *Mahātamaḥ-prabhā* (having the color of thick darkness).

B. The middle or terrestrial world (*madhya-loka*) consists of innumerable concentric island-continents (*dvīpa-samudra*), with Jambūdvīpa in the center. This is the abode of humans (manuṣya) and animals (tiryañca). Human beings are not found beyond the middle of the third continent from the center.[59]

C. In the higher or celestial world (*ūrdhva-loka*) are found the abodes of heavenly beings (Vaimānika-deva, gods endowed with celestial vehicles).[60] These gods fall into two categories: those born in kalpa heavens (*kalpopapanna*), and those born beyond them (*kalpātīta*). The former are ordinary beings who may or may not have entered the holy Jaina path of insight (samyak-darśana—see Chapter V); the latter are invariably endowed with this insight and are destined to attain mokṣa within two or three births after returning to human existence. There are sixteen possible abodes,

59. See Ch. I n. 66.

60. It should not be thought that all "gods" (deva) dwell in the celestial realm. In addition to the Vaimānika-devas there are three lower orders (*nikāyas*), as follows. (1) Bhavanavāsī (those who reside in mansions), comprising ten classes: Asurakumāra, Nāgakumāra, Vidyutkumāra, Suparṇakumāra, Agnikumāra, Vātakumāra, Stanitakumāra, Udadhikumāra, Dvīpakumāra, Dikkumāra. The mansions of the Asurakumāras are said to lie in the upper level of the first hell, while those of the other nine classes appear either between earth and hell or between earth and heaven. (2) Vyantaravāsī (the peripatatic), comprising eight classes: Kinnara, Kiṃpuruṣa, Mahoraga, Gandharva, Yakṣa, Rākṣasa, Bhūta, Piśāca. These demigods actually dwell on earth, but in continents far beyond those accessible to human beings. (3) Jyotiṣka (the stellar), i.e., devas residing in the sun, the moon, the constellations and the scattered (*prakīrṇaka*) stars. These luminary beings are characterized by their continuous movement around Mount Meru, which stands at the very center of the loka-ākāśa.

situated one above the other, for kalpopapanna beings: (1) Saudharma; (2) Īśāna; (3) Sānatkumāra; (4) Māhendra; (5) Brahma; (6) Brahmottara; (7) Lāntava; (8) Kāpiṣṭha; (9) Śukra; (10) Mahāśukra; (11) Śatāra; (12) Sahasrāra; (13) Ānata; (14) Prāṇata; (15) Āraṇa; (16) Acyuta. The kalpātīta beings on the other hand, have fourteen: (1–9) nine Graiveyakas; (10) Vijaya; (11) Vaijayanta; (12) Jayanta; (13) Aparājita; (14) Sarvārthasiddhi (those born in the latter, the highest heaven, are said to be in their penultimate existence; they will be reborn as human beings and will attain mokṣa in that life).

D. *Siddha-loka* is the permanent abode of the liberated souls.[61] This crescent-shaped region, lying beyond the celestial realms, constitutes the apex of world-space (loka-ākāśa).

E. Some abodes are restricted to habitation by *ekendriyas* (beings with only one sense faculty). These organisms may occupy all parts of the loka-ākāśa, but trasas (beings having two or more senses) are restricted to areas (A)–(D), the so-called *trasa-nāḍī*; hence there are only ekendriyas in (E).

61. The siddhas abide in the tanu-vāta, just at the edge of the aloka-ākāśa. This region, also known as *īśat-prāgbhārā-bhūmi* ("slightly bent," like an inverted umbrella), is said to be of the same circumference as the realm of human beings: "edāe bahumajjhe khettaṃ ṇāmeṇa Īsipabbhāraṃ/ . . . uttāṇadhavalachattovamāṇasaṃṭhāṇasuṃdaraṃ edaṃ/ . . . aṭṭhamabhūmajjhagado tapparihī maṇuvakhettaparihisamo//" Quoted in *JSK*: III, 334.

TYPES OF KARMA

Karmic Matter "Bound" with the Soul[62]

A. Four ghātiyā (destructive karmas):

1. mohanīya:
   - (a) darśana-mohanīya (insight-deluding), engendering mithyātva (false views)
   - (b) cāritra-mohanīya (conduct deluding), preventing samyak-cāritra (pure conduct)
     - (b-1) kaṣāya (passions)—anger (krodha), pride (māna), deceit (māyā), greed (lobha)—of four types:
       - —anantānubandhī (pursuers through endless times), always operating with darśana-mohanīya
       - —apratyākhyānāvaraṇa (obstructers of partial renunciation), those which prevent the proper conduct of a man taking the layman's vows
       - —pratyākhyānāvaraṇa (obstructers of complete renunciation), those which prevent the conduct of a mendicant
       - —saṃjvalana (smoldering), producing apathy (pramāda) in meditation and causing subtle attachment to life
     - (b-2) no-kaṣāya (subsidiary passions, or sentiments), of nine kinds: laughter (hāsya), pleasure (rati), displeasure (arati), sorrow (śoka), fear (bhaya), disgust (jugupsā), sexual cravings for male, female, and hermaphrodite (strīveda, puṃveda, napuṃsakaveda)
2. jñānāvaraṇīya (knowledge-obscuring), of five kinds:
   - —matijñānāvaraṇīya, obstructing the function of senses and mind

62. For a comprehensive treatment of the doctrines of karma and rebirth, see Guérinot 1926: 186–205; Glasenapp 1942; *SJP*: 220–260; Kalghatgi 1971.

—śrutajñānāvaraṇīya, obstructing the ability to use reasoning
—avadhijñānāvaraṇīya, obstructing the ability of clairvoyance
—manaḥparyayajñānāvaraṇīya, obstructing the ability to be aware of thought forms of others
—kevalajñānāvaraṇīya, obstructing the ability of omniscience

3. darśanāvaraṇīya (perception-obscuring), of four kinds:
—cakṣurdarśanāvaraṇīya, obstructing perception by means of eyes
—acakṣurdarśanāvaraṇīya, obstructing perception by means of other senses
—avadhidarśanāvaraṇīya, obstructing perception preceding avadhijñāna
—kevaladarśanāvaraṇīya, obstructing perception associated with kevalajñāna
4. antarāya (restricter), that is, of the quality of energy (vīrya); also, generator of yoga (vibrations) of body mind, and speech

B. Four aghātiyā (nondestructive, that is, secondary karmas):
1. vedanīya (feeling-producing), twofold:
—sātāvedanīya, producing pleasant feelings
—asātāvedanīya, producing unpleasant feelings
2. nāma (name), that by which a soul is identified as being a man, animal, heavenly being, or hell being; this karma determines these births and provides the appropriate body, senses, mind, sex, and color
3. āyu (longevity); this karma determines longevity in a given birth
4. gotra (family); this karma determines environmental circumstances conducive or detrimental to leading a spiritual life.

Of the four ghātiyā karmas, the darśana-mohanīya is first destroyed in the fourth *guṇasthāna* and the cāritra-mohanīya is next destroyed in the twelfth guṇasthāna. The remaining three ghātiyā karmas are then destroyed automatically in the thirteenth guṇasthāna. The aghātiyā karmas are all simultaneously destroyed at the time of death in the fourteenth guṇasthāna. (See Chapter VIII.)

V

Samyak-Darśana: The First Awakening

The Problem

Man's attempts to describe comprehensively the human condition have yielded religious and philosophical systems of incredible diversity. Within a given cultural matrix, however, it is usually possible to discover certain core beliefs, "givens" accepted by nearly all thinkers of that culture, which underlie the multitude of conflicting doctrinal developments. The history of Indian thought provides a clear example of this phenomenon; indeed, we can properly understand the doctrines of virtually all Indian schools (excepting that of the Cārvāka or "materialist" tradition) as efforts to encompass consistently, within a soteriological framework, the implications of two basic assumptions: that man has been forever bound in a state of suffering, and that this bondage is fundamentally due to some kind of spiritual ignorance.

This ignorance receives various names: *avidyā* for the Buddhists, *aviveka* for the Sāṃkhya, *mithyātva* for the Jainas.[1] In every case, however, it represents a misunderstanding or lack of awareness of one's "true nature" (however this may be defined by a given school), as well as of the factors which cause that nature to be hidden from view. Thus it follows that elimination of ignorance provides the only key whereby the shackles of bondage, hence of suffering, can be removed.

1. On the problem of avidyā in different Indian systems, see *SJP*: 81–219.

Certain difficulties come immediately to mind. If one has been in a state of bondage since beginningless time, why will he suddenly turn away from delusion and set out upon a new course? What are the conditions that could bring about this momentous shift, conditions which have never been present before? These are among the most difficult questions that any soteriological system must face, for each possible answer presents its own set of problems. If, for example, the factors required to turn a soul away from delusion and towards salvation have been eternally present in that soul in some potential form, then we must seek the crucial external causes which bring those potentialities into a manifest state. Can the soul, moreover, in any way influence the appearance of such "efficient causes," or does it remain totally at their mercy, languishing helplessly in bondage until some force beyond its control brings them into play?

The Theistic Solution

Most Indian traditions, with the notable exception of the monistic (Advaita) Vedānta, have dealt with these problems by recourse to a theistic doctrine; the intervention of some divine agency is here seen to provide the "helping hand" that lifts human souls from the mire of transmigration. This divine grace is not in any way subject to human influence; even the ability to engage in devotional practices (*bhakti*) is considered a gift from the Lord.[2] Grace can be neither compelled nor rejected; hence the soul's salvation is completely out of its own hands. While the workings of grace are shrouded in mystery, the result produced thereby is said to be perfectly clear: the soul's eyes are opened, truth is perceived, and one enters upon the path of salvation.

A theistic point of view deals well with the question of how a soul can suddenly turn away from an eternity of

2. Compare: nāyam ātmā pravacanena labhyo na medhayā na bahunā śrutena/ yam evaiṣa vṛuṇute tena labhyas tasyaiṣa ātmā vivṛṇute tanūṃ svām// *Kaṭhopaniṣat*: k 22.

ignorance; the totally external nature of grace seems in some way to "explain" such an apparently arbitrary event. For the non-Vedic śramaṇa traditions of the Ganges Valley, however, the theory of divine intervention generated even more logical problems than it solved. The agent of grace, it was said, would have to be a special sort of being (*puruṣa-viśeṣa*), unlike all other living things in that it has been forever free of bondage (*sadā-mukta*).[3] But how could an unbound being ever come into contact with the world of sāṃsāra—or influence it—since such actions are by definition limited to the embodied state?[4] If it is admitted, moreover, that even a single being can exist outside the framework of karmic entrapment, that same possibility must be admitted for any number of other beings as well. Thus one would be driven into the theory that all souls are *in reality* unbound, and that we must understand "bondage" as illusory.[5] But if this is so, if bondage is unreal, then why is there the experience of suffering?

The Fatalist Solution

A radical alternative to theism was propounded by the śramaṇa school known as Ājīvika, whose most influential teacher was the rather notorious Makkhali Gosāla. The Ājīvikas held that a soul could suddenly escape from bondage because the extent of its time therein was specifically predetermined; it simply passed through a linear series of births whose point of termination was absolutely fixed.

The precise doctrines of this sect have not come down to us; we have only the descriptions provided by rival

3. kleśakarmavipākāśayair aparāmṛṣṭaḥ puruṣaviśeṣa īśvaraḥ/ avidyādayaḥ kleśāḥ, kuśalākuśalāni karmāṇi, tatphalaṃ vipākaḥ, tadanuguṇā vāsanā āśayāḥ . . . yo hy anena bhogenāparāmṛṣṭaḥ sa puruṣaviśeṣa īśvaraḥ . . . sa tu sadiava muktaḥ sadaiveśvaraḥ. *Yoga-sūtra* [*Vyāsa-bhāṣya*]: i, 24.

4. For a Jaina critique of the Vaiśeṣika doctrine of a world-creator God, see *SM*: k 6; Thomas 1960: 29–36.

5. Compare: tasmān na badhyate 'ddhā na mucyate nāpi saṃsarati kaścit/ saṃsarati badhyate mucyate ca nānāśrayā prakṛtiḥ// *Sāṃkhyakārikā*: k 62.

schools, such as the following passage from the Buddhist Sāmaññaphala-sutta of the *Dīghanikāya*:

> There is no cause, either ultimate or remote, for the depravity of beings; they become depraved without reason and without cause. There is no cause, either proximate or remote, for the rectitude of beings; they become pure without reason and without cause. The attainment of any given condition, of any character, does not depend on one's own acts, or on the acts of another, or on human effort. There is no such thing as power, energy, human strength or human vigor. All animals, all creatures (with one, two or more senses), all beings (produced from eggs or in womb), all souls are without force and power and energy of their own. They are bent this way and that by their fate (*niyati*), by the necessary conditions of the classes to which they belong, by their individual natures, and it is according to their positions in one or another of the six classes that they experience ease or pain . . .[6]
>
> Having wandered in transmigration through eighty-four hundred thousand periods [that is, states of existence], both fools and wise alike shall at last make an end of suffering. Though the wise may hope: "By this virtue or this performance of duty, or this penance, or this righteousness will I bring to maturity the (inherited) karma that is not yet mature," and though the fool may hope, by the same means, to get gradually rid of karma that has matured, neither can do it. The measure of ease and pain cannot be altered in the course of transmigration; there can be neither increase nor decrease thereof, neither excess nor deficiency. Just as when a ball of string is cast forth it will spread out only as far as, and no farther than, it is able to unwind, just so shall both fools and

6. n'atthi . . . hetu, n'atthi paccayo sattānaṃ saṃkilesāya, ahetu-apaccayā sattā saṃkilissanti. n'atthi hetu, n'atthi paccayo sattānaṃ visuddhiyā, ahetu-apaccayā sattā visujjhanti. n'atthi atta-kāre, n'atthi para-kāre, n'atthi purisakāre, n'atthi balaṃ, n'atthi viriyaṃ, n'atthi purisathāmo, n'atthi purisaparakkamo. sabbe sattā, sabbe pāṇā, sabbe bhūtā, sabbe jīvā, avasā abalā aviriyā niyati-saṅgati-bhāva-pariṇatā chass'evābhijātisu sukha-dukkhaṃ paṭisaṃvedenti. *Dīghanikāya*: I, 53.

wise alike, having wandered in transmigration . . . make an end of suffering.[7]

The universal process thus described stands in sharp contrast to the beginningless cyclic one perceived by all other Indian schools. More important, however, the Ājīvikas contradicted the most dearly held belief of their śramaṇa counterparts: that all human actions generate appropriate karmic reward or retribution. By postulating real bondage and automatic liberation they overcame several of the philosophical difficulties mentioned above but aroused the vehement antagonism of Buddhists, Jainas, and others for whom conduct was directly and intimately related to eventual suffering or salvation.

The Jaina Solution

Perhaps more than any other Indian religious tradition, Jainism is imbued with an emotional commitment to self-reliance. Thus Jainas have found both theistic and fatalistic doctrines repugnant, for these doctrines not only negate the efficacy of the Tīrthaṅkaras' path, but they totally deny the soul's ability to influence its own future. Although Jaina philosophers have made much of the burden of karma, this burden is not to be construed as an inescapable, unalterable, externally imposed effect.

We have seen that the soul itself is the material cause (upādāna-kāraṇa) of defilement and obscuration, and that its energy quality (vīrya) actively differentiates the karmic matter into appropriate efficient causes (nimitta-kāraṇa).

7. cuddasa kho pan' imāni yoni-pamukha-satasahassāni . . . cullāsīti mahākappuno sata-sahassāni, yāni bāle ca paṇḍite ca sandhāvitvā saṃsaritvā dukkhass' antaṃ karissanti. tattha n'atthi: "imināhaṃ sīlena vā vatena vā tapena vā brahmacariyena vā aparipakkaṃ vā kammaṃ paripācessāmi, paripakkaṃ vā kammaṃ phussa-phussa vyantikarissāmī" ti. h'evaṃ n'atthi. doṇa-mite sikha-dukkhe pariyantakaṭe saṃsāre, n'atthi hāyana-vaḍḍhane, n'atthi ukkaṃsāvakaṃse. seyyathā pi nāma suttaguḷe khitte nibbeṭhiyamānam eva phaleti, evam eva bāle ca paṇḍite ca sandhāvitvā saṃsaritvā dukkhass' antaṃ karissanti. Ibid.: I, 54. For a discussion on the terms *niyati* and *saṅgati* in the Ājīvika system, see Basham 1951: 225–239.

But the capacities of the soul do not end here. Jainas in fact set forth a total of eight different functions into which the energy quality[8] can be directed: (1) *bandhana*, energy that brings about karmic influx; (2) *saṃkramaṇa*, energy that contributes to karmic differentiation or transformation; (3) *udvartanā*, energy that delays the time and increases the intensity of karmic fruition; (4) *apavartanā*, energy that hastens the time and decreases the intensity of karmic fruition; (6) *udīraṇā*, energy that makes possible the actual event of premature fruition; (6) *upaśamanā*, energy that temporarily prevents karmas from rising to fruition; (7) *nidhatti*, energy that renders karmas incapable of all processes except change in fruition time and intensity; (8) *nikācanā*, energy that renders karmas incapable of all processes whatsoever. All of this is a far cry from the Ājīvika position that the soul, with every action predetermined and involuntary, can neither prolong nor decrease the karmic influences upon it.[9]

The Idea of Capability

Jainas grant the soul great powers of manipulation with regard to the karmas. But these powers alone are not considered sufficient to effect the incredible shift from ignorance to insight that makes eventual salvation possible. Such an event, we are told, can occur only in the presence of a further element, an extraordinary quality of the soul called *bhavyatva*, capability to become (free). This quality is said to exist within the soul and yet remain totally untouched by the karmas also present there. It is a sort of inert catalyst, awaiting the time when it will be activated and thus trigger an irrevocable redirection of the soul's energy: away from delusion and bondage, towards insight and freedom.

8. See Ch. IV n. 17 for the manifold functions of vīrya.

9. For details on the various processes involved in these operations, see *SJP*: 254–255.

The mysterious nature of bhavyatva is compounded by the assertion that not all souls possess it. Those which do not are designated *abhavya*; they can never attain salvation.[10] Why the Jainas should harbor such a theory of absolute, permanent bondage for certain beings is not at all clear; it has been dogmatically accepted on the basis of scripture, and may simply reflect the commonplace observation that some individuals show no interest whatsoever in their salvation. Later Buddhist schools (the Yogācāra-Vijñānavādins, for example) held a similar view, comparing such unfortunate beings to "rotten seeds" forever incapable of spiritual growth.[11]

The abhavya doctrine appears to be tinged with fatalism. Jainas minimize this tendency by stressing that an abhavya *is* able to manipulate karmas and may attain births in the higher heavens; only mokṣa is denied to him. It is further said in the same vein that even a *bhavya* soul, which has the potential to reach salvation, will not *necessarily* realize that potential. The bhavyatva can be aroused, thus initiating an irreversible turning of the soul towards mokṣa, only when that soul encounters a particular set of outside conditions while being itself sufficiently "ready" to respond to them; such a confluence of external and internal factors may or may not ever take place.

Thus the Jainas exclude from their doctrine any notion of "automatic" salvation. They must still explain, however, the nature of those conditions the coming together of which does in fact activate the bhavyatva quality. Here the texts are quite vague, suggesting only that at some time when the soul is *relatively* less bound and more oriented towards its own well-being, thanks to fluctuations in the

10. For a discussion of the nature of these two categories of souls, see *Gaṇadharavāda*: k 1820–1836; P. S. Jaini 1977c.

11. Compare: varṣaty api hi parjanye naivābījaṃ prarohati/ samutpāde 'pi buddhānāṃ nābhavyo bhadram aśnute// *Abhisamayālaṅkāra*: viii, 10. Compare: agotrastho pudgalo gotre 'sati cittotpāde 'pi yatnasamāśraye saty abhavyaś cānuttarāyāḥ samyaksaṃbodheḥ paripūraye. *Bodhisattvabhūmi*: 1. See P. S. Jaini 1977c.

ongoing interaction of vīrya and karma, certain experiences (especially an encounter with a Jina or his image, hearing the Jaina teachings, or remembering past lives)[12] *may* bring the bhavyatva out of its dormant state and thus initiate the process that leads eventually to mokṣa.

We must bear in mind, however, that for a Jaina the knowledge, bliss, and energy of the soul can never be totally extinguished, whereas karmic influence is subject to complete elimination. Hence the soul possesses a sort of built-in advantage, an everpresent tendency to develop its qualities and temporarily reduce the influence of the karmas.[13] When Jainas say that a soul is free to work for its own salvation, it is this inherent tendency towards self-improvement that is referred to. Thus a soul will again and again progress to transitory states of relative purity and insight, only to be driven back by onrushing karmas, until a moment when the attainment of such a state coincides with the sort of external "activating" conditions mentioned above. We do not know precisely what happens at that moment; it would appear, however, that the bhavyatva is moved to exert its catalytic influence upon the energy quality, thereby redirecting it towards mokṣa. This mysterious event completely alters the future of the soul; its bonds of saṃsāra begin to unravel, and ultimate salvation is assured.

Samyak-Darśana (Having the Correct View)

Jainas have given us a detailed picture of the ladder one must climb as he progresses from the depths of delusion and entrapment to the pinnacle of omniscience and freedom. This ladder has fourteen rungs, called *guṇasthāna*,[14] stages of purification. The state of *mithyādṛṣṭi* (the incorrect view of reality) is designated as the first of these rungs;

12. Compare: "titthayara-kevali-samaṇa-bhavasumaraṇa-satthadevamahimādī/ iccevamāi bahugā bāhiraheu muṇeyavvā//" Quoted in *JSK*: IV, 364.

13. The scriptural term for this tendency is yathā-pravṛtta-karaṇa: "anādikālāt karmakṣapaṇapravṛtto 'dhyāśayaviśeṣo yathāpravṛttakaraṇam ity arthaḥ." Quoted in *SJP*: 269 (from *Bṛhadvṛtti, Viśeṣāvaśyaka-bhāṣya*: k 1202).

14. See the list at the end of Ch. VIII.

it is here that every embodied soul must dwell until it undergoes the momentous shift described above. This event is followed very quickly by the experience called samyak-darśana, having the correct view, in which the soul for the first time glimpses its true nature.[15] Such an experience is compared to that of a blind man who is suddenly able to see; although the event is momentary, it involves nothing less than an absolutely undistorted view of reality.

THE ATTAINMENTS

Kṣayopaśama-Labdhi.—Certain attainments (*labdhi*), involving increased purity, are said to provide a necessary transition from the moment of turning from bondage to the flash of samyak-darśana.[16] First and most important of these is *kṣayopaśama-labdhi,* in which large numbers of obscuring karmas (for example, vīryāntarāya, jñānāvaraṇa) are forced to dissociate themselves from the soul while others are placed under temporary suppression. The increased energy and knowledge thus made available allows the soul to progress quickly in the search for its own nature. It withdraws attention from the possessions, body, and psychological states with which it had formerly identified itself; gaining thereby a certain distance or detachment from passions, it attains the pure and peaceful state called *viśuddhi.*

Deśanā-labdhi.—This feeling of peace is followed in turn by a longing for instruction concerning the true nature of the soul. Any teachings which the individual may have heard prior to this time were as if meaningless, for he had not then developed sufficient spiritual awareness to comprehend or benefit from them. Now, however, he is ready

15. It is maintained that only souls endowed with five senses and mind are capable of having this experience: bhavyaḥ pañcendriyaḥ saṃjñī paryāptakaḥ sarvaviśuddhaḥ prathamasamyaktvam utpādayati. *SS*: §258.

16. Five labdhis are mentioned: "labdhiḥ kālakaraṇopaśamopadeśayogyatābhedāt pañcadhā." Quoted in *JSK*: III, 426 (from *Niyamasāra-vṛtti*). For details, see *SJP*: 269–270.

to receive properly the words of a Jina, an advanced mendicant, or for that matter anyone who has gained at least a brief insight into reality. Actually a very wide range of experiences, such as the loss of a beloved one, or the sight of extreme suffering, can serve as "instruction," exerting a profoundly awakening effect upon the receptive soul. Ordinarily, however, we imagine a being who longs for the true teachings coming into the presence of a Jina and there attaining his goal. This attainment is *deśanā-labdhi*; it can be experienced by any soul endowed with at least five senses and a mind. Thus Jainas depict animals receiving Mahāvīra's teachings in the holy assembly (samavasaraṇa) and even suggest that Mahāvīra himself was awakened while he existed as a lion.[17]

Prāyogya-labdhi.—Having been brought to an even higher level of insight and purity by the attainment of instruction, the soul generates an unprecedented surge of energy whereby further masses of accumulated karmas are drastically reduced, melting away like ice before a flame. Such karmic reduction is called *prāyogya-labdhi*; it sets the stage, as it were, for the actual attainment of samyak-darśana, true insight.

This attainment is itself divided into several steps. There first arises an extreme manifestation of the urge, present to some extent in even the lowest nigodas, to loosen the shackles of desire. This brings the soul face to face, for the first time, with the knot (*granthi*) of the gross (anantānubandhi) passions and deluding factors (darśana-mohanīya karmas), which have clung to it through beginningless eons of existence.[18] The "enemies" of the soul are thus identified; one becomes suddenly aware of the powerful forces that have controlled one's activities for so many

17. Compare: vidhāya hṛdi yogīndrayugmaṃ bhaktibharāhitaḥ/ muhuḥ pradakṣiṇīkṛtya prapraṇamya mṛgādhipaḥ// tattvaśraddhānam āsādya sadyaḥ kālādilabdhitaḥ/ praṇidhāya manaḥ śrāvakavratāni samādade// *UP*: lxxiv, 207–208.

18. On the conditions under which this granthi is cut, see *SJP*: 270.

lifetimes. The confrontation with one's karmic impediments is technically called *yathā-pravṛtta-karaṇa,* a term normally referring to the soul's ineradicable tendency towards spiritual growth. Its usage here suggests how significant a stage in the development of this tendency is represented by the first awareness of the granthi.

Once the oppressive forces have been recognized, there is a further increase in energy aimed at their removal. A higher state of purity is thus obtained, and the duration (sthiti) and intensity (anubhava) of all bound karmas are reduced; this process is known as *apūrva-karaṇa.* Finally, the darśana-mohanīya karmas are subjected to a brief but total suppression (*upaśama*), by means of *anivṛtti-karaṇa.* All obstructions to insight are thereby prevented from rising (*udaya*), and the soul instantaneously experiences the glorious vision of reality that is samyak-darśana.[19]

The significance of samyak-darśana in the life of the soul is second only to that of attaining Jinahood itself. So great is the purity generated by this flash of insight that enormous numbers of bound karmas are driven out of the soul altogether, while future karmic influx is severely limited in both quantity and intensity. Thus it is said that a soul which retains its samyak-darśana at the time of death will not fall into the hells or the lower tiryañca destiny. Even more important, it will remain in bondage *no longer* than the amount of time required to take in and use up half of the available karmas in the universe (*ardha-pudgala-parāvartana-kāla*).[20] While this may seem a tre-

19. Attainment of the "correct view" is thus not an accretion of something external to the soul; rather, it is the unfolding of "true vision" in the soul when the forces of mithyā-darśana are prevented from being active: tatra yasyodayāt sarvajñapraṇītamārgaparāṅmukhas tattvārthaśraddhānanirutsuko hitāhitavicārāsamartho mithyādṛṣṭir bhavati tan mithyātvam. tad eva samyaktvaṃ śubhapariṇāmaniruddhasvarasaṃ yadaudāsīnyenāvasthitam ātmanaḥ śraddhānaṃ na niruṇaddhi, tad vedayamānaḥ puruṣaḥ samyagdṛṣṭir ity abhidhīyate. *SS*: §749.

20. "darśanamohasyāpi sampanno jinendrabimbādi dravyaṃ, samavasaraṇādi kṣetraṃ, kālaś cārdhapudgalaparāvartanaviśeṣādir bhāvaś cādhāpravṛttakaraṇādir iti niścīyate. tadabhāve tadupaśamādipratipatteḥ." Quoted in *JSK*: IV, 363 (from *Tattvārtha-Ślokavārttika*).

mendous period, it is miniscule by comparison with that already gone through. Moreover, the fact of its finitude constitutes an absolute guarantee of eventual liberation.

We have seen that during the samyak-darśana itself, all darśana-mohanīya karmas are suppressed. Thus it would appear that the level of insight attained at this time is identical for all souls. But the specific *results* that this insight will generate for a given soul are not fixed; they depend upon the type, number, and intensity of karmas which remained in that soul at the moment of suppression, as well as upon the precise length of time that the insight was maintained.[21] The first experience of samyak-darśana brings the soul to the fourth guṇasthāna, the state called *samyak-dṛṣṭi.* This state is itself not permanent; nevertheless, even its temporary attainment heralds the soul's irreversible entry onto the path that leads to mokṣa.

Jainas believe that the *first* experience of undeluded insight must be the result of suppression (upaśama) rather than elimination (*kṣaya*) of the karmic forces. After a brief period the "suppressed" darśana-mohanīya karmas will surface (udaya) and the soul will fall back to the state of mithyātva, with its accompanying bondage of anantānubandhi passions. As this fall occurs, there may be a short pause at the third guṇasthāna, an ambiguous stage called *samyak-mithyātva,* in which insight is no longer clear but the passions have not yet reasserted themselves. Just below this stage is another called *sāsvādana,* the second guṇasthāna. Actually no longer than a single instant in duration, it marks the point at which the anantānubandhi passions rise up and overpower the soul once more. This having occurred, the return to mithyātva guṇasthāna is complete.

21. Jainas suggest that the duration of any such insight, particularly if attained through meditational experience, varies with the amount of energy available to the soul; it may last from a single instant up to a maximum of forty-eight minutes (*antar-muhūrta*). See *JSK*: I, 30.

It should be stressed that this "return" by no means erases the effects of the samyak-darśana. The deluding karmas still dominate the soul, but they have been so weakened that further true insights can be generated much more easily than the first one was. These will be of greater duration, and will involve not only the keeping down but also the actual removal of certain darśana-mohanīya karmas and the anantānubandhi passions; thus they are characterized as *kṣāyopaśamika* (due to elimination-and-suppression).[22] Some darśana-mohanīya karmas remain active (are neither suppressed nor eliminated) during such experiences, but they are unable to overcome the soul's awareness of reality; they function only to produce certain faults or imperfections (doṣa), which make the true perception somewhat unstable.

Imperfect as they may be, insights of the kṣāyopaśamika type nevertheless form the basis for the spiritual disciplines of the fifth, sixth, and seventh guṇasthānas. Such insights will eventually lead, moreover, to one so pure that it obliterates (kṣaya) the total mass of the darśana-mohanīya karmas as well as the total mass of the anantānubandhi passions, thus making it impossible for the soul to ever again fall below the fourth guṇasthāna. This is the *kṣāyika samyak-darśana;*[23] it will be followed within no more than four lifetimes (and perhaps in that very life, should a Jina then be present) by the attainment of mokṣa. Thus even the most brief initial experience of samyak-darśana is enormously significant in the spiritual progress of the soul; indeed, it is said that only one who has undergone such an experience should be called "Jaina," for only he has truly entered upon the path that the Jinas have followed.

22. This is also known by the name of *vedaka-samyaktva*: 'samyaktva'grahaṇena vedakasamyaktvaṃ gṛhyate. anantānubandhikaṣāyacatuṣṭayasya mithyātvasamyaṅmithyātvayoś codayakṣayāt sadupaśamāc ca samyaktvasya deśaghātispardhakodaye tattvārthaśraddhānaṃ kṣāyopaśamikaṃ samyaktvam. *SS*: §263.

23. "athocyeta—kṣīṇasaptako gatyantaraṃ saṅkrāman katitame bhave mokṣam upayāti? ucyate—tṛtīye caturthe vā bhave." Quoted in *SJP*: 276, n. 1.

The Signs of Awakening

Suppression or elimination of karmas by the soul are purely internal functions, which cannot be perceived either by the person in whom they occur or by others (save the omniscient Jina). It may well be asked, then, whether there exist any outward signs that identify one who has experienced samyak-darśana. We should perhaps expect certain fruits of this attainment, observable through changes of attitude, thought process, social behavior, and so forth. Jainas have been very concerned with this issue, setting forth in great detail the "new" characteristics of an individual transformed by true insight. Such externally evident characteristics are called *dravya-samyaktva*, as opposed to the internal *bhāva-samyaktva* states which they are supposed to reflect. The fact of their presence does not in itself prove that one has undergone samyak-darśana; it is said, however, that any being who *has* experienced true insight will thereafter be endowed with all of them.

THE ATTITUDES

The first major type of dravya-samyaktva pertains to a person's attitude towards himself. Previously he has identified his being with the external signs of life—the body, states, possessions; thus he has been in the state known as *bahirātman*,[24] seeing the self in externals dominated by the consciousness which is aware only of the results of karma (*karma-phala-cetanā*). He has also dwelt constantly on activities (*karma-cetanā*), thinking "I have done this," "I am doing this now," "I will do this." This orientation depends on the false notion that one can be the agent (*kartā*) of change in other beings; hence there is constant (and futile) effort to manipulate the thought and behavior

24. Three states of the soul are described: bahir antaḥ paraś ceti tridhātmā sarvadehiṣu/ upeyāt tatra paramaṃ madhyopāyād bahis tyajet// bahirātmā śarīrādau jātātmabhrāntir, āntaraḥ/ cittadoṣātmavibhrāntiḥ, paramātmā 'tinirmalaḥ// *Samādhiśataka*: k 4–5.

of these others, accompanied by a failure to work towards the only kind of change that *is* possible: self-transformation.

Consciousness attuned only to actions or the results of actions generates perpetual continuation of the sāṃsāric cycle. Upon the attainment of samyak-darśana, the soul turns away from such concerns; it undergoes a deliberate and mindful reorientation of attention, coming to focus upon nothing but its own nature (svabhāva). The body, the possessions, even the ever-changing psychological states (anger, the passions, pride, self-pity, and so forth), are no longer identified with the self. The functioning of consciousness is now characterized as *jñāna-cetanā*; here, the individual dwells only upon the innate and pure qualities of the soul, realizing that he is not *doing* anything in the world beyond simply *knowing* it.[25] Finally, his awareness of objects no longer generates a tendency to grasp or manipulate them; he remains in the state called *antarātman*, seeing the self within, thereby greatly increasing his mindfulness and pure awareness. This highly developed jñāna-cetanā will enable him to undertake the pure conduct (*samyak-cāritra*) necessary to overcome ingrained negative tendencies, tendencies which have persisted from beginningless time. Thus he will attain eventually to the state of constant self-awareness and purity called *paramātman*, the highest (the liberated) self.[26]

THE BEHAVIOR

The profound changes in consciousness generated by attainment of samyak-darśana are accompanied by equally significant transformations of an individual's behavior

25. jñānād anyatredam aham iti cetanaṃ ajñānacetanā. sā dvidhā—karmacetanā karmaphalacetanā ca. tatra jñānād anyatredam ahaṃ karomīti cetanaṃ karmacetanā; jñānād anyatredaṃ vedaye 'ham iti cetanaṃ karmaphalacetanā. sā tu samastā 'pi saṃsārabījaṃ, saṃsārabījasyāṣṭavidhakarmaṇo bījatvāt. tato mokṣārthinā puruṣeṇājñānacetanāpralayāya sakalakarmaphalasaṃnyāsabhāvanāṃ ca nāṭayitvā svabhāvabhūtā bhagavatī jñānacetanaivaikā nityam eva nāṭayitavyā. *Samayasāra* [*Ātmakhyāti-ṭīkā*]. k 387–389.

26. nirmalaḥ kevalaḥ śuddho viviktaḥ prabhur avyayaḥ/ parameṣṭhī parātmeti paramātmeśvaro jinaḥ// *Samādhiśataka*: k 6.

pattern. Having come to "dwell in himself" (*ātmānubhava*),[27] he experiences extraordinary bliss (sukha); this kind of bliss, although far removed from the pure sukha of a Jina, is not contaminated by dependence upon the body or psychological states and thus reaches a level hardly imaginable to an ordinary person. The experience of such a state, coupled with the fact that gross forms of anger, pride, deceitfulness, and greed (the anantānubandhi passions) have been rendered inoperative, gives rise to a new quality called *praśama*, ease.[28] One who is endowed with this quality shows great tranquillity; he is invariably relaxed and "at peace" with himself, never subject to the fits of anger, devouring greed, and other torments of others. Thus he becomes able to see behind the veil of illusion that has previously obscured the true nature of worldly objects and events; he no longer perceives things as "attractive" or "desirable," but rather he penetrates to the fact that every aspect of life is transitory and mortal.

This realization has a tremendous impact; it fills him with extreme agitation (*saṃvega*), an inner turmoil that is expressed in the form of strong disenchantment with worldly things. He may at this point still lack the strength required for renunciation; nevertheless, he will never again be drawn to the world as he once was. Thus he leads a seemingly normal life, acting out ordinary societal roles, but is subject to terrific internal conflicts which must sooner or later bring him to some act of renunciation, either partial (taking the layman's vows) or complete (taking the vows of a monk).

The understanding of bondage that comes with true insight is followed by a strong feeling of identification with

27. ātmānubhūtir iti śuddhanayātmikā yā jñānānubhūtir iyam eva kileti buddhvā/ ātmānam ātmani niveśya suniṣprakampam eko 'sti nityam avabodhaghanaḥ samantāt// *Samayasārakalaśa*: k 13.

28. sadyaḥ kṛtāparādheṣu yad vā jīveṣu jātucit/ tadvadhādivikārāya na buddhi-praśamo mataḥ// hetus tatrodayābhāvaḥ syād anantānubandhinām/ . . . samyaktvenāvinābhūtaḥ praśamaḥ paramo guṇaḥ// *Pañcādhyāyī*: II, k 427–430.

all beings, an awareness that they too suffer from such entrapment but remain ignorant of their plight. Further grasped is the essential fact that all diversity among beings, though real, exists simply on the level of modes (paryāya); fundamentally, every living being possesses a soul that may be capable of attaining omniscience. This awareness of the basic worth of all beings, and of one's kinship with them, generates a feeling of great compassion (*anukampā*) for others. Whereas the compassion felt by an ordinary man is tinged with pity or with attachment to its object, anukampā is free of such negative aspects; it develops purely from wisdom, from seeing the substance (dravya) that underlies visible modes, and it fills the individual with an unselfish desire to help other souls towards mokṣa. If this urge to bring all tormented beings out of saṃsāra is particularly strong and is cultivated, it may generate those auspicious karmas that later confer the status of Tīrthaṅkara upon certain omniscients. When present to a more moderate degree, anukampā brings an end to exploitative and destructive behavior, for even the lowest animal is now seen as intrinsically worthwhile and thus inviolable.

While every Indian doctrinal system stresses the importance of perception and reasoning in validating its position on a given issue, it is nevertheless true that certain fundamental problems—for example, the nature of death, the possibility of salvation, the operational laws of the universe—are simply not subject to the direct or rational approach. Speculations concerning these problems must, if they are to be accepted, become objects of faith. According to the Jainas, one who has not attained samyak-darśana is likely to fall prey to nihilism or skepticism, refusing to believe in the existence of anything which he has not seen with his own eyes, as it were. If he is prone to the desire for heavens or supernatural boons, on the other hand, he may develop a dogmatic, blind faith in theories propounded by one or another of the "one-sided" (ekāntavādin) religious systems. The experience of true insight is said to save a person from drifting into these wrong views.

While Jainas do not claim that samyak-darśana brings answers to *all* the great mysteries of existence, they do hold that it generates an important quality called *āstikya*, affirmation; this in turn becomes the basis for the "educated faith" (*śraddhā*) of the Jaina.[29] Specifically, one who possesses āstikya will manifest a firm belief in the reality of nine things (*tattva*): the sentient (jīva), the insentient (ajīva), karmic influx (āsrava), unwholesome karmas (*pāpa*), wholesome karmas (*puṇya*), bondage (bandha), stoppage of karmic influx (saṃvara), dissociation of bound karmas (nirjarā), and liberation (mokṣa). Accepting the existence of these nine is the final behavioral "mark" of having attained samyak-darśana; thus we may understand the famous Jaina sūtra which says: *tattvārtha-śraddhānaṃ samyak-darśanaṃ*:[30] "True insight *is* faith in the tattvas."

THE "LIMBS" OF SAMYAK-DARŚANA

In addition to the transformation of consciousness and behavior described above, Jainas set forth a third category of marks following attainment of the fourth guṇasthāna. This final group is called *aṣṭāṅga*, "eight limbs" that arise after samyak-darśana and are then to be cultivated to the point of perfection.[31] The first of these is *niḥśaṅkita*, freedom from doubt. Filled with the affirming tendency of āstikya, the individual becomes free of skepticism and perplexity regarding the teachings of the Jina. He accepts these teachings without reservation, partly because of his own glimpse into reality and partly because he realizes that a Jina, totally omniscient and free of all passions, can preach nothing but the absolute truth. Thus he not only affirms Jaina doctrine but is careful to avoid any "extremist" ideas whatsoever.

29. āstikyaṃ tattvasadbhāve svataḥ siddhe viniścitiḥ/ dharme hetau ca dharmasya phale cāstyādi dharmavit// svātmānubhūtimātraṃ syād āstikyaṃ paramo guṇaḥ/ . . . *Pañcādhyāyī*: k 452–453.

30. *TS*: i, 2. arthaśraddhānam iti . . . tad dvividham, sarāgavītarāgaviṣayabhedāt. praśamasaṃvegānukampāstikyādyabhivyaktilakṣaṇaṃ prathamam; ātmaviśuddhimātram itarat. *SS*: §12.

31. For narratives illustrating these eight virtues, see *Bṛhatkathākośa*: nos. 4-12, 52-55, 63-71, 111; *Upāsakādhyayana*: 49-103.

The second limb is called *niḥkāṃkṣita,* freedom from anticipation. This means that one entertains no desire with regard to the future; although he accepts the fact of transmigration, the existence of heavens, and so on, he remains free of any wish to be reborn as a highly placed person or as a god. The tranquil disposition resulting from attainment of samyak-darśana has rendered nearly all his activities wholesome (puṇya)—capable of bringing him to such desirable rebirths; even so, he must transcend the lure of these happy states lest he become interminably bound up in worldly life. Indeed, the niḥkāṃkṣita quality will eventually carry one beyond desire for any worldly thing.

The ordinary person distinguishes between good and bad, pleasant and unpleasant, and so forth, because he has not yet perceived the true relation between substance (dravya) and modes (paryāya); thus he retains a deep attachment for things which please the senses and an aversion for those which do not. In one who has gained true insight, however, there arises a quality called *nirvicikitsā,* freedom from disgust, which entails overcoming of such dualities. The individual possessed of nirvicikitsā will feel no revulsion at the sight of human sickness, insanity, or ugliness. Having gone beyond a merely physical view of beings, he will not find them "better" or "worse," "delightful" or "disgusting." Rather, he will view as unpleasant anything that furthers the binding tendencies of saṃsāra, while all that tends to carry one away from attachment to the world will be seen as pleasant.

The fourth aṅga is *amūḍhadṛṣti,* freedom from delusive notions, which refers to the abandonment of three particular types of false belief. The first of these is *devamūḍhatā,* delusion pertaining to gods; this indicates the common tendency towards indiscriminate worship of any god claimed to lead human beings to salvation. Faced with the widespread popularity of Vedic and Purāṇic gods, Jaina monks have undertaken to expose the inferior nature of these deities. Pointing out that such beings are still subject to the passions and hence themselves not free from bondage, they held that only a Jina, sitting in totally detached meditation, is fit to lead others to mokṣa.[32] Many people may see the logic of this claim and yet are still prevented from breaking their attachments to particular gods by fear or simply ingrained habit. For one who has reached samyak-darśana, however, all such commitment to the worship of "inferior" god-figures is abandoned; he knows that salvation can be attained only through the path of the Jina.

A second type of false belief overcome through true insight is that pertaining to teachers (guru) and their teachings; this is called *guru-mūḍhatā*. India has long abounded in ascetics and spiritual preceptors of all sorts, preaching numerous doctrines and engaging in an incredible diversity of practices. Although most such teachers profess to be free from attachment to the world, their activities are said by the Jainas to belie this claim. Tantric practitioners, for example, are widely known to engage in sexual activity and in consumption of meat and alcohol, while many so-called gurus emphasize the development of occult powers that are useful only within the context of saṃsāra.[33] But more important than such considerations is the fact that from the Jaina standpoint the practices of non-Jaina

32. Somadeva criticizes the alleged "divinity" of the popular brahmanical "Trinity" (Brahmā, Viṣṇu, and Śiva) in the following manner: Ajas Tilottamācittaḥ śrīrataḥ Śrīpatiḥ smṛtaḥ/ ardhanārīśvaraḥ Śambhus tathāpy eṣāṃ kilāptatā// Vasudevaḥ pitā yasya savitrī Devakī Hareḥ/ svayaṃ ca rājadharmasthaś citraṃ devas tathāpi saḥ// . . . bhaikṣanartananagnatvaṃ puratrayavilopanam/ brahmahatyākapālitvam etāḥ krīḍāḥ kileśvare// gehinā samavṛttasya yater apy adharasthiteḥ/ yadi devasya devatvaṃ na devo durlabho bhavet// *Upāsakādhyayana*: k 62–63, 68, 93. Jinasena stipulates that a person with samyak-darśana should remove images of these "false gods" from his residence: nirdiṣṭasthānalābhasya punar asya gaṇagrahaḥ/ syān mithyādevatāḥ svasmād viniḥsārayato gṛhāt// "iyantaṃ kālam ajñānāt pūjitāḥ sma kṛtādaram/ pūjyās tv idānīm asmābhir asmat samayadevatāḥ// tato 'pamṛṣitenālam anyatra svairam āsyatām"/ iti prakāśam evaitān nītvā 'nyatra kvacit tyajet// *AP*: xxxix, 45–47.

33. Compare: "ajñānijanacittacamatkārotpādakaṃ jyotiṣkamantravādādikaṃ dṛṣṭvā . . . kudevāgamaliṅgināṃ bhayāśāsnehalobhair dharmārthaṃ praṇāmavinayapūjāpuraskārādikaraṇaṃ samayamūḍhatvam iti." Quoted in *JSK*: III, 326 (from *Dravyasaṅgraha-ṭīkā*).

mendicants are simply not effective in bringing spiritual progress. The idea that purity can be gained through bathing in a particular river, by ingesting certain drugs, or by similar activities seems simpleminded to one who has reached the fourth guṇasthāna. Having seen the validity of the Jina's path, he will never again be tempted to take anyone but a Jaina mendicant as his teacher.

Finally, true insight brings abandonment of *loka-mūḍhatā,* false notions pertaining to everyday religious practices. This term encompasses a wide range of superstitious behavior indulged in by the Hindu populace, such as making food offerings (*śrāddha*) to the manes, worshipping trees or mountains, or touching the tail of a cow. All these practices are thought to better a person's worldly situation.[34] But to one who has truly understood the operation of karma, it is clear that such behavior can neither bring favors nor avert disasters and is thus useless.

Each of the four *aṅgas* discussed above—niḥśaṅkita, niḥkāṃkṣita, nirvicikitsā, and amūḍhadṛṣṭi—is formulated in a negative sense, pointing out certain views or tendencies absent from an individual who has penetrated to reality. The remaining four are stated in a positive manner, designating new attributes of a social nature. The first of this group is *upagūhana,* protecting; what is meant here is a tendency to cover up or hide from public view the shortcomings of a fellow Jaina when such shortcomings are observed; thus he may be saved from the sort of shame that could drive him from the order and place him beyond

34. Somadeva lists the following practices under this heading: sūryārgho grahaṇasnānaṃ saṃkrāntau draviṇavyayaḥ/ saṃdhyā sevāgnisatkāro gehadehārcano vidhiḥ// nadīnadasamudreṣu majjanaṃ dharmacetasā/ tarustūpāgrabhaktānāṃ vandanaṃ bhṛgusaṃśrayaḥ// gopṛṣṭhāntanamaskāras tanmūtrasya niṣevaṇam/ ratnavāhanabhūyakṣaśastraśailādisevanam// samayāntarapākhaṇḍavedalokasamāśrayam/ evamādivimūḍhānāṃ jñeyaṃ mūḍham anekadhā// varārthaṃ lokavārtārtham uparodhārtham eva vā/ upāsanam amīṣāṃ syāt samyagdarśanahānaye// *Upāsakādhyayana*: k 136–140.

the reach of private, "corrective" instruction. This does not mean that faults are to be overlooked, but simply that the order is to be maintained and self-improvement encouraged.

The second "social" aṅga is *sthitīkaraṇa*, promoting stability. This involves working to make others more secure in their religious convictions when they are severely shaken; such efforts may take the form of consolation or material aid at a time of calamity, logical persuasion in the face of intellectual doubts, or criticism of the tempting doctrines set forth by other traditions.

Next is *prabhāvanā*,[35] illumination, which leads to such positive actions as building temples, erecting Jina images, celebrating holy days (such as anniversaries of the Tīrthaṅkaras' births and nirvāṇas), arranging for the distribution of the sacred texts, undertaking pilgrimages to Jaina holy places, and donating money for hospitals, animal shelters, and the like. All such activities "illuminate" the Jaina religion to the world, as well as doing good for others. Those who show extreme development of this tendency are thought to be destined for an eventual career as a Tīrthaṅkara.

The final aṅga is *vātsalya*, disinterested affection,[36] which involves a selfless love for the high ideal of mokṣa and thus for the monks who strive to attain that ideal. Hence one might dedicate his life to the service (*vaiyāvṛttya*) of Jaina ascetics, recognizing their exalted nature and the fact that they have no families who contribute to their support. This service is especially important when monks become ill, for their vows prevent them from entering a hospital. Even more significant is the fact that a monk who receives such devoted assistance is able to undertake the ritual death by fasting (*sallekhanā*), the most holy ending

35. ajñānatimiravyāptim apākṛtya yathāyatham/ jinaśāsanamāhātmyaprakāśaḥ syāt prabhāvanā// *RŚr*: i, 18.

36. vātsalyaṃ nāma dāsatvaṃ siddhārhadbimbaveśmasu/ saṃghe caturvidhe śāstre svāmikārye subhṛtyavat// *Pañcādhyāyī*: II, k 806.

possible for a mendicant's career.[37] Thus the quality of vātsalya is held in high regard by the Jaina community.

This concludes the Jaina list of new characteristics evidenced by a person who has reached the fourth guṇasthāna, the state of true insight. Although these characteristics indicate a high degree of wisdom, purity, and compassion, they also entail activities which prolong involvement with the mundane world. Further spiritual development, therefore, requires voluntary restriction of such activities; only thus may one progress beyond the fourth guṇasthāna. Jainas have laid down two specific sets of restraints for this purpose, the lay and the mendicant disciplines. It is to these disciplines, and the states to which they lead, that we must now turn our attention.

37. See Ch. VII.

VI

Vrata and Pratimā: The Path of the Layman

The Fourteen Stages of Spiritual Purification

mithyādarśana-avirati-pramāda-kaṣāya-yogāḥ bandhahetavaḥ/[1]

Perverted views, nonrestraint, carelessness, passions, and activities: the causes of bondage.

With this brief aphorism the great ācārya Umāsvāti has summarized the entire Jaina explanation of the bondage process. We have already seen how "perverted views," false notions pertaining to the nature of the soul, are eliminated with the attainment of samyak-darśana, the fourth guṇasthāna. This is equivalent to saying that the soul has here effectively triumphed over the insight-deluding (darśana-mohanīya) karmas and must now overcome the conduct-deluding (cāritra-mohanīya) forces blocking its way to mokṣa. In fact this battle has already been joined at the fourth guṇasthāna, for true insight renders the gross passions (the anantānubandhis) inoperative and generates sufficient energy in the soul to guarantee rapid progress on the path of conduct.

More specifically, this increased energy allows the individual to overcome for the first time the two subtle forms of passions called apratyākhyānāvaraṇa and pratyākhyānāvaraṇa, passions which have theretofore prevented him

1. *TS*: viii, 1.

from taking the vows of a layman or of a mendicant, respectively. This inability to refrain voluntarily from "evil" actions (those which harm oneself or others) is thus the nonrestraint (avirati) of Umāsvāti's aphorism. A person's adherence to the partial restraint (deśa-virati) of the layman (*śrāvaka*) or the total restraint (*sarva-virati*) of the monk (muni) therefore reflects his soul's subjugation of the apratyākhyānāvaraṇa or the pratyākhyānāvaraṇa passions. Thus it is said that deśa-virati is the fifth guṇasthāna and sarva-virati the sixth, and that one who has entered the mendicant order must be considered to have overcome all but the most subtle forms of the passions, those called saṃjvalana.

As noted earlier, the saṃjvalana (smoldering) passions find expression in a basic attachment to the state of embodiment. They also generate a certain apathy or lack of vigor with regard to strict observance of the vows. This is the carelessness (pramāda) to which Umāsvāti refers. By repeated meditative suppression of carelessness, the spiritual aspirant can render this tendency less and less effective, until finally it is overcome altogether; at this point, he is said to have reached the seventh guṇasthāna, restraint free of carelessness (*apramatta-virata*).

Thus his purity and energy are increased, enabling him to pursue meditation with constant vigor. He now enters into several highly refined trance states through which the saṃjvalana passions themselves, along with the sexual sentiments and other subsidiary passions (no-kaṣāya) that they produce, are progressively weakened. Three levels of trance or meditational attainment are set forth: apūrva-karaṇa, anivṛtti-karaṇa,[2] and *sūkṣma-sāmparāya*; these constitute the eighth, ninth, and tenth guṇasthānas, respectively.

If one passes through these states via mere *suppression* (upaśama) of the saṃjvalana passions and the sentiments,

2. For a discussion of these two *karaṇas*, see *SJP*: 277–278.

he will be able to attain only the temporary level called *upaśānta-moha*, the eleventh guṇasthāna, in which all cāritra-mohanīya karmas are briefly rendered inoperative. A fall from this level is inevitable. One may progress beyond it only if the subtle passions and their effects are actually *eliminated* (kṣaya) during the trances. In that case, the eleventh guṇasthāna will be passed over altogether, and the aspirant will reach *kṣīṇa-moha*, permanent dissociation from all cāritra-mohanīya karmas and the passions (kaṣāya) which they engender. This is the twelfth guṇasthāna; its attainment leads instantly and automatically to the elimination of the three remaining ghātiyā karmas, the jñānāvaraṇa, the darśanāvaraṇa, and the antarāya. With this elimination one is fixed in the thirteenth guṇasthāna, the state of embodied Jinahood or "omniscience with activities" (*sayoga-kevalin*).

Of the five "causes of bondage" set forth by Umāsvāti, only yoga, the activities that necessarily accompany embodiment, now remain. These no longer have any defiling effect upon the soul, for the body of a kevalin does not contribute to future bondage; it is simply the "fruit" of prior aghātiyā karmas, destined to pass away forever when those karmas are exhausted. In the last few moments of embodiment, even yoga is brought to cessation; this state of utter immobility is called omniscience without activities (*ayoga-kevalin*), the fourteenth guṇasthāna. At the instant of death (nirvāṇa) itself, the soul is freed forever from the last vestige of sāmsāric influence; thus it reaches in the very next moment the state of infinite bliss and omniscience called siddha.[3]

This is a brief overview of the steps leading from samyak-darśana to complete liberation. Let us now look more closely at the actual practices and experiences that certain of these steps involve.

3. For a schematic list of the guṇasthānas, see Ch. VIII.

Path of the Layman

THE LAY IDEAL

Books of the Jaina discipline preach the conduct in which a true follower of the Jina should engage. This preaching is of course aimed at those who have already attained the fourth guṇasthāna, for only such individuals can really benefit from religious practice; practice without insight is fruitless. We might expect to find the aspirant directed first to partial renunciation (deśa-virati), assuming that a certain period of lay discipline provides a necessary transition from an unrestrained way of life to one of complete asceticism. But in fact, the books of discipline call for a person of insight to immediately take up the great vows (mahāvrata) of the mendicant's discipline (sarva-virati); life is short, and one should progress as quickly as one is able.

Strictly speaking, then, the vows of the layman are really just a modified, relatively weak version of the *real* Jaina vows; they may curb evil behavior to some extent, but they cannot bring a person to liberation. In practice, however, this point has not been stressed. Jaina teachers have been realistic enough to see that most new converts will be emotionally ready only for the layman's path.[4] They have correctly perceived, moreover, that no religious institution can survive without the strong involvement of the laity; hence they have not only downplayed the "inferior" nature of the lay path, but have shown their high regard for this path by producing numerous tracts (called śrāvakācāra) on the particulars of lay conduct.[5] Despite this trend, the ascetic orientation of Jainism has certainly not been lost; not only does the way of the mendicant retain premier status among Jainas, but even the lay discipline is far more strict than that of any other Indian religious community.

4. Compare: tyājyān ajasrān viṣayān, paśyato 'pi jinājñayā/ mohāt tyaktum aśaktasya gṛhidharmo 'numanyate// *SD*: ii, 1.

5. Williams (*JY*: intro. xxvii–xxx) lists over forty śrāvakācāras, beginning with the *Cāritra-prābhṛta* of Kundakunda (second century) and ending with the *Dharmasaṅgraha-ṭīkā* of Yaśovijaya (seventeenth century).

In constructing a framework for the conduct of the laity, the authors of the śrāvakācāra texts were very systematic and specific. They defined numerous kinds of evil conduct, then instituted separate vows of renunciation for each. Set forth, in addition, were all the ways in which one might accidentally or intentionally break each vow,[6] and how he might expiate such infractions. The books of discipline also employ narrative tales that show the great virtue of keeping the vows, even if only temporarily.[7] Finally, they set up a "ladder," analogous to that of the guṇasthānas,[8] representing the process whereby a layman can make ready for the mendicant vows. The eleven "steps" of this ladder are called *śrāvaka-pratimā;*[9] they lead one through progressively greater restrictions upon his worldly activities, until at last the complete renunciation of the ascetic is within his grasp.

Darśana-Pratimā.—The "marks" of one who has attained the insight prerequisite to entry upon the path of the Jina have been discussed earlier. Even these marks, however, are not so apparent as to identify a person's "spiritual status," as it were. The degree of his advancement on the path, indeed the very fact of his commitment to the Jaina ideal, is indicated by the religious practices which he undertakes—particularly those involving various self-imposed restraints. Certain practices of this type are so basic that they functionally define membership in the Jaina community; failure to adhere to these "fundamentals," subsumed under the designation *darśana-pratimā,* means simply that one is not a practicing Jaina. (Children of Jaina households, prior to their initiation into the darśana-pratimā, are referred to as nominal (*nāma*) Jainas.)

6. See *JY*: App.

7. For example, *Bṛhatkathākośa*: nos. 46, 72–79 (Upadhye intro. 83ff.).

8. Compare: dṛṣṭyā mūlaguṇāṣṭakaṃ vratabharaṃ sāmāyikaṃ proṣadham/ saccittānnadinavyavāyavanitārambhopadhibhyo matāt// uddiṣṭād api bhojanāc ca viratim prāptaḥ kramāt prāgguṇa-/ -prauḍhyā darśanikādayaḥ saha bhavanty ekādaśopāsakāḥ// *SD*: i, 17.

9. See the list at the end of this chapter.

The Pañca-Namaskāra-Mantra: Darśana-pratimā consists of two modes of religious observance, one devotional and the other renunciatory. The devotional aspect involves acceptance of the Jina as the ultimate divinity (deva), of the Jina-āgamas as the only valid scriptures (*śāstra*), and of the Jaina mendicants as the only proper teachers (guru).[10] This taking refuge in the Jina and his path is formalized by initiation into the holy litany (mantra) called pañca-namaskāra, reverent salutation to the five (holy beings). The initiate chants:

ṇamo arahaṃtāṇaṃ[11]
(I bow before the worthy ones [arhat]—the Jinas);
ṇamo siddhāṇaṃ
(I bow before the Perfected beings [siddha]—those who have attained mokṣa);
ṇamo āyariyāṇaṃ
(I bow before the [mendicant] leaders [ācārya] of the Jaina order);
ṇamo uvajjhāyāṇaṃ
(I bow before the [mendicant] preceptors [*upādhyāya*]);

10. These three are defined as follows: kṣutpipāsājarātaṅkajanmāntakabhayasmayāḥ/ na rāgadveṣamohāś ca yasyāptaḥ sa prakīrtyate// āptopajñam anullaṅghyam adṛṣṭeṣṭavirodhakam/ tattvopadeśakṛt śārvaṃ śāstraṃ kāpathaghaṭṭanam// viṣayāśāvaśātīto nirārambho 'parigrahaḥ/ jñānadhyānataporaktas tapasvī sa praśasyate// *RŚr*: i, 6, 9–10.

11. A variant of arahanta is *arihanta;* both are Prakrit forms of the Sanskrit arhat or *arhaṃ*. In the medieval period the term arhaṃ formed the nucleus for a large number of tantric works. Jaina ācāryas sought to explore the mystical attributes of the seed syllables *a* and *h* (the first and last sounds in the Sanskrit syllabary) found in this word. Compare: "akārādi-hakārāntā prasiddhā siddhamātṛkā/ yugādau yā svayaṃ proktā Ṛṣabheṇa mahātmanā// . . . akāraḥ prathamaṃ tattvaṃ sarvabhūtābhayapradam/ kaṇṭhadeśaṃ samāśritya vartate sarvadehinām// . . . hakāro hi mahāprāṇaḥ lokaśāstreṣu pūjitaḥ/ vidhinā mantriṇā dhyātaḥ sarvakāryaprasādhakaḥ// . . . trīṇy akṣarāṇi binduś ca yasya devasya nāma vai/ sa sarvajñaḥ samākhyātaḥ arhaṃ tad iti paṇḍitaḥ//" *Dharmopadeśamālā* (quoted in *Namaskāra-svādhyāya* [Sanskrit]: 21–24). In his famous lexicon of the twelfth century. Hemacandra praises arhaṃ in exalted terms: "arhaṃ" iti. etad akṣaraṃ parameśvarasya parameṣṭhino vācakaṃ, siddhacakrasyādibījaṃ, sakalāgamopaniṣadbhūtaṃ . . . āśāstrādhyanādhyāpanāvadhi praṇidheyaṃ . . . ayam eva hi tāttviko namaskāra iti. *Śabdānuśāsana* [*Svopajña-ṭīkā*]: I, i, 1.

ṇamo loe savva-sāhūṇaṃ

(I bow before all the [Jaina] mendicants [*sādhu*] in the world)

eso paṃca ṇamokkāro savva-pāvappaṇāsaṇo/
maṃgalāṇaṃ ca savvesiṃ paḍhamaṃ havai maṃgalaṃ//[12]

(This fivefold salutation, which destroys all sin, is preeminent as the most auspicious of all auspicious things).

The fact that first salutations go not to the perfected siddhas, but rather to the Jinas (arhats) who teach in the world, indicates the extent to which Jainas have glorified the virtue of compassion.[13] It is also significant that no particular being, not even Mahāvīra, receives mention as the object of veneration. Jaina devotionalism is oriented not towards a chosen deity (*iṣṭa-devatā*) but toward an ideal, the attainment of kevalajñāna; thus reverence is given to all beings who have been or are actively engaged in pursuit of that ideal. Even so, the Hindu concept of iṣṭa has exerted a certain amount of influence, evident in such Jaina practices as referring to their five "holies" as *parameṣṭhin*, the supreme divinities.[14]

Jainas sometimes venerate the holy syllable oṃ as well, though their analysis of this utterance differs from that of the brahmanical tradition. Whereas Vedic scripture suggests that the *a*, *u*, and *m* of which oṃ is composed repre-

12. See Glasenapp 1925: 367; and *JY*: 184–185. The origin of the pañcanamaskāra litany is not known. In the inscription of King Khāravela (circa 150 B.C.—see p. 278), only the arahaṃta and the siddha are invoked. A fivefold salutation is attested in the *Bhagavatī-sūtra* (i, 1), but the fifth of these is to the Brāhmī script (ṇamo bambhīe livīe) instead of to the sādhus as in the standard formula. There is a Digambara tradition that the namaskāra-mantra was composed by Puṣpadanta (circa A.D. 157), since it appears as a *maṅgala* (auspicious) verse in the beginning of his *Ṣaṭkhaṇḍāgama*. For details, see *JSK*: III, 258–259.

13. vigatāśeṣalepeṣu satsv arhatāṃ salepānām ādau kimiti namskāraḥ kriyata iti cen na doṣaḥ . . . asaty arhaty āptāgamapadārthāvagamo na bhaved asmadādīnām . . . *Dhavalāṭīkā*: 54–55. Compare *SM*: k 31.

14. "aruhā siddhāyariyā ujjhāyā sāhu paṃca parameṭṭhī/ te vi hu ciṭṭhahi āde tamhā ādā hu me saraṇaṃ// Quoted in *JSK*: III, 23 (from *Mokṣapāhuḍa*: k 104).

sent earth, the atmosphere, and heaven respectively,[15] Jaina texts (probably postcanonical) derive the same sound by connecting the initial syllables of the epithets for each being addressed in the *namaskāra-mantra*: hence *a* (arhat), *a* (*aśarīra* [the siddha]), *ā* (ācārya), *u* (upādhyāya), *m* (muni [sādhu]).[16] Repetition of oṃ thus becomes a legitimate practice for the Jaina, serving to remind him of the five holy beings of his creed.

The Four Refuges (*Catuḥ-Śaraṇa*): Equally popular is catuḥ-śaraṇa, a chant in which the initiate is reminded of the supremacy of the dharma preached by the kevalin. This chant forms an important part of daily prayers and runs as follows:

cattāri saraṇaṃ pavvajjāmi
(I take refuge in the four):
arahaṃte saraṇaṃ pavvajjāmi
(I take refuge in the arhats)
siddhe saraṇaṃ pavvajjāmi
(I take refuge in the siddhas)
sāhū saraṇaṃ pavvajjāmi
(I take refuge in the sādhus)
kevali-paṇṇattaṃ dhammaṃ saraṇaṃ pavvajjāmi
(I take refuge in the dharma [Holy Law] preached by the omniscient Jina).

It should be pointed out that the third refuge, sāhu (sādhu), is a cover term for ācāryas, preceptors, and mendicants,[17] all of whom are saluted in the pañca-namskāra-mantra; thus the catuḥ-śaraṇa formula is hardly more than a variation on that mantra.

The Hymns of Praise: In addition to these rather brief

15. See *Māṇḍūkyopaniṣat*: k 8–10. The given combination of letters yields oṃ in accord with the rules of euphony that govern the Sanskrit language.

16. " 'oṃ' ekākṣaraṃ pañcaparameṣṭhinām ādipadam. tat katham iti cet: "arihaṃtā asarīrā āyariyā taha uvajjhayā muṇiṇā/ paḍhamakkharanippaṇṇo oṃkāro paṃcaparameṭṭhī//9//" iti gāthākathitaprathamākṣarāṇāṃ . . . svarasandhividhānena oṃ śabdo niṣpadyate." Quoted in *JSK*: I, 500 (from *Dravyasaṅgraha-ṭīkā*).

17. "sādhuśabdenācāryopādhyāyasarvasādhavo labhyante." Quoted in *JSK*: III, 259 (from *Bhāvapāhuḍa-ṭīkā*).

ritual utterances, the initiate ordinarily performs several *stavas*, or hymns of praise. These are directed either towards all Jinas or towards the twenty-four Tīrthaṅkaras in particular. Of the several forms a stava may take, three deserve special mention, since they probably date back to canonical times and have been preserved in both the Śvetāmbara and Digambara traditions. The first, called *Śakra-stava* (ostensibly spoken by Śakra, king of the gods), describes the Jinas in the grandest of terms:

> Praise to the arhats, the blessed ones, who are the cause of the beginnings [of the Holy Law], who provide the path across, who have themselves attained enlightenment, the best among men . . . the lights of the world, those who give the right direction, who give refuge, who give enlightenment (*bodhi*), who give the sacred doctrine . . . the monarchs of the sacred doctrine, those who are endowed with unobstructed knowledge and insight . . . the Jinas, who have crossed over, who help others to cross, the enlightened and the enlighteners, the liberated and the liberators, the omniscient, the all-seeing, those who have reached the place that is called *siddha-gati* [destiny of the siddha], that from which there is no return, and which is bliss immutable, inviolable, endless, imperishable, and undisturbed; praise to the Jinas who have overcome fear. In the threefold way I worship all the siddhas, those who have been, and those who in future time will be.[18]

The second, *Nāma-Jina-stava*, praises the twenty-four Jinas by invoking their names individually.[19] Daily recitation of the names has contributed to their memorization

18. "namo 'tthu arihantāṇaṃ bhagavantāṇaṃ āigarāṇaṃ titthayarāṇaṃ sayaṃsambuddhāṇaṃ, purisuttamāṇaṃ purisasīhāṇaṃ purisavarapuṇḍarīyāṇaṃ purisavaragandhahatthīṇam, loguttamāṇaṃ loganāhāṇaṃ logahiyāṇaṃ logapaīvāṇaṃ logapajjoyagarāṇaṃ, abhayadayāṇaṃ saraṇadayāṇaṃ bohidayāṇaṃ, dhammadayāṇaṃ dhammadesayāṇaṃ dhammanāyagāṇaṃ dhammasārahīṇaṃ dhammavaracāurantacakkavaṭṭīṇaṃ, appaḍihayavaranāṇadaṃsaṇadharāṇaṃ viyaṭṭachaumāṇaṃ, jiṇāṇaṃ jāvayāṇaṃ tiṇṇāṇaṃ tārayāṇaṃ buddhāṇaṃ bohayāṇaṃ muttāṇaṃ moyagāṇaṃ, savvannūṇaṃ savvadarisīṇaṃ sivam ayalam aruyam aṇantam akkhayam avvābāham apunarāvattisiddhigaināmadheyaṃ ṭhāṇaṃ sampattāṇaṃ namo jiṇāṇaṃ jiyabhayāṇaṃ. je ya āīyā siddhā je ya bhavissanti 'nāgate kāle/ sampai ya vaṭṭamāṇā savve tiviheṇa vandāmi//" Quoted in *JY*: 193. Compare *KS*: §16.

19. Following is a list of the twenty-four Tīrthaṅkaras of the present half-

by the community and thus has helped to preserve the "historical" character of even the most ancient teacher-Jinas. They are glorified as those who have "illuminated the world" (*logassa-ujjoyagare*) and who have "laid out the sacred ford of doctrine as a way across" (*dhamma-titthayare*). The hymn closes with the words:

> May the siddhas, purer than the moons, more radiant than the suns, and profound as the oceans, give me protection.[20]

The third, *Śruta-stava*, praises the sacred canon (śruta), as well as the Tīrthaṅkaras who are even now living in the continents of Videha. A typical invocation runs as follows:

> O siddhas . . . may the eternal sacred doctrine bring prosperity . . . may it be victorious and may it enhance the primacy of the dharma.[21]

The "Basic Restraints" (Mūlaguṇa): The renunciatory aspect of darśana-pratimā is eightfold, comprising the so-called basic restraints (*mūlaguṇa*), which are observed

---

cycle. The symbols by which their iconographic representations can be identified are given in parentheses; these symbols usually appear on the pedestal of a given sculpture. 1) Ṛṣabha (bull), 2) Ajita (elephant), 3) Sambhava (horse), 4) Abhinandana (ape), 5) Sumati (partridge), 6) Padmaprabha (lotus), 7) Supārśva (*nandyāvarta* figure), 8) Candraprabha (moon), 9) Suvidhi/Puṣpadanta (crocodile), 10) Śītala (svastika), 11) Śreyāṃsa (rhinoceros), 12) Vāsupūjya (male buffalo), 13) Vimala (boar), 14) Ananta (hawk/bear), 15) Dharma (thunderbolt), 16) Śānti (deer), 17) Kunthu (goat), 18) Ara (fish), 19) Malli (water jar), 20) Munisuvrata (tortoise), 21) Nami (blue lotus), 22) Nemi (conch shell), 23) Pārśva (snake), 24) Vardhamāna/Mahāvīra (lion). For detailed information on these Tīrthaṅkaras (names of their parents, geographical data, physical descriptions, identity of attendant demi-gods (yakṣas), nature of their congregations) see *JSK*: II, 376–391. See also Jas Burgess 1903 and Stevenson 1915: 312–314. For a similar discussion on the Tīrthaṅkaras of the past and future half-cycles, as well as of the twenty Tīrthaṅkaras who are now alive in the Videha "continent" (Ch. I n. 70), see *JSK*: II, 376ff.

20. logass' ujjoyagare dhamma-titthayare jiṇe/ arihaṃte kittaissaṃ cauvīsaṃ pi kevalī// . . . kittiya-vaṃdiya-mahiyā je e logassa uttamā siddhā/ ārogga-bohi-lābhaṃ samāhivaram uttamaṃ dentu// candesu nimmalayarā āiccesu ahiyaṃ pabhāsayarā/ sāgaravaragambhīrā siddhā siddhiṃ mama disantu// *Suttāgame*, II, Āvassaya-sutta: §2. See *JY*: 195. For a Digambara version of this stava, see *NNP*: 8.

21. *JY*: 196.

almost automatically by members of the Jaina community.[22] All of these restraints are dietary in nature; the Jaina must never partake of meat (*māṃsa*), alcohol (*madya*), honey (*madhu*), or any of five kinds of figs (*udumbara*).[23] The Jaina will of course be asked why these particular substances came to be considered unfit for human consumption.

To answer this question, as well as to properly understand the restraints applied at later stages of the Jaina path of purification, we must be aware of one basic fact: the Jaina preoccupation with ahiṃsā, the avoidance of giving injury. Great importance has been attached to this concept by every Indian school, but none has carried it to the extreme of the Jainas. For them it is not simply the first among virtues but *the* virtue; all other restraints are simply elaborations of this central one.

Hiṃsā has ordinarily been understood in India as harm done to others; for Jainas, however, it refers primarily to injuring *oneself*—to behavior which inhibits the soul's ability to attain mokṣa.[24] Thus the killing of animals, for example, is reprehensible not only for the suffering produced in the victims, but even more so because it involves intense passions on the part of the killer, passions which bind him more firmly in the grip of saṃsāra. The Jaina concept of hiṃsā, then, is very broad in terms of the actions to which it refers; and the need for abandonment of such actions becomes of paramount importance to the spiritual aspirant.

22. tatrādau śraddadhaj jainīm ājñāṃ hiṃsām apāsitum/ madya-māṃsa-madhūny ujjhet, pañca kṣīriphalāni ca// *SD*: ii, 2. For the variations of the mūlaguṇas, see *JY*: 51. Williams is of the opinion that the mūlaguṇas, although not unknown to the Śvetāmbaras, were probably integrated into the pratimā ladder only by Digambara writers.

23. "The *udumbaras* are the fruits of five trees of the genus *Ficus*: (i) umbara, udumbara—*Ficus glomerata* Roxb.; (ii) vaṭa, nyagrodha—*Ficus bengalensis*; (iii) pippala, aśvattha—*Ficus religiosa* Linn.; (iv) plakṣa—*Ficus infectoria* Roxb.; (v) kakombari, guphala—*Ficus oppositifolia* Willd." *JY*: 53.

24. Compare: aprādurbhāvaḥ khalu rāgādīnāṃ bhavaty ahiṃseti/ teṣām evotpattir hiṃseti jināgamasya saṃkṣepaḥ// *Puruṣārthasiddhyupāya*: k 44.

Seen within this context, the forbidden substances mentioned above begin to show certain features in common. Most important is the fact that, in the Jaina view, partaking of any of these necessarily involves killing and so must be avoided. This fact is of course most obvious with regard to meat; thus it is not surprising that the taboo against eating animal flesh is enforced more strongly in the Jaina community than in any other. To perceive the violence supposedly inherent in partaking of the other prohibited foods, we must recall the Jaina belief in nigoda, the myriad single-sense creatures which inhabit almost every corner of the universe.[25] Such creatures are said to be especially prevalent in substances where fermentation or sweetness is present; hence the consumption of liquor or honey brings untold millions of these organisms to an untimely and violent end. The tissues of certain plants, especially those of a sweet, fleshy, or seed-filled nature, are also thought to serve as hosts for the nigoda; plants of this type are termed sādhāraṇa, "those which share their bodies." The avoidance of figs as part of the mūlaguṇa practice seems to represent a symbolic renunciation of all nigoda-ridden vegetable substances; indeed, later stages of the path involve the abandonment of any such food whatsoever.[26]

While Jainas take very seriously the destruction of nigoda, it should be noted that violence against these creatures is considered far less terrible than that against higher animals. Thus a Jaina layman may on rare occasions consume medicinal preparations made with honey or wine, but under *no* circumstances may he take meat. If there is a single practice which can be called the hallmark of the Jaina, it must be this strict adherence to vegetarianism; his refusal to eat meat constitutes the most basic expression of his commitment to ahiṃsā.

25. See Ch. IV n. 7.

26. For a long list of plants and substances forbidden to a devout Jaina, see *JY*: 110–116.

Certain modern scholars have suggested that the mūlaguṇa restraints actually represent a reaction to ancient Vedic sacrificial practices.[27] Such a view implies that Jainism began as an ahiṃsā-oriented protestant sect within the Vedic tradition, becoming defined as a separate religion only after developing this orientation into an all-out ban on sacrifice and killing of every sort. It is true that Jaina attacks on Vedic ritual have at times reached the proportions of a crusade, and also that the specific food substances forbidden to Jainas were all commonly employed in ceremonial offerings to the manes. Such apparent connections, however, must be weighed against the fact that Jainas themselves have no memory of a time when they fell within the Vedic fold.[28] Any theory which attempts to link the two traditions, moreover, fails to appreciate the rather unique and very anti-Vedic character of Jaina cosmology, soul theory, karmic doctrine, and atheism.

Whatever may be the origin of the great Jaina concern with nonviolence, or of the expression of this concern through dietary restrictions, we *do* know that Jainas became the primary exponents of vegetarianism in India. They rejected even the Buddhist notion that meat is acceptable if an animal has died of natural causes, contending that the dead flesh itself is a breeding ground for innumerable nigodas and hence must not be consumed.[29] It may well be that Jainism was the first Indian tradition to preach so strongly against the taking of meat; in any case, it certainly contributed much to the eventual triumph of vegetarianism throughout the subcontinent.

Vrata-Pratimā (Stage of Restraints).—Once a person has

27. *JY*: 52–53. See also Schmidt 1968.

28. "As to Jainas being Hindu dissenters, and, *therefore* governable by Hindu Law, we are not told the date of this secession . . . Jainism certainly has a longer history than is consistent with its being a creed of dissenters from Hinduism." J. L. Jaini 1916a: 12–13. See below, Ch. IX n. 30.

29. yad api kila bhavati māṃsaṃ svayam eva mṛtasya mahiṣavṛṣabhādeḥ/ tatrāpi bhavati hiṃsā tadāśritanigodanirmathanāt// *Puruṣārthasiddhyupāya*: k 66.

taken refuge in the five kinds of holy beings and has become fixed in the eight mūlaguṇas, he is considered able to appreciate the value of restraints (*vrata*). Vratas (from the Sanskrit *vṛ*, to fence in) provide the means whereby karmic influx can be placed within certain limits, thereby ensuring that the worldly activities inevitable for the householder do not lead to passions which deepen his involvement in saṃsāra. Jainas set forth twelve "partial" vratas (those appropriate for the layman); vows of adherence to these constitute the second or vrata-pratimā. The twelve partial vratas are in three categories: five *aṇuvratas*, three *guṇavratas*, and four *śikṣāvratas*. Of these, the aṇuvratas are basic.[30] Restraints of the second category are elaborations of those included in the first, while those of the third are actually spiritual exercises of a ritual sort. Let us now examine each category in some detail.

The First Aṇuvrata: Ahiṃsā—The first aṇuvrata is called ahiṃsā. One here vows to undertake a set of restraints which further deepen his commitment to this most central concept of Jaina ethics. As we have seen, hiṃsā refers to any action accompanied by the giving of pain or the rise of passions. Recognizing that total avoidance of such actions would be impossible for a householder, Jaina teachers have drawn a distinction between injurious activities which are totally forbidden and those which may be tolerated within strict guidelines. The first of these categories is designated as *saṃkalpajā-hiṃsā*, and includes all deeds involving intentional, premeditated violence.[31] Such deeds are contrasted with those of the *ārambhajā-hiṃsā*

30. While all Jaina sects agree on the identity and nature of the aṇuvratas, there has been some argument as to precisely which restraints make up the guṇavratas and śikṣāvratas, respectively. Here I have followed the most widely accepted tradition; for variant lists, see *JY*: 56ff. See the list of vratas at the end of this chapter.

31. pramattayogāt prāṇavyaparopaṇaṃ hiṃsā/ *TS*: vii, 13. pramādaḥ sakaṣāyatvaṃ tadvān ātmapariṇāmaḥ pramattaḥ . . . tasya yogaḥ pramattayogaḥ. tasmāt pramattayogāt indriyādayo daśaprāṇās teṣāṃ yathāsambhavaṃ vyaparopaṇaṃ viyogakaraṇaṃ hiṃsety abhidhīyate . . . 'pramattayogāt' iti viśeṣaṇaṃ kevalaṃ prāṇavyaparopaṇaṃ nādharmāyeti jñāpanārtham. *SS*: §687.

variety, which either occur accidentally or may result from the performance of an "acceptable" occupation. A murderer, for example, clearly sets out to end the life of his victim, hence commits saṃkalpajā-hiṃsā. Surgeons, on the other hand, may cause pain or even death during a delicate operation, but are guilty only of the much less serious ārambhajā-hiṃsā. As for occupations, Jainas should not choose one involving intentional destruction, such as that of a hunter or a fisherman. Though even a farmer may destroy insects during the course of his work, such harm is done unwittingly and so does not render this means of livelihood unacceptable.

During the performance of any task, one who has taken the vow of noninjury must exercise a high degree of care in order to minimize even ārambhajā-hiṃsā. This becomes especially important when caste duties demand violent action, as in the case of a kṣatriya (warrior) whose country becomes involved in warfare. Jainas have not been blind to the importance of resisting injustice and aggression. Hence they have considered even killing, when done in self-defense or during a purely defensive war, to involve not saṃkalpajā-hiṃsā but a less serious variety called *virodhī-hiṃsā* (injury generated by standing in opposition).[32] Under more ordinary circumstances, however, the lay Jaina would not have found himself confronted by the necessity for such drastic behavior.

Six modes of livelihood—government (*asi*), writing

32. "daṇḍo hi kevalo lokam imaṃ cāmuṃ ca rakṣati/ rājñā śatrau ca putre ca yathā doṣasamaṃ dhṛtaḥ//" Quoted in *JSK*: IV, 537 (from *Sāgāradharmāmṛta-ṭīkā* iv, 5). The concept of virodhī-hiṃsā appears to be a noncanonical one, as the word is not attested in any ancient works. It does not appear even in the *Nītivākyāmṛta* of Somadevasūri (tenth century), the only book on polity by a Jaina author. In this avowedly nonsectarian work, Somadeva holds that kings should regard warfare as a "last resort," but he does not go so far as to specify that it may be undertaken only on a defensive basis: buddhiyuddhena paraṃ jetum aśaktaḥ śastrayuddham upakramet/4/ praharato 'pasarato vā same vināśe varaṃ prahāro yatra naikāntiko vināśaḥ/12/ sa dharmavijayo rājā yo vidheyamātreṇaiva santuṣṭaḥ prāṇārthamāneṣu na vyabhicarati/70/ *Nītivākyāmṛta*: xxx (yuddhasamuddeśa). For a discussion on the Jaina attitude towards the concept of kṣatriya-dharma, see below, Ch. IX n. 62.

(*maṣi*), farming (*kṛṣi*), the arts (*vidyā*), commerce (*vāṇijya*), and various crafts (*śilpa*)—have been designated as "respectable" by Jaina teachers.[33] In practice, however, followers of the Jina have been strongly encouraged to enter those professions which have the least potential for violence; hence statecraft and agriculture have come to be considered somewhat less desirable occupations, while the career of a merchant is seen as most appropriate. Even within the context of commercial activity, certain varieties of trade have been specifically prohibited for one who has entered upon the path of restraint.[34] These include dealing in charcoal; selling timber; selling or driving oxcarts; charging fees for transport by oxcart; excavation, plowing, and quarrying; dealing in animal by-products, for example, ivory; trading in lac; manufacturing or selling alcohol or other substances prohibited under the mūlaguṇa; trading in slaves or livestock; dealing in poisons or weapons; operating mills or oilpresses; gelding and branding animals; burning fields to encourage subsequent agricultural production; draining water so that crops can be planted; breeding destructive animals.

Acceptance of the first vrata entails much more than simply an expansion of the basic commitment to ahiṃsā. Once a layman has taken this vow, he must scrupulously avoid all practices in violation thereof. Whereas the restrictions of the first pratimā operate mainly on the level of attitude—generating a *tendency* to avoid certain activities—those of the vrata-pratimā constitute a lifelong code of conduct to which one must pay meticulous attention at every moment. With full awareness of the obligation involved, the aspirant approaches a Jaina mendicant and begs to be given the vow. In the presence of the holy person he repeats the ancient formula:

33. asir maṣiḥ kṛṣir vidyā vāṇijyaṃ śilpam eva ca/ karmāṇīmāni ṣoḍhā syuḥ prajājīvanahetavaḥ// *AP*: xvi, 179.

34. Fifteen trades forbidden to a Jaina are listed in *JY*: 117–123; and *SD*: v, 21–23.

> I will desist from the knowing or intentional destruction of all great lives [trasa, souls embodied with two or more senses]. As long as I live, I will neither kill nor cause others to kill. I shall strive to refrain from all such activities, whether of body, speech, or mind.[35]

Vows for each of the other lay or partial vratas, whenever these are undertaken, involve a similar declaration. Immediately after administering the vow, the teacher instructs the aspirant concerning related infractions which he must be careful to avoid, as well as on the proper means of expiation should such transgressions occur. A further distinction is made, in terms of seriousness and expiatory procedure, between infractions committed intentionally (*bhaṅga*) and those which take place by accident (*aticāra*).[36] Five infractions are listed with regard to the ahiṃsā-vrata; these pertain mainly to the treatment of humans and animals in one's care and include holding beings in captivity, beating, mutilating or branding, loading an excessive weight on the back or head, and providing insufficient food or water. The great Jaina concern with protection of animals is seen clearly in these prohibitions. Indeed, one who has taken the first vrata asserts the inviolability of *all* life, aligning himself with this principle to an extent probably unmatched by laymen of any other religious tradition.

The Second Aṇuvrata: Satya—The second aṇuvrata is that of *satya*, truth; it involves the vow to abstain from lying (*asatya*) of any sort. Jainas see a close connection between asatya and hiṃsā, since all lying is volitional and tainted by some operation of the passions; thus the soul

35. This declaration is modeled on the words used by certain of Mahāvīra's outstanding lay disciples (Ānanda, e.g.; see below, Ch. VII): Āṇande gāhāvaī samaṇassa bhagavao Mahāvīrassa aṃtie . . . thūlagaṃ pāṇāivāyaṃ paccakkhāi, "jāvajjīvāe duvihaṃ tiviheṇaṃ na karemi na kāravemi maṇasā vayasā kāyasā." *Upāsakadaśāḥ*: i, §4.

36. For a chart listing five infractions pertaining to each vrata, see *JY*: 58–62.

is injured by such activity.[37] In its broader sense, the satyavrata requires great care with regard to *all* acts of speech, lest they have destructive consequences; thus even a truthful statement cannot be uttered if it will lead to the destruction of a living being. This requirement would seem to create the possibility of a double-bind situation for one who has undertaken the satya restraint. When, for example, he is asked the direction that a deer has gone by someone hunting the creature, pointing out the proper path endangers the life of the deer; pointing elsewhere, on the other hand, involves a deliberate untruth.

Once again, the Jaina teachers have taken the exigencies of worldly existence into account, functionally defining asatya for the layman as a lie *for one's own sake.* The hypothetical situation described above, therefore, should ordinarily be resolved by misleading the hunter; since the untruth has been spoken purely for the sake of the deer, injury to the soul of the speaker will be minimal.[38] In the case of a monk, however, the vow applies in its "complete" form; hence no such expedient solution is available. Faced by a choice between lying and abetting the destruction of another being, he must simply maintain silence, even if this behavior brings the wrath of the questioner down upon him.

The honesty of the Jaina businessman has long been proverbial in India; that this should be so reflects not only the pervasive effect of the satyavrata spirit on the worldview of the Jainas, but also the fact that their teachers have emphasized application of this spirit to the activities of the merchant class.[39] Thus a layman who undertakes the satya

37. sarvasminn apy asmin, pramattayogaikahetukathanaṃ yat/ anṛtavacane 'pi tasmān niyataṃ hiṃsā samavasarati// *Puruṣārthasiddhyupāya*: k 68.

38. "saṃkaṭākīrṇajīvānām uddhārakaraṇecchayā/ kathitā sādhubhir jātu mṛṣoktir amṛṣaiva sā//" Quoted in *JSK*: II, 273 (from *Ārādhanāsāra*).

39. "The honesty of the Jain trader was famous. Their wealth was also famous: formerly it has been maintained that more than half the trade of India passed through their hands." Weber 1958: 200. "Not all Jainas are merchants but many merchants happen to be Jainas because the qualities highlighted in the ideal layman are also those which generally contribute to success in business, and so a creed of complete otherworldliness has offered a background

restraint is specifically cautioned against untruths pertaining to ownership, the quality of goods, or the repayment of debts. Avoidance of such infractions plus those of a more general sort (bearing false witness, spreading unkind rumors, divulging confidences, using harsh language, and so on) comprises the everyday discipline entailed by the satya vow. Whether one who has taken this vow is indeed the "truly honest man" for whom Diogenes searched in vain may be open to question; even so, the high degree of respect accorded such a person by Jainas and non-Jainas alike bears adequate witness to the great dedication and strength of character which his discipline requires.

The Third Aṇuvrata: Asteya—The third of the aṇuvratas is *asteya*, not stealing; this has been more broadly defined as adattādāna-virati, refraining from taking anything that is not given. "Given" is generally understood here to mean "acquired in a legitimate transaction" or "received through inheritance." Thus, for one who embraces this restraint, it is not allowed even to pick up goods which have been lost or forgotten.[40] More important, he must not indulge in such immoral or illegal practices as employing thieves to obtain things for him, receiving stolen merchandise, using false weights and measures, secretly adulterating commodities or substituting inferior ones for the original, or gaining or storing goods without paying the required taxes. All such acts of "stealing" are said to involve hiṃsā, since they necessarily reflect the presence of greed (lobha). In its partial form this vow does allow the collection of water, firewood, and similar materials from public lands. For a mendicant, however, even these activities are forbidden; he may obtain such necessities only if they are gathered by others and presented to him as a gift.[41]

---

for the successfully worldly." Williams in *JY*: intro. xxii. For a comparison of the Jainas with the Quakers in this context, see Nevaskar 1971.

40. nihitaṃ vā patitaṃ vā suvismṛtaṃ vā parasvam avisṛṣṭam/ na harati yan na ca datte tad akṛśacauryyād upāramaṇam// *RŚr*: iii, 11.

41. See the story of Ammaḍa's mendicant disciples in Ch. II.

The Fourth Aṇuvrata: Brahma—Fourth is the *brahmavrata*, in accord with which an aspirant refrains from all "illicit" sexual activities (those which occur outside of marriage). The specific prohibitions set forth under this restraint speak directly to men, who are clearly considered much more prone to sexual license than are women. Thus we read that one who undertakes the brahma vow should "avoid the wives of others" and be "content with his own wife."[42] (The use of the singular here does not imply prohibition of polygamy; Jainas have traditionally accepted this practice, but consider monogamous marriage as the ideal.) Further, he must not take a woman as his wife only temporarily, purely to legitimize a short-term sexual involvement. He must view all women other than his wife as he would his mother or sister, thus overcoming sexual desire for them. Beyond the duty of finding suitable mates for his own children, he should not engage in matchmaking of any sort, as this would necessitate excessive contact with women. Finally, even with his wife he must eschew all "deviations," as well as any tendency towards overindulgence in carnal pleasures. The sexual code of the Jaina laity, then, focuses upon "marriage and moderation." The importance of loyalty to one's spouse is strongly emphasized, as is the need to provide an outstanding moral example for children.

As seen earlier, sexuality has no place in the life of a Jaina mendicant. This prohibition on the expression of so basic a human urge again connects to the problem of avoiding hiṃsā. The fact that sexual activity involves passion, hence from the Jaina perspective injures the soul, is of course obvious. It is further held, however, that the very act of intercourse slaughters great numbers of single-sense creatures, thought to dwell in the generative organs of the female and the ejaculate of the male.[43] Thus, while various

42. na tu paradārān gacchati, na parān gamayati ca pāpabhīter yat/ sā paradāranivṛttiḥ svadārasantoṣanāmāpi// *RŚr*: iii, 13.

43. yad vedarāgayogān maithunam abhidhīyate tad abrahma/ avatarati tatra hiṃsā vadhasya sarvatra sadbhāvāt// hiṃsyante tilanālyāṃ taptāyasi

Indian religious sects have praised sexual restraint on grounds ranging from the social to the mystical, Jainas see this practice as simply one more facet in the universal implementation of ahiṃsā.

The Fifth Aṇuvrata: Aparigraha—The fifth and final aṇuvrata is that of aparigraha, nonpossession or nonattachment. The Jaina scriptures often define *parigraha* as the delusion (*mūrcchā*) of possession—that is, harboring such false notions as "this is mine" or "I made that" and imagining that one can hold on forever to what he now "has."[44] The term is further made synonymous with the four passions (kaṣāya) and nine sentiments (no-kaṣāya) discussed earlier; these are called the "internal possessions," and their renunciation (the avoidance of activities which generate them) constitutes the essence of the aparigraha-vrata.

But such renunciation is not possible until a person has detached himself from the ten "external possessions,"—land, houses, silver, gold, livestock, grain, maidservants, manservants, clothing, and miscellaneous goods (furniture, and so on). With the exception of clothing in sects other than the Digambara, Jaina mendicants must give up all of these things entirely. For the layman, aparigraha is expressed by the setting of limits upon what he may own. Having once established reasonable upper bounds on the quantity of goods in each of the ten categories, he must not exceed these at any time. The śrāvakācāra texts list five devious means by which certain people may try to "get around" such limits: (1) gaining new land by "incorporation," (extending one's boundaries and then saying "I haven't acquired anything beyond the limits of my property line"); (2) disguising an excess accumulation of gold or

---

vinihite tilā yadvat/ bahavo jīvā yonau hiṃsyante maithune tadvat// *Puruṣārthasiddhyupāya*: k 107–108. See also *SM*: k 23.

44. mūrcchā parigrahaḥ/ *TS*: vii, 17. bāhyānāṃ gomahiṣamaṇimuktāphalādīnāṃ ca . . . ābhyantarāṇāṃ ca rāgādīnām upadhīnāṃ saṃrakṣaṇārjanasaṃskārādilakṣaṇāvyāvṛttir mūrcchā . . . teṣu saṃkalpaḥ parigraha iti yujyate. *SS*: §695.

silver by "donating" it to one's wife; (3) going beyond the volume limit on grain and foodstuffs by repackaging these commodities in more compact containers; (4) not counting the newborn offspring of one's livestock as an increase in overall holdings, since they were "not purchased"; (5) "diminishing" the amount of household goods by combining them, welding plates together, for example. Such practices are of course to be avoided, as are the four infractions set forth under aparigraha: driving cattle over excessive distances or with too heavy a load in order to increase profits, hoarding grain to drive up the price, hoping for greater than reasonable profit in any transaction, and falling into dejection after having sold something at a low price.

All of these prohibitions are clearly oriented towards the situation of a merchant community, where greed and attachment to goods are likely to become major problems. By undertaking the aparigrahavrata, a Jaina layman systematically reduces his tendencies to fall into such passions; thus he protects his soul from increased karmic entanglement and lays the groundwork for complete nonattachment, the path of the mendicant.

The Guṇavratas—The five aṇuvratas discussed above are expanded by the so-called guṇavratas,[45] which aim to limit the area of a person's activities and the number of beings and objects with which he comes into contact. Jaina teachers have likened a layman to a heated iron ball, "burning" (injuring) everything it touches. Hence it becomes important to restrict the sphere of his activities as well as the activities themselves; only thus can karmic influx be reduced to a minimum. The first such restriction is called *digvrata*, by which an individual voluntarily curtails the distance he will travel in any given direction. He sets definite boundaries, marked by the position of well-known rivers, seas, mountains, or he simply limits the

45. yad guṇāyopakārāyāṇuvratānāṃ vratāni tat/ guṇavratāni trīṇy āhur digviratyādikāny api// *SD*: v, 1.

radius of his movements to a specific number of miles. By spending his lifetime within such boundaries, one can at least prevent himself from perpetrating violence in the areas beyond them.

Second is the *bhogopabhoga-parimāṇavrata*, which legislates against the use of certain items or the performance of certain tasks. The fifteen undesirable professions, for example, are specifically forbidden by this restraint; so is partaking of numerous foods (turmeric, ginger, garlic, carrot—thirty-two are listed) normally allowed the layman.[46] But the most important aspect of this vrata is its ban on eating (or cooking) at night (*rātri-bhojana*). Indeed, the practice of preparing and consuming food only before sunset has become so widespread among Jainas that it is popularly considered one of the mūlaguṇas. This rule can be readily understood if one recalls the large numbers of flying insects which populate the Indian household after dark; a cooking fire will certainly draw many to their deaths, and others may be inadvertantly consumed along with any food taken at that time.[47] Jainas also subscribe to the widely held folk belief that going to bed with a full stomach tends to increase the level of one's passions, hence should be avoided. Finally, the second guṇavrata prohibits the drinking of unfiltered water (which may contain small creatures); this rule, like the one pertaining to nighttime dining, is almost universally followed in Jaina households.

Third of the guṇavratas is that called *anarthadaṇḍa-vrata*, which comprises injunctions against five "minor" types of evil activity: brooding (contemplating harm to oneself or others), purposeless mischief (gambling, cutting trees or digging in the ground just for fun, and so forth), facilitation of destruction (keeping or distributing poisons, weapons, and so on), giving harmful advice (encouraging warfare, helping hunters to find animals, or in any way

46. See *JY*: 110–123.

47. arkālokena vinā bhuñjānaḥ pariharet kathaṃ hiṃsām/ api bodhitaḥ pradīpe bhojyajuṣāṃ sūkṣmajantūnām// *Puruṣārthasiddhyupāya*: k 133.

offering counsel which leads others to commit hiṃsā), and "purposeless listening" (such as to the *Kāma-sūtra*, public shows, or other things which can only increase one's tendencies towards lust and violence).

Lists of infractions are also set forth for each guṇavrata. Those for the first two generally admonish the aspirant to keep the appropriate "limits" always in mind, lest he inadvertantly exceed them, while those for the third warn against various kinds of immoderate activity: libidinous speech, buffoonery, living in great luxury, and so forth.

The Śikṣāvratas—The final set of restraints, called śikṣāvrata, contains four varieties of ritual activity.[48] In undertaking any one of them, the layman vows to engage therein on a regular basis. The specific frequency may vary, but whether it be daily, weekly, or otherwise, the point is the same: practice is now *required* rather than optional. First of the four is *deśāvakāśika,* in which one elects to remain within an area even narrower than that called for by the digvrata. This restraint is necessarily temporary, lasting no more than a day or two. During that time the aspirant does not go beyond his "normal surroundings,"—his dwelling place, the temple, the fasting hall, or the confines of the village. He is also encouraged (though not required) to cut down on as many worldly activities as possible, particularly those that originate beyond the spatial and temporal limits of the vrata.

The second śikṣāvrata is *sāmāyika*; literally meaning equanimity, or (the process of) coming to oneness, it refers here to brief periods spent in meditation. Third is *poṣadhopavāsa,* which mainly entails fasting on the four *parvan* (holy) days, the eighth and fourteenth days of the moon's waxing and waning periods. (For a Jaina, fasting ordinarily means total abstention from food and water; this is usually done in a special fasting hall or some other place of seclusion.) Both sāmāyika and poṣadhopavāsa are

48. For details of the rituals involved, see Ch. VII.

very ancient practices, perhaps dating back to the time of Pārśva.

Last of these vratas is dāna. Here the aspirant pledges to give alms to mendicants or to spiritually advanced laypeople. In order to perform this activity, one must become aware of the qualities which mark a proper donor, then strive to embody those qualities. He must be able to determine which individuals are worthy to receive his gifts. Finally, he must be careful to offer only those kinds of food and other requisites which are suitable for the recipient, and to do so in strict accordance with the methods prescribed by ritual.

For the individual who has trained himself in these practices, the śrāvakācāras recommend a supplementary vrata, probably the most sacred ritual act that a layman can undertake. This is *sallekhanāvrata,* the decision to meet one's natural death in a controlled and peaceful manner by recourse to fasting and meditation during the last days of earthly existence. Since the precise moment when sallekhanā will become appropriate cannot be known in advance, it is customary for the aspirant to take an "informal" vow of adherence to this vrata, resolving to undertake its actual practice at some future time. In this way he becomes emotionally prepared, over the years, for the profound experience that such a holy death entails.[49]

The four śikṣāvratas and sallekhanā have been referred to here as "rituals." This designation actually describes the activities involved, but it must be kept in mind that these five are practices of an exalted nature, not to be

49. Compare: sallekhanāṃ kariṣye 'haṃ vidhinā māraṇāntikīm/ avaśyam ity adaḥ śīlaṃ sannidadhyāt sadā hṛdi// *SD*: vii, 57. The individual may also prepare himself for sallekhanā by vowing each night, e.g., that he will take no further food until morning. Should death thus come during sleep, it will be in a sense sanctified by this sincere, albeit temporary, form of restraint.

categorized with such rituals as marriage or birth ceremonies, funerals, and so on. (These will be discussed in the last chapter.) Indeed, the śikṣāvratas are seen by Jainas as the holiest of lay activities. For the mendicant, too, rigorous performance of these vratas constitute the most significant aspect of his spiritual life. He will engage in sāmāyika at least three times each day, fast regularly, and prepare himself at all times for the sacred practice of sallekhanā. (Deśāvakāśika and dāna of course do not apply to a monk, since he has no fixed place of residence and is, moreover, possessionless, hence unable to engage in donation.)

The Remaining Pratimās.—This completes the list of twelve vratas. Having undertaken all of these in their prescribed form, one becomes fully established in Jaina lay discipline at the level of the second (namely the vrata) pratimā. Progress through the higher pratimās, ending just short of actual mendicancy, basically involves increased rigor in the performance of the vows already taken at this level. By resolving to practice sāmāyika three times each day, for example (thereby equaling the minimum amount of meditation required for a monk), one attains the third or *sāmāyika-pratimā*. This stage also entails daily performance of *pūjā* (Jina-worship and similar temple rituals) prior to the morning meal. Similarly, vowing to fast on every parvan day (as well as abandoning business, domestic, and social activities during these periods) constitutes establishment in the *poṣadha-pratimā,* fourth stage on the ladder of progressive renunciation.

The fifth stage, called *sacittatyāga-pratimā,* involves giving up all forms of green leaves and shoots, as well as roots and tubers, and certain other edibles normally allowed the layman. The use of unboiled water, moreover, is now forbidden. Having thus extended the bhogopabhoga restraint, the aspirant lives mainly on lentils and similar dried foodstuffs.

The sixth and seventh pratimās represent an increasing commitment to the spirit of the brahmavrata (vow of sexual restraint). In the first of these, called the *rātribhakta-pratimā,* one resolves to limit one's sexual activity to the nighttime hours. He thus becomes gradually prepared for the seventh or *brahmacarya-pratimā,* in which absolute continence is observed. Also referred to as *abrahma-varjana* (abandonment of [all] incontinence), this stage represents near-total renunciation of the household life; one who has attained so high a level of restraint receives the title *brahmacāri* and commands great respect in his community. In addition to ceasing from all physical contact with members of the opposite sex, the brahmacāri may no longer wear tailored clothing; he dons only simple garments consisting of two or three long pieces of cloth. He further abandons all devices ordinarily used to increase one's attractiveness: soap, oil, jewelry, and the like.

Having functionally ended his marital life in the seventh stage, the aspirant withdraws from all professional commitments in the eighth (called *ārambhatyāga-pratimā*). Whatever his job has been, he ceases entirely from its performance; receiving support from his children, he spends the major portion of each day engaged in spiritual practices and reading of the scriptures. Eventually he may hand over all his property to other members of the household (children, brothers), thereby abandoning the cares of worldly possession and arriving at the ninth or *parigrahatyāga-pratimā.*[50] At this stage he still participates in matters of family business, but he gains increasing detachment from such affairs since they no longer concern him directly. In the tenth of *anumatityāga-pratimā,* even this "advisory" role is abandoned; though still living in the

50. This stage is followed by a ceremony called *sakala-datti,* in which a man's property is transferred to his son in the presence of community leaders: athāhūya sutaṃ yogyaṃ, gotrajaṃ vā tathāvidham/ brūyād idaṃ praśān sākṣāj jātijyeṣṭhasadharmaṇām// tātādya yāvad asmābhiḥ pālito 'yaṃ gṛhāśramaḥ/ virajyainaṃ jihāsūnāṃ tvam adyārhasi naḥ padam// *SD*: vii, 24–25.

household, the layman remains totally uninvolved with its activities. Thus he becomes ready for the final (eleventh) stage, called *uddiṣṭatyāga-pratimā*, in which there is renunciation of all food and lodging specifically prepared (*uddiṣṭa*) for him. At this point he turns away from the world, leaves home forever, and goes to live in a temple or a public hall for renunciants.[51]

Within the Śvetāmbara tradition, one who has thus reached the eleventh pratimā is called *śramaṇabhūta* (about to become a mendicant).[52] He carries the requisites of the monk, begging bowl and whisk broom, and may even go so far as to shave his head and don monk's clothing. Thus he lives almost exactly as would a Śvetāmbara mendicant, but remains technically a layman in that he has not yet taken the mahāvratas.

Among Digambaras, the aspirant who has reached this level repairs to an ascetic retreat and subsists on alms. Initially he will wear three "garments": a loin cover, a sarong-like waist wrap, and a large piece of cloth thrown about the shoulders. Although carrying no begging bowl, he does not eat from his bare hands as monks do; rather, he is allowed to partake from a plate (which belongs to the householder who gives him the alms). One who has reached this stage is called *kṣullaka* (minor, junior), and is considered almost ready to undertake the mendicant vows.[53] First, however, he must pass through the stage known as ailaka,[54] wherein he reduces his possessions to a single piece of cloth (the loin cover) and thus prepares for total ascetic nudity, the defining practice of the Digambara monk.[55]

51. uddiṣṭaṃ piṇḍam apy ujjhed utkṛṣṭaḥ śrāvako 'ntimaḥ/ Ibid.: vii, 37.
52. See *JY*: 178. See the story of Ānanda below, Ch. VII.
53. For the variant practices prescribed for a kṣullaka, see *JY*: 178–181.
54. See Ch. I n. 45.
55. Actually, Digambara monks and eleventh-pratimā laypersons carry a peacock-feather whisk broom (called *piñchī*), used to clear their sitting place lest small creatures be harmed; since this broom is necessary to the observance of ahiṃsā, it is not considered a "possession." The same exemption applies to a gourd pot used to carry water for toilet purposes. See pl. 24.

It seems that in ancient times the vows for each of the eleven pratimās were initially undertaken for a period of months equal to the "step number" of that pratimā; hence one would practice the vratas for two months, then sāmāyika for three, fasting for four, and so on up to eleven months as a kṣullaka or śramaṇabhūta.[56] Such a progression, with each stage including those already undertaken, would require five-and-a-half years for completion; thereafter, the aspirant would usually (but not necessarily) decide to take the vows permanently. Today this practice is no longer observed; once accepted, the restraints of a particular pratimā are binding for life.

By passing through all eleven of the pratimā "ladder," a layman shows that he has totally overcome the apratyākhyānāvaraṇa passions and is fully established in the fifth guṇasthāna. Thus he is ready for the exalted practices of the mendicant path, a path which may at last carry his soul to the brink of liberation.

56. See the story of Ānanda, Ch. VII.

THE PRATIMĀS

THE ELEVEN STAGES OF SPIRITUAL PROGRESS PRESCRIBED FOR A LAYMAN[57]

1. Darśana-pratimā
   The stage of right views
2. Vrata-pratimā
   The stage of taking the vows (see chart on vratas)
3. Sāmāyika-pratimā
   The stage of practicing the sāmāyika
4. Poṣadha-pratimā
   The stage of fasting on certain holy days
5. Sacittatyāga-pratimā
   The stage of purity of nourishment
6. Rātribhakta-pratimā
   The stage of continence by day
7. Brahmacarya-pratimā
   The stage of absolute continence
8. Ārambhatyāga-pratimā
   The stage of abandonment of household activity
9. Parigrahatyāga-pratimā
   The stage of abandonment of acquisitiveness (by formally disposing of one's property)
10. Anumatityāga-pratimā
    The stage of abandonment of approval for activities connected with household life
11. Uddiṣṭatyāga-pratimā
    The stage of renunciation of specially prepared food or lodging (the stage of renouncing all connections with one's family). In the Śvetāmbara tradition this is known as the stage of the śramaṇabhūta. In the Digambara tradition this stage is divided into two steps: (1) kṣullaka (the junior, one with three pieces of cloth), (2) ailaka (one with only the loincloth).

57. For variations in the Śvetāmbara and the Digambara lists, see *JY*: 172–178.

THE ŚRĀVAKA-VRATAS

THE VOWS PRESCRIBED FOR A LAYMAN

a. The eight mūlaguṇas (basic restraints)
   Refraining from partaking of meat, alcohol, honey, and five kinds of figs
b. The five aṇuvratas (limited or restricted vows)
   1. Ahiṃsāvrata: refraining from causing injury to beings with more than one sense faculty
   2. Satyavrata: refraining from false speech
   3. Asteyavrata: refraining from theft
   4. Brahmavrata: refraining from illicit sexual activities
   5. Aparigrahavrata: limiting one's possessions
c. The three guṇavratas (vows that strengthen the aṇuvratas)
   1. Digvrata: restricting one's activities to a specific area in any given direction
   2. Bhogopabhogavrata: restricting the objects of one's enjoyment (items of food, clothing, and so forth)
   3. Anarthadaṇḍavrata: refraining from all "unwholesome" activities (hunting, gambling, and so forth)
d. The four śikṣāvratas (vows of spiritual discipline)
   1. Sāmāyikavrata: attainment of equanimity through meditation
   2. Deśāvakāśikavrata: further restrictions on the area defined by digvrata
   3. Poṣadhopavāsavrata: fasting on certain holy days each month
   4. Dānavrata: performing "charity"—offering food, residence, medicine and books to mendicants and others
e. A supplementary vrata, sallekhanāvrata
   "emaciating the body by fasting," a nonobligatory practice highly recommended for a layman on his deathbed.

VII

Jaina Rituals and Ceremonies

The Practices of the Jaina Laity

The rules of lay conduct discussed in the previous chapter are severe; indeed, even the clerics of many religions do not live so strict a life as these rules demand. One would expect, under such conditions, that the number of persons able to adhere to such conduct would be small. Observation of a typical Jaina community bears out this expectation; the partial vratas and the pratimās, while theoretically set down for all laymen, tend to constitute an ideal path followed only by a highly select few. Certainly the ethical codes which underlie these disciplines strongly influence the outlook of the community at large, but it is a rare individual who actually *vows* to accept the restraints or perform the holy activities described here. Even the widespread practice of the namaskāra-mantra and the mūlaguṇas is due more to the weight of social convention than to that of spiritual obligations formally undertaken.

If we wish, therefore, to comprehend the religious life of the Jaina laity in real terms, we must look beyond the paradigmatic statements of the śrāvakācāra texts. For most Jainas, practice of their faith centers upon a diverse group of daily rituals and periodic ceremonies. Many of these may be equivalent in substance to aspects of the "ideal" lay path, but they differ significantly in that no compulsion attaches to them; unbound by any vow, the layman performs such activities only if and when he desires to. These rituals serve not merely to bring members of a family or community together in a context imbued with religious meaning, but they also provide a sense of group identity—that is, the particular ritual forms adopted by members of a given community clearly distinguish them from their Hindu neighbors and from rival Jaina sects as well.

In view of this latter function, we must bear in mind that the designation applied to a given practice by Śvetāmbaras, for example, may refer to something very different among Digambaras or even among the "protestant" offshoots of the Śvetāmbara tradition. (The history and doctrine of these subsects will be discussed in Chapter IX.) Such sectarian differences are evident both in terms of litany and of the nonverbal actions which constitute a particular ceremony. The Śvetāmbaras, having managed to preserve most of their original Prakrit scriptures, still employ virtually the same liturgical formulas and practices that were in use during the time of the Valabhi council (fifth century A.D.). The Digambaras, on the other hand, possessed almost no ancient canonical materials upon which their recitations or ceremonial procedures could be based. Hence they composed new litanies in Sanskrit and developed ritual forms which were sometimes borrowed, through an ongoing process of "Jaina-ization," from those of the surrounding Hindu majority.[1] In this way there arose many of the surface differences now observable between the lay activities of the two great Jaina traditions. Such differences should not, however, blind us to the common spirit which informs a given ritual regardless of its particular sectarian mode of expression. Thus it is often possible to speak in a general way of "the practices of the Jaina laity" without falling into any profound inaccuracy.

The Six Obligatory Duties

The canonical texts set forth six so-called obligatory duties (*āvaśyakas*) for members of the mendicant order. These are *recommended* to the laity as well, and although no

1. In his *Ādipurāṇa*, for example, Jinasena introduces several mantras which have no parallel in the Jaina canon. See *AP*: xl, 1–77.

actual obligation applies in the case of a nonascetic, the āvaśyakas in modified form are performed regularly in many Jaina households.[2] These are, in brief: (1) sāmāyika, the practice of equanimity (meditation); (2) *caturviṃśati-stava*, praise of the twenty-four Tīrthaṅkaras; (3) *vandana*, veneration (of the mendicant teachers); (4) pratikramaṇa, expiation (for transgressions); (5) *kāyotsarga*, abandonment of the body (standing or sitting motionless for various lengths of time); (6) *pratyākhyāna*, renunciation (of certain foods, indulgences, or activities, for a specified period). In medieval times the concept of sāmāyika seems to have broadened to include worship of Jina images at various shrines.[3] This sort of "meditation by worship (*pūjā*)" led to similar notions—meditation by fasting, meditation by expiation, and so on—until at last sāmāyika became, for many Jainas, a cover term for *all* types of spiritual activity.

Digambaras developed a list of practices quite similar to those of the canonical āvaśyaka scheme, but moved towards a greater emphasis upon the popular or secular aspects of ritual. Mainly responsible for this trend were the great teachers Jinasena (circa A.D. 840) and Somadeva (tenth century), both of whom laid down sixfold sets of practices which laymen were to perform as regularly as possible. Somadeva's list became the standard one, including: (1) *devapūjā*, worship of the Tīrthankaras; (2) *guru-upāsti*, venerating and listening to the teachers; (3) *svādhyāya*, study (of the scriptures); (4) saṃyama, restraint (including observance of the mūlaguṇas, the aṇuvratas, the guṇavratas, and the first śikṣāvrata, sāmāyika); (5) tapas, austerities (especially fasting on holy days, as in the second śikṣāvrata); (6) dāna, charity (giving alms to mendicants).[4]

2. "sāmāyikaṃ stavaḥ prājñair vandanā sapratikramā/ pratyākhyānaṃ tanūtsargaḥ ṣoḍhāvaśyakam īritam//" Quoted in *JSK*: IV, 51 (from *Amitagati-śrāvakācāra*: viii, 29). For details on the āvaśyakas, see Schubring 1962: §151; and *JY*: 184.

3. In his discussion on the sāmāyikavrata, Somadeva deals at length with the worship of the parameṣṭhins. See *Upāsakādhyayana*: k 459–565; Handiqui 1949: 269–282; *JY*: 137–138.

4. Jinasena's list is very similar, except that it has *vārtā* (an acceptable profession) rather than guru-upāsti: ijyāṃ vārtāṃ ca dattiṃ ca svādhyāyaṃ

It can readily be seen that the ritual practices recommended here come very close to those in canonical sources, particularly when the sāmāyika of the āvaśyaka list is understood to include pūjā, and so on, as noted above. These practices therefore constitute the fundamental modes of religious expression for the Jaina laity and must be examined in greater detail.

Worship of the Tīrthaṅkaras (Devapūjā)

Foremost among the six lay rituals is devapūjā, worship of the Tīrthaṅkaras. This normally takes place before an image of one of these omniscient teachers (any of the twenty-four is considered suitable); such images are most often (but not always) located within a temple. Since the most ancient Jaina texts seem to make no reference to Jina-images (or to temples, for that matter), we must assume that the practice of erecting these icons dates from the postcanonical period. (Indeed one Jaina sect, the Sthānakavāsi, condemns image-worship altogether on the basis that it is extracanonical and thus heterodox.[5])

Construction of images and active veneration of the omniscient teachers whom they represented may well have begun during the Mauryan period (circa 300 B.C.), sometime after Mahāvīra had been elevated by many of his followers to the status of a quasi-divine cult figure. But the oldest known Jaina stone inscription suggests that images of the Jinas may have been worshiped at an earlier date. This inscription, commissioned by one King Khāravela of Kalinga (modern Orissa) around 150 B.C., tells how that king engaged in warfare to regain a famous image of Ananta Jina (the fourteenth Tīrthaṅkara), which had been carried off by agents of the Nanda dynasty.[6] The Nandas are known to have ruled in Bihar around 400 B.C.; crediting

---

saṃyamaṃ tapaḥ/ śrutopāsakasūtratvāt sa tebhyaḥ samupādiśat// *AP*: xxxviii, 24.

5. For a brief history of the Sthānakavāsi sect, see Ch. IX.

6. "Naṃdarājanītaṃ Kāliṃgajinaṃ saṃnivesaṃ . . . ca nayati." Quoted in Sahu 1964: I, 402. See Ch. IX n. 8.

the veracity of Khāravela's inscription, therefore, would mean that a full-blown cult of image-worship existed among Jainas even in Mahāvīra's time.[7]

Further evidence concerning the history of devapūjā in Jainism is provided by various stone remains unearthed at Mathura. These cover perhaps a thousand years of Jaina history; a few may date back to the second century B.C. The most significant items in the Mathura collection are certain votive slabs (*āyāga-paṭa*) of the type usually donated to a temple by a group of several lay-devotees.[8] Some of these depict Jinas seated in meditation, surrounded by various auspicious signs—svastikas, fish, trees—as well as by gods, men, and animals. This scene, of course, is the samavasaraṇa so often described in Jaina literature. It is especially noteworthy for the lotus (meditative) posture of its central figure, which conforms strictly to the Jaina doctrine that an omniscient being no longer sleeps (as Buddha, for example, is often shown doing), and certainly does not engage in passionate worldly activities. (Compare the dancing, warring, or sportive poses used by Hindus in depicting their various gods.) Even the well-known statues of Jaina saints standing erect, arms and hands pointed downward, illustrate a form of deepest meditation (in this case conjoined with the practice of kāyotsarga). Indeed no Jina-image has ever been found which shows the great being in any but one of these two "orthodox" positions, positions suggesting omniscient awareness and complete nonvolition.

7. There is an ancient legend among the Śvetāmbara Jainas that a sandalwood image of Mahāvīra prior to his renunciation was carved during the Jina's lifetime (hence it became known as Jīvantasvāmī). For literary evidence in support of this tradition, as well as a discussion of a certain bronze figure (circa sixth century) considered a replica of the original Jīvantasvāmī image, see U. P. Shah 1951–52a, b. For a more general history of Jaina iconography and architecture, see Fergusson 1891: 207–278; Smith 1901; Sankalia 1939; Lohuizen-de Leeuw 1949; U. P. Shah 1955; Dhaky 1968; Nigam 1968; Prasad 1968; Bruhn 1969; Ghosh 1974–1976; Fischer 1975.

8. See Smith 1901: pl. VII–XIII. For a full discussion of the inscriptions on these tablets, see Lohuizen-de Leeuw 1949: 65–72; U. P. Shah 1955: 77–94. See pl. 16.

Another group of votive slabs taken from Mathura depicts what appear to be Jaina *stūpas* (reliquary mounds); this is particularly interesting since neither the śrāvakācāras nor the current practices of Jainism give any indication that a cult of relic-worship once flourished within the tradition.[9] No stūpas housing the remains of Jaina teachers have yet been discovered;[10] those shown on slabs, however, are very similar in design to the Buddhist ones which survive at Sanchi and elsewhere. In any case, we know that Jainas never carried the stūpa cult to a great extreme; their efforts seem to have been directed more towards the straightforward construction and veneration of images (or some variation thereof); for a time it seems to have been popular to commemorate the great teachers by placing footprints (*pādukā*) in stone and paying homage to these artifacts.

Whatever the particulars of the development of these practices, building, consecrating, and regularly venerating images of the Tīrthaṅkaras today constitute the primary religious activities of lay Jainas. The popularity of these practices should not, however, be construed to mean that Jainas expect worldly help of any sort from the Jinas thus worshiped; they know full well that these perfected beings are forever beyond the pale of human affairs. In other words, there is basically no "deity" present in a Jaina temple; a one-way relation obtains between the devotee and the object of his devotion. Hence we must understand

9. Smith 1901: pl. XII, XV. One of the Mathura inscriptions (circa A.D. 157) refers to a stūpa "built by gods" (*thūpe devanirmite*). Commenting on this designation, Smith has suggested that the structure referred to "was probably erected several centuries before the Christian era, and may have been at least as ancient as the oldest Buddhist stūpa." Smith 1901: 12. Somadeva (tenth century) narrates a story concerning a stūpa at Mathura and says that "even now it is called Devanirmita": ata evādyāpi tat tīrthaṃ Devanirmitākhyayā prathate. *Upāsakādhyayana*: 92–93. See Handiqui (1949: 432) for a Śvetāmbara version of the stūpa legend, as preserved in Jinaprabhasūri's *Tīrthakalpa* (fourteenth century).

10. The so-called tombs of priests at Mudbidri (Fergusson 1891: 275), while clearly of a commemorative nature, were most likely dedicated to local *bhaṭṭārakas*, Jaina clerics (see below, Ch. IX n. 56) rather than to any more exalted figure.

Jaina image-worship as being of a meditational nature; the Jina is seen merely as an ideal, a certain mode of the soul, a state attainable by all embodied beings.[11] Through personification of that ideal state in stone, the Jaina creates a meditative support, as it were, a reminder of his lofty goal and the possibility of its attainment.

Even Jainas, however, have not been totally immune to the lure of "divine powers." Under the influence of Hindu devotionalism, there appeared certain god-images in Jaina temples during the medieval period. The divinities chosen were those associated in a benevolent manner with the careers of various Jinas—for example, the snake god Dharaṇendra and his consort Padmāvatī, who protected Pārśva from several extraordinary calamities which threatened him.[12] Such beings, referred to as *śāsana-devatā*, guardian spirits, *are* considered able to fulfill mundane wishes; they may often be appealed to on this level by "weaker" segments of the Jaina community.[13] Even so, they have never been allowed to usurp the primary position occupied by the Jina himself, despite the fact that Jina-worship promises no reward whatsoever save the turning of one's mind towards the goal of mokṣa.[14]

11. Excepting, of course, the abhavyas (see P. S. Jaini 1977c). It should be mentioned here that the abhavya doctrine has no real bearing upon the religious practices of a Jaina, since it is not possible to know whether one falls into this category.

12. See Zimmer 1951: 198.

13. On the iconographic representation of the śāsana-devatās, see Jas Burgess 1903. Each Tīrthaṅkara is said to be attended by two such demi-gods, but of the forty-eight figures thus enumerated only a few have gained prominence in the popular imagination: Cakreśvarī (belonging to Ṛṣabha), Jvālāmālinī (belonging to Candraprabha), Ambikā or Kūṣmāṇḍinī (belonging to Nemi), Padmāvatī (belonging to Pārśva), and finally Brahmadeva (belonging to Śītala). In addition to their place in the main temple itself, these famous devatās may sometimes have small adjoining shrines dedicated exclusively to them (see pl. 22). It is interesting to note that of the five figures listed here, all but the last are female; and also that neither of the attendants of Mahāvīra has managed to attain to such great popular esteem.

14. Somadeva, cognizant of the possibility that these devatās might tend to replace rather than merely complement the Jinas as objects of worship, cautions that anyone who considers them equal to a Jina is "heading downwards": devaṃ jagattrayīnetraṃ vyantarādyāś ca devatāḥ/ samaṃ pūjāvidhāneṣu paśyan dūraṃ vrajed adhaḥ// tāḥ śāsanādhikārārthaṃ kalpitāḥ paramāgame/

The "unreachable" nature of a Jina renders the presence of any priest or other intermediary, such as one normally finds in traditions more oriented towards the hope of divine intervention, virtually unnecessary in a Jaina temple. Hence the Jaina community has for the most part never developed a special priestly caste analogous to that of the brahmans in Hinduism. Laymen are encouraged to carry out ritual services on their own, either individually or in a group.

Śvetāmbaras in particular have been loath to give over the performance of ceremonial functions to a caste of specialists; they may delegate to certain individuals the regular responsibility for cleaning the temple and washing and decorating the images, but such people are by no means priests. Among Digambaras in the north, a similar situation has prevailed. But those in the south have developed a class of so-called "Jaina-brahmans"; members of this group were permanently attached to temples or temple lands, and were usually entrusted with the actual performance of rituals held within their domain.[15] The presence of Jaina-brahmans was of course intimately connected with worship of the "guardian spirits" and various yakṣas (demigods) who could be "reached" by means of complex religious procedures. But even where such ceremonial specialists did exist within Jainism, they never assumed the sacred status or exclusive sway over religious functions accorded brahmans in the Hindu community. An ordinary layperson was always free, provided he had taken the mūlaguṇas and sanctified himself with a ritual bath, to perform pūjā in any Jaina temple; this held true even if a Jaina-brahman was "in charge" there.

---

ato yajñāṃśadānena mānanīyāḥ sudṛṣṭibhiḥ// *Upāsakādhyayana*: k 697–698. Āśādhara proclaims that a person with "true insight" would never worship yakṣas even when beset with great calamities, thus suggesting that only weak-minded and ignorant people fall into such worship: "āpādākulito 'pi dārśanikaḥ tan nivṛttyarthaṃ śāsanadevatādīn kadācid api na bhajate, pākṣikas tu bhajaty api . . ." Quoted in *Upāsakādhyayana*: intro. 58.

15. For a discussion of the possible origin of this group in the Jaina community, see below, Ch. IX. See also Sangave 1959: 109ff.

The Jaina temple is perhaps most accurately viewed as a replica of the samavasaraṇa (holy assembly of the Tīrthaṅkara).[16] The layman comes near as though he were actually approaching the spot where a living Jina sits immobile, bathed in omniscient glory, "preaching" by means of the miraculous sound emanating from his body. The Jina-image itself is used as a tangible aid to visualization of such a sacred being; thereby one can hope to awaken his soul's potential for samyak-darśana, as so often supposedly happened to those fortunate enough to have encountered a real Jina in ancient times.[17]

The Great Ceremony of the Five Auspicious Occasions

The visualization rationale discussed above is carried still further by the important temple ritual which, using an image as its "central character," re-enacts the five auspicious events (*pañca-kalyāṇa*) in the life of a Tīrthaṅkara (conception, birth, renunciation, attainment of omniscience, and nirvāṇa).[18] This ceremony is not a daily or regularly scheduled one; it is ordinarily performed only when a new image or set of images is to be installed. Thus it not only provides a "vision of the Jina" (the kind of symbolic "encounter" discussed above) for the lay participants, but it also serves to sanctify the new icons. Jainas believe that erecting a Jina-image is the noblest of worldly activities; one who commissions the building of such an image, as well as its

16. For literary and iconographic sources providing a description of samavasaraṇa, as well as for a discussion of the role of this image in the Jaina temple architecture, see U. P. Shah 1955: 85–95. See pl. 10.

17. As he approaches the image of the Jina, a worshiper recites the following verses: adya me saphalaṃ janma, netre ca saphale mama/ tvām adrākṣaṃ yato deva, hetum akṣayasampadaḥ// adya karmāṣṭakajvālaṃ vidhūtaṃ sakaṣāyakam/ durgater vinivṛtto 'haṃ jinendra tava darśanāt// *JP*: 11 (*Adyāṣṭaka-stotra*).

18. yo garbhāvatarotsavo bhagavatāṃ janmābhiṣekotsavo/ yo jātaḥ pariniṣkramenạ vibhavo yaḥ kevalajñānabhāk// yaḥ kaivalyapurapraveśamahimā saṃbhāvitaḥ svargibhiḥ/ kalyāṇāni ca tāni pañca satataṃ kurvantu te maṅgalam// Ibid.: 5 (*Maṅglāṣṭaka*).

proper consecration by performance of the "great ceremony of the five auspicious occasions" (*pañca-kalyāṇa-mahotsava*), is considered very likely to be born in a world blessed with a living Tīrthaṅkara.

The ceremony itself strikes the outsider as a sort of stylized dramatic production. The person who has requested (and financed) this event takes the part of Śakra (Indra), king of gods; he is accompanied by his wife in the role of Indrāṇī, Śakra's consort, who is thought to come to earth to greet the birth of each Jina-to-be. Certain members of his family play the parents of the illustrious baby. The "mother" witnesses the sixteen auspicious dream-images which portend so extraordinary a conception; artistic representations of these images (see Chapter I) are displayed within the temple. During the "birth" phase (*janma-kalyāṇa*), "Śakra" places the Jina-image atop a five-tiered pedestal, silver in color, which symbolizes Mount Meru, the center of the Jaina universe. Local women close to the family that commissioned the ceremony then gather water from four different wells, signifying the waters drawn by the gods from the various oceans described in Jaina cosmology; the "baby Jina" is sprinkled with this holy liquid. The sequence of actions in this and certain other stages of the ritual is fairly complex; thus a person of advanced religious standing (a Jaina-brahman, a kṣullaka, or a layman who has reached at least the seventh pratimā) "officiates," instructing the participants in their roles as the ceremony proceeds.

A pañca-kalyāṇa-mahotsava continues for several days. Its third phase begins when the Jina-image, now seen as a full-grown "prince," is adorned with jewelry and silken clothing. Various "kings" come to pay him tribute, and the Laukāntika-devas[19] (played by certain young people of the community) remind him that the time for his renunciation is at hand. The image is then decorated still further and

19. See Ch. I n. 21.

carried in grand procession to a park outside the town. If the image, or images, being sanctified is too large to be moved easily, a smaller one represents it in this procession. In the park the ornaments are removed and further consecration procedures (sprinkling with more holy water and sandalwood paste, for example) are carried out. Soon thereafter, the renunciant is considered to attain omniscience; this event is celebrated with great pomp, for it marks the point at which a Jina-image becomes worthy of worship. The fifth kalyāṇa, attainment of nirvāṇa, is of course duly celebrated, but not until after the image has been formally installed. As noted above, the Jina within a temple is considered to be still alive, seated in the samavasaraṇa; hence, the marking of his departure from the worldly realm has little relevance to the religious practice of the layperson.

The ritual actions of the pañca-kalyāṇa-mahotsava are accompanied by great festivity and merrymaking, especially at the time of the birth ceremony. Music, temple dancing, and feasts are provided by the person installing the image; thus only a rich man can hope to undertake this meritorious activity. If he carries out the entire event in a grand fashion, such a man will receive the title of *saṃgha-pati* (leader of the community) and will command great respect from his fellows.

When the new image is finally placed upon its pedestal, perhaps flanked by various guardian deities, it obtains the very exalted status of a real Tīrthaṅkara. In a Digambara temple it will of course be devoid of all clothing and decoration. Śvetāmbaras, on the other hand, will have carved it in such a way as to suggest certain garments and will provide ornamentation by, for example, using crystal for the eyes. In either case, the image now becomes the object of regular worship by members of the community.

The importance of the occasional pañca-kalyāṇa-mahotsava, and of the temple images consecrated thereby, should not blind us to the fact that much of Jaina lay practice occurs beyond the confines of the temple. Many homes have their own shrines, complete with small Jina-images; so it is within the household that the daily rituals of the devout layperson are often carried out. A Jaina is advised to awaken before dawn and immediately recite the five salutations of the namaskāra-mantra. He should then ponder his religious duties, reminding himself to adhere closely to whatever vratas he has taken and to strive towards the eventual taking of those which he has not. Having bathed and donned newly washed clothing, he is likely to sit in his household shrine and begin the day in a holy manner by performing devapūjā.[20] Other rituals may also be regularly carried out at home; hence the role of the temple in the religious life of a Jaina community, while very important, is by no means exclusive.

The Devapūjā Ritual

Specific customs pertaining to devapūjā, especially when it is practiced within a temple, vary among Jaina sects and even from one locality to another within the same sect. This is especially true for the Digambaras, whose southern majority has developed a relatively elaborate form of the ritual. Such elaboration is to be expected in view of the role played by Jaina-brahmans within this group, since increased complexity of any ceremony can only render their presence more essential.

But certain fundamental features characterize the performance of devapūjā for all sects. As a Jaina enters the temple, he typically wears only three simple pieces of clothing and carries a plate filled with flowers, fruit, camphor, uncooked rice, and incense. Having approached the main shrine, he will bow down, utter the namaskāra litany,

20. brāhme muhūrta utthāya, vṛtta-pañca-namaskṛtiḥ/ ko 'haṃ, ko mama dharmaḥ, kiṃ vrataṃ ceti parāmṛśet// . . . ity āsthāyotthitas talpāc chucir ekāyano 'rhataḥ/ nirmāyāṣṭatayīm iṣṭiṃ, kṛtikarma samācaret// *SD*: vi, 1–3.

and circumambulate the image three times (keeping the Tīrthaṅkara always to his right). He then sits on a mat before the image and, using rice grains, forms a svastika on a plate or wooden plank. (This ancient symbol, as we have seen, signifies the four possible saṃsāric destinies.) Above it he places three dots, standing for the "three jewels" (*ratnatraya*): true insight (samyak-darśana), right knowledge (samyak-jñāna), and proper conduct (samyak-cāritra). These three provide the means of escape from the cycle of bondage represented by the svastika. Finally, at the very top, he makes a small crescent with a dot mounted upon it; thus is suggested the uppermost portion of the universe, with the liberated soul resting just within its edge. The completed figure appears below. (See also, pl. 17.)

By forming these symbols prior to actual worship of the Tīrthaṅkara, one shows that his pūjā has as its ultimate purpose the attainment of liberation. Such preliminaries completed, he performs the *snāpana* or *abhiṣeka* ceremony, in which holy water is sprinkled over a small image placed near the foot of the main one for this purpose. The water thus used for "bathing" the Jina must first have been strained and made pure, either by boiling or by the use of a "sterilizing" substance such as cloves. (It is thought that nonsterile water still harbors water bodies; its use would therefore entail violence, making it unfit for a sacred act.) While engaging in abhiṣeka, the devotee visualizes himself as Śakra (a sandalwood paste mark on his forehead signifies this role); thus his action becomes, as in the pañca-kalyāṇa ceremony, a re-enactment of the baby Jina's ritual bath atop Mount Meru.[21] After the holy water, he pours

21. śrīmanmandarasundare śucijalair dhaute sadarbhākṣate/ pīṭhe muktivaraṃ nidhāya racitaṃ tvatpādapadmasrajā// indro'haṃ nijabhūṣaṇārthakam idaṃ yajñopavītaṃ dadhe/ mudrā-kaṅkaṇa-śekharāṇy api tathā jainābhiṣekotsave// *JP*: 13 (*Laghu-abhiṣeka-pāṭha*).

sandalwood paste and milk over the image; the latter substance reminds him of the pure, milky-white color which suffuses the Jina's body as he sits in the samavasaraṇa.[22] The abhiṣeka is concluded with purified water and a shower of blossoms.

Thereafter, the worshiper wipes the image dry and begins the second phase of devapūjā, a ritual called *arcana*. Invoking the name of the particular Tīrthaṅkara represented, he pays homage by offering up eight substances: (1) water (*jala*), for the attainment of cleanliness; (2) sandalwood paste (*candana*), for the attainment of purity; (3) uncooked rice (*akṣatā*), for the attainment of immortality; (4) flowers (*puṣpa*), for the attainment of freedom from passion; (5) sweets (*caru*), for the attainment of contentment; (6) a lamp or camphor light (*dīpa*), for the attainment of omniscience; (7) incense (*dhūpa*), for the attainment of great fame; and (8) fruits (*phala*), for the attainment of the fruit of liberation, mokṣa. Next, small amounts of all eight substances are offered together on a single plate; this gesture, called *arghya*, completes the second portion of the pūjā.[23]

The third involves a recitation known as *jayamālā*, the garland of victory. Here, one repeats the names of all twenty-four Tīrthaṅkaras, sits in silence for a few moments, and then chants the namaskāra litany as he did prior to beginning the entire ceremony.

At last the worshiper moves to the fourth and final portion of devapūjā, a waving of lamps before the image; this process is designated by the term *ārati* (Sanskrit *ārātrika*). Having thus completed his worship, the lay devotee returns home and takes his first food of the day.

Services similar to those just described are sometimes repeated just before the evening meal, but on a much

22. See Ch. I n. 79.

23. vārdhārā rajasaḥ śamāya padayoḥ samyak prayuktā 'rhataḥ/ sadgandhas tanusaurabhāya vibhavācchedāya santy akṣatāḥ// yaṣṭuḥ sṛgdivijasraje carur umāsvāmyāya dīpas tviṣe/ dhūpo viśvadṛgutsavāya phalam iṣṭārthāya cārghyāya saḥ// *SD*: ii, 30.

smaller scale; they are normally restricted to an ārati ceremony performed to the tune of temple music. This combination of regular morning and occasional evening worship comprises the usual pattern of devapūjā for the Jaina layperson.

It should be noted that for women the overall procedure is greatly simplified. They seldom touch the Jina-image, engaging in abhiṣeka only on such special occasions like the pañca-kalyāṇakas. In general, female devotees express their veneration mainly through the offering of the eight substances.

In performing devapūjā, both Śvetāmbaras and Digambaras add certain characteristic practices to the basic ones discussed above. For Śvetāmbaras, the most important of these involves showing respect by covering the mouth with a piece of cloth when approaching the image. They may also ask a temple attendant to adorn the Jina with various ornaments (gold or jeweled necklaces or a crown, for example) normally kept in storage; this will be done for a small fee which is then applied to upkeep of the temple. The act of thus decorating a Tīrthaṅkara is called *aṅga-pūjā,* veneration of the limbs (of the Lord). The omniscient being is of course not considered to have any attachment to such ornaments; Śvetāmbaras may thus have begun aṅgapūjā in imitation of rituals popular among the Gujarati Kṛṣṇa cults, with which they have had extensive contact since the seventh century. In any case, they consider this practice to be a form of prabhāvanā (illumination).

Digambaras have no such practice; it would violate the ascetic nudity of their images. They do, however, complement their worship of the Tīrthaṅkara by ornamenting the various guardian deities which surround him; these figures, being "laity," are considered proper recipients of such gifts. We have already seen, moreover, the important role which guardian spirits and demi-gods often play in Digambara religious life. Lavish expenditure on their beautification therefore has a dual function, symbolically honoring the

Jina whose teachings they "protect," and placing the donor in the good graces of the deities.

Jaina Holy Days

Worship of the omniscient beings sometimes assumes a scale much larger than that of the services so far described. On the third day of the waxing moon of Vaiśākha (May/June) (called Akṣaya-tṛtīyā, the immortal third), for example, Jainas everywhere engage in extensive pūjā, commemorating the first giving of alms to a mendicant in the current avasarpiṇī. The mendicant in question was of course Ṛṣabha, founder of asceticism for our age. It is said that he went totally without food for six months following his renunciation. Members of the community, lacking any precedent, were not aware either of their proper role as donors or of the ritually acceptable means by which alms could be given. At last a prince by the name of Śreyāṃsa had a dream in which he witnessed himself, during a previous lifetime, offering food to a Jaina monk. Inspired by this example, he later presented a small quantity of sugar cane juice to Ṛṣabha; thus was initiated the relation between layman and mendicant which is still so fundamental to Jaina life. Observance of the Akṣaya-tṛtīyā,[24] then, does not simply memorialize a single event; it also celebrates the great spiritual benefits which the laity can gain through free and proper donation of alms to members of the ascetic order.

Other annual holy days marked widely by pūjā are the anniversaries of Mahāvīra's birth (Mahāvīra-jayantī) and death (Vīra-nirvāṇa), observed during April/May and October/November, respectively. Digambaras additionally set apart the fifth day of the waxing moon of Jyeṣṭhā (June), thus commemorating the day in A.D. 150 when, it is said, Bhūtabali and Puṣpadanta first put the scriptures of

24. rādhaśuklatṛtīyāyāṃ dānam āsīt tad akṣayam/ parvākṣayatṛtīyeti tato 'dyāpi pravartate// *TSPC*: I, iii, 301. Compare *AP*: ii, 89–120.

their sect into written form. On that date (called Śrutapañcamī, the scripture-fifth), image worship is supplemented by the donation of ancient manuscripts and other forms of scriptural material to the temples. These texts become objects of veneration, symbolizing as they do the sacred teachings of the Jinas.

Mastakābhiṣeka: The Head-Anointing Ceremony

Perhaps the most famous example of pūjā performed on a grand scale in Jainism is the *mastakābhiṣeka* (head-anointing) ceremony held every twelfth year in Shravanabelgola. This honors the spiritual hero Bāhubali, who is represented by a colossal fifty-seven-foot image carved from the living rock nearly a thousand years ago. Digambaras claim that Bāhubali, the son of Ṛṣabha, was the first individual to attain siddhahood in the present time cycle. Śvetāmbaras deny this, suggesting that Bāhubali's paternal grandmother, Marudevī, actually attained the exalted state before he did; hence the veneration of his image is less important to them than to their Digambara counterparts.[25] Even so, thousands of Jainas of both traditions come to pay homage during the several weeks that the ceremony goes on; Bāhubali thus receives the kind of adoration otherwise reserved exclusively for Tīrthaṅkaras.[26]

25. While Ṛṣabha was of course the first to have reached kevalajñāna, he is thought to have outlived both his son and his mother: thus neither sect regards him as the first in our age to go to the siddha-loka. As for Marudevī, she is said by Śvetāmbaras to have attained mokṣa upon catching sight of the holy assembly of Ṛṣabha from her chair on the back of the royal elephant: sā 'paśyat tīrthakṛllakṣmīṃ sūnor atiśayānvitām/ tasyās tad darśanānandāt tanmayatvam ajāyata// sāruhya kṣapakaśreṇim apūrvakaraṇakramāt/ kṣīṇāṣṭakarmā yugapat kevalajñānam āsadat// kariskandhādhirūḍhaiva svāminī Marudevy atha/ antakṛtkevalitvena prapede padam avyayam// etasyām avasarpiṇyāṃ siddho 'sau prathamas tataḥ/ *TSPC*: I, iii, 529–532. This version is unacceptable to Digambaras not only because it depicts a *woman* becoming an arhat, but also because it suggests that such a state is possible for one who had not left the household life.

26. Although only an arhat, Bāhubali can in many ways be said to occupy a prime position in the Digambara mind. The Jaina purāṇas devote a great deal of attention to his exploits, particularly those concerning the dispensation of Ṛṣabha's kingdom after the latter had taken to mendicancy. It seems that Bharata, unwilling to share the wealth with his younger brothers, set out to

The image depicts Bāhubali as standing erect, free of clothing and immersed in deepest meditation. For the period of the mastakābhiṣeka a temporary scaffolding is built behind the huge statue, terminating in a platform just atop the head; thus the faithful can anoint Bāhubali in the proper manner, pouring various sacred substances (such as purified water and sandalwood paste) over him from above. (See pl. 20.) The festivities associated with this ceremony can continue for several weeks; participation in them is felt to engender great merit and perhaps to make possible the experience of samyak-darśana itself.

Pilgrimage to Holy Places

It should be noted that numerous devotees worship at the site of Bāhubali's image, and at other famous holy places, even when no ceremony is being held there. Jainas place great value upon pilgrimage to such shrines; indeed, the layman considers it an important goal of his life to make at least one visit, with his family if possible, to one or more of the several areas that his faith holds sacred. Such exalted sites fall into three categories: *nirvāṇa-bhūmi* (where certain Tīrthaṅkaras left the embodied state forever), *tīrtha-kṣetra* (where countless arhats—liberated non-Tīrthaṅkaras—attained a similar glorious end), and *atiśaya-kṣetra*

---

consolidate all the family lands under his personal control. But Bāhubali held fast to his own legitimate claim, until war between the two factions became imminent. Rather than sacrifice the lives of soldiers, the two brothers undertook personal contests of strength and skill, with Bāhubali emerging the clear victor. Suddenly realizing that lust for wealth and power had led him to badly humiliate his elder brother, Bāhubali became filled with remorse and renounced all his possessions, entering immediately into the houseless life. Many months later, perceiving Bharata approaching with the aim of effecting a reconciliation, the young mendicant was able to root out the last vestiges of pride and anger from his heart, thus attaining to kevalajñāna on the spot.

Accounts of the battle between the brothers, and of the incredible austerities which Bāhubali performed as an ascetic, occur again and again in Jaina literature (*AP*: xxxvi; *TSPC*: I, iv–v; *Bharateśavaibhavasaṃgraha*: xlii–xlix). Iconographic representation of Bāhubali in standing meditation, moreover, is not limited to the great image at Shravanabelgola; similar statues, albeit of somewhat smaller dimensions, are common in Digambara communities; they invariably depict the mediator as so unshakable in his practice that creepers have grown about his arms and legs. (See Frontispiece.)

(where miraculous events associated with the lives of great monks are said to have occurred).[27] Most famous of the nirvāṇa-bhūmis is Sammedaśikhara, the Parasnath Hills region of Bihar, where Pārśva and nineteen other Jinas passed away. Four other such bhūmis are recognized; Mt. Kailāsa in the Himalayas, Campāpuri in Bihar, Girnār in Saurashtra, and Pāvāpuri near modern Patna. These sites saw the attainment of nirvāṇa by Ṛṣabha, Vāsupūjya (the twelfth Tīrthaṅkara), Nemi (the twenty-second), and Mahāvīra, respectively. Important tīrtha-kṣetras are Śatruñjaya[28] in Gujarat and Mount Abu in Rajasthan, while the best-known atiśaya-kṣetra is at Shravanabelgola in Karnataka State. The fame of the latter derives from its having been, according to legend, the place where the Digambara pontiff Bhadrabāhu reached a holy death in sallekhanā; perhaps even more significant, from the pilgrim's point of view, is the fact that the great image of Bāhubali is located there.

For Jainas living at great distances from such sacred areas, the cost of traveling to one of them may well be prohibitive. Thus has developed the institution of the *yātrā,* a large-scale pilgrimage organized and paid for by some wealthy member of a community. In ancient times this took the form of a caravan; today, several specially commissioned trains may carry the lay devotees to their destination. (Monks and nuns, of course, cannot employ such modern conveyances; they ordinarily undertake extended walks to the holy sites, stopping to perform pūjā at various minor shrines along the way.) The individual who finances a yātrā is accorded great reverence by other Jaina laypeople; like one who has initiated a pañca-kalyāṇa celebration, he earns the extensive merit attached to large-scale

27. Two texts, the *Vividhatīrthakalpa* of Jinaprabhasūri and the anonymous *Nirvāṇabhakti,* enumerate the holy places of the Śvetāmbara and Digambara sects, respectively. For details on these sites, see Premi 1956: 422–477. For a state-by-state regional history of tīrtha-kṣetras of the Digambara sect, see B. Jain 1974.

28. On the temples of Śatruñjaya, see Burgess 1869.

acts of illumination (prabhāvanā) and is therefore considered a saṃgha-pati by all who know him. His status may be enhanced still further if he erects an image upon the sacred spot, thereby making a "vision of the Jina" possible for many more people than could benefit from an icon in a local temple.[29]

This account of devapūjā in Jainism has thus far focused upon the external aspects of the practice, emphasizing public activities and the expenditure of large amounts of goods and money. To take this as a comprehensive picture of Jaina worship would be misleading. The Jaina teachers have stressed time and again that such pūjā with external objects (*dravya-pūjā*) is not efficacious unless accompanied by great peace of mind and devotion to the virtues of the Jina-ideal; these internal states, referred to as *bhāva-pūjā*, *must* obtain if other devotional practices are to be meaningful. The various forms of ostentation sometimes displayed in the pañca-kalyāṇa and other ceremonies, moreover, are tolerated only on the grounds that they contribute to prabhāvanā; their lack of significance to the ritual per se is well-recognized. We have already seen the social benefits which follow from making offerings, erecting Jina-images, and the like; but such practices are fundamentally intended as a means whereby the layperson can withdraw from worldly occupations and dwell for a time in the peaceful presence of the holies. Bhāva-pūjā, therefore, is the real devotional activity of the Jaina laity, while for the ascetic it is the *only* acceptable form of worship.

Veneration of the Teachers

The second important ritual duty of a Jaina layperson is guru-upāsti, visiting and venerating the mendicant teachers. An unusually close relation has always obtained between ascetic and householder in the Jaina tradition; monks and

29. This rationale explains the seemingly "excessive" number of images set up by devotees in Jaina holy places, a phenomenon often remarked by uninitiated visitors.

nuns have acted as the spiritual teachers of the lay followers and have in turn been revered, often to the point of adoration, as the only "true propagators" of the Jina's message. This honored status has carried with it the expectation of a very high standard of conduct; every layman is well-informed on the sorts of behavior appropriate to a mendicant, and constant vigilance by the lay community has usually enforced strict adherence to this code. Unlike their counterparts in certain other religious groups, moreover, Jaina clerics have scrupulously avoided involvement in the social activities of the laity; the image of the "nagging preacher," questioning his parishioners about the conduct of their daily lives, is totally foreign to Jainism. The monks' involvement has been of a nonmanipulative sort, concerning itself only with the spiritual well-being of the people. Hence the relation between these two groups has never been tinged with fear or guilt; to the contrary, a very real feeling of mutual respect and affection has prevailed.

It should be noted that members of the Digambara laity have had far less exposure to bona fide "ascetic" teachers than have those of the Śvetāmbara. The extreme severity of restraints incumbent upon a Digambara monk, especially as regards clothing, has tended to keep the number of individuals who undertake this path to a select minimum. Hence the teaching function has fallen mainly upon the shoulders of eleventh-pratimā laymen—kṣullakas, ailakas, and the female *āryikās*; in terms of guru-upāsti such preceptors typically receive the same treatment accorded an actual (naked) monk.

The ritual of teacher veneration shows some sectarian variation. For Digambaras it involves bowing, and beseeching the teacher to utter the formula blessing "may your righteousness increase."[30] The layman may also take this opportunity to confess any vrata-infractions of which he is guilty, or perhaps to assume still further restraints. Śvetāmbaras have retained a very ancient and rather more

30. "saddharma-vṛddhir astu" or "dharma-lābha."

complex procedure. Called vandana (reverent salutation), this ceremony begins when a lay man or woman approaches a mendicant (preferably of the same sex) and greets him or her as *kṣamāśramaṇa*, ascetic who suffers with equanimity. There follows a ritual exchange in ancient Prakrit, with both individuals reciting their parts from memory.[31] The content of this exchange gives a clear picture of the sort of relation obtaining between Jaina monk and layperson:

> I desire to worship you, kṣamāśramaṇa, with very intense concentration. (The guru: so be it.) You will have spent the whole day, fortunately, little disturbed. (The guru: yes.) You are making spiritual progress. (The guru: yes, and so are you.) You are unperturbed by your sense organs? (The guru: yes.) I ask pardon, kṣamāśramaṇa, for my daily transgressions. (The guru: I too ask pardon.) I must engage in pratikramaṇa [confession] to you, kṣamāśramaṇa, for any day-by-day lack of respect . . . anything done amiss through mind, speech, or body, through anger, pride, deceit, or greed, through false behavior and neglect of the sacred doctrine at any time; whatever offence may have been committed by me, forbearing monk, I confess and reprehend and repent of it and cast aside my past self.[32]

The Annual Rite of Confession

The vandanaka also includes certain forms of further confession (pratikramaṇa) and renunciation (pratyākhyāna),

31. In the absence of a teacher the layman may use a sacred book or small bookstand as a substitute, referred to as *sthāpanācārya*. The vandanaka formula is repeated in full before this object, just as it would be before the teacher. See *JY*: 202.

32. "icchāmi khamāśamaṇo vandiuṃ jāvaṇijjāe nisīhiyāe (*the guru*: chandeṇa) aṇujāṇaha me miy'-oggahaṃ (*the guru*: aṇujāṇāmi) nisīhi aho kāyaṃ kāya-saṃphāsaṃ khamaṇijjo bhe kilāmo appa-kilantāṇaṃ bahu-subheṇa bhe divaso vaikkanto (*the guru*: taha tti) jattā bhe (*the guru*: tubbhaṃ pi vaṭṭai) javaṇijjaṃ ca bhe (*the guru*: evaṃ) khāmemi khamāsamaṇo devasiyaṃ vaikkamaṃ (*the guru*: ahaṃ avi khāmemi) āvassiyāe paḍikkamāmi khamāsamaṇāṇaṃ devasiyāe āsāyaṇāe tettīs' annayarāe jaṃ kiṃci micchāe maṇa-dukkaḍāe vaya-dukkaḍāe kāya-dukkaḍāe kohāe māṇāe māyāe lobhāe savva-kāliyāe savva-micchovayārāe savva-dhammāikkamaṇāe jo me aiyāro kao tassa khamāsamaṇo paḍikkamāmi nindāmi garihāmi appāṇaṃ vosirāmi." Quoted in *JY*: 199–200. See Leumann 1934: 7–10.

as we have seen in the case of the Digambaras. The confessional aspect of guru-upāsti is very important to the conscientious layman who has taken one or more of the pratimās; he is likely to approach the teacher nearly every day in order to ritually clear his conscience and strengthen his spiritual resolve. In addition to the twenty or more formulas used for this regular practice, there are others to be employed on a fortnightly (*pākṣika*) basis and some intended especially for the great annual rite known as saṃvatsarī.

The latter ceremony is observed on a large scale by Jainas of all sects. It takes place during the rainy season, since monks are at that time required to maintain a fixed abode for several months; thus an extended ritual involving their continuous presence is possible during that time.

15. The twenty-four symbols associated, respectively, with each of the twenty-four Tīrthaṅkaras (see p. 165n).

16. Āyāga-paṭa with fish-tailed svastika motif, Mathura. Lucknow Museum. Courtesy of American Institute of Indian Studies, Varanasi (see p. 192).

17. Use of the svastika diagram in pūjā (see p. 200). Courtesy of Gary Tartakov.

18. Inner shrine of the Lūṇa-vasahī [Śvetāmbara] temple, Abu (13th century). Courtesy of Jagan Mehta.

19. Tribhuvana-tilaka-cūḍāmaṇi ("The Crest-jewel of the Three Worlds"), a 15th-century [Digambara] temple, Mudbidre, South Kanara. Courtesy of Robert J. Del Bonta.

20. Mastakābhiṣeka (head-anointing ceremony) of Bāhubali (see p. 205). Courtesy of C. B. M. Chandriah.

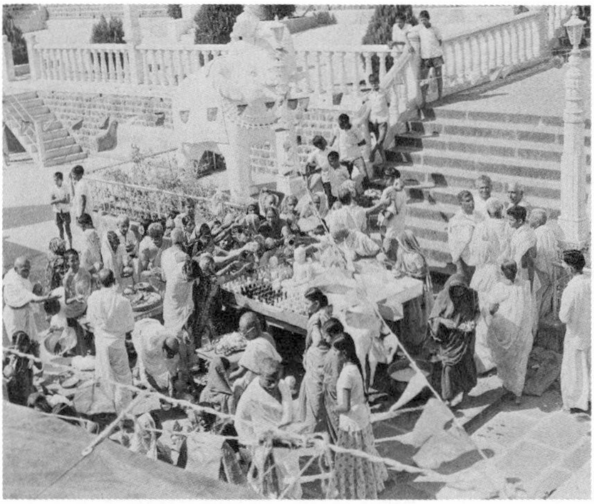

21. Digambara ceremony of setting up a new image of the Jina (see p. 196).

22. Five-pillared "yakṣa-residence" (Brahmadeva at top, Kṣetrapāla at bottom) adjoining a Digambara Jaina temple (see p. 194n13) at Guruvayanakere, South Kanara. Courtesy of Martha Ashton.

23. Mānastambha, the characteristic Jaina pillar (see p. 35n81), Mulki, South Kanara. Courtesy of Martha Ashton.

For an eight- to ten-day period, known as *paryūṣaṇa-parva,* the laypeople take various temporary restraints from food, fasting altogether, eating only one meal a day, and so on; towards the end of this period they go through confession. The admissions of sins, and accompanying pleas for forgiveness (*kṣamā*), are directed not only to a teacher but to all of one's family and friends, irrespective of age or sex. Letters are written to those relatives and acquaintances not in attendance, repeating the same acknowledgements of wrongdoing and solicitations of pardon. Finally, the participant in a saṃvatsarī extends his own forgiveness to all beings and asks that they grant the same favor to him; this is done by repetition of a famous verse which points up the real spirit of pratikramaṇa—the establishment of universal friendship and goodwill:

> khāmemi savvajīve savve jīvā khamantu me/ metti me savvabhūesu veraṃ majjha na keṇavi//[33]

> I ask pardon of all living creatures; may all of them pardon me. May I have a friendly relationship with all beings and unfriendly with none.

The pratyākhyāna aspect of visiting one's teacher never developed into any rituals so elaborate as the saṃvatsarī; even so, it is considered a highly important practice. In accordance with the great Jaina emphasis on fasting, the layman typically performs pratyākhyāna by renouncing certain kinds of food. This usually involves only temporary abstention, but in some cases it can be undertaken for life. It is accomplished by utterance of a formula similar to the following:

> When the sun is risen I renounce for the duration of a day (or certain portion thereof, as the case may be) the fourfold aliments (cooked food, water, snacks, and pastes) and except for cases of unawareness or of force majeure . . . or of in-

33. Quoted in *JY*: 207 (from *Pratikramaṇa-sūtra*).

structions from a monk or except in order to attain full tranquillity of mind, I abandon them.[34]

Fasting and Presentation of Alms

Ritual fasting is also associated with lay observance of the parvan days, referred to earlier in connection with the poṣadhavrata. The virtue of going without food or drink on these days has long been stressed by Jaina teachers; even the early Buddhist texts refer to it as a characteristic practice of the Nigaṇṭhas. Fasting actually begins after a single meal on the day prior to the parvan period. The layman takes breakfast on the morning of the seventh, for example, then retires to a temple or fasting hall for some thirty-five to fifty hours. During this interval he remains in strict seclusion from his family. Sleeping very little at night, he may chant the namaskāra litany or read the scriptures; for the most part, however, he will observe silence and meditate upon the virtues of the Jina. Bathing, or even washing of the mouth, is not allowed unless one plans to perform dravya-pūjā. (Bhāva-pūjā is more strongly recommended while fasting, but the "external" ceremony, requiring prior purification by bathing, is not proscribed.) He returns home on the morning of the ninth, does devapūjā at his home shrine, gives alms to begging mendicants, and then breaks his fast.[35]

Voluntary abstinence from food and water contributes directly to a person's spiritual progress by reducing his attachment to the body. Less direct but equally important benefits result from the widespread practice of *sharing* one's food with others. This activity, closely connected to the dāna śikṣāvrata, is called *atithi-saṃvibhāga,* sharing with guests. The term *atithi* literally means "no date"; such

34. "porisīyaṃ paccakkhāmi uggae sūre cauvvihaṃ pi āhāraṃ asanaṃ pāṇaṃ khāimaṃ sāimaṃ annatth' aṇābhogeṇaṃ sahasāgāreṇaṃ . . . sāhuvayaṇeṇaṃ savva-samāhi-vattiy'-āgāreṇaṃ vosirāmi." Quoted in ibid.: 209.

35. For details and variations in the observance of this kind of fasting in the different Jaina sects, see ibid.: 142–149.

a "guest," therefore, is one who arrives without invitation, who is simply passing by the door in search of alms.[36] In Indian society only those who are brahmacārins (celibate students) or who have renounced the world altogether are allowed to beg food. A normal householder must never do so; his position is to give, not take. In those cases where extreme poverty drives ordinary people into a beggar's role despite this cultural restriction, it is understood that alms will be offered them only out of compassion on the part of the donor; no great spiritual merit accrues to such charity, since householders are not considered "worthy recipients." Presenting alms to an ascetic, on the other hand, is thought to bring one closer to salvation. Thus can be understood the fact that, while most beggars thank the person who gives them food, in the case of feeding holy men it is the *donor* who expresses his gratitude. For a Jaina, the inherent benefits of charity to a monk are increased by the holy man's conferring a blessing upon him each time a gift is received. (This blessing involves the same "may your righteousness increase" formula noted earlier with regard to guru-upāsti.)

Hence the act of sharing food with a worthy "guest" has assumed the form of an important ritual among Jaina laity. Only those who observe at least the mūlaguṇas are "qualified" to engage in this ritual. The Jaina mendicant must therefore avoid begging at any household, whether Jaina or Hindu, not confirmed in the basic practices of the Jina's path (not observing strict vegetarianism). Although atithi can refer to any mendicant, it is ordinarily understood by the Jaina laity to indicate only those of their own faith, who are held to be the holiest of ascetics and therefore most worthy to receive gifts. Whereas non-Jaina mendicants may accept invitations, ask for specific foods, or eat that which has been prepared especially for them, the Jaina monk or nun must eschew all such "lax" practices, arriving

36. Compare: jñānādisiddhyarthatanusthityarthānnāya yaḥ svayam/ yatnenātati gehaṃ vā, na tithir yasya so 'tithiḥ// *SD*: v, 42.

only "by surprise" and taking only "surplus" food. Jainas claim superior status for their ascetics partly on the basis of these differences; even so, there is no doubt that many Jaina households do in fact set food aside to be given as alms. This is justified by saying that the layman cannot know in advance *which* monk or nun will come to his door; hence the food has not been made for anyone in particular, and the mendicant's vows are not violated.

The actual presentation of alms is a rather simple matter. Śvetāmbara mendicants, as we have seen in an earlier chapter, carry begging bowls and may not eat in the home of the donor. They are received at the door with respect, brought into the house (but not the kitchen), and offered suitable food and water by the householder and his wife together. The couple makes obeisance both before and after the actual offering is given. Finally the monks, who invariably go on their begging rounds in pairs, are escorted to the door. They proceed to other houses until their bowls are filled, then return to the monastery to eat. Digambara monks, kṣullakas, and ailakas, on the other hand, carry no bowls and visit only a single house each day. As one of them approaches, the householder (who knows that the mendicants in his neighborhood will pass by his residence) stands outside his door, takes a few steps in the holy man's direction, bows, and says: "Salutations to you, sir. Please stop." This offer may or may not be accepted, since Jaina monks make it a point to avoid visiting the same house too often (which would deprive other families of the great privilege of alms-giving). It is also common for them to make some arbitrary decision, prior to setting out on begging rounds, that aims not only to ensure impartiality but also to maintain the "surprise" or "uninvited" element in their appearance at a particular layman's door. This involves such resolutions (*abhigraha*) as "I will stop only at the fifth house I pass" or "I will stop only for a householder dressed in red"; hence it is not at all unusual for one or more invitations to be refused.

In any case, when a Digambara mendicant does respond affirmatively to someone's performance of *sthāpana* (the ritual greeting quoted above), indicating his assent by silence, that person proceeds to the second phase of the food-sharing ceremony. This is called *śuddhi,* purity, and entails the declaration that the layman's mind, speech, and body are pure (in other words, that he is a proper donor) and that the food being offered is similarly "faultless." The mendicant is then invited into the house, where he is reverenced by a ritual foot-bathing (*pāda-udaka*) and by having flowers placed before him (*arcana*).[37] Kṣullakas or ailakas may next be seated on a low wooden stool and given food on a plate belonging to the householder. A monk, however, must remain standing and take the offering in his palms, fingers interlaced. Upon finishing, he will be given additional water with which to wash his hands; thereafter, he may sit for a few moments before departing in order to deliver a short religious discourse and to confer a blessing upon the family. (Prior to this time he has uttered no sound whatsoever.)

While atithi-saṃvibhāga is the most important form of dāna, members of the laity are encouraged to perform other acts of charity as well. These should involve the "proper items, proper time, proper recipient(s), and proper cause"; in other words, contributions should go towards one of the seven *puṇya-kṣetras*[38] (fields of merit) designated by Jaina teachers. These fields, some of which we have seen earlier, are: (1) *Jina-bimba,* setting up Jina-images; (2) *Jina-bhavana,* building a temple or hall to house an image; (3) *Jina-āgama,* causing the Jaina scriptures to be copied and circulated; (4) giving alms to monks; (5) giving alms to nuns; (6) providing spiritual assistance to male members of the lay community—for example, offering alms to those advanced on the pratimā ladder,

37. pratigrahoccasthānāṅghrikṣālanārcānatir viduḥ/ yogānnaśuddhīṃś ca vidhīn navādaraviśeṣataḥ// Ibid.: v, 45.

38. See *JY*: 165.

encouraging various religious activities, building schools and fasting halls, distributing clothes to the poor; (7) identical to the sixth, but with reference to women. By donating his wealth and energy to as many of these meritorious pursuits as possible, the Jaina layman may hope to gain rebirth in a heaven or a bhoga-bhūmi. As for charity to non-Jainas, such practice is considered somewhat beneficial but not really conducive to meaningful spiritual progress.

Sāmāyika: The Attainment of Equanimity

The actions associated with guru-upāsti and dāna bring the layman into continuous contact with a teacher, who serves as both example and counselor. But performance of what is perhaps the most highly regarded of Jaina rituals is by nature rather more solitary. This is sāmāyika (seen earlier as the first śikṣāvrata and the fourth pratimā), a practice of great antiquity wherein the layman's religious activities are integrated with the yogic methods of the ascetic path. The term sāmāyika was first used in canonical texts with reference to a restraint (saṃyama) undertaken by Mahāvīra when he renounced the world; there it involved nothing less than the lifetime abandonment of all evil acts. For ordinary laymen, however, it indicates a restraint of short duration and functions mainly as a meditational exercise. The derivation of the term is not completely clear. Proceeding from the root *i, aya* to go, it has been understood both as "attaining equanimity" and as "fusion with the true self" (becoming fixed in jñāna-cetanā, pure self-awareness). Both of these definitions render sāmāyika equivalent to the progressive detachment of one's consciousness from all external objects. The famous Digambara ācārya Jaṭāsiṃhanandi supports this interpretation with the following verse:

> Equanimity towards all beings;
> self-control and pure aspirations;
> abandonment of every thought

> which is tainted by desire or aversion;
> that, truly, is considered sāmāyika.[39]

Śvetāmbaras have preserved a certain ritual formula through which a layman begins sāmāyika in the presence of a teacher. This is ordinarily done at sunset, when the day's activities are over and one is well-composed and ready to pull himself away from worldly preoccupations.[40] Approaching a monk (and perhaps carrying a whisk broom [*rajoharaṇa*] to symbolize his temporary "ascetic" status), he makes obeisance and says:

> I undertake, venerable one, the sāmāyika, renouncing for as long as I worship the mendicants (that is, remain in your company) all harmful activities, both those which might be done by myself or which I might cause to be done by others. I will not engage in such activities with either mind, speech, or body, nor will I cause others to engage in them (in those ways.) I confess, sir, all my blameworthy acts; I accept censure and truly repent for every one of them, and I cast aside my former self (which committed these deeds).[41]

Having made the resolve, the layman sits in a yogic posture and begins his meditation.

Digambaras retain this ancient formula only for the use of monks and advanced laypeople; hence they have composed a number of recitations suitable for the ordinary householder. These may include confession of past misdeeds, the pledge to undertake further restraints, or hymns in praise of the Jinas; in every case, the point of such recitations is the "dwelling in one's self" towards which the overall ritual is aimed.

39. samatā sarvabhūteṣu saṃyame śubhabhāvanāḥ/ ārtaraudraparityāgas taddhi sāmāyikaṃ matam// *Varāṅgacaritra*: xv, 122. Compare: tyaktārtaraudradhyānasya tyaktasāvadyakarmaṇaḥ/ muhūrtaṃ samatā yā tāṃ viduḥ sāmāyikavratam// *Yogaśāstra*: iii, 82.

40. A person who has undertaken the sāmāyikavrata will, of course, engage in this practice more frequently: at dawn and noon as well as sunset.

41. "karemi bhante sāmāiyaṃ savvaṃ sāvajjaṃ jogaṃ paccakkhāmi jāva sāhu pajjuvāsāmi duvihaṃ tiviheṇaṃ maṇeṇaṃ vāyāe kāyeṇaṃ na karemi karāvemi tassa bhante paḍikkamāmi nindāmi appāṇaṃ vosirāmi." Quoted in *JY*: 132

The temporary renunciation that constitutes lay sāmāyika must be a very ancient practice in Jainism, since it is referred to in the Buddhist scripture. The Buddhist reference is a derisive one, stating that:

> The Nigaṇṭhas call their laypeople on the uposatha (fasting) days, saying "Come here, sir. Abandoning all your clothes, speak thus: 'I belong to no one; I am nothing to anyone. I own nothing; nothing owns me.'" Having spoken thus, and having thus renounced all his possessions, (the layman) later returns and reclaims all that he has "given away." This kind of renunciation is nothing but a sham![42]

Representing a hostile point of view, this account of sāmāyika ignores, or is unaware of, the true spirit of the ceremony. By undertaking such a temporary practice the layman ritually expresses his determination to ultimately renounce everything forever; he gains, moreover, a real taste (however brief) of the ascetic experience. Even today a Digambara performing sāmāyika in the privacy of his household takes off most or all of his clothes prior to arranging his limbs in the meditative posture. Jainas of all sects, having once assumed this posture, repudiate all goods and relations and resolve to sit, unmoving and undistracted, for up to forty-eight minutes. The tranquillity of the mind is at first increased by forgiving, and begging forgiveness of, the entire world of beings. We have already observed, with reference to the saṃvatsarī festival, the great importance which Jainas attach to such pleas for forgiveness. Even in the absence of the beings addressed and even though most of those beings (the lower animals and single-sense life forms) remain unaware that they have ever been harmed, these pleas are believed to remove from

42. atthi, Visākhe, Nigaṇṭhā nāma samaṇajātikā, te . . . tadah' uposathe sāvakaṃ evaṃ samādapenti: ehi tvaṃ, ambho purisa, sabbacelāni nikkhipitvā evaṃ vadehi, 'nāhaṃ kvaci kassaci kiñcanatasmiṃ, na ca mama kvacani kassaci kiñcanaṃ n'atthī 'ti . . . so tasmā rattiyā accayena bhoge adinnaṃ yeva paribhuñjati. idaṃ tassa adinnādānasmiṃ vadāmi. evaṃ kho, Visākhe, Nigaṇṭhuposatho na mahapphalo . . . *Aṅguttaranikāya*: I, 206.

one's heart all anger and resentment caused by or directed towards others.

Having thus put his mind at ease, the aspirant further expresses his feelings for others by saying:

> Friendship towards all beings,
> Delight in the qualities of virtuous ones,
> Utmost compassion for afflicted beings,
> Equanimity towards those who are not
> well-disposed towards me.
> May my soul have such dispositions as these
> forever.[43]

Finally, he carries his mind to a deep level of meditation on the self by inwardly repeating one of the many recitations (sāmāyika-pāṭha) intended for this purpose, such as the one that follows.[44]

> As long as I am seated in this meditation,
> I shall patiently suffer all calamities
> that may befall me, be they caused
> by an animal, a human being, or a god.
> I renounce, for the duration (of this meditation),
> my body, all food, and all passions.[45]
> Attachment, aversion, fear, sorrow, joy,
> anxiety, self-pity . . . all these
> I abandon with body, mind, and speech.
> I further renounce all delight and all repulsion
> of a sexual nature.[46]
> Whether it is life or death, whether gain or loss,
> Whether defeat or victory, whether meeting
> or separation,

43. sattveṣu maitrīṃ guṇiṣu pramodaṃ, kliṣṭeṣu jīveṣu kṛpāparatvam/ mādhyasthabhāvaṃ viparītavṛttau, sadā mamātmā vidadhātu deva// Amitagati's *Dvātriṃśatikā*: k 1. See *NNP*: 21.

44. These verses are quoted from *NNP*: 21–24.

45. tairaścaṃ mānavaṃ daivam upasargaṃ sahe 'dhunā/ kāyāhārakaṣāyādīn pratyākhyāmi triśuddhitaḥ// k 9.

46. rāgaṃ dveṣaṃ bhayaṃ śokaṃ praharṣautsukyadīnatāḥ/ vyutsṛjāmi tridhā sarvām aratiṃ ratim eva ca// k 10.

Whether friend or enemy, whether pleasure or pain,
I have equanimity towards all.[47]
In (the attainment of) knowledge, insight,
and proper conduct,
(the cause) is invariably nothing but
my own soul;
(Similarly), my soul (is the primary cause) for both
the influx (of karmas) and the stopping[48] (of that influx).
One and eternal is my soul,
Characterized by intuition and knowledge;
All other states that I undergo are external to me,
for they are formed by associations.[49]
Because of these associations
My soul has suffered the chains of misery;
Therefore I renounce with body, mind, and speech,
all relationships based on such associations.[50]
Thus have I attained to equanimity
and to my own self-nature.
May this state of equanimity be with me
until I attain to salvation.[51]

Extensive practice enables the meditator to enter, by this means, states in which his mind is withdrawn from all results of karmas and from any belief in the self as effective agency ("I caused this," "I did that"). Such a temporary experience of abandoning the body (kāyotsarga) is reputed to be quite common among lay practitioners of sāmāyika. Jaina lawbooks repeatedly commend this ritual as the highest form of spiritual discipline. One ancient commentary goes so far as to claim that "during the time

47. jīvite maraṇe lābhe 'lābhe yoge viparyaye/ bandhāvarau sukhe duḥkhe sarvadā samatā mama// k 11.

48. ātmaiva me sadā jñāne darśane caraṇe tathā/ pratyākhyāne mamātmaiva tathā saṃvarayogayoḥ// k 12.

49. eko me śāśvataś cātmā jñānadarśanalakṣaṇaḥ/ śeṣā bahirbhavā bhāvāḥ sarve saṃyogalakṣaṇāḥ// k 13.

50. saṃyogamūlaṃ jīvena prāptā duḥkhaparamparā/ tasmāt saṃyogasambandhaṃ tridhā sarvaṃ tyajāmy aham// k 14.

51. evaṃ sāmāyikāt samyak sāmāyikam akhaṇḍitam/ vartatāṃ muktimāninyā vaśīcūrṇāyitaṃ mama// k 15.

of sāmāyika, a layman indeed becomes an ascetic." Or again: "He who practices sāmāyika is like a monk over whom clothes have been draped."[52] This is high praise indeed for one who has not actually taken the mahāvratas. And yet it is warranted, from the Jaina perspective, for such an individual has had at least some taste of the tranquillity and bliss which prevail once the pratyākhyānāvaraṇa passions (those which prevent an aspirant from taking the great vows) have been overcome. This sublime experience will sustain him even when he returns to his family and to the bustle of everyday life, drawing him again and again to the inner refuge he has discovered. Thus the very austerity which makes the mendicant path seem so difficult initially tends at last to become its primary attraction; by moving towards full-time practice of sāmāyika, the layman may find peace in the midst of whatever worldly problems surround him. Clearly, then, the purpose of this ritual goes beyond mere temporary attainment of equanimity; it aims, finally, at leading the layman voluntarily and irrevocably into the vows and life of an ascetic.

The sāmāyika is concluded with the universal prayer of the Jainas:

Dukkhakkhavo kammakkhavo
samāhimaraṇaṃ ya bohilāho ya/
ṃama hou jagadabandhava
jiṇavara tava caraṇasaraṇena//[53]

Cessation of sorrow,
Cessation of karmas,
Death while in meditation,
The attainment of enlightenment;

52. "sāmāiyammi u kae samaṇo iva sāvao havai jamhā/ eeṇa kāraṇeṇaṃ bahuso sāmāiyaṃ kujjā." Quoted in *JY*: 133 (from *Āvaśyaka-niryukti*). Compare: sāmayike sārambhāḥ parigrahā naiva santi sarve 'pi/ celopasṛṣṭamunir iva gṛhī tadā yāti yatibhāvam// *RŚr*: iv, 12.

53. *NNP*: 89.

O holy Jina! friend of the entire universe,
  let these be mine,
For I have taken refuge at your feet.

Sallekhanā: The Holy Death

The third line of the prayer just quoted, "Death while in meditation" (*samādhi-maraṇa*), expresses a rather extraordinary aspiration which may truly be said to be held by every Jaina. Indeed, all Indian religions consider the last moments of a person's life to be of utmost importance in determining the condition of his subsequent incarnation. Many Hindus, for example, believe that one is reborn in a state reflecting his strongest attachment at the moment of death. Hence they may name their children after certain divinities, hoping that, should one's last thoughts fall upon these beloved family members, the names will remind him or her to concentrate instead upon the gods and thus gain rebirth in heaven. Buddhists have developed several rituals which aim to give a certain amount of influence over one's destiny; these pertain not only to the time just prior to death, but also to the so-called *antarā-bhava* (Tibetan *bar-do*),[54] or "intermediate state" between leaving one body and assuming another. Both Hindu and Buddhist approaches to this problem involve "outside help"—divine intervention or the efforts of a tantric master, respectively.

For Jainas, who have emphasized the importance of control over the life-to-life transition far more than any other Indian school, the process depends completely upon the aspirant himself. By dying in meditation he is able to choose the precise circumstances of his end. The point is to meet death with all of one's faculties functioning properly, in a state of complete awareness and freedom from infractions against whatever vratas have been undertaken. If, for example, a person allows his vows to fall into disuse

54. See *Abhidharmakośa-bhāṣya*: 120–127 (III, k 10–16); Evans-Wentz 1971: 85–196.

due to the onset of infirmity or senility, he will pass his final hours in *asaṃyama*, nonrestraint; such an unfortunate circumstance, it is believed, will adversely affect his next birth.

Having spent a lifetime in pursuit of proper conduct (cāritra), it behooves a Jaina to prevent the process of aging from undermining his practice. Thus he may seek death in the holy manner called sallekhanā; following this procedure is strongly recommended for mendicants and forms an important goal among numerous laymen as well.[55] (The latter may often choose to take the mahāvratas during performance of this final ritual.) In every case, Jaina teachers are careful to stress the need for "pure means" in undertaking a "controlled" death. They object strenuously, for example, to the sort of practice described in certain Hindu scriptures wherein yogins of young age and good health are voluntarily entombed while in meditation, hoping to please their gods and attain endless bliss by this "self-offering." Jumping from holy peaks or disappearing into the sea while in deep trance are similarly decried. Though Jainas are willing to ascribe good (spiritual) *motives* to individuals who commit such acts, they nevertheless consider these forms of suicide to be absolutely improper and to lead one only to rebirth in hell. Jaina tradition is adamant on this point; even the famous King Śreṇika,[56] a contemporary of Mahāvīra and a great patron of Jainism, is said to have fallen into a hellish destiny when, after having been imprisoned by his son, he took his own life in an "impure" manner.

There is only one way, then, that a Jaina can legitimately attain samādhi-maraṇa: by gradual fasting, carried out in strict accord with ritual prescription and in most cases under the close supervision of his mendicant teachers. The

55. Āśādhara goes so far as to declare that even lay discipline is fully completed only by sallekhanā: samyktvam amalam amalāny aṇuguṇaśikṣāvratāni maraṇānte/ sallekhanā ca vidhinā pūrṇaḥ sāgāradharmo 'yam// *SD*: i, 12.

56. See Seṇiya in Mehta 1970–1972: II, 856–857; *UP*: lxxiv, 388–452.

term sallekhanā applies here in the sense of "properly thinning out (the passions and the body)."[57] Jaina lawbooks list four situations in which sallekhanā can be performed: (1) *upasarga*, an unavoidable calamity (for example, captivity by an enemy) that makes keeping one's vows impossible; (2) *durbhikṣā*, a great famine, during which there is no way to obtain acceptable food, much less to do so in the proper manner; (3) *jarā*, old age, defined by the onset of such problems as blindness, inability to walk without help, or senility, any of which make one likely to fall away from his vratas; (4) *niḥpratīkārā rujā*, a terminal illness from which death is imminent.[58]

Any one of these situations can be considered grounds for undertaking a fast unto death, but it is almost always the third or fourth that lead an aspirant to perform this sacred ritual. For Jainas the essential difference between a "pure" and an "impure" suicide is that the latter always involves an *increase* in the passions, hence it cannot be a holy death. But in sallekhanā, it is said that one does not actively engage in any destructive, passion-tinged activity; he merely withdraws conscientiously from the taking of food, doing so in a gradual manner which never disrupts his inner peace or dispassionate mindfulness.[59] Whether or not this distinction can be justified, there is no doubt that over the centuries many Jainas of both sexes have in fact fasted to death, invariably secure in the belief that theirs was a noble and sacred act; hundreds of inscriptions all over India record and glorify such cases.[60]

57. upavāsādibhiḥ kāyaṃ kaṣāyaṃ ca śrutāmṛtaiḥ/ saṃlikhya gaṇamadhye syāt samādhimaraṇodyamī// *SD*: viii, 15.

58. upasarge durbhikṣe jarasi rujāyāṃ ca niḥpratīkāre/ dharmāya tanuvimocanam āhuḥ sallekhanām āryāḥ// *RŚr*: v, 1.

59. syān matam ātmavadhaḥ prāpnoti, svābhisandhipūrvakāyurādinivṛtteḥ. naiṣa doṣaḥ, apramattatvāt. "pramattayogāt prāṇavyaparopaṇaṃ hiṃsā" ity uktam. na cāsya pramādayogo 'sti. kutaḥ? rāgādyabhāvāt. rāgadveṣamohāviṣṭasya hi viṣaśastrādyupakaraṇaprayogavaśād ātmānaṃ ghnataḥ svaghāto bhavati. na sallekhanāṃ pratipannasya rāgādayaḥ santi tato nātmavadhadoṣaḥ. *SS*: §705. On the legal aspects of sallekhanā, see Tukol 1976.

60. For a few records of sallekhanā at Shravanabelgola, see inscription nos. 67, 118, 258, 389 in Narasimhachar 1923.

It has been seen that sallekhanā is most often undertaken by mendicants; even so, it has been common enough among laymen to be properly regarded as a significant aspect of lay ritual. Any Jaina facing death or an unavoidable falling away from his vows can approach a teacher and express the wish to embark upon this sacred path by saying:

> Please instruct me, sir. I have come forward to seek . . . sallekhanā, (the vow of) which will remain in force as long as I live. I am free of all doubts and anxieties in this matter. I renounce, from now until the moment of my last breath, food and drink of all kinds.[61]

If the teacher agrees to administer the vow of sallekhanā, he first informs the aspirant that the vow will not be properly kept if it is tainted by any desires pertaining to rebirth (wishing to go to heaven, and so on), to the extension of the current life-span, to a rapid death (if the aspirant is unhappy or in pain), or to the prospect of sensual pleasures in the future which were not attained in this life.[62] Such bartering of penances for worldly gain or pleasure (known as *nidāna*) is viewed with the greatest repugnance. Although mundane benefits are said to accrue automatically to the performance of virtuous deeds, performing such deeds *in order to obtain* these benefits can only be counterproductive; Jainas at all levels of spiritual development are warned against doing so. Even the wish to be reborn as a Tīrthaṅkara would be, strictly speaking, a form of nidāna.

The Jaina must turn away from the results of his deeds, renouncing these "fruits" as he does everything else. Having understood this admonition, the aspirant receives the

61. ahaṃ bhaṃte, apacchimamāraṇaṃtiyasaṃlehaṇājhūsaṇā-ārāhaṇāsamae . . . ṇissallo hoūṇa . . . jāvajjīvāe . . . savvaṃ asaṇaṃ pāṇaṃ khāimaṃ sāimaṃ cauvvihaṃ pi āhāraṃ paccakkhāmi . . . carimehiṃ ussāsaṇissāsehiṃ vosirāmi . . . *Suttāgame*: II, App. III.

62. jīvitamaraṇāśamse bhayamitrasmṛtinidānanāmānaḥ/ sallekhanāticārāḥ pañca jinendraiḥ samādiṣṭāḥ// *RŚr*: v, 8.

vrata and then proceeds to engage in confession (pratikramaṇa), self-censure (*ālocanā*), and the ritual of forgiving and asking forgiveness discussed earlier. He next embarks upon a program of gradual renunciation with regard to eating. The teacher, judging his ability to withstand hunger and thirst, stipulates a certain amount of food and water to be allowed at the outset, then sets down the extent to which this should be decreased each day. Eventually the intake of solid food is reduced to nothing; the aspirant then subsists on liquids of a progressively less sustaining nature, for example, from milk to fruit juice to plain boiled water. It is at the "water only" stage that a layman, perceiving that his death is near, often takes the mahāvratas as noted above.

In ancient times it may well have been permitted for any Jaina to initiate the sallekhanā fast on his own, but the practice seems to have come under greater ecclesiastical supervision in the postcanonical period. Today only a mendicant is normally given this freedom; lay aspirants must first receive the vow of sallekhanā from a member of the clergy (except in the rare circumstances of calamity or famine referred to earlier). If the layperson is too ill to move, a monk comes to his bedside to administer the vow. Jainas are quick to point out the difference between such a practice and that of the common suicide, wherein a person tells no one of his deed and commits it in secret.

Occasionally, it may happen that a supposedly "fatal" illness undergoes remission or complete cure during the course of progressive fasting. In such cases the vows which have been taken cannot be rescinded; the aspirant must continue to take no more food per day than his current allotment for as long as he lives. This possibility explains the usual practice of refraining from a vow of *total* fasting until such time as death is clearly at hand.

A prolonged and eventually terminal withdrawal from food may strike the reader as a very unpleasant process. It must be borne in mind, however, that those who follow such a course will have already gained extensive experience of fasting during their prior religious practice, hence will be able to tolerate the rigors of sallekhanā with their contentment and mindfulness undisturbed. Indeed, a request to undertake this holy fast is not granted lightly; part of the teacher's role is to determine whether a given individual has in fact attained the level of discipline and spiritual development required.[63]

The fasting is done either at one's home or in a special fasting hall where certain mendicants reside. In either case, though the aspirant remains in virtual seclusion, his act is in a real sense a public one; the family has given its consent, and every person in the local community is aware of what is happening. In conjunction with sallekhanā, there is renunciation of all possessions and associations; thus one is left totally free of worldly concerns and spends his final hours silently repeating the namaskāra mantra or perhaps listening to it being chanted by others. In this way, it is hoped, he will draw his last breath fully conscious and uttering the names of the holy beings in whom he has taken refuge since the day of his first awakening (samyak-darśana).

Jainas believe that the entire spiritual life of a layman (and, to an even greater extent, of a mendicant) is in fact preparation for such a sacred death. Any person who might waver on this occasion and revert at the very last to a state of nonrestraint (desire) is compared to a warrior who, after years of practicing for battle, flees at the moment when he must actually face it.[64] Those who do pass away in the proper manner are considered to be close to salvation. It is said that their next birth will be in a heaven

63. "It is not unusual to see one of them (as I have) freely choose to die in the way characteristic of the Jainas, ending a life of austerities by abstaining from food altogether. Nevertheless, it is a way of life that many aspire after eagerly; postulants beseech the Master to admit them to it; relations and friends add their entreaties on the applicant's behalf." Renou 1953: 124.

64. nṛpasyeva yater dharmo ciram abhyastino 'stravat/ yudhīva skhalato mṛtyau svārthabhraṃśo 'yaśaḥ kaṭuḥ// *SD*: viii, 17.

or similarly exalted abode, and that within a very few lifetimes they will gain incarnation in the presence of a Tīrthaṅkara, thus being enabled to complete the path which they have so bravely followed.

It is possible to recount any number of well-known cases involving Jainas who crowned a highly spiritual life with the consecrated act of sallekhanā; indeed the death of ācārya Śāntisāgara, with which this book begins, is perhaps the most celebrated modern example. But there is one story that stands apart from all others. This forms the first of the *Ten Lectures on the Religious Profession of a Layman* (*Upāsaka-daśāḥ*),[65] which comprise the seventh aṅga of the Jaina canon; it recounts the career of Ānanda, a lay disciple of Mahāvīra who attained all eleven pratimās and finally undertook sallekhanā. Ānanda's life has long been regarded as a model to be emulated by all Jaina laymen; the fact that he renounced great wealth to follow the Jina's path has an especially strong impact upon a community whose members are so often affluent. In addition to illustrating the proper approach to lay practice and setting forth the benefits which result therefrom, this story provides a great insight into the kind of relation that has traditionally existed between layman and mendicant. Thus it serves as an appropriate conclusion to this discussion of lay ritual in Jainism.

The Story of Ānanda, a Lay Disciple of Mahāvīra

During the time of Mahāvīra, in a city called Vāṇijagrāma, capital of the Licchavi nation, there lived a householder called Ānanda. He was a very prosperous man, with wealth unequalled by any person in that city. He possessed forty million measures of gold buried in a safe place, another forty million put out at interest, a well-stocked estate of equivalent value, and forty thousand cattle divided into

65. Text and tr. Hoernle 1888.

four herds. Ānanda was consulted by numerous kings and merchants with regard to every sort of business. He was the pillar of his family, ministering to them and guiding them in all matters. His wife was called Śivānandā—a woman dear to her husband, devoted, attached, and loving. The two of them lived together very happily as householders. Their respective families too, being large and well-established, lived in pleasure and contentment.

At that time the venerable ascetic Mahāvīra visited Vāṇijagrāma and took up residence in a park outside the city. Large numbers of people, together with their king, went to pay their respects and listen to his sermons. The householder Ānanda, having heard this news, reflected thus: "Truly the venerable one is staying here on a visit. This is a most auspicious event. Let me go to pay my respects."

Having made this decision he bathed, adorned himself with his finest clothing, and went out on foot, surrounded by a great retinue and protected by an umbrella held over his head. Walking all the way through the city, he arrived at the park; there, Mahāvīra was residing in a *caitya* (temple) called Dvipalāsa. Approaching this spot, Ānanda circumambulated the sage three times and, having thus expressed his veneration, sat down to listen to the sermon. Then the venerable Mahāvīra expounded the law to the householder Ānanda, and to the large company of people present on that occasion. When the congregation had departed, Ānanda, pleased and elated, spoke thus:

> Venerable sir, I believe in the doctrine of the Nigaṇṭhas; I am convinced of the Nigaṇṭha doctrine; I am delighted with it. It is so, sir, it is exactly so. It is true. It is what I accept. Indeed, sir, it is really so, just as you have declared it. Venerable sir, although many nobles, bankers, and merchants have, upon hearing your sermon, renounced the household life and entered the monastic state, I, sir, cannot do the same. But I will, in your presence, take upon myself the twelve-fold restraint of a householder, consisting of the five aṇuvratas, three

guṇavratas, and the four śikṣāvratas. May it so please you, venerable sir, not to deny me this honor.

Then the householder Ānanda, in the presence of the venerable ascetic Mahāvīra, renounced all gross forms of injury to living beings, saying: "As long as I live . . . [see Chapter VI, n. 35] I will not do it, nor cause it to be done, either in thought, word, or deed."

Next he renounced all grossly lying speech and all gross taking of things not given; he also limited himself to contentment with his wife and restricted his possessions by pledging not to accumulate further wealth in any form. Similarly, he renounced the various kinds of activities dealt with by the other vratas. At this point the venerable Mahāvīra addressed Ānanda, saying: "Truly, Ānanda, you have now become a disciple of the ascetic [*śramaṇopāsaka*]; you must now be aware of the transgressions pertaining to all twelve vratas, and must avoid them."

Then the householder Ānanda, having formally taken the vows administered to him, praised and worshiped the venerable ascetic Mahāvīra and solemnly spoke to him thus:

> Truly, venerable sir, it does not befit me, from this day forward, to praise or worship any man of a heterodox community, or any of the objects of reverence of a heterodox community. Neither should I address nor converse with one of their teachers unless he first addresses me, nor give food or drink to such teachers, except if it be required by the king, or by the elders, or by the exigencies of life. On the other hand, it behooves me, venerable sir, to devote myself to providing the ascetics of the Nigaṇṭha faith with pure and acceptable food and other provisions permitted to them: clothes, blankets, alms bowls, medicines, and the like.[66]

66. tae ṇaṃ se Āṇande gāhāvaī samaṇassa bhagavao Mahāvīrassa antie pañcāṇuvvaiyaṃ sattasikkhāvaiyaṃ duvālasavihaṃ sāvayadhammaṃ paḍivajjai . . . evaṃ vayāsī: "no khalu me, bhante, kappai ajjappabhiiṃ annautthie vā annautthiyadevayāṇi vā vandittae vā namaṃsittae vā, puvviṃ aṇālatteṇaṃ ālavittae vā saṃlavittae vā, tesiṃ asaṇaṃ vā pāṇaṃ vā khāimaṃ vā sāimaṃ

Having thus promised and having engaged in religious discourse with his teacher, Ānanda respectfully took leave of the venerable ascetic Mahāvīra and returned from the park to his home. Calling his wife to him, he said:

> Truly, beloved of the gods, I have listened to the law in the presence of the venerable ascetic Mahāvīra, and that dharma is what I desire, what I accept, what I am pleased by. So now, beloved of the gods, go and praise the venerable ascetic and listen to his sermon, and take upon thyself in his presence the twelve-fold restraint of the householder.

Then Śivānandā did as he said, receiving the same vratas in a similar manner as had her husband. After some time, the venerable ascetic Mahāvīra went away to a different part of the country. Ānanda and Śivānandā, having become his disciples, devoted themselves to mindfully keeping their vows and honoring the Nigaṇṭha mendicants with due charity. Fourteen years passed thus, during which time the śramaṇopāsaka Ānanda trained himself with constant exercise in the moral restraints imposed by his vows, as well as in those called for under the various seasonal abstentions. Then, during one night in the fifteenth year of his discipline, as he reflected upon his progress, it occurred to him:

> Truly I am the support of numerous families in this city; I have many responsibilities. But because of this situation I have been hindered from living in complete conformity with the teachings and restraints received in the presence of the venerable ascetic Mahāvīra. It is better, indeed, that after sunrise tomorrow I should place my eldest son in charge of my household; then I may repair to the fasting hall of my community and live there, leading a life in which I fully observe the vratas of a householder.

---

vā dāuṃ vā aṇuppadāuṃ vā, nannattha rāyābhiogeṇaṃ gaṇābhiogeṇaṃ balābhiogeṇaṃ devayābhiogeṇaṃ gurūniggaheṇaṃ vittikantāreṇaṃ. kappai me samaṇe nigganthe phāsueṇaṃ esaṇijjeṇaṃ asaṇapāṇakhāimasāimeṇaṃ vatthapaḍiggahakambalapāyapuṃchaṇeṇaṃ . . . paḍilābhemāṇassa viharittae" tti kaṭṭu eyārūvaṃ abhiggahaṃ abhigiṇhai . . . uvāgacchai. *Upāsakadaśāḥ*: i, §6.

Accordingly, on the next morning he invited all his friends and relatives to his home and fed them abundantly. The meal completed, he appointed his son the head of the family, and addressed them all, saying: "Do not thou, my beloved son, nor you, my dear friends, any of you, from this day onwards, ask me or consult me regarding any of the manifold affairs with which I was hitherto connected. Nor should you cook or prepare any food for my sake."

Then Ānanda took leave of his friends and kinsmen, went out of the house, and walked to a suburb of the city in which was located the fasting hall belonging to his own community.[67] He swept the grounds of the hall, spread a bed of grass, and placed himself upon it. He continued to live there, in accord with the rules, taking one after another of the eleven pratimās for a full period of five-and-a-half years; he persevered in the performance of ascetic practices (mainly fasting), and became extremely thin. Then Ānanda reflected as follows:

> Truly, through these ascetic exercises, I have become reduced to a skeleton. While there is still within me the vigor and energy of faith, therefore, I should, after sunrise tomorrow, devote myself to a determined sallekhanā that ends in death, renouncing all food and drink and patiently awaiting my end.[68]

Then the śramaṇopāsaka Ānanda, by reason of his splendid transformation and the purity of his extraordinary resolution, gained a supernatural vision which enabled him to see, from where he sat, an area of five-hundred *yojanas* (a yojana is eight or nine miles) across the earth, as well as upwards to the first heaven and downwards to the first hell.

67. It is evident that Śivānandā did not accompany her husband to the fasting hall. She apparently led the life of a widow keeping the vows she has assumed earlier.

68. taṃ jāva me atthi uṭṭhāṇe saddhādhiisaṃvege jāva ya me dhammāyarie dhammovadesae samaṇe bhagavaṃ Mahāvīre jiṇe suhatthī viharai tāva tā me seyaṃ kallaṃ jāva jalante apacchimamāraṇantiyasaṃlehaṇājhūsaṇājhūsiyassa bhattapāṇapaḍiyāikkhiyassa kālaṃ aṇavakaṃkhamāṇassa viharittae . . . *Upāsakadaśāḥ*: i, §12.

Now it happened that at that very time the venerable ascetic Mahāvīra again arrived in Vāṇijagrāma for a visit, accompanied by his gaṇadhara, the venerable Indrabhūti Gautama. This Gautama was given to the habit of taking food only once every six days. On one such day he went around the city with his begging bowl, moving from house to house collecting alms. There he heard from various people of the great austerities of the householder Ānanda and about his vow of sallekhanā. The venerable Gautama decided to go and see him, and so proceeded to the place where Ānanda was residing in seclusion. When Ānanda saw the venerable Gautama approaching, his heart was filled with happiness and he spoke to him thus:

> Truly, venerable sir, I have now become, through my vratas, reduced to a skeleton. I am therefore unable to come forward into your presence in order to salute you and bow my head to your feet. So please, venerable sir, graciously take the trouble to come near me so that I may do so.

And when the venerable Gautama had approached, Ānanda respectfully saluted him and asked: "Is it so, venerable sir, that a householder, one who has not become a monk, can indeed win the power of supernatural sight?"

And Gautama answered, "Yes, it is so."

Then Ānanda continued: "If that is so, venerable sir, I would like to inform you that I can see an area of five-hundred yojanas across the earth, and upwards to the first heaven, and downwards to the first hell."

Then the venerable Gautama said to Ānanda, the disciple of the ascetic: "I do maintain, Ānanda, that a householder can indeed possess supernatural sight, but not to such an extent as you claim. Therefore, Ānanda, it is only fitting that you should acknowledge your infraction in this matter [exaggeration, a violation of the satya-vrata] and perform a penance in expiation."

Then the householder Ānanda answered: "Is it required by the law of the Jina, sir, that one should take upon oneself a penance for speaking of things which are real and actual?"

Gautama replied, "No, it is not so required."

And Ānanda said: "If, sir, what you have said is true, then you, venerable one, should indeed yourself acknowledge an infraction in this matter and undertake a penance in expiation thereof."[69]

Then the venerable Gautama, having been spoken to thus by Ānanda the householder, was unsettled and filled with doubt. He departed from that place and returned to the Dvipalāsa caitya, where the venerable ascetic Mahāvīra was residing. Having reported the entire incident, he asked: "Venerable sir, tell me, is it for Ānanda, your lay disciple, to acknowledge his transgression in this matter and to take a penance upon himself, or is it for me to do so?"

Then the venerable ascetic Mahāvīra, turning to Gautama, said without hesitation: "Indeed Gautama, it is you who should acknowledge transgression in this matter and take a penance upon yourself. And you should forgive his rudeness in contradicting you."[70] The venerable Gautama, saying "so be it," humbly accepted the decision of the venerable ascetic Mahāvīra. Having done so, he acknowledged his transgression, took an expiation upon himself, and forgave Ānanda.

Mahāvīra and his gaṇadharas then went away to live in another place. At that time the śramaṇopāsaka Ānanda, having persevered for twenty years as a lay servant of the ascetic and having conscientiously observed the twelve vratas and eleven pratimās of a layman, undertook the course of sallekhanā, which ends in death, for a period of one month. During this period he consumed only water.

69. That is, Gautama showed carelessness of the truth by expressing his view on the possible extent of a layman's supernatural vision in a most positive manner, when in fact he was incorrect. He should have said: "I do not know."

70. samaṇe bhagavaṃ Mahāvīre bhagavaṃ Goyamaṃ evaṃ vayāsī: "Goyamā, tumaṃ ceva ṇaṃ tassa ṭhāṇassa āloehi jāva paḍivajjāhi, Āṇandaṃ ca samaṇovāsayaṃ eyamaṭṭhaṃ khāmehi." *Upāsakadaśāḥ*: i, §15.

At the end of the month, having confessed his transgressions and begged forgiveness of all beings, he sank into deep meditation and thus attained his mortal end. He was reborn as a celestial being in the first heaven.

When the venerable Gautama came to know of this, he inquired of the venerable ascetic Mahāvīra: "Venerable sir, Ānanda the heavenly being, upon making his descent from the world of the gods, after the termination of his life in heaven, will be reborn in what realm?"

And Mahāvīra replied: "Gautama, he will take human form in the great Videha country, and there he will attain to arhatship."[71]

71. Āṇande ṇaṃ bhante, deve tāo devalogāo . . . caittā kahiṃ . . . uvavajjihii? Goyamā, Mahāvidehe vāse sijjhii. Ibid.: i, §15.

VIII

The Mendicant Path and the Attainment of the Goal

The Meaning of Total Renunciation

The rigorous and extensive restraints undertaken by an advanced Jaina layperson may well seem virtually identical to those of the bona fide mendicant. On what basis, then, are the latter described as sarva-virati, "total" renunciation, in contradistinction to the "partial" renunciation of the laity? It was seen in an earlier chapter that only the actual taking of the mendicant vows can indicate "internal attainment of the state of proper conduct," the overcoming of the pratyākhyānāvaraṇa passions. Even an eleventh-pratimā layman, therefore, cannot claim to have reached this state.

In terms of daily practice, moreover, the mendicant is set apart mainly by the manner of his observance of ahiṃsā. Whereas this vrata in its partial form applies only to beings with two or more senses (trasa), it is extended for the monk or nun to include the infinitely larger group of single-sense beings (ekendriya) and element bodies (sthāvara). The importance of recognizing the inviolability of even such subtle creatures is stressed, for example, in the opening portions of the *Ācārāṅga-sūtra*, where it is said:

> Take note—there are innumerable tiny beings individually embodied in earth. Take note—there are some men who truly control themselves, safeguarding even these beings, while

others, (such as the monks of other sects) fail to do so and thus are only pretending to be renunciants.[1]

The *Ācārāṅga-sūtra* goes on to state that the element bodies suffer as do all other living things; their torment is compared to that of a blind and mute person, who can neither see who it is that hurts him nor express his pain. One who injures these minute creatures, therefore, has failed to fully renounce sinful activities; the wise man will neither indulge in nor countenance such behavior.

It has sometimes been suggested that Jaina holy men are overly preoccupied with beings of a lower order, to the detriment of their concern for higher animals or with humankind. But this criticism fails to take into account the fact that a mendicant has *already*, as part of his lay vows, established a pattern of absolutely nonharmful behavior towards the more highly evolved creatures; his attention to the well-being of the ekendriya and element bodies by no means excludes this prior commitment, but rather carries it to the widest possible extent. Indeed, Jainas consider their practice of ahiṃsā unique in the universality of its application.

Bearing these factors in mind, the following rules to which a monk is subject can be properly understood: (1) He must refrain from all acts of digging in the earth, in order to avoid the destruction of earth bodies; (2) he must refrain from all forms of bathing, swimming, wading, or walking in the rain, thus showing proper concern for water bodies; (3) he must protect fire bodies by never extinguishing fires; nor may he light a match or kindle any flame, for such is the evanescent nature of the fire bodies that the very act of producing them is virtually equivalent to causing their destruction; (4) he must refrain from fanning himself, lest he injure air bodies by creating a sudden change of temperature in the air; (5) he must avoid walking on

1. santi pāṇā puḍho siyā, lajjamāṇā puḍho pāsa; aṇagārā 'motti ege pavayamāṇā, jaṃ iṇaṃ virūvarūvehiṃ satthehiṃ puḍhavikammasamārambheṇaṃ . . . aṇegarūve pāṇe vihiṃsai. *AS*: §11–12.

greenery or touching a living plant, since either action might injure certain vegetable bodies.[2]

Perhaps every culture teaches its children to behave with regard for the well-being of other persons and of domestic animals. The normal socialization process, however, provides little or no basis for extending this consideration to the single-sense creatures. Hence the Jaina mendicant must put forth a tremendous effort of mindfulness, consciously establishing a totally new pattern of behavior for which his prior training has in no way prepared him. Undertaking ahiṃsā and the other great vows forces him to become constantly aware of his every action, always on guard against the possibility of committing an infraction. But if the obstacles to such a discipline are great, the rewards are no less so; not only does the spiritual aspirant become established in the holy pattern of proper conduct, but he learns a technique of perpetual attentiveness which will ultimately help him to overcome pramāda (carelessness), the third great cause of bondage.

The question concerning the distinction between mendicants and advanced laypeople, then, can be answered with reference to several criteria: the internal state, the range of applicability of vows, the degree of effort required to avoid transgressions. We are now ready to examine more closely the actual process through which the unique path of the Jaina monk or nun is entered upon.

Initiation into Mendicancy

Formal assumption of the mahāvratas[3] occurs in a ceremony called *dīkṣā* (initiation) or *pravrajyā* (renunciation).

2. For a comprehensive treatment of Jaina monastic law, see Deo 1956; Caillat 1975; Dixit 1976; and above, Ch. II n. 54.

3. In a famous section of the *Ācārāṅga-sūtra* known as Bhāvanā, Mahāvīra is said to have laid down five great vows (mahāvratas) together with their specific practices (*bhāvanā*): tao ṇaṃ samaṇe bhagavaṃ Mahāvīre uppaṇṇaṇāṇadaṃsaṇadhare Goyamāīṇaṃ samaṇāṇaṃ ṇiggaṃthāṇaṃ paṃca mahavvayāiṃ sabhāvaṇāiṃ chajjīvanikāyāiṃ āikkhai . . . taṃ jahā—puḍhavikāe jāva tasakāe// paḍhamaṃ bhaṃte mahavvayaṃ: paccakkhāmi savvaṃ pāṇāivāyaṃ se suhumaṃ vā bāyaraṃ vā . . . tasaṃ vā thāvaraṃ vā ṇeva sayaṃ

This ritual constitutes the symbolic rebirth of the individual; in addition to casting off all lay possessions, he forever abandons the name by which he has theretofore been known. (Ordinarily, the new mendicant will take on the lineage name of his teacher, for example, -nandi, -kīrti, -sena, -candra, -sāgara, -vijaya.)[4] Among the Śvetāmbara, dīkṣā is normally barred to those who are physically or mentally incapacitated, who lack the consent of their parents, who are exconvicts, or who are under eight years old.[5] Similar guidelines determine fitness for admission to the Digambara monkhood; in practice, however, these are supplemented by general understanding among members of this sect that only those of rather advanced age should leave the household life altogether.

Every dīkṣā ceremony is accompanied by great pomp and by the performance of various religious acts in the lay community: Jina-worship, charity in honor of the new initiate, and so forth. Particulars of the ceremony itself vary somewhat among sects. An aspiring Digambara monk, for example, will stand before the teacher and renounce every possession, even his loincloth. (It will be recalled that only thus may the Digambara definition of aparigraha be fulfilled.) He further declares his lifelong acceptance of the mahāvratas, and is given a small whisk

---

pāṇāivāyaṃ karejjā . . . jāvajjīvāe tivihaṃ tiviheṇa maṇasā vayasā kāyasā, tassa bhaṃte paḍikkamāmi niṃdāmi garahāmi appāṇaṃ vosirāmi// . . . ahāvaraṃ doccaṃ mahavvayaṃ, paccakkhāmi savvaṃ musāvāyaṃ . . . taccaṃ mahavvayaṃ, paccakkhāmi savvaṃ adiṇṇādāṇaṃ . . . cautthaṃ mahavvayaṃ, paccakkhāmi savvaṃ mehuṇaṃ . . . paṃcamaṃ mahavvayaṃ, savvaṃ pariggahaṃ paccakkhāmi . . . jāva vosirāmi// icceehiṃ . . . sampaṇṇe aṇagāre āṇāe ārāhie yāvi bhavai// *AS*: §1024–1074. See Jacobi 1884: 202–210. For a discussion on the tradition of the five great vows, see above, Ch. I nn. 32–42.

4. Members of the Sthānakavāsi sect (see Ch. IX) are exceptions to this rule; they retain their household names even as ascetics—a practice which may have originally served to distinguish them from the Śvetāmbaras.

5. In the ancient scriptures, only those who have attained to at least young adulthood appear as members of the monastic order; the practice of admitting eight- or nine-year-old children seems to have first gained legitimacy during medieval times. There have recently been numerous attempts among the Śvetāmbara Jainas to curb this practice. For the monastic rules governing the admission of a layman to the community of monks and nuns, see Deo 1956: 139–142.

broom (rajoharaṇa) made of peacock feathers (*piñchī*), with which to gently remove insects from his sitting or sleeping place. Lengthy chanting of the namaskāra-mantra by those in attendance, both monks and laypeople, accompanies the entire procedure. Certain devotional texts may also be recited at this time, especially the *Siddhabhakti* (In praise of the perfected ones), *Śrutajñānabhakti* (In praise of scriptural knowledge), *Cāritrabhakti* (In praise of proper conduct), *Ācāryabhakti* (In praise of the teachers and their qualities), and *Nirvāṇabhakti* (In praise of mokṣa and of the places where various saints have achieved this state).[6]

Among Śvetāmbaras, the aspirant is given three large pieces of cloth, which constitute his new wardrobe. He also receives a rajoharaṇa made of woolen tufts, a begging bowl, a blanket, a staff, and some volumes of scripture. Sthānakavāsi custom is virtually identical, except that the new monk is given, in addition to the articles noted above, a small strip of cloth called *muh-patti*; this is tied in place over his mouth at all times save during meals, and serves to protect air bodies which might be injured by an unimpeded rush of warm breath. All such "marks" of a monk—whisk broom, face-mask, or whatever—function perhaps as much to identify his sect as to aid him in keeping the mahāvratas.

One aspect of dīkṣā is of special interest in that it is totally unique to Jainism among the mendicant traditions of India. This is *keśa-loca*, the ancient practice (said to have been performed by Mahāvīra himself) of slowly and painfully pulling the hair from one's head in five handfuls. In this manner an aspirant signifies his determination to successfully meet the severe demands of the ascetic life.

We have already noted lay involvement in the ordination process through chanting, devotional and charitable works, and so forth. Much excitement is also generated

6. For the texts of these various *bhaktis*, see *NNP*: 1–28.

among members of a Jaina village on the day following the dīkṣā, for at that time the new monk completes his obligatory initiation-day fast and goes abroad in search of alms for the first time. The householder who provides these alms is considered to earn great merit; indeed, his action not only affirms the traditional bond of interdependence between monk and layman, but symbolically recapitulates the profound moment when Ṛṣabha first received offerings proper to a Jaina holy man.

After taking the mahāvratas, a monk must become totally obedient to his upādhyāya (preceptor) and to his ācārya (the head of his order). He may neither live alone nor seek alms on his own, but should join with two other ascetics to form a *gaṇa*, or residence unit.[7] These three will remain together at all times, staying in a temple, fasting hall, or other suitable quarters and going on their begging rounds as a group. Digambara mendicants, being so few in number, are permitted to live with kṣullakas, ailakas, or brahmacārins. A monk must not share his residence with a nun, nor should he be alone with a nun on any occasion; indeed, all interaction with women is to be kept to a minimum. As for the nuns, they are governed by a kind of "mother superior" who is in turn ultimately responsible to a male ācārya. It will be remembered in this connection that Digambara "nuns" are technically of a lower status than monks in the mendicant order, since they cannot enter a state of ascetic nudity. Śvetāmbara and Sthānakavāsi nuns, however, take the same vows as do their male counterparts and are considered their spiritual equals.[8]

7. The community of monks is divided into various kinds of groups such as *gaṇa, gaccha, gumma, phaḍḍaga, kula.* For details, see Deo 1956: 337ff.

8. It should be noted that brahmanical society has never approved of mendicancy for women; even a widow is required by law to stay in the household under the protection of her son (cf. *Manusmṛti*: ix, 3). As for the Buddhists, it is well known that Śākyamuni agreed only reluctantly to the establishment of a *bhikṣuṇī-saṃgha*; this saṃgha lasted but a few centuries within India and is now practically defunct in the Buddhist countries of Southeast Asia. Thus it appears that Jainism alone favored the idea of an order of nuns. The canon

The Eight Matrices of Doctrine

The purpose of assuming the mahāvratas is to reduce to a minimum the sphere and frequency of activities that would otherwise generate the influx of karmas and the rise of fresh passions. The stopping of karmic influx, called saṃvara,[9] is achieved by various methods; these basically involve control of the senses and the development of extreme mindfulness. More specifically, the Jainas set forth three restraints (*gupti*) and five rules of conduct (*samiti*); taken together these comprise the so-called eight matrices of doctrine (*aṣṭa-pravacana-mātṛkā*),[10] exercises that prepare a monk for the advanced meditational states through which karmic matter is finally eliminated from the soul.

The term gupti refers to a progressive curbing of the activities of mind, body, and speech; hence the monk undertakes long periods of silence, remains motionless for hours on end, strives for the one-pointedness that stills the intellective process, and so forth. The samitis include: (1) care in walking (*īryā-samiti*)—a mendicant must neither run nor jump, but should move ahead slowly, gaze turned downwards, so that he will avoid stepping on any creature no matter how small; (2) care in speaking (*bhāṣā-samiti*)—in addition to observing the vow of truthfulness,

---

speaks of a large number of female mendicants (*sādhvīji*) in the order of Mahāvīra (see above, Ch. I), and even today nuns constitute a majority in both the Śvetāmbara and Sthānakavāsi sects. (See pls. 28 and 30.) According to the most recent census, taken in 1977, the Śvetāmbaras had approximately 1,200 monks and 3,400 nuns, the Stānakavāsis 325 monks and 522 nuns. Among Digambaras, where the number of mendicants has always been small, there were at last count about 65 monks (munis), and sixty kṣullakas and ailakas, and fifty nuns (*āryikās* and *kṣullikās*). [These figures are based upon personal communication from Dr. Nagin J. Shah (Śvetāmbaras), Mr. Kantilal D. Kora (Sthānakavāsis and Terāpanthis), and Pandit Narendra J. Bhisikar (Digambaras).] The preponderance of women (most of whom are widows) in the Jaina mendicant order has yet to be examined from a sociological perspective.

9. abhinavakarmādānahetur āsravaḥ. tasya nirodhaḥ saṃvara ity ucyate. tatra saṃsāranimittakriyānivṛttir bhāvasaṃvaraḥ. tan nirodhe tatpūrvakakarmapudgalādānavicchedo dravyasaṃvaraḥ. *SS*: §785.

10. samyagyoganigraho guptiḥ/ īryābhāṣaiṣaṇādānanikṣepotsargāḥ samitayaḥ/ *TS*: ix, 4-5. "edāo aṭṭhapavayaṇamādāo ṇāṇadaṃsaṇacarittaṃ/ rakkhaṃti sadā muṇio mātā puttaṃ va payadāo//" Quoted in *JSK*: III, 149.

he should speak only when absolutely necessary and then in as few words as possible; (3) care in accepting alms (*eṣaṇā-samiti*)—only appropriate food may be taken, and it should be consumed as if it were unpleasant medicine, that is, with no sense of gratification involved; (4) care in picking up things and putting them down (*ādāna-nikṣe-paṇa-samiti*)—whether moving a whisk broom, bowl, book, or any other object, the utmost caution must be observed lest some form of life be disturbed or crushed; (5) care in performing the excretory functions (*utsarga-samiti*)—the place chosen must be entirely free of living things.

The Cultivation of Righteousness and Reflection

A mendicant is encouraged to reinforce his practice of the guptis and samitis by constantly manifesting ten forms of righteousness (*daśa-dharma*):[11] perfect forbearance, perfect modesty, perfect uprightness, perfect truthfulness, perfect purity, perfect restraint, perfect austerity, perfect renunciation, perfect nonattachment, and perfect continence. Each of these is of course already included in some aspect of the mahāvratas; the purpose of their restatement is to remind the aspirant at *every* moment of the necessity to remain fixed in proper conduct. He must also engage repeatedly in twelve mental reflections (*anuprekṣā*)[12] upon certain conditions of the universe, of human existence, and so forth; contemplation of such things will ostensibly increase his detachment from the world, protect him from any tendencies toward heretical views, and spur his efforts towards final enlightenment.

The twelve anuprekṣā are: (1) The transitoriness of everything that surrounds one; (2) the utter helplessness of beings in the face of death; (3) the relentless cycle of rebirth, with its attendant suffering; (4) the absolute aloneness of

11. uttamakṣamāmārdavārjavaśaucaśatyasaṃyamatapastyāgākiñcanya-brahmacaryāṇi dharmaḥ/ *TS*: ix, 6.

12. Ibid.: ix, 7. See *Kārtikeyānuprekṣā* (Upadhye intro.).

each individual as he moves through this cycle; (5) the fact that soul and body are completely separate from each other; (6) the filth and impurity which in reality permeate a seemingly attractive physical body; (7) the manner in which karmic influx takes place; (8) how such influx can be stopped; (9) how karmas already clinging to the soul can be driven out; (10) fundamental truths about the universe, namely, that it is beginningless, uncreated, and operates according to its own laws—thus each person is responsible for his own salvation, for there is no divinity that might intervene; (11) the rarity of true insight (*bodhi-durlabha*), and the number of creatures who, because they have not been so fortunate as to attain human embodiment, are currently denied the wonderful opportunity to attain mokṣa; (12) the absolutely true teachings of the Jinas (*dharma-svākhyātatva*), how they are most fundamentally expressed through the practice of ahiṃsā, and how they can lead one to the ultimate goal of eternal peace.

Victory over the Afflictions

His resolve bolstered by dwelling upon these thoughts, a new Jaina monk mentally prepares himself to quietly endure all the tribulations that accompany the ascetic life. More than twenty such "typical hardships" are set down for systematic contemplation in a schema called *parīṣaha-jaya*,[13] victory over the afflictions. The aspirant must recall that he is no longer socially acceptable to many people, that he must depend upon the good will of others for even his most basic physical needs, that many discomforts which he has never before experienced will now be his lot forever. Specifically, he must strive for equanimity in the face of hunger, thirst, cold, heat, insect bites, and, for a Digambara, problems which accompany the state of nudity. There can be no ill-feeling over the absence of those

13. mārgācyavananirjarārthaṃ pariṣoḍhavyāḥ parīṣahāḥ/ kṣutpipāsāśīto-ṣṇadaṃśamaśakanāgnyāratistrīcaryāniṣadyāśayyākrośavadhayācanālābharo-gatṛṇasparśamalasatkārapuraskāraprajñājñānādarśanāni/ *TS*: ix, 8–9.

many small pleasures to which he was once accustomed. Further, the sight of a lovely woman must leave him totally unmoved. The pain produced by the constant walking and difficult meditative postures required of a monk must be ignored.

And so the list of discomforts and difficulties to be patiently borne goes on: a hard wooden bed; the scolding, injury, or indignity often visited upon beggars; the disappointment of receiving no alms; the pains of illness, of thorns, of dirt which gathers for want of a bath; the failure of certain persons to approve or praise what he has undertaken or to show the reverence ordinarily due a holy man. One must abandon, moreover, any conceit which might arise from knowing that he has greater spiritual insight than most people; conversely, he should not feel despair because he understands less than a Jina or ācārya. Finally, the monk may never allow himself to succumb, even in the face of great frustration, to the most pernicious of wrong beliefs: that his practices are not efficacious, that austerities bring no spiritual benefit, that he is in fact making a monumental error by following the ascetic path.

Ordering the difficult aspects of monkish existence into a list for contemplation by the beginning ascetic has a dual function. He becomes better able to deal with the reality of these discomforts by virtue of having coped so often with the images thereof. Perhaps even more important, he is reminded by the very existence of such a list that he is not alone in his quest; countless others have undergone similar trials, and have emerged victorious.

Austerities: Internal and External

In addition to observing the restrictions called for by the mahāvratas, Jaina monks ordinarily perform certain voluntary austerities (tapas) intended to aid their spiritual progress. Twelve such practices are considered especially useful; of these, six are "external" and six "internal." The former group involves the deliberate generation of physical afflictions.[14] Hence the aspirant may fast (*anaśana*) for extended periods, or perhaps reduce his food intake to as little as one morsel a day (*avamaudarya*). He may limit to four or five the number of houses to be visited on begging rounds (*vṛtti-parisaṃkhyāna*), thereby making it unlikely that he will receive his normal daily ration. He may refuse to accept stimulating or delicious food (*rasa-parityāga*); thus taking only dry and tasteless fare, he overcomes any undue interest in eating and curbs the tendency to sleep during daylight hours (to nap after a heavy meal). He is encouraged to stay in lonely places (*vivikta-śayyāsana*)—caves, abandoned houses, forests—in order to avoid becoming dependent upon the companionship of others. Finally, he may engage in various mortifications of the body (*kāya-kleśa*); these must be in no way injurious to other beings, so they take such forms as standing in the mid-day sun, maintaining difficult postures for very long periods, or sitting outside during cold weather.

The internal austerities include[15]: repentence (*prāyaścitta*) of transgressions due to negligence; reverence to the elders (*vinaya*); service to other monks, especially when they are ill (vaiyāvṛttya); study of the scriptures (svādhyāya); renunciation of all egoistic thoughts (*vyutsarga*); and the cultivation of trance states (*dhyāna*). Of these, dhyāna is by far the most significant. The long hours of the night are often passed by the mendicant in a state of deep meditation; thus he not only attains great peace of mind but also develops the internal control so necessary to reach the higher guṇasthānas.

Dhyāna: Jaina Meditational Practices

Jaina texts provide surprisingly little information on the details of dhyāna practice. In part this is due to the ācāryas'

14. anaśanāvamaudaryavṛttiparisaṃkhyānarasaparityāgaviviktaśayyāsanakāyakleśāḥ bāhyaṃ tapaḥ/ Ibid.: ix, 19.

15. prāyaścittavinayavaiyāvṛttyasvādhyāyavyutsargadhyānāny uttaram/ Ibid.: ix, 20.

traditional emphasis upon those austerities which lie within the reach of a majority of aspirants; the more refined trance states are normally attainable only by a select group of skilled contemplatives. The very nature of meditation itself, moreover, tends to discourage written exposition; so esoteric a teaching is best conveyed on a personal basis.

What few references to the subject that do exist classify dhyāna into four types.[16] Two of these are cases of one-pointed concentration which may occur spontaneously and which focus upon objects unsuitable for spiritual progress; they are, therefore, to be eliminated. The first, *ārtadhyāna*, involves preoccupation with something unpleasant or sorrowful—the necessity of contact with that which is disagreeable, the loss of loved ones or valued possessions, physical or psychic pain, the desire for theretofore unattained pleasures. The second, *raudradhyāna*, is a sort of "cruel concentration," wherein the individual may dwell upon the perverse pleasures of causing injury to others. It is said that these negative mental states may persist even into the sixth guṇasthāna; they are best avoided by careful practice of the guptis.

The two remaining forms of dhyāna require continuous cultivation and contribute directly to the soul's quest for liberation; they are designated as *dharmadhyāna* (virtuous concentration) and *śukladhyāna* (pure concentration). Dharmadhyāna entails the intense contemplation, for a short period (up to forty-eight minutes), of one of several objects:[17] (1) the teachings of the Jina on the nine tattvas (see Chapter V, n. 30) and how these teachings can best be communicated to others (*ājñāvicaya*); (2) the great misery suffered by other beings (whose minds are impelled by passions and blinded by ignorance) and the means by which these beings can be saved (*apāyavicaya*); (3) the mysterious mechanisms of karmic influx, binding, duration, and outcome and the fact that the soul is funda-

16. ārtaraudradharmyaśuklāni/ pare mokṣahetū/ Ibid.: ix, 28–29.
17. ājñāpāyavipākasaṃsthānavicayāya dharmyam/ Ibid.: ix, 36.

mentally independent of these processes and thus able to disengage itself therefrom (*vipākavicaya*); (4) the structure of the universe and the interplay of causes that brings souls to their particular destinies (*saṃsthānavicaya*).

Diligent practice of these dharmadhyānas leads one to seek more and more the states of omniscience and perfect purity which characterize a Jina; thus he will eventually begin to cultivate the śukladhyānas, through which such states become accessible. Before describing these higher forms of meditation, the relation of dharmadhyāna to the overall scheme of spiritual development must be considered.

It will be recalled that acceptance of the mahāvratas automatically places an aspirant in the sixth guṇasthāna. This stage is called *pramatta-virata,* indicative of the fact that the bond of carelessness (pramāda), as well as the passions (kaṣāya) which produce it, have not yet been overcome. During the short periods when one of the dharmadhyānas is achieved, pramāda is suppressed and the meditator dwells temporarily in the seventh guṇasthāna (called apramatta-virata, restraint free of carelessness); hence the dedicated practitioner of these dhyānas will be constantly moving back and forth between the sixth and seventh guṇasthāna stages. Such experiences of trances free from pramāda are considered by Jainas to be *preparatory* to salvation, but are not in themselves sufficient to overcome the subtle passions which constitute the most tenacious forms of cāritra-mohanīya-karma. Thus it is only with attainment of the *eighth* guṇasthāna (called apūrva-karaṇa, unprecedented spiritual progress) that one actually mounts the *śreṇi* or ladder leading inevitably to mokṣa.[18] Attainment of apūrva-karaṇa cannot occur except through the practice of śukladhyāna.

It is interesting to note that, although Jainas have developed such meditative exercises as sāmāyika and the aforementioned types of dharmadhyāna, they have traditionally

18. For details on the various processes involved in climbing the śreṇi, see *SJP*: 275–280.

paid scant attention to the more magical paths of awakening so heavily favored by other Indian schools. Thus we find in their ancient texts no mention of yogic control over respiration (*prāṇāyāma*), or of the mystical centers of psychic energy (the *kuṇḍalinī* or the *cakras*, for example). Jaina teachers seem to have felt a pronounced repugnance for occult powers and the practices which aimed specifically to generate them; such techniques are considered suitable mainly for destructive purposes, hence to be avoided.[19] Perhaps this attitude can be traced back to Makkhali Gosāla's attempt to kill Mahāvīra with yogic heat; in any case, Jainism has remained for the most part untouched by the sort of tantric practices which typified many Śaivite cults and eventually permeated the Buddhist community as well.[20]

Indeed, we might have remained unaware that the Jainas had been exposed to any tantric influences whatsoever were it not for the fact that four mystical trances, somewhat parallel to those of the dharma type, are recommended by certain authors of medieval times as useful preliminaries to higher (śukla) forms of meditation. These trances, which can be cultivated either by monks or laypeople, are as follows: (1) *piṇḍastha-dhyāna*, concentra-

19. We should not infer that Jainas have been altogether unfamiliar with supernatural abilities. Texts from the earliest times ascribe seemingly magical powers (especially moving without touching the ground) to eminent monks; but these powers are said to be the by-products of meditation and superior insight, rather than a result of "occult" practices.

20. In the medieval period the Jainas did develop a large number of mystical diagrams (*yantras*), as well as rituals (*vidhāna*) associated with them. The yantras, inscribed on metal, contained the names of Tīrthaṅkaras, the syllables of the namaskāra-mantra, and various "seed" syllables sacred to the manifold śāsana-devatās (see Ch. VII n. 13) of the Jaina pantheon. Over forty such yantras are known to exist (see *JSK*: IV, 354–383), although only a few, notably the Ṛṣimaṇḍala, Kalikuṇḍadaṇḍa, Gaṇadharavalaya (see pl. 11), and Siddhacakra are still in use for rituals of propitiation. These rituals were supervised by advanced laymen (yatis, kṣullakas, bhaṭṭārakas, etc.) and were kept strictly within the discipline enjoined by the śrāvakācāras. Mendicants could not take part in the ceremonies, but they could chant the mantras. Lacking the basic ingredient of the tantric cult—fusion of the mundane and the supermundane—such practices seem to have had little effect upon the development of Jainism.

tion upon certain imaginary objects; (2) *padastha-dhyāna*, concentration upon holy chants; (3) *rūpastha-dhyāna*, concentration upon the form of the Jina; (4) *rūpātīta-dhyāna*, concentration upon that which transcends form—the nature of the siddha.[21]

Piṇḍastha-dhyāna basically involves the mystical purification of the physical self. This is accomplished through visualization of certain scenes constructed in the mind from "material" of the four physical elements, earth, fire, air, and water. (The elements must be understood here as the gross types of earth, water, fire, and air encountered in everyday experience, rather than the subtle, invisible elements of all worldly objects postulated by certain brahmanical schools.) Using the earth element, for example, an aspirant mentally creates a vast ocean with a thousand-petalled lotus at its center; he then "enters" this picture, imagining himself seated on a white throne atop the lotus and fully prepared to eliminate all karmas.

Such an exercise (called *pārthivī-dhāraṇā*) is followed by one employing the element of fire. Here the meditator envisions a lotus in his navel, inscribed with sacred syllables from the namaskāra-mantra. He further imagines another lotus possessed of eight petals, representing the four ghātiyā and four aghātiyā karmas, situated in his heart. Flames rise from the navel-lotus to the heart-lotus, burning the eight karma-petals of the latter to ashes. The next step is, of course, to visualize the elimination of even these "ashes" or symbolic residual karmas. This is done in two phases. First the practitioner creates the image of a whirlwind from the element of air; concentrating upon this wind, he causes it to blow into his heart and carry off

21. For a detailed description of these four dhyānas, taken from the Digambara text *Jñānārṇava* (by Śubhacandra, eleventh century) and the Śvetāmbara text *Yogaśāstra* (by Hemacandra, twelfth century), see *SJP*: 285–290. The terms piṇḍastha, padastha, rūpastha, and rūpātīta are not attested in the *Tattvārtha-sūtra* of Umāsvāti, and in the opinion of Tatia are not to be found "anywhere in the Jaina works earlier than the *Jñānārṇava*." Ibid.: 288.

most of the ashes. The few that remain are then washed away completely by a great internal rainstorm, generated from the water element by the process called *vāruṇī-dhāraṇā*. Finally, the yogin completes his practice of piṇḍastha-dhyāna by engaging in *tattva-rūpavatī*, wherein the body is envisioned as totally pure, devoid of all "unclean" substances (phlegm, pus, blood, and so on) and possessing a luster like that of the Jina.

In padastha-dhyāna, the syllables of the namaskāra-mantra are rearranged into various mystical formulas, which the aspirant chants continuously; this procedure is said to confer extraordinary powers, corresponding to the *siddhis* described in yogic texts of other schools. Such powers generally involve control of the physical world—the ability to fly, to produce fire at will, and so forth.

The rūpastha-dhyāna is generated by picturing a Jina in the holy assembly (samavasaraṇa), with particular attention to his overwhelming majesty and splendor. Intensive contemplation of this inspiring image will move the earnest seeker to ever higher levels of spiritual endeavor.

Finally, in rūpātīta-dhyāna, one concentrates upon the various abstract qualities—omniscience, perfect bliss, infinite energy—which constitute the "body" of the siddha or totally liberated being. The visualization skills developed through the previous exercises are here employed to give the meditator a kind of experiential contact with the "ultimate self" (paramātman); that is, he "perceives" a soul in that formless, unfettered state to which he too may someday attain. This experience is of course not equivalent to that of siddhahood; actual perfection of the siddha-qualities can come about only by mounting the śreṇi ladder and climbing upwards through rigorous cultivation of the "pure trances," the śukladhyānas mentioned above. Let us turn now to this final and all-important phase of the Jina's path, for which all the devotions, restraints, and austerities described thus far have been nothing more than preparation.

ŚUKLADHYĀNA: THE "PURE TRANCES"

Four types of śukladhyāna are described in Jaina texts. Of these, the first two are said to operate in the "lower" portions of the śreṇi, the eighth through tenth guṇasthānas, during which there is progressive overcoming (either by suppression or outright elimination) of both the subsidiary passions (no-kaṣāyas) and those very subtle passions described as "smoldering" (saṃjvalana-kaṣāya; see Chapter IV). Specifically, the no-kaṣāyas are rendered inoperative in the eighth and ninth guṇasthāna stages and the saṃjvalana passions in the tenth. As noted earlier, if these processes occur via the mechanism of suppression (upaśama), the aspirant will subsequently reach only the temporary stage called upaśānta-moha, the eleventh guṇasthāna, and will fall again to a lower stage when the passions "resurface," as it were. But eventually his soul will gain sufficient energy to mount the śreṇi with actual *elimination* (kṣaya) of the passions at each stage; thus he will pass over the eleventh guṇasthāna altogether and become established in the twelfth, called kṣīṇa-moha, wherein all mohanīya-karmas will have forever ceased to afflict him.

The two dhyānas through which these attainments are made possible involve discursive concentration upon the nature of the tattvas (existents) as set forth in the Jaina scriptures; thus both are described by the term *savitarka* (accompanied by conceptual thinking). Each of these dhyānas will focus upon a single existent. In the first, however, the meditator's attention continually shifts from one of that existent's countless modes to another, a process known as *vicāra*. Hence this form of concentration is labeled *pṛthaktva-savitarka-savicāra*: accompanied by conceptual thinking applied to various aspects.[22] The second form, by contrast, attests only to a single mode of the

22. tatra dravyaparamāṇuṃ bhāvaparamāṇuṃ vā dhyāyan . . . arthavyañjane kāyavacasī ca pṛthaktvena saṃkramatā manasā . . . mohaprakṛtīr upaśamayan kṣapayaṃś ca pṛthaktvavitarkavīcāradhyānabhāg bhavati. sa eva punaḥ samūlatūlaṃ mohanīyaṃ nirdidhakṣann anantaguṇaviśuddhiyogaviśe-

existent under examination, thus it is called *ekatva-savitarka-avicāra*: accompanied by conceptual thinking applied to one aspect. The correlation between these two types of śukladhyāna and the spiritual processes of the eighth, ninth, and tenth guṇasthānas, especially regarding the precise mechanism whereby the passions are negated, is not fully explained by the Jaina texts. There is no doubt, however, that without cultivating such trances the attainment of the twelfth guṇasthāna would not be possible.

The State of Arhat

Upon entering this twelfth stage, an aspirant reaches the upper portion of the śreṇi; here, his spiritual career is nearly at an end. Having destroyed the mohanīya karmas, which had afflicted him from beginningless time, he realizes the state of perfect purity called *yathākhyāta-cāritra* (conduct exactly conforming to that which has been stated). With the falling away of all factors which prevent proper conduct, moreover, there is a simultaneous end to those which block omniscience, total bliss, and unlimited energy, for all of these varieties of karmic matter have existed in a state of complete interdependence.

Thus the individual now rises spontaneously to the thirteenth guṇasthāna, called sayoga-kevali (possessing omniscience while in the state of embodiment and activity). Characterized by the "four infinities" (knowledge, perception, bliss, energy), this level is in effect the highest possible as long as the state of embodiment persists, and it is one that can be reached only from the human destiny (that is, gods cannot achieve it). A being in the thirteenth guṇasthāna is referred to as arhat, he who is worthy of worship, and kevalin, alone, since he has become fully isolated from the ghātiyā karmas; similarly, the omniscient cognition with which he is endowed is called kevalajñāna.

ṣam āśritya . . . śrutajñānopayogo nivṛttārthavyañjanayogasaṃkrāntiḥ avicalitamanāḥ kṣīṇakaṣāyo vaiḍūryamaṇir iva nirupalepo dhyātvā punar na nivartata ity uktam ekatvavitarkam. *SS*: §906.

Attainment of the Tīrthaṅkara Status

If one who attains to the thirteenth guṇasthāna has previously acquired "the ability to teach"—those wholesome (śubha) nāma-karmas which confer the "nature of a fordmaker" (*tīrthaṅkara-prakṛti*), he will become a propagator of the Jaina tradition, one of the twenty-four Tīrthaṅkaras of his half-cycle. The notion that only so limited a number of arhats achieve Tīrthaṅkarahood seems rather arbitrary; it is tempting to suggest, therefore, that the Jaina teachers have considered certain souls to possess some innate differentiating factor that has made their attainment of this status possible.[23]

Such a distinction *was* well-developed among certain Buddhist sects. The Vaibhāṣikas, for example, defined a Buddha as an enlightened *teacher*, by way of contrast with the enlightened *disciples* or arhats; they further held that only twenty-five Buddhas could appear during a given world-period, and that these beings possessed a quality of omniscience which the arhats lacked.[24] Mahāyānists carried this dichotomy to its logical extreme, eventually denying that the arhat could be called enlightened or liberated at all.[25] Nevertheless, there is no textual evidence that the

23. This possibility has been suggested by Dr. Gopinath Kaviraj: ". . . so is *siddhi* open to all, though the status of Īśvara or tīrthaṅkara is reserved for a chosen few only. What the special qualifications of these few are and how they were originally acquired we do not know. The Jaina view seems to point to radical differences inherent in the souls in spite of their essential sameness of qualitative perfection. Apart from the basic difference due to *bhavyatā* in a soul there are other differences as well, which in fact tend to make each soul unique." *SJP*: foreword, xxi.

24. Compare: ajñānaṃ hi bhūtārthadarśanapratibandhād andhakāram. tac ca bhagavato Buddhasya pratipakṣalābhenātyantaṃ sarvathā sarvatra jñeye punar anutpattidharmatvād hatam. ato 'sau sarvathā sarvahatāndhakāraḥ. pratyekabuddhaśrāvakā api kāmaṃ sarvatra hatāndhakārāḥ, kliṣṭasaṃmohātyantavigamāt? na tu sarvathā. tathā hy eṣāṃ buddhadharmeṣv ativiprakṛṣṭadeśakāleṣu, artheṣu cānantaprabhedeṣu bhavaty evākliṣṭam ajñānam. *Abhidharmakośabhāṣya*: 1.

25. Compare: traidhātukān niḥsṛtasya śrāvakasya vijānataḥ/ bhavaty evaṃ mayā prāptaṃ nirvāṇam amalaṃ śivam//63// tām eva tatra prakāśemi naitan nirvāṇam ucyate/ sarvadharmāvabodhāt tu nirvāṇaṃ prāpyate 'mṛtam//64// maharṣayo yathā tasmai karuṇāṃ saṃniveśya vai/ kathayanti ca mūḍho 'si mā te 'bhūd jñānavān aham//65// . . . tvaṃ mohād apy akiṃcijñaḥ sarvajño 'smīti bhāṣase//71// *Saddharmapuṇḍarīka-sūtra*: v, 63–71.

Jainas ever tried to set the Tīrthaṅkaras apart in such a manner. Indeed, absolute omniscience is in their tradition the fundamental criterion for liberation; thus it would have made no sense for the ācāryas to have spoken of an arhat who was "not omniscient" or who was somehow "less omniscient" than the teacher-Jina. The only differences between arhats and Tīrthaṅkaras, therefore, were of a worldly (hence not ultimately significant) nature; although the teacher possessed certain miraculous powers, especially the divyadhvani, the quality of his enlightenment was in no way superior. As for these powers themselves, we have seen that they follow karmically from particular modes of conduct cultivated in past lifetimes.

Specifically, Jaina texts set forth sixteen forms of action conducive to the production of tīrthaṅkara-prakṛti-karmas:[26] (1) purity of right faith; (2) reverence to elders; (3) proper observance of vows; (4) ceaseless pursuit of knowledge; (5) intense desire of emancipation; (6) charity; (7) practicing austerities to the best of one's ability; (8) removal of obstacles that threaten the equanimity of ascetics; (9) serving the meritorious ones (monks and nuns) in their times of illness with one's whole heart and body; (10) devotion to the arhats; (11) devotion to the ācāryas; (12) devotion to the learned monks; (13) devotion to the scriptures; (14) practicing the six essential daily duties (āvaśyakas); (15) illumination of the teachings of the Jina; (16) fervent affection for brothers in faith (those following the same spiritual path).[27] Of the sixteen, three are considered especially significant in fostering tīrthaṅkara-nature: charity, service to sick mendicants, and illumination of the teachings.

26. darśanaviśuddhir vinayasampannatā śīlavrateṣv anaticāro 'bhīkṣṇajñānopayogasaṃvegau śaktitas tyāgatapasī sādhusamādhir vaiyāvṛttyakaraṇam arhadācāryabahuśrutapravacanabhaktir āvaśyakāparihāṇir mārgaprabhāvanā pravacanavatsalatvam iti tīrthakaratvasya/ *TS*: vi, 24.

27. Compare the list of six perfections (*pāramitā*) considered as prerequisites to Buddhahood in Mahāyāna texts: 1) charity (dāna); 2) moral conduct (*śīla*); 3) forbearance (*kṣānti*); 4) effort (vīrya); 5) meditation (dhyāna); 6) wisdom (*prajñā*).

24. Ācārya Śāntisāgara (top row, center; see p. 1) surrounded by mendicant and ailaka disciples (circa 1934). Note the peacock feather whisk brooms and water gourds, the sole possessions of Digambara monks.

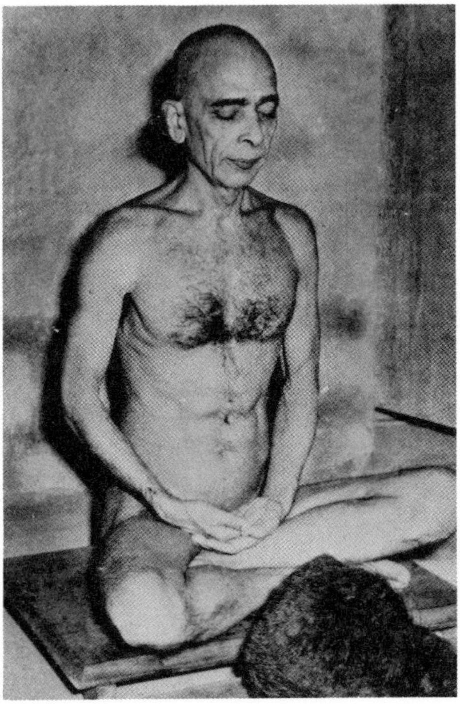

25. A Digambara muni in meditation.

26. A group of Śvetāmbara monks (1934). Courtesy of the Mahāvīra Jaina Vidyālaya, Bombay.

27. Initiation of a Śvetāmbara nun. Courtesy of Kantiroy Photo Studio, Bombay.

28. Svetāmbara nuns attending to a sermon. Courtesy of Kantiroy Photo Studio, Bombay.

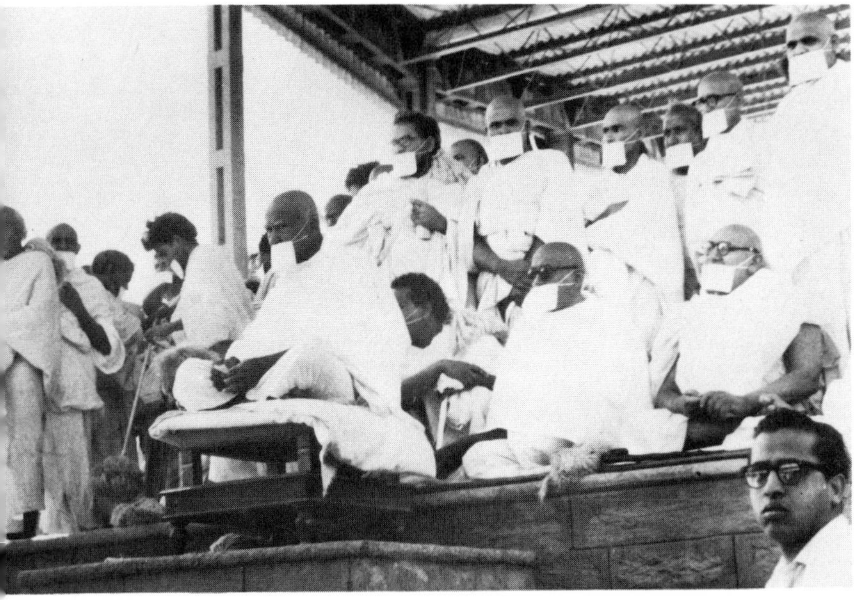

29. Sthānakavāsi monks. Note the use of muh-pattis (see p. 245).

30. Sthānakavāsi nuns. Courtesy of *The Times of India*, Bombay.

31. A siddha, represented as nothing more than an external outline in order to suggest that such beings are without material forms yet retain the shape of their final embodied existence (see p. 270). Courtesy of the Horniman Museum, London.

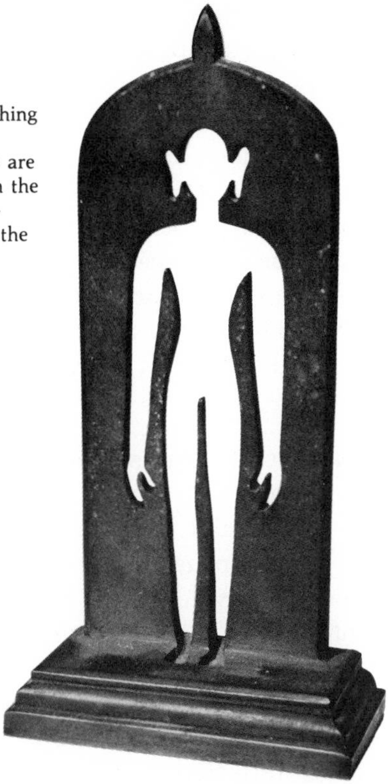

32. Raychandbhai Mehta with Mahatma Gandhi (right; see p. 315). Courtesy of the Bombay Jain Yuvak Sangh, Bombay.

It is important to remember that no Jaina should pursue these meritorious activities with the aim of becoming a Tīrthaṅkara; to do so would, strictly speaking, constitute a nidāna or forbidden wish (that is, desiring worldly gain in return for one's deeds).[28] It is assumed, therefore, that one becomes a Tīrthaṅkara all unawares, as it were; this destiny has ordinarily not been predicted for him, and he has directed neither his attention nor his energy towards it.

The Nature of Omniscience (Kevalajñāna)

We have said that any arhat, whether destined to be a Tīrthaṅkara or not, is endowed with the quality of omniscience. What, precisely, does this quality entail? The actual term used is kevalajñāna, 'knowledge isolated from karmic interference"; occasionally we find *anantajñāna*, "infinite knowledge." Such knowledge is compared to a mirror in which every one of the innumerable existents (dravyas), in all its qualities (guṇas) and modes (paryāyas), is simultaneously reflected.[29] These "knowables" are cognized without any volition whatsoever on the part of the arhat. Furthermore, no activity of senses or mind is involved; there is only direct perception by the soul.[30]

Omniscience as defined by the Jainas, then, is clearly in the realm of the supermundane; indeed, one finds similar qualities ascribed to God by the theistic schools. Virtually no tradition other than Jainism has dared to attach so cosmic an attribute to a human being. (Later Buddhist

28. This is in strong contrast to the *bodhisattva* path in Buddhism, wherein the aspirant resolves over and over again to achieve Buddhahood and even dedicates the karmic fruits of all his good deeds to that end.

29. yadīye caitanye mukura iva bhāvāś cidacitaḥ/ samaṃ bhānti dhrauvyavyayajanilasanto 'ntarahitāḥ// jagatsākṣī mārgaprakaṭanaparo bhānur iva yo/ Mahāvīrasvāmī nayanapathagāmī bhavatu naḥ// *NNP*: 17 (*Mahāvīrāṣṭaka-stotra*).

30. The sense organs and the physical basis of mind (called *dravya-mana*), which form part of the human body, must continue to exist as long as the kevalin remains alive; but they are rendered inoperative as soon as the soul is able to cognize objects directly: "samanaskatvāt sayogakevalino 'pi saṃjñina iti cet, na. teṣāṃ kṣīṇāvaraṇānāṃ mano'vaṣṭambhabalena bāhyārthagrahaṇābhāvatas tad asattvāt." Quoted in *JSK*: I, 163 (from *Dhavalāṭīkā*).

schools, perhaps in an attempt to compete with their Jaina rivals, did refer to the Buddha as *sarvajña*, "he who knows everything." But this term implies a sequential, or one-at-a-time knowledge of existents, rather than the feat of grasping them all simultaneously. A Buddha, in other words, *could* know about any given thing simply by turning his attention towards it, but he would not be aware of that thing otherwise. The denial of the soul in Buddhist doctrine, moreover, meant that a sarvajña's knowledge was necessarily a function of his ever-fluctuating mental process, rather than of some permanent or essential self.)[31] Jainas have never felt compelled to produce apologetics for this doctrine, despite the fact that others have often portrayed it as extreme or even preposterous.[32] To the contrary, they cite the very uniqueness of the claims made for Mahāvīra and the other arhats as evidence for the exalted nature of their path.

In examining these claims, we must be careful not to overemphasize the aspect of "knowing all existents at once." Jainas themselves have generally placed little importance upon this ability; they have stressed, rather, that the Jina's soul in fact *perceives only itself*. But the absence of karmic obstructions in such a soul means that, as noted above, all external objects will be reflected therein; hence these objects become "known" in an indirect, and relatively insignificant, sense. It is complete *self*-knowledge, then, which constitutes the defining mark of the omniscient being; any other description is simply a worldly or "conventional" one.[33]

31. The difficulties raised by postulating omniscience in the absence of a permanent soul were recognized even by certain Buddhists (the Pudgalavādins): yady evaṃ tarhi na Buddhaḥ sarvajñaḥ prāpnoti. na hi kiñcic cittaṃ asti caittā vā yat sarvaṃ jānīyāt, kṣaṇikatvāt. pudgalas tu jānīyāt. *Abhidharmakośabhāṣya*: 467. For a comparison of the omniscience of Mahāvīra and that of the Buddha, see P. S. Jaini 1974.

32. Kumārila mounts a vigorous attack on the Jaina claims regarding omniscience in his *Ślokavārttika*; Buddhist critiques appear in the *Pramāṇavārttika* of Dharmakīrti and the *Tattvasaṅgraha* of Śāntarakṣita. For full details on this controversy, see *Pramāṇamīmāṃsā* (Sanghavi's comments on pp. 27–33); and Singh 1974.

33. jāṇadi passadi savvaṃ vavahāraṇayeṇa kevalī bhagavaṃ/ kevalaṇāṇī

Samudghāta: The Yogic "Thinning" of Karmic Matter

Endowed with such knowledge and pure bliss (*ananta-sukha*), the arhat will remain in the thirteenth guṇasthāna until the time for his death is at hand. The two major Jaina traditions are at odds concerning his mode of existence during this period. Doctrinal conflicts over the post-enlightenment career of a Tīrthaṅkara have already been discussed in some detail (see Chapter I, n. 78); not surprisingly, a parallel divergence characterizes the sectarian descriptions on nonteaching arhats. Digambaras hold that these beings dwell in isolated glory, requiring no food or drink, totally free from impurities of any sort. Śvetāmbaras, however, see the arhat as one who still needs food and who continues to lead the normal life of a mendicant, except of course that he generates no karmic influx in doing so.

Both traditions agree that no arhat, whether a Tīrthaṅkara or not, need resort to sallekhanā, since he is already free of passions and will not be reborn.[34] Only one kind of bondage remains for him: that produced by the fourfold aghātiyā karmas (see Chapter IV, n. 47), which necessitates the continuing state of embodiment and its resultant activities of body, speech, and mind. (Hence the kevalin is said to be sayoga, with activities.) Of these karmas, three types (nāma, gotra, and āyu) are thought to be of equal duration; they will all be "used up" at precisely the same time, namely, the last moment of embodied existence. Vedanīya ("pertaining to pleasure and pain"), however, may have been accumulated in such vast quantities as to now be "in excess," sufficient to last through several more lifetimes.

---

jāṇadi passadi ṇiyameṇa appāṇaṃ// *Niyamasāra*: k 159. paśyaty ātmā sahajaparamātmānam ekaṃ viśuddhaṃ/ svāntaḥ śuddhyāvasathamahimādhāram atyantadhīram// svātmany uccair avicalatayā sarvadāntarnimagnaṃ/ tasmin naiva prakṛtimahati vyāvahāraprapañcaḥ// *Niyamasāra*[*ṭīkā*]: k 282.

34. The Śvetāmbara description of the gaṇadharas fasting during their final month (see Ch. II) should not be taken to mean that these enlightened beings practiced sallekhanā. The proper interpretation is, rather, that any kevalin, knowing the time of his death in advance, will cease to take food when the maintenance of his body is no longer necessary.

Because karmic matter cannot fall away of its own accord until it has yielded its fruits or appropriate results, the kevalin (who will of course have no further births during which such fruition might occur) must reduce the amount of the vedanīya factors, bringing it "into line" with that of the other aghātiyā karmas. This is accomplished through a process called *samudghāta*, which means "bursting forth," in which the soul is yogically expanded to the very limits of the universe (loka-ākāśa) while retaining its connection with the physical body. Samudghāta lasts only for eight instants, after which there is "contraction" to the previous size and shape.[35] Jainas hold that such an expansion of the soul is analogous to the spreading out of a wet cloth; just as increasing the exposed surface area of the cloth promotes more rapid drying, so will samudghāta make it possible for karmas to be "thinned out," or brought to instant fruition.

One might expect this unique moment of omnipresence to correspond to final liberation. But Jaina doctrine denies that this is the case, since not every arhat must go through such an experience; samudghāta is called for only in those cases where, as we have seen, vedanīya karmas are overly abundant. It is from the human form, therefore, that the soul undertakes its final task: elimination of those activities (yoga) which necessarily accrue to the condition of embodiment. Here at last are employed the third and fourth types of śukladhyāna, to which the kevalin resorts just a few moments before physical death.[36] In the trance called *sūkṣmakriyā-anivartin* (the state of subtle movement), all gross and subtle activities of mind and speech, as well as the gross activities of the body, are absolutely stopped. There now remain only the autonomic processes: breathing, heartbeat, and the like. Even these are brought to cessation by attainment of the highest meditational state,

35. Compare: . . . daṇḍakapāṭaprataralokapūraṇāni caturbhiḥ samayaiḥ kṛtvā punar api tāvadbhir eva samayaiḥ . . . pūrvaśarīrapramāṇo bhūtvā . . . sūkṣmakriyāpratipātidhyānaṃ dhyāyati. *SS*: §906.

36. It will be recalled that the first two forms of the śukladhyāna brought the aspirant to the thirteenth guṇasthāna.

vyuparatakriyā-anivartin (absolute nonmotion). Both of these dhyānas are designated as *anivartin*, meaning "that from which there can be no falling back."

Thus the soul *must* proceed from the state of subtle movement into that of nonmovement, the latter being identical with the fourteenth guṇasthāna (ayoga-kevali—isolated from all ghātiyā karmas and free of all activities). This guṇasthāna lasts only for an instant; suddenly, as the āyu karmas are exhausted and death occurs, the soul leaves the body, darting upward by its very nature to the highest point of the universe (loka-ākāśa).[37] There it will reside, totally free of either bondage or movement, for all eternity.

The Siddha: The Liberated Soul

Souls in this final abode (referred to as *īṣat-prāgbhārā-bhūmi*,[38] "the slightly bending place," because of its dome-like appearance) are thought by Jainas to possess a definite shape. (See pl. 31.) This shape is identical to that of the last incarnation, though on a slightly reduced scale (the empty spaces found in an earthly body are no longer present). No clear explanation is offered for this seeming association of the totally liberated soul with its former condition.[39] We can only surmise that, in addition to preserving the individuality of siddhas in the state of mokṣa

37. This rather dramatic departure from the realm of embodiment is sometimes explained as due to an "inherent tendency" of the soul to "break away from" or "rise above" all karmas. Alternatively, its arrow-like flight to the summit of the universe is ascribed to "momentum" originally set up by the bodily activities; a similar phenomenon occurs, we are told, when the potter's wheel continues to rotate long after the potter has ceased to turn it: kulālaprayogāpāditahastadaṇḍacakrasaṃyogapūrvakaṃ bhramaṇam. uparate 'pi tasmin pūrvaprayogād ā saṃskārakṣayād bhramati . . . kiñca tathāgatipariṇāmāt. yathā . . . pradīpaśikhā svabhāvād utpatati tathā muktātmāpi nānāgativikārakāraṇakarmanirvāraṇe saty ūrdhvagatisvabhāvād ūrdhvam evābhirohati. *SS:* §933.

38. See Ch. IV n. 61.

39. The technical discussion of this phenomenon suggests that contraction and expansion of a soul's pradeśas are due to the presence of the nāma-karma; the latter having been destroyed at the time of death, the liberated soul remains forever in the "shape" of its last body: syān mataṃ, yadi śarīrānuvidhāyī jīvaḥ,

where all souls are otherwise of identical nature, such a concept serves to emphasize the fact that every siddha was previously an ordinary human being; hence the Jaina aspirant will be encouraged to pursue the path of purification ever more rigorously, for he will be reminded that even the most exalted souls were once trapped in bondage just as he is now.[40] But again, it must be borne in mind that any description of the perfected being, or of the infinite cognition and bliss which characterize him, is purely conventional. In reality such things, lying as they do beyond the space-time limitations of ordinary human consciousness, cannot be described at all. As Mahāvīra is reported to have said:

> All sounds recoil thence, where speculation has no room, nor does the mind penetrate there. The liberated is not long or small or round or triangular . . . he is not black . . . or white . . . he is without body, without contact (of matter), he is not feminine or masculine or neuter; he perceives, he knows, but there is no analogy (whereby to know the nature of the liberated soul); its essence is without form; there is no condition of the unconditioned.[41]

---

tadabhāvāt svābhāvikalokākāśapradeśaparimāṇatvāt tāvad visarpaṇaṃ prāpnotīti. naiṣa doṣaḥ. kutaḥ? kāraṇābhāvāt. nāmakarmasambandho hi saṃharaṇavisarpaṇakāraṇam. tadabhāvāt punaḥ saṃharaṇavisarpaṇābhāvaḥ. *SS*: §928. See pl. 31.

40. Compare the Sāṃkhya-Yoga notion of Īśvara, a soul which has never experienced any form of bondage (see above, Ch. V n. 3) and yet serves as a kind of model for the spiritual efforts of those who are themselves bound.

41. savve sarā ṇiyaṭṭaṃti, takkā jattha ṇa vijjai/ maī tattha ṇa gāhiyā, oe appatiṭṭhāṇassa kheyanne// se ṇa dīhe ṇa hasse ṇa vaṭṭe ṇa taṃse ṇa cauraṃse ṇa parimaṃḍale, ṇa kiṇhe ṇa nīle ṇa lohie ṇa halidde ṇa sukkille . . . ṇa itthī ṇa purise ṇa annahā. pariṇṇe saṇṇe uvamā ṇa vijjai, arūvī sattā, apayassa payaṃ ṇatthi. *AS*: §330–332.

THE FOURTEEN GUṆASTHĀNAS

1. Mithyādṛṣṭi: The lowest state, in which the soul suffers from "wrong views" (mithyā-darśana) because of the presence of darśana-mohanīya karmas and the anantānubandhī type of passions (kaṣāya).
2. Sāsvādana: The state of "mixed taste," reached only during a fall to the first guṇasthāna from one of the higher states.
3. Samyak-mithyātva: The state of transition from the first to the fourth guṇasthāna and vice versa.
4. Samyak-dṛṣṭi: The first rung in the ladder to salvation, the state of true vision (samyak-darśana). This is attained by overcoming both the darśana-mohanīya and the anantānubandhī passions. Mithyā-darśana, the first cause of bondage, is also overcome at this stage.
5. Deśa-virata: The state attained by receiving the vratas prescribed for a layman. Here avirati (non-restraint) is partially overcome by rendering the apratyākhyānāvaraṇa passions inoperative.
6. Sarva-virata: The state attained by receiving the mahāvratas (total restraint) of the mendicant. Here avirati is fully overcome by bringing an end to the function of the pratyākhyānāvaraṇa passions. Due to the presence of "carelessness," this stage is also known as pramatta-virata.
7. Apramatta-virata: The state in which pramāda (carelessness), the third cause of bondage, is overcome by means of dharmadhyāna.
8. Apūrva-karaṇa
9. Anivṛtti-karaṇa
10. Sūkṣma-sāmparāya } These three comprise the śreṇi (ladder), in which the aspirant may either suppress (upaśama) or eliminate (*kṣapaṇa*) the no-kaṣāyas (secondary passions) and the subtle forms of the saṃjvalana passions.

11. Upaśānta-moha: The state attained through the *suppression* of the saṃjvalana passions; from here a fall to the lower states is inevitable. Progress is possible only for those who are able to *eliminate* the passions, a process which must begin at the eighth guṇasthāna.
12. Kṣīṇa-moha: The state in which even the subtle forms of saṃjvalana passions (that is, the remaining portion of mohanīya karma) are completely eliminated. Thus kaṣāya, the fourth cause of bondage, is overcome. The soul must now inevitably proceed to the higher stages.
13. Sayoga-kevalin: The state of omniscience (kevalajñāna), wherein the remaining three ghātiyā (knowledge-obscuring, perception-obscuring, and energy-restricting) karmas are eliminated. This is the state of an arhat, kevalin, Jina, or Tīrthaṅkara.
14. Ayoga-kevalin: The state attained by an arhat in the instant prior to his death. Here yoga (activity), the last cause of bondage, comes to an end. Death itself is accompanied by elimination of the four aghātiyā (feeling-producing, body-producing, longevity-determining, and environment-determining) karmas.

MOKṢA: This state, characteristic of the siddha (perfected being), involves total freedom from embodiment and thus is not included among the guṇasthānas.

IX

Jaina Society through the Ages: Growth and Survival

Causes for the Survival of Jaina Society

In charting the Jaina path of purification, from its philosophical basis to the particulars of its actual practice, we have dealt with the very core of Jaina religious experience. The circumstances of Jainism as a social institution, functioning for over two millennia within the great cultural mosaic of Indian life, have remained largely unexamined; indeed, such an examination would require a book in itself and lies mainly beyond the purview of this work. Nevertheless, there are certain sociohistorical issues which are too significant to be passed over completely here. These issues revolve around the basic question of just how Jainism, alone among the non-Vedic śramaṇa traditions, has been able to survive and prosper in India up to the present day.

Most of the antibrahmanical sects died out soon after the passing of their respective founders; even Buddhism, with its centers of learning in ruins and the Buddha himself being described by brahmanical writers as simply an avatar of Viṣṇu, disappeared from the subcontinent by perhaps the fourteenth century.[1] But the Jainas somehow managed

1. Of the six titthiyas (Pali for Tīrthaṅkara) mentioned in the Sāmaññaphalasutta of the *Dīghanikāya* (Pūraṇa Kassapa, Makkhali Gosāla, Ajita Kesakambalī, Pakudha Kaccāyana, Nigaṇṭha Nātaputta, Sañjaya Belaṭṭhiputta), only the Ājīvikas and the Nigaṇṭhas seem to have survived the deaths of their masters. On the disappearance of the Ājīvika sect, see Basham 1951: 187ff. On the decline of Buddhism in India, see Mitra 1954. For a contrast of the fortunes of Buddhism and Jainism, see P. S. Jaini, forthcoming (a).

to keep both their tradition and their community intact, despite the myriad forces operating against the continued existence of so tiny a heterodox minority. Let us now consider certain of the factors underlying this rather puzzling phenomenon; whether or not we are able to come to some "explanation," it may at least be possible to gain a better understanding of how Jainas, struggling as much for institutional survival as for the attainment of the noble spiritual goals set forth by the Tīrthaṅkaras, have in fact lived and applied (or failed to apply) their religious principles in the realm of everyday worldly experience.

Royal Patronage

A cardinal feature of the śramaṇa movements which arose in India circa 550 B.C. was their emphasis upon the superiority of the princely class (kṣatriya), whether in a spiritual context or a secular one.[2] Hence these movements tended to find common cause with local kings, who were themselves engaged in a constant fight against the claims to supremacy of the brahman class; while custom demanded that a king always be of kṣatriya origin, he might all too easily find himself reduced to little more than a figurehead for his brahman ministers. Furthermore, by opening their ranks to members of any age group or caste (and, in the case of the Jainas, even to women), the śramaṇa groups in fact created an entire separate society, parallel to the Vedic one. They were able to recruit large numbers of mendicant and lay followers and thus constituted a significant force—social, political, and economic, as well as spiritual—within the large cities where they were concentrated.

It is not surprising, therefore, to find that Indian kings commonly formed alliances (in the form of generous patronage or even outright conversion to the faith) with one or another of these groups. Such rulers may sometimes have acted out of genuine religious conviction, but often

2. Recall the story of Mahāvīra's "change of womb," and the prediction that Gautama would become either a saint or a great king (these two possibilities in fact represent two sides of the same kṣatriya coin).

they simply aimed to strengthen their position against the powerful brahmanic elements with which they had to contend. Whatever motives might have been involved, it is clear that the granting or withholding of royal support often effectively determined a sect's ability to survive in a given region. The Jaina movement was by no means an exception to this pattern; indeed, its development was from the beginning tied to the fortunes of various ruling houses, and it is in the rather remarkable ability of the Jainas to have repeatedly won kingly favor that we find the first important key to their long and relatively prosperous existence.[3]

Whether or not one credits the suggestion that Mahāvīra himself was of royal blood, it does seem certain that even during his time the Nigaṇṭhas were actively cultivating local monarchs, particularly King Śreṇika of Magadha. Though not a Jaina by birth, this king seems to have been converted by his wife Celanā (perhaps an aunt of Mahāvīra), and his capital at Rājagṛha became the major center of Mahāvīra's assembly. When Śreṇika's throne was usurped by his son Ajātaśatru, however, Jaina influence

3. Several regional histories of the Jainas have appeared, each drawing upon the literary and inscriptional evidence of specific periods and locations. For the ancient era, beginning with Mahāvīra and ending with the Valabhi council, one finds useful information in Smith's work (1901) on the Jaina antiquities at Mathura and in B. L. Rice's collection (1909) of epigraphic materials from Mysore and Coorg. J. C. Jain (1947) presents a clear idea of the Jaina community as depicted in the canon; and J. P. Jain (1964) attempts a chronological survey of the main events preceding the onset of the medieval period. For this period itself, the best resources are C. J. Shah (1932) on Jainism in North India, and Saletore (1938) on developments in the south, especially during the Vijayanagara epoch. These are supplemented by Desai's new collections of South Indian epigraphy (1957) and K. C. Jain's study of Jainism in Rajasthan (1963). Handiqui's critique of the *Yaśastilaka-campū* (1949) offers new material concerning the interrelation of Jainas and Śaivites around the tenth century.

On the modern period, Stevenson's *Heart of Jainism* (1915), despite the numerous defects arising from her Christian missionary zeal, is still the only study based on actual field work, in this case among the Śvetāmbara Jaina community of Gujarat. Sangave (1959) has collected a great deal of useful data pertaining to the kinds of social divisions typically found among both Śvetāmbaras and Digambaras. Finally, Sharma has contributed an article (1976) on the Jainas as a minority in Indian society; and Nevaskar (1971) attempts to compare the Jaina role in India with that of the Quakers in the West.

suffered a temporary decline in the area; Ajātaśatru was rather pro-Buddhist,[4] and though Indian kings were duty-bound to support all religions, their active patronage of a particular sect invariably brought a tremendous increase in that sect's power and prestige. This took the form not only of greater popularity among the common people, but also of material benefits (the king's annual taxes from a particular village, for example, might be turned over to a mendicant community) and of access to the court, hence to the machinery of political power.

Ajātaśatru's line was soon replaced by the pro-Jaina Nanda dynasty;[5] the Nandas reigned until around 324 B.C., when they were swallowed up by the newly emerging empire of Candragupta Maurya. Candragupta is said to have become a disciple of the famous Jaina pontiff Bhadrabāhu, and to have accompanied him on the southward migration described in Chapter I. Certain inscriptional evidence may support this claim;[6] in any case, the period of Jaina ascendancy was fast drawing to a close, for the throne was soon to be occupied by Candragupta's grandson Aśoka, perhaps India's greatest ancient king and an ardent patron of Buddhism.[7]

4. Malalasekera 1937: I, 35. See above, Ch. VII n. 56.

5. *Pariśiṣṭaparva*: viii, 240. For a critical evaluation of this version, see Trautman 1971: 21-30.

6. In light of the great distance separating the Mauryan capital from Shravanabelgola, where Bhadrabāhu is claimed to have met his end (see Ch. I n. 6), certain critics have tended to discount the authenticity of this entire story. B. L. Rice, however, has discovered Aśokan edicts in Mysore very close to the area in question, and he takes them as an indication that the Mauryan empire did extend this far south even in such ancient times. (B. L. Rice 1909: 1–16.) Hence, the possibility of Candragupta's visit there cannot simply be rejected out of hand.

7. Śvetāmbara tradition holds that one Samprati, a grandson of Aśoka, succeeded to the throne and became an important benefactor of the Jainas, particularly in terms of increasing their influence among the Dravidian peoples of the Andhra region: Sampratiś cintayāmāsa niśīthsamaye 'nyadā/ anāryeṣv api sādhūnāṃ vihāraṃ vartayāmy aham//89// . . . evaṃ rājño 'tinirbandhād ācāryaiḥ ke 'pi sādhavaḥ/ vihartum ādidiśire tato 'ndhradamilādiṣu//99// *Pariśiṣṭaparva*: xi, 89–99. There is no inscriptional evidence to support this claim; even so, there is no reason to doubt that it rests upon at least some historical basis.

Thus the Jainas began slowly to move away from Magadha, becoming established in various cities along the two great caravan routes; one of these led northwest, towards Delhi and Mathura, thence south and west through Saurashtra and into Gujarat, while the other followed the east coast southward into Kalinga (modern Orissa), finally reaching even to the Dravidian lands around Madras and Mysore. Migration along these routes increased greatly around 150 B.C. with the advent of the Śunga dynasty, which brought with it a brahmanical resurgence and hard times for all non-Vedic groups in and around Magadha. The Kalinga area was more hospitable, at least initially; inscriptional evidence suggests that the installation of large Jina-images, patronage to Jaina monks, and other such works were known there as early as the second century B.C., especially in connection with a certain King Khāravela (see Chapter VII, n. 6). This king ostensibly took the vows of a layman, and described himself in terms that would become the ideal for many Jaina rulers in the future:

> Thus reigned that king of bliss . . . of prosperity . . . of dharma . . . worshipper of all religious orders, champion of shrines to all gods, possessor of invincible armies, administrator of the rule of law, guardian of the law, executor of the law . . . having seen, heard, experienced, and done that which is good.[8]

But in Kalinga too the Jainas eventually lost ground as they had in Magadha and were forced once again to seek the favor of other kings in distant regions.

As for the northwest, a major śramaṇa center seems to have developed in Mathura between 100 B.C. and A.D. 100;

8. The inscription of King Khārevela begins with salutations to the arhats and siddhas, the two most auspicious figures for Jainas: "namo arahaṃtānaṃ/ namo savasiddhānaṃ/ Aireṇa mahārājena Mahāmeghavāhanena . . . Kaliṃgādhipatinā siri Khāravelena . . ./ . . . khemarājā sa baḍharājā sa bhikhurājā dhamarājā pasaṃto sunaṃto anubhabaṃto kalāṇāni guṇavisesakusalo savapāsaṃḍapūjako savadevāyatana saṃkārakārako . . . mahāvijayo rājā Khāravelasiri." Sahu 1964: I, 398–404.

the Śakas and Scythians who ruled the area around that time produced at least one Buddhist king (Kaniṣka), and were in general favorably disposed to nonbrahmanical groups. Many Jaina migrants continued on past Mathura, tending especially to settle in or around the city of Valabhi in Saurashtra; it was here that their canon was first put into written form.

Valabhi served for many years as the primary location from which Jaina teachings were disseminated. Though the city housed many members of both Jaina sects, it eventually became the main stronghold of the Śvetāmbaras; large members of Digambara adherents, perhaps following their monks, moved to the coast of the Arabian Sea, thence into the Deccan, and finally even further south to Shravanabelgola (where Bhadrabāhu had arrived so many years before). Others came to the same locale from Kalinga in the east. Thus by the fifth or sixth century a situation had developed in which the ancient centers of Jaina power —Kalinga and the Ganges Valley—were almost totally bereft of Jaina elements, while at the same time the Jaina community itself had become irrevocably divided along geographical lines, Digambaras in the south (modern Maharashtra and Karnataka) and Śvetāmbaras in the west (Gujarat, Rajasthan, and Punjab). These regional concentrations prevail, for the most part, even today; although a certain number of Jaina communities can be found in every part of India, most members of the faith still live in or near one of the two "home areas" in which the migrants originally settled.

Jaina Royal Houses in Karnataka

While numerous examples of Jaina involvement with ruling houses may be cited, perhaps the most striking is that pertaining to the Ganga dynasty in what is now Karnataka State. This dynasty was apparently established by a Digambara monk called Siṃhanandi, who somehow contrived to set up one Mādhava Konguṇivarma as the local ruler in A.D. 265.[9] Various fantastic legends surround the circumstances of this event, some suggesting that it involved the use of great occult powers by the monk. Whatever actually transpired, it does seem clear that Siṃhanandi commanded sufficient political influence to effectively function as a king-maker, and further that the subsequent Ganga rulers were all staunch Jainas. The fact that Jaina inscriptions simply report and do not condemn the monk's activities—despite their obvious unsuitability for one who has taken the mahāvratas—points out the moral ambivalence created by the need for royal support on the one hand and the demands of the spiritual life on the other. Whatever spiritually negative results Siṃhanandi may have brought upon himself by his behavior, there can be no doubt that he greatly benefited the Digambara community as a whole. The Ganga dynasty, centered in the city of Gangavāḍī, provided almost seven centuries of uninterrupted pro-Jaina rule.

With the need for repeated migration thus eliminated, Digambara life attained a degree of stability unprecedented in its history. Some of the Ganga kings went so far as to take the vratas and to meet their deaths in sallekhanā; most engaged in extensive temple building and generally attempted to follow the rules of kingship which Siṃhanandi himself had laid down for his protege:

> If you fail in what you have promised
> If you do not approve of the Jaina teachings
> If you seize the wife of another
> If you eat honey or flesh
> If you form relationships with low people
> If you do not give your wealth to the needy
> If you flee from the battlefield
> Then your race will go to ruin.[10]

9. "Gaṅgarājyamaṃ māḍida Siṃhanandiācāryar," quoted (from the *Epigraphica Carnatica*: vii, no. 46, 139) in Saletore 1938: 11.
10. Ibid.: 12.

It is interesting to note that, while this formula promotes ahiṃsā in the form of vegetarianism, it does not rule out warfare: another example of doctrine coming to terms with social and political reality. Indeed, military men were often strong supporters of the Jaina faith and were by no means excoriated for practicing their profession. Most famous of such individuals was the Ganga general Cāmuṇḍarāya, a successful field commander who gained the Jaina epithet *samyaktvaratnākara*, meaning "ocean of true insight," for commissioning erection of the great Bāhubali image at Shravanabelgola in 948.[11]

Two other dynasties deserve mention in the context of Jaina history in South India. The first, that of the Rāṣṭrakūṭas, ruled in the Deccan (just north of the Ganga kingdom) from the eighth until the twelfth century. One of its kings, known as Amoghavarṣa, abdicated the throne around the year 800 in order to become a mendicant disciple of the famous ācārya Jinasena (circa 770–850); another, called Indra IV, is said to have performed sallekhanā at the Shravanabelgola shrine in 982.[12] During the Rāṣṭrakūṭa period, Jaina adherents were able to establish a large number of cave temples dedicated to their Jinas; located in the Ellora hills near Ajanata, these can still be seen today, side by side with others sacred to the Buddhists and the Hindus.

The second important dynasty arose in Karnataka as the successor to the Gangas. Once again the Jaina mendicant community seems to have been instrumental in its establishment. A well-known legend, often represented in art, tells how at one time the monk Sudatta was in the company of a local tribal chieftain called Sala, when suddenly

11. Cāmuṇḍarāya was also a very able general and had won such titles as *vairikulakāladaṇḍa* (the club which brings death to the host of enemies), *bhujavikrama* (valliant in arms), and *samara-Paraśurāma* (the incarnation of Paraśurāma on the battlefield). Ibid.: 107ff.

12. Ibid.: 105.

they were confronted by a raging tiger. Sudatta immediately handed over his staff and shouted "poy [smite him], Sala!" whereupon the animal was struck down and killed. This event apparently proved to be a great inspiration to the chieftain, who soon thereafter founded a Jaina kingdom and named it Poyasala (later Hoysala).[13] The story is especially interesting because it depicts a monk not only participating in worldly affairs, but even going so far as to encourage hiṃsā. We may assume that with Ganga power in a state of decline, it behooved the Jaina elders to do whatever was necessary to ensure the continuation of a government sympathetic to their cause; whether or not the tale of Sudatta has any basis in fact, the theme of doctrinally improper monkish involvement in the political fortunes of the nation certainly rings true.

The Hoysalas held sway in Karnataka until the fourteenth century, at which time they were absorbed into the brahmanical Vijayanagara empire.[14] Thus the Jainas were forced out of whatever seats of power they had gained; even so, hundreds of years of uninterrupted royal patronage had left them with sufficient wealth (particularly in the form of numerous well-endowed temples) to permit their continued prosperous existence, albeit on the fringes rather than at the heart of prevailing society.

Śvetāmbara Jaina Rulers of Gujarat

Members of the Śvetāmbara community seem to have been less aggressive initially in seeking influence within the court than were their Digambara brethren; nevertheless, several incidents illustrate the fact that even in early times they were able to marshal strong political support when the need arose. A particularly famous story describes the response of the Śvetāmbara ācārya Kālaka (first century B.C.) to the unpardonable behavior of a certain King Gar-

13. Ibid.: 58–86.
14. On the Jaina celebrities in the Vijayanagara empire, see ibid.: 366–387.

dabhila of Ujjain.[15] This king, whose name suggests that he may have been of Indo-Greek origin, apparently displayed sexual interest in Kālaka's sister, a Jaina nun. Ignoring the ācārya's remonstrations, Gardabhila ordered the woman brought to his harem and proceeded to have his way with her. Kālaka, outraged, went immediately to the neighboring Sāhi kings (probably Scythians or Persians) and incited them to invade Ujjain, hoping to punish Gardabhila and to obtain the release of his sister. This chain of events led to the establishment of Sāhi rule in Ujjain, a situation which continued until the triumph there of Vikramāditya (said to be a Jaina) in A.D. 57.[16]

Perhaps inspired by Kālaka's example (but more likely through having realized the tenuous sociopolitical position of so small a minority group as their own), Śvetāmbaras began to actively pursue royal favor around the beginning of the Christian era. But it was not until the eighth century that a Jaina ruler came to power in West India. This was made possible when the orphan of a displaced Śaivite royal lineage in Gujarat was found and raised by a Śvetāmbara monk called Śīlaguṇasūri. Upon reaching adulthood this orphan managed to regain his throne, taking the name Vanarāja and establishing a Jaina kingdom centered in Anahilanagara.[17] During his long reign (746–806), the Jainas moved into positions of great influence as ministers and financiers; thus they were able to establish a power base which remained relatively effective for many years, despite the fact that Vanarāja's successors soon reverted to Śaivism.

At one point (mid-twelfth century) the Śvetāmbaras even brought about a brief "golden age" of their own in the Saurashtra area. It seems that the Śaivite king Jayasiṃha-Siddharāja died without an heir; after various ma-

15. For a critical study of the Kālaka story, see Brown 1933.
16. For evidence in support of this claim, see C. J. Shah 1932: 190ff.
17. Account based on Hemacandra's *Kumārapālacarita*, first reported by Colonel James Tod in 1839 (see Tod, repr. 1971: 149–155); Premi 1956: 481.

neuverings, the throne passed to a distant cousin called Kumārapāla. This accession was engineered largely through the combined efforts of a certain Jaina minister and the great ācārya Hemacandra.[18] Kumārapāla was at that time already deeply in Hemacandra's debt, for the latter had once saved him from execution at the hands of Jayasiṃha-Siddharāja's minions by hiding him in the monastery (supposedly beneath a pile of holy manuscripts). Thus we cannot be absolutely sure whether his actions as king sprang mainly from a sense of obligation or reflected a sincere commitment to the Jaina world-view. In any case, Kumārapāla took the aṇuvratas of a layman, forbade the sacrifice of animals in his kingdom, and built a large number of temples in honor of the Jinas. His rule ended with the Muslim invasions of 1165; though the dynasty was eventually restored, it once again became firmly Śaivite in its sympathies, and no other Jaina king ever arose. The Śvetāmbara community did retain a certain measure of political and economic influence in the kingdom, but for the most part its members contented themselves with local affairs, religious activities centering around their many wealthy temples, and the promotion of *amāri* (prohibition of animal sacrifice) in the Muslim kingdoms of the north.[19]

18. For a biography of Hemacandra, see Buhler 1889 (tr. Patel 1936); for a complete bibliography, see Sharma 1975. On Kumārapāla, see Alsdorf 1928; and Satyaprakash 1972.

19. Jainas have taken great pride in the degree to which they have been able to gain political support for the practice of ahiṃsā, even among non-Indian kings whose own religions were in no way opposed to the killing of animals. The most striking example of this phenomenon took place in the late sixteenth century, when the Mughal potentate Akbar (1556–1605) became closely involved with a famous Śvetāmbara monk called Hīravijaya-Sūri. According to the historian Vincent Smith, the Sūri "persuaded the Emperor to release prisoners and caged birds, and to prohibit the killing of animals on certain days. In the following year (1583) those orders were extended, and disobedience to them was made a capital offence. Akbar renounced his much-loved hunting and restricted the practice of fishing." Smith adds that "Akbar's action in abstaining almost wholly from eating meat and in issuing stringent prohibitions, resembling those of Aśoka, restricting to the narrowest limits the destruction of animal life, certainly was taken in obedience to the doctrine of his Jain teachers." Smith 1917: 119–120.

Preoccupation of the Jainas with efforts of this sort was not restricted to the

Jainas and the Class/Caste System (Varṇa/Jāti Vyavasthā)

The Jainas were by no means alone in their ability to gain royal patronage; Buddhists, in particular, often received lavish support for extended periods, perhaps to an even greater degree than did their Nigaṇṭha rivals. And yet, as we have noted, Buddhism as a social institution could not withstand the combined onslaught of Muslim invasion and Hindu devotional fervor in the twelfth century; its development thereafter was limited to the Himalayan states, Southeast Asia, and the Far East. Thus, while the support of ruling houses was extremely important, it was not in itself sufficient to ensure a sect's long-term survival. Clearly, one must look further to discover the factors that enabled Jainism to endure while its closest counterparts disappeared from the scene.

A comparative examination of the great bodies of Buddhist and Jaina literature initially gives a rather striking impression of similarity. In particular, both traditions produced numerous works presenting the teachings of their respective founders and elucidating the complex systems which developed therefrom. For the Buddhists, however, dealing with philosophical issues seems to have become the chief preoccupation of the learned ācāryas. Jaina teachers, while also deeply interested in such questions, nevertheless showed equal or perhaps even greater concern with the creation of works intended for the ordinary layperson. We have already seen, for example, the kind of systematic instructions for lay conduct set forth in the śrāvakācāra texts. Virtually nothing of similar nature and scope was produced by Buddhist authors.[20]

Mughal court. (See Majmudar 1969.) They have brought similar pressures to bear whenever and wherever it has been possible for them to do so; the most recent example is their successful drive, during the 2,500th anniversary of Mahāvīra's nirvāṇa, to ban animal sacrifice in nearly every Indian state.

20. Williams (1963) lists more than forty Jaina texts on lay discipline. Theravāda Buddhists apparently came up with only one such work, the *Upāsakajanālaṃkāra* of Ānanda (twelfth century); the concern of the Mahāyāna tradition

On the social level, an analogous distinction prevailed. Whereas Buddhist monks congregated in great scholastic enclaves (Nālandā and Vikramaśīla, for example), Jaina holy men remained relatively dispersed in their temples, constantly in close touch with the many laymen who worshipped there. Indeed, the very term "Buddhist" originally referred only to those who had donned the yellow robes; the rich merchants and others who supported these monks and nuns were said to gain merit through generosity, but they probably never participated fully in either the organization or the religious practice of the Buddhist community. Such a situation never prevailed in Jainism; from earliest times the complete integration of lay followers into the religious life was strongly emphasized. As Weber has accurately observed, the Jainas were

> . . . perhaps the first, certainly . . . among the older confessions of cultured intellectuals who were . . . successful in carrying out the typical dualistic organization . . . : the community of monks as the nucleus, the laity (upāsaka, adorers) as a community under the religious rule of the monks.[21]

There can be little doubt that this high degree of lay involvement was significant in enabling Jainism to persevere amidst a veritable sea of Hindu influence. Furthermore, as observed in the tale of Ānanda, a Jaina's identification with his community could often be carried to extraordinary lengths; for example, Ānanda's pledge not only to refuse alms to non-Jaina mendicants, but even to avoid, whenever possible, any teachers, practitioners, or places of worship associated with other traditions.

But such behavior could not have been the general rule; we can assume that this "exclusivist" trend was ordinarily tempered by the necessity of dealing with the larger society outside. Whether involved in a government career (politics, the military), influence-gathering in the court, or simply

---

with lay matters found literary expression only in a small portion of Śāntideva's *Śikṣāsamuccaya* (ninth century).

21. Weber 1958: 196.

the pursuit of business or pleasure, Jainas were constantly forced to mingle with non-Jaina elements, hence to confront systems of custom and belief which invariably called their own into question. It fell to the Jaina ācāryas to strike a reasonable balance between these two priorities—on the one hand, the perpetuation of orthodoxy, perhaps best achieved through enforced isolation; on the other, the need for fruitful intercourse with Hindu society. They appear to have handled the task with considerable skill and wisdom, compromising often with heretical practices but always striving (and usually managing) to retain the spirit of their own tradition. This phenomenon was perhaps most obvious among Digambaras in the south, owing to their heavy involvement, both social and political, with non-Jaina society; but it sometimes occurred among Śvetāmbaras as well.

Considering the Digambara case as an example, we find that elders of the community allowed cautious "integration" with the surrounding Hindu populace in three main ways: by adopting certain local customs outright, by reinterpreting the doctrine of the caste system so that Jaina society could be organized along the lines similar to those of its neighbors, and by instituting new sets of ceremonial practices, called *kriyās,* which pertained to the changing phases of secular life. As for the first of these, the Jaina attitude towards the incredible diversity of social forms which they encountered during their years of migration and colonization is well expressed by the following dictum: "All worldly practices [those not related to salvation] are valid for the Jainas, as long as there is neither loss of pure insight nor violation of the vratas."[22] Thus a Jaina layman could, in general, adopt the day-to-day patterns of life in a given area—staple foods, gift-giving customs, holidays, clothing, the language—with a clear conscience.

22. dvau hi dharmau gṛhasthānāṃ laukikaḥ pāralaukikaḥ/ lokāśrayo bhaved ādyaḥ paraḥ syād āgamāśrayaḥ// . . . sarva eva hi Jainānāṃ pramāṇaṃ laukiko vidhiḥ/ yatra samyaktvahānir na yatra na vratadūṣaṇam// *Upāsakādhyayana*: k 477–480.

One such pattern, however, presented special problems to the ācāryas; while its observance was universal among Hindu communities, thus putting strong pressure upon other groups to conform thereto, the doctrine upon which it was based stood in sharp contradiction to Jaina scripture. This was of course the caste system, which in Hindu terms placed all persons into one of four fixed social classes (brahman, kṣatriya, vaiśya, or śūdra), classes determined by birth and said to have originated as part of the divine creation of the world.

The traditional Jaina denial of a theistic creation, as well as of brahmanic supremacy in either the spiritual or the secular realm, has already been noted. Jaina teachers had to develop a system that would not violate these basic tenets. This feat was accomplished largely through the ingenuity and literary skill of the ācārya Jinasena, whose massive *Ādipurāṇa* was nothing less than a Jaina version of the history of the world. Exploiting the rich potentialities in the tale of Ṛṣabha, the first king and the first Tīrthaṅkara, Jinasena made of this figure a virtual "Jaina Brahmā," one who pronounced a set of "Jaina Vedas" and, most germane to the present discussion, *instituted the division of the castes.* Ṛṣabha's status, reflected in such epithets as *prajāpati* (lord of creatures) and *ādi-deva* (first lord), became that of "creator" in a sense acceptable to Jaina tradition; he was not held to have made the world, but he did supposedly create the organization of human society.[23]

As for the castes, these are depicted not as part of the cosmic order but as a system politically imposed upon the single jāti (birth or destiny) to which all human beings belong.[24] Jinasena tells us that Ṛṣabha, while still a layman, responded to the excessive lawlessness and disorder

23. On the Vaiṣṇava attempts to integrate Ṛṣabha into the Bhāgavata cult, see *Śrīmad Bhāgavata*: V, i–v; and P. S. Jaini 1977a.

24. manuṣyajātir ekaiva jātināmodayodbhavā/ vṛttibhedāhitād bhedāc cāturvidhyam ihāśnute// *AP*: xxxviii, 45.

prevalent among the people of those ancient times by taking up arms and assuming the powers of a king; thus was established the kṣatriya caste. The vaiśya (merchant) and śūdra (craftsman) castes arose subsequently as the new king invented different means of livelihood and as people were trained in various arts and crafts. It is significant that Jainas place these events prior to the time of Ṛṣabha's attainment of Jinahood, thereby emphasizing the mundane and conventional nature of caste distinctions.[25]

The point is made especially clear with regard to the establishment of the priestly class; all Jaina sources agree that this was done not by Ṛṣabha at all, but by his son Bharata. Bharata became the first cakravartin after his father had reached enlightenment and had established the tīrtha, the path of Jaina practice, for our age. In order to determine the level of religious devotion and diligence among those who had taken the lay vows prescribed by this path, the young king arranged a kind of "ahiṃsā-test." Bharata had the courtyard of his palace strewn with fresh flowers and sprouting grain; then he invited the citizens for a feast on a sacred day. Those who were careless in the observance of their vows walked across the courtyard, disregarding the vegetable life beneath their feet. Those who were most virtuous refused to enter the palace lest they should harm the growing things and violate the vow of ahiṃsā.

The latter group Bharata then invited to enter by a suitable path; honoring each of its members, he encouraged them to accept one or more of the pratimās (thereby coming closer to the discipline of a monk). In recognition of their new status he gave them the title dvija, twice-born; this was confirmed by a ceremonial investiture with sacred

25. asir maṣiḥ kṛṣir vidyā vāṇijyaṃ śilpam eva ca/ karmāṇīmāni ṣoḍhā syuḥ prajājīvanahetavaḥ// tatra vṛttiṃ prajānāṃ hi sa bhagavān matikauśalāt/ upādikṣat *sarāgo hi sa tadāsīj* jagadguruḥ// . . . utpāditās trayo varṇās tadā tenādivedhasā/ kṣatriyā vaṇijaḥ śūdrāḥ kṣatratrāṇādibhir guṇaiḥ// Ibid.: xvi, 179–183.

threads, indicating the number of pratimās that each had assumed.[26] Speaking of such dvijas, Jinasena states that *these* are indeed the true children of the Jina and thus deserve to be called *deva-brāhmaṇa*, divine brahmans worthy of worship. Perhaps anticipating a hostile reaction to this notion of "Jaina-brahmans" from members of the traditional brahman caste, he adds:

> Now should a so-called brahman through his vanity of birth confront him [a Jaina-brahman] and say: Well, sir, did you suddenly become a god [deva] today? Are you not the son of so-and-so, is not your mother daughter of so-and-so, that you should put your nose in the air and dare to walk about ignoring a person like me? What great miracle happened to you by your initiation into the Jaina order?—you still walk on earth and not in the sky! Let him be told: Please listen, you so-called brahman, to our divine origin. Lord Jina is our father, and his pure knowledge is our womb. We are therefore truly born as gods, but if you find others of similar description, be free to call them also by the same title.[27]

26. ye 'ṇuvratadharā dhīrā dhaureyā gṛhamedhinām/ tarpaṇīyā hi te 'smābhir īpsitair vasuvāhanaiḥ// iti niścitya rājendraḥ satkartum ucitān imān/ parīcikṣiṣur āhvāsta tadā sarvān mahībhujaḥ// sadācārair nijair iṣṭair anujīvibhir anvitāḥ/ adyāsmat utsave yūyam āyāteti pṛthak pṛthak// haritair aṅkuraiḥ puṣpaiḥ phalaiś cākīrṇam aṅgaṇam/ saṃrāḍ acīkarat teṣāṃ parīkṣāyai svaveśmani// teṣv avratā vinā saṃgāt prāvikṣan nṛpamandiram/ tān ekataḥ samutsārya śeṣān āhvayayat prabhuḥ// te tu svavratasiddhyartham īhamānā mahānvayāḥ/ naiṣuḥ praveśanaṃ tāvad yāvad ārdrāṅkurāḥ pathi// . . . santy evānantaśo jīvā hariteṣv aṅkurādiṣu/ nigotā iti sārvajñaṃ devāsmābhiḥ śrutaṃ vacaḥ// . . . iti tadvacanāt sarvān so 'bhinandya dṛḍhavratān/ . . . teṣaṃ kṛtāni cihnāni sūtraiḥ padmāhvayān nidheḥ/ upāttair brahmasūtrāhvair ekādyekādaśāntakaiḥ// guṇabhūmikṛtād bhedāt klṛptayajñopavītinām/ satkāraḥ kriyate smaiṣām avratāś ca bahiḥ kṛtāḥ// Ibid.: xxxviii, 8–22.

27. atha jātimadāveśāt kaścid enaṃ dvijabruvaḥ/ brūyād evaṃ kim adyaiva devabhūyaṃ gato bhavān// tvam āmuṣyāyaṇaḥ kin na kiṃ te 'mbā 'muṣya putrikā/ yenaivam unnaso bhūtvā yāsy asatkṛtya madvidhān// jātiḥ saiva kulaṃ tac ca so 'si yo 'si pragetanaḥ/ tathāpi devatātmānam ātmānaṃ manyate bhavān// devatātithipitragnikāryeṣvaprayato bhavān/ gurudvijātidevānāṃ praṇāmāc ca parāṅmukhaḥ// dīkṣāṃ jainīṃ prapannasya jātaḥ ko 'tiśayas tava/ yato 'dyāpi manuṣyas tvaṃ pādacārī mahīṃ spṛśan// ity upārūḍhasaṃrambham upālabdhaḥ sa kenacit/ dadāty uttaram ity asmai vacobhir yuktipeśalaiḥ// śrūyatāṃ bho dvijammanya tvayā 'smad divyasambhavaḥ/ jino janayitā 'smākaṃ jñānaṃ garbho 'tinirmalaḥ// tatrārhatīṃ tridhā bhinnāṃ śaktiṃ traiguṇyasaṃśritām/ svasātkṛtya samudbhūtā vayaṃ saṃskārajanmanā// ayonisambhavās tena devā eva na mānuṣāḥ/ vayaṃ, vayam ivānye 'pi santi cet brūhi tadvidhān// Ibid.: xxxix, 108–116.

The rise among Digambaras of a class of "Jaina brahmans," individuals entrusted with care of the temples and the performance of elaborate rituals, was noted earlier, in Chapter VII. Whether this class originated, as Jinasena suggests, with a group of ordinary laymen who were on the basis of great merit or spiritual advancement appointed to such positions—or perhaps with a group of traditional brahmans who were converted to Jainism—we cannot be sure. It is clear, however, that the Jaina-brahmans eventually developed into a caste nearly as rigid as its Hindu counterpart; membership became strictly hereditary, and the range of rituals requiring the "supervision" of one of these "specialists" was greatly expanded. Faithful Digambaras in the south even today regard Jaina-brahmans as descendants of those honored by Bharata at the beginning of human civilization; Hindu brahmans are of course labeled "renegades" or "apostates," brahmans who have "fallen away from the true path."[28]

Thus the Jainas converted the varṇa system into what was for them an acceptable form. The role of theistic creation was eliminated, and the existence of a class of "spiritually superior laymen" analogous to the Hindu brahmans was justified on the basis of *conduct,* rather than of some irrevocable cosmic order. This second accomplishment was perhaps most important, for it allowed the community to have its own secular "priests" while still rejecting the supposed supremacy of the traditional brahman caste.

Jaina Integration of the Hindu Saṃskāras

Jinasena's efforts to "Jaina-ize" certain pan-Indian social norms were by no means confined to the area of varṇa. He also addressed himself to rituals celebrating the important events of everyday life: birth, marriage, and so forth. Prior to the appearance of the *Ādipurāṇa,* Jaina writings on lay

28. This was prophesied by Ṛṣabha: tataḥ kaliyuge 'bhyarṇe jātivādāvalepataḥ/ bhraṣṭācārāḥ prapatsyante sanmārgapratyanīkatām// te 'mī jātimadāviṣṭā vayaṃ lokādhikā iti/ purā durāgamair lokaṃ mohayanti dhanāśayā// Ibid.: xli, 47–48.

conduct dealt only with the vratas and pratimās, in other words, with matters of a specifically spiritual nature.[29] Hence it seems likely that until Jinasena's time, important secular ceremonies among Jainas of both sects were simply taken directly from the traditional Hindu *saṃskāras* (rites); indeed, Hindu brahmans may often have been called upon to perform such ceremonies, especially those pertaining to marriage. Jinasena must have perceived the dangers inherent in this tendency, for such blatant penetration of Hindu practices into those activities which formed the very heart of secular existence could only contain the seeds of Jainism's eventual and irrevocable absorption by the Hindu community.

We have already seen how the Jaina ācāryas had to walk a thin line between the need for social intercourse with non-Jainas and the dangers that invariably accompanied such contact. This problem was further complicated by the fact that brahmanical society, while traditionally tolerant of *doctrinal* heterodoxy, has often shown marked hostility towards deviation from accepted patterns of *social* behavior. So it was that those Jainas who held positions of power in the larger non-Jaina society must have found it to their advantage to encourage at least a surface similarity between the everyday conduct of their own community and that of the Hindu majority. Such similarity would have served not only to reduce intercommunity friction, but also to raise the status of the politically or financially prominent Jaina in the eyes of his brahmanical counterparts. The work of Jinasena, therefore, can perhaps be best understood as an attempt to deal with this situation, to devise a system whereby Jainas would evidence apparent conformity with Hindu practices and yet somehow remain uniquely Jaina. It seems, moreover, that he was eminently successful in this endeavor; whereas scholars from outside

29. "It is in the *Ādi-purāṇa* that the first description of these is to be found . . . For the first time in Jaina history the *rites de passage* are incorporated in the religious framework instead of being thrust aside as proper only for the deśācāra . . ." Williams in *JY*: 274–275.

the Jaina community have often observed that Jainas are "indistinguishable from Hindus" and should not be considered an independent group at all, Jainas themselves have adamantly denied any such claim, insisting again and again that they are not and never have been Hindus in any meaningful sense of the term.[30]

The reality beneath these divergent views is perhaps to be sought in an examination of the actual rules for secular life prescribed by Jinasena. We have seen, for example, that a Jaina varṇa system was developed on the Ṛṣabha-Bharata legend; Jinasena even went so far as to incorporate a brahmanical prejudice by asserting that members of the śūdra varṇa were excluded from certain higher religious practices. With regard to marriage customs, he again followed the Hindu model, allowing men to marry women of a lower caste, but not vice versa. The five essential elements of Hindu ritual—presence of a deity, availability of a priest capable of invoking that deity, use of a holy chant or mantra, ritual offering, and most important, holy fire—were all made a part of Jaina ceremonies as well. Finally, the sixteen Hindu saṃskāras were incorporated almost in their entirety, becoming part of a larger list of fifty-three kriyās (actions) which marked all the important events of life.[31] It is true that these practices are clearly brahmanical

30. The term "Hindu" is employed in several ways. As a cultural designation, it becomes almost synonymous with "Indian"; thus we have "Hindu drama," "Hindu poetry," and the like. From the constitutional standpoint, it includes all Indians save those belonging to the several religious minorities which have their roots in foreign traditions—Muslims, Christians, and Zoroastrians (Parsis)—and who are thus eligible for special privileges under the law. It is clear that in both these senses even Jainas must be classified as Hindus. Speaking within a purely religious context, however, the term denotes only those theistic movements or traditions which are either of Vedic origin or have long since been incorporated into the brahmanical fold. Jainism, as the sole surviving example of the śramaṇa religions once prevalent in the Ganges Valley (see Ch. I n. 2), meets neither of these criteria. It is in this context, then, that the Jaina claim to non-Hindu status must be understood. For more light on this controversy, see V. R. Gandhi 1893: 15; J. L. Jaini 1916a; C. R. Jain 1926; Chopade 1946; R. N. Shah 1950; Sangave 1959: 267–270.

31. On the variant enumerations of these saṃskāras, see Pandey 1969: 23. The standard list is as follows: 1) *garbhādhāna* (conception); 2) *puṃsavana* (quickening of a male child); 3) *sīmantonnayana* (hair-parting); 4) *jātakarma*

in appearance; the meaning-scheme which underlies their performance, however, is one which no Hindu could even begin to accept.

Consider for example, the meaning of the term dvija. Among Hindus this denotes a status which is available only to members of the three higher varṇas, and which may be attained simply by undergoing a ceremony of initiation (*upanayana*); dvijahood is, in other words, here seen as a rather automatic perquisite of the higher castes. For Jainas, however, becoming a dvija requires the taking of certain lay vows (at least the eight mūlaguṇas) in addition to mere initiation; hence there must be a more radical transformation of conduct than that entailed by the brahmanical upanayana.

As stated earlier, moreover, Jinasena took up the Hindu bias against śūdras. This is true to the extent that he denied the possibility of their becoming mendicants, as well as withholding from them the right to receive the sacred threads indicative of a dvijahood.[32] Even so, a sharp distinction remained between the Jaina śūdra and his Hindu counterpart. Whereas the latter was given no saṃskāras whatsoever, the former typically performed nearly all the lay ceremonies and could even attain the quasi-mendicant

(birth ceremony); 5) *nāmakaraṇa* (name-giving); 6) *niṣkramaṇa* (first outing); 7) *annaprāśana* (first feeding); 8) *cūḍākaraṇa* (tonsure); 9) *karṇavedha* (boring the ears); 10) *vidyārambha* (learning the alphabet); 11) *upanayana* (initiation); 12) *vedārambha* (beginning of Vedic study); 13) *keśānta* (shaving the beard); 14) *samāvartana* (end of studentship); 15) *vivāha* (marriage ceremony); 16) *antyeṣṭi* (funeral ceremony). For the Jaina lists, see below, n. 40.

32. adīkṣārhe kule jātā vidyāśilpopajīvinaḥ/ eteṣām upanītyādisaṃskāro nābhisammataḥ// teṣāṃ syād ucitaṃ liṅgaṃ svayogyavratadhāriṇām/ ekaśāṭakadhāritvaṃ saṃnyāsamaraṇāvadhi// *AP*: xl, 170–171. Recent research by the Digambara scholar Phoolchandra (1963) has led to the conclusion that this view originated with Jinasena; it does not appear to have been held by previous ācāryas, and it was certainly never preached by Mahāvīra. It is thus noncanonical, and not to be considered binding upon modern Jainas. Similarly, the idea of class (varṇa) in general, and of the caste (jāti) of Jaina-brahmans in particular, should not be understood as fundamental Jaina doctrine. These class distinctions were, as we have seen (n. 25 above), established by Ṛṣabha and Bharata when they were still worldly kings and not yet spiritual leaders; such distinctions are thus of a sociopolitical nature and cannot be taken as valid on the religious level.

status of an ailaka. Thus, although Jinasena's rules prohibited a śūdra from becoming either a dvija or a monk, they did not prevent him from taking an active role in most aspects of the religious life of the community.

Next it must be understood clearly what is meant by the Jainas' use of the five ritual elements referred to above.

1. *The deity*: As noted with reference to pūjā (see Chapter VII), the worship of an image or "invoking" of a holy figure by the Jaina has a far different signification than does a similar act carried out by a Hindu. The Jinas take the *place* of Hindu gods, but do not play a similar *role* in the Jaina ritual; they are seen as noble examples of the highest state to which man can aspire, and never as iṣṭa-devatā, the personal deity with whom one can enter into an intimate relationship. Although a Jina may be referred to as deva, this is never construed as an avatar; for Jainas, in other words, no deity is ever *present* in a real sense.[33]

2. *The priest*: The Hindu creation myth describes the origin of the four varṇas from various parts of the body of Prajāpati, the Creator. It is on the basis of this myth, in which their own lineage is said to proceed from the mouth of the Lord, that brahmans have claimed a special status relative to the gods: *only they* are fit to communicate, in a ritual context, with the powers of the nonhuman realm. The position of a Jaina-brahman, however, carries with it no such status; it is, as we have seen, a purely occupational (albeit hereditary) role.[34] A "brahmanical" caste conceived in this way, then, does not constitute true Hinduization; indeed, it undercuts the very assumptions upon which the Hindu conception of brahmanhood is based.

3. *The offering*: Jinasena reduced the hiṃsā inherent in

33. For the role of the śāsana-devatās, which may seem to contradict this view, see Ch. VII nn. 13–14.

34. brāhmaṇò 'sya múkham āsīd bāhū́ rājaníaḥ kṛtáḥ/ ūrū́ tád asya yád váiśyaḥ padbhyā́ṃ śūdró ajāyata// *Ṛgveda*: x, 90, 12. Jinasena is emphatic in his claim that the Jaina "dvijas" are not part of the Vedic "varṇa" system: viśuddhavṛttayas tasmāj Jainā varṇottamā dvijāḥ/ varṇāntaḥpātino naite jaganmānyā iti sthitam// *AP*: xli, 142.

Vedic sacrifice simply by stipulating that for Jainas only plants or milk products could be "offered" to the Jinas. And again, the whole relation of the "offering" to the "deity" is changed. Nothing is "received," no one is "propitiated"; the flowers or fruit laid upon the altar serve simply to honor the memory of the Jina, to reaffirm his exalted status as a model for human behavior.

4. *The mantra*: Jinasena provides a set of seven holy chants,[35] any of which is (with minor changes) applicable to nearly all ritual occasions. These chants are for the most part simply variations on the pañca-namaskāras or the catuḥ-śaraṇas and thus do not even make the pretence of "invoking" any of the "deities" associated with Hindu rites. The *jāti-mantra*, for example, is typically recited during the celebration of a Jaina birth-ceremony:

I take refuge in one who is born [has realized] the truth
I take refuge in the mother [the enlightenment] of the arhats
I take refuge in the sons [the disciples] of the arhats
I take refuge in those whose knowledge is infinite
I take refuge in those who have reached the incomparable birth [who have attained the state of a kevalin, and will thus become siddhas after death]
I take refuge in the three "jewels"
O Sarasvatī [the goddess of knowledge—that is, a personified way of referring to kevalajñāna], you who are embodiment of knowledge, the embodiment of true insight, may this ritual redound to the service of those who have attained the high status [the siddhas, arhats, and so on], may it eliminate [the possibility of] premature death [may he live long].[36]

35. See Ibid.: xl, 1–77.

36. satyajanmanaḥ śaraṇaṃ prapadyāmi, arhajjanmanaḥ śaraṇaṃ prapadyāmi, arhanmātuḥ śaraṇaṃ prapadyāmi, arhatsutasya śaraṇaṃ prapadyāmi, anādigamanasya śaraṇaṃ prapadyāmi, anupamajanmanaḥ śaraṇaṃ prapadyāmi, ratnatrayasya śaraṇaṃ prapadyāmi, he samyagdṛṣṛe, he samyagdṛṣṭe, he jñānamūrte, he jñānamūrte, he sarasvati, he sarasvati, svāhā, sevāphalaṃ ṣaṭparamasthānaṃ bhavatu, apamṛtyuvināśanaṃ bhavatu. jātimantro 'yam āmnāto jātisaṃskārakāraṇam/ Ibid.: xl, 31.

The dependence of this formula upon that of the pañca-namaskāra is very clear; moreover, Vedic or brahmanical mantric elements are conspicuously absent.

5. *The holy fire (agni)*: No ancient śramaṇa sect regarded any of the material elements (earth, water, air, fire) as sacred; hence they gave no great importance to fire in their ritual activities. Jinasena seems to have been the first śramaṇa ācārya to elevate fire to a "holy" status; but his rationale for doing so, as we might expect, could easily be considered blasphemy from the Hindu point of view. Speaking on this question, he says:

> Fire has no inherent sacredness, and no divinity. But because of its contact with the divine body of the arhat [at the time of his cremation], it can be considered pure. Therefore, the best among the dvijas make offerings into it. Such worship of the fire, like the worship of places made sacred by a saint's having attained nirvāṇa there, is not in any way blameworthy. By the twice-born, however, fire is to be considered suitable for worship only on a conventional level. It is in this wise that Jainas worship fire as part of their worship of the Jinas.[37]

Jinasena also asserts that three fires (corresponding, at least in name, to the *gārhapatya, āhavanīya,* and *dākṣiṇa* fires of the Hindu *śrauta* ritual) should be set up by the Jaina-brahmans at the beginning of any ceremony. Expanding the idea stated above, he suggests that each of these flames derive a certain holiness as a result of the role played by fire in three great events: the cremations of Ṛṣabha and other Tīrthaṅkaras, of the gaṇadharas, and finally of all other kevalins of our age.[38] By lighting three

37. na svato 'gneḥ pavitratvaṃ devatārūpam eva vā/ kintv arhaddivya-mūrtījyāsambandhāt pāvano 'nalaḥ// tataḥ pūjāṅgatām asya matvā 'rcanti dvijottamāḥ/ nirvāṇakṣetrapūjāvat tatpūjā 'to na duṣyati// vyavahāranayā-pekṣā tasyeṣṭā pūjyatā dvijaiḥ/ Jainair adhyavahāryo 'yaṃ nayo 'dyatve 'grajan-manaḥ// Ibid.: xl, 88–90.

38. trayo 'gnayaḥ praṇeyāḥ syuḥ karmārambhe dvijottamaiḥ/ ratnatritaya-saṃkalpād agnīndramukuṭodbhavāḥ// tīrthakṛt-gaṇabhṛc-cheṣakevaly-anta-mahotsave/ pūjāṅgatvaṃ samāsādya pavitratvam upāgatāḥ// kuṇḍatraye praṇetavyās traya ete mahāgnayaḥ/ gārhapaty-āhavanīya-dākṣiṇāgni-prasiddhayaḥ// asminn agnitraye pūjāṃ mantraiḥ kurvan dvijottamaḥ/ āhitāgnir iti jñeyo nityejyā yasya sadmani// Ibid.: xl, 82–85. The Śvetāmbara tradition agrees

fires, then, a Jaina pays homage to the memory of these departed ones who reached the highest goal. Two things must be noted here: First, it is not the fire qua fire that becomes the object of worship, but rather those beings of whom one is reminded by association therewith. Second, the source of whatever holiness fire does "possess" is based upon its function in a funereal context; although it has become "pure" by contact with holy beings, the point is nevertheless made that this contact took place only with the dead bodies of those beings. Thus we find Jinasena not only denying the divinity of *agni*, but even linking any religious significance attributed to fire with something that is for Hindus ritually impure in the extreme: the funeral pyre.[39]

As for the specific kriyās to be performed in the course of a lifetime, Jinasena was not content to simply take over the Hindu saṃskāras. He supplemented them with almost forty additional events worthy of being marked by a ceremony.[40] Certain of these differ in important ways not only

---

substantially with the above belief as can be seen from Hemacandra's account of Ṛṣabha's funeral ceremony: prācīnabarhiḥ prācīnacitāyāṃ svāminas tanum/ śanakaiḥ sthāpayāmāsa svaputra iva kṛtyavit// citāyāṃ dākṣiṇātyāyām ikṣvākukulajanmanām/ vapūṃṣi sthāpayanti sma sanābhaya ivāmarāḥ// anyeṣām anagārāṇāṃ śarīrāṇy apare surāḥ/ pratīcīnacitāyāṃ tu samīcīnavido nyadhuḥ// atra gotrabhidādeśān nākono 'gnikumārikāḥ/ citāsu tāsu tatkālam agnikāyān vicakrire// . . . mārgantaḥ śrāvakā devair dattakuṇḍatrayāgnayaḥ/ tataḥ prabhṛty abhūvāṃs te brāhmaṇā agnihotriṇaḥ// *TSPC*: I, vi, 546–556.

39. Related to the Jaina notion that the arhat's funeral pyre is sacred was their practice of stūpa worship, a common phenomenon among śramaṇas. Although this practice has died out in India, it is still found elsewhere among Buddhists, who were its main proponents even in ancient times. Worship of relics, however, has remained unknown within the brahmanical tradition. Regarding stūpa worship among the Jainas, see above, Ch. VII n. 9.

40. Jinasena enumerates fifty-three kriyās, as follows: ādhānaṃ prīti-suprītī dhṛtir modaḥ priyodbhavaḥ/ nāmakarma-bahiryāna-niṣadyāḥ prāśanaṃ tathā// vyuṣṭiś ca keśavāpaś ca lipisaṃkhyānasaṅgrahaḥ/ upanītir vrataṃcaryā vratāvataraṇaṃ tathā// vivāho varṇalābhaś ca kulacaryā gṛhīśitā/ praśāntiś ca gṛhatyāgo dīkṣādyaṃ jinarūpatā// maunādhyayanavṛttatvaṃ tīrthakṛttvasya bhāvanā/ gurusthānābhyupagamo gaṇopagrahaṇaṃ tathā// svagurusthānasaṃkrāntir nissaṅgatvātmabhāvanā/ yoganirvāṇasamprāptir yoganirvāṇasādhanam// indropapādābhiṣekau vidhidānaṃ sukhodayaḥ/ indratyāgāvatārau ca hiraṇyotkṛṣṭajanmatā// mandarendrābhiṣekaś ca gurupūjopalambhanam/ yauvarājyaṃ svarājyaṃ ca cakralābho diśāṃ jayaḥ// cakrābhiṣekasāmrājye niṣkrāntir yogasaṃmahaḥ/ ārhantyaṃ tadvihāraś ca yogatyāgo 'granir-

from the letter, but also from the spirit, of Hindu custom. The *varṇalābha* ritual, for example, celebrates a married son's establishment of his own household and business, separate from those of his father.[41] For the brahmanical community, which followed the traditional Dharmaśāstras (*Manusmṛti* and others), such a breaking away from the family might well have been frowned upon and would certainly not have provided occasion for a ceremony. Moreover, by listing among kriyās such things as the taking of lay vows (vratas and pratimās), and even certain posthumous events (for example, the attainment of heaven due to prior right conduct), Jinasena integrated his entire secular system into the larger context of a soul's progress towards mokṣa.

It is interesting to note that among the fifty-three rituals prescribed in the *Ādipurāṇa*, two—investiture with the sacred thread and marriage—receive particular emphasis. The first of these, called *upanīti* (corresponding to the brahmanical upanayana ceremony), is initiation into the adult religious community. The male child, at approximately eight years of age, is furnished with three threads indicative of ratnatraya (three jewels: right faith, right

---

vṛtiḥ// trayaḥ pañcāśad etā hi matā garbhānvayakriyāḥ/ garbhādhānādinirvāṇaparyantāḥ paramāgame// *AP*: xxxviii, 55–63.

For a complete description of these kriyās, see Sangave 1959: 259–262. It is evident that only the first eighteen, ending with varṇalābha, mark particular occasions in the life of a householder. Numbers nineteen through twenty-one are merely extensions of the eighteenth, while those beginning with gṛhatyāga (abandoning the household) and ending with nirvāṇa (fifty-three) have no direct relevance to lay existence. It is therefore not surprising that a later Digambara work, the *Traivarṇikācāra* of Somasena (seventeenth century) enumerates only the first twenty-three of Jinasena's kriyās—or that Śvetāmbara texts like the *Ācāradinakara* of Vardhamāna (circa 1411) ignore them altogether and provide for a new set of eighteen saṃskāras almost indistinguishable from that of the brahmanical tradition (see above, n. 31). For further details on the Śvetāmbara list, see Glasenapp 1925: 408–416; for a critical evaluation of all three lists and their relation to brahmanical rites, see *JY*: 274–287.

41. evaṃ kṛtavivāhasya gārhasthyam anutiṣṭhataḥ/ svadharmānativṛttyarthaṃ varṇalābham atho bruve// ūḍhabhāryo 'py ayaṃ tāvad asvatantro guror gṛhe/ tataḥ svātantryasiddhyarthaṃ varṇalābho 'sya varṇitaḥ// guror anujñayā labdhadhanadhānyādisampadaḥ/ pṛthakkṛtālayasyāsyai vṛttir varṇāptir iṣyate// *AP*: xxxviii, 135–137.

knowledge, and right conduct); he also receives the holy pañca-namaskāra litany. He then takes the mūlaguṇas (see Chapter VI), becoming thereby a bona fide Jaina layman with the status of a dvija.[42] It must be noted, however, that this particular practice persists only among the Digambaras of South India, who came most directly under Jinasena's influence. Neither Śvetāmbaras nor those Digambaras who remained in the north have developed any initiation ceremony per se; while members of these communities do receive the pañca-namaskāra-mantra from a mendicant teacher, no fire is lit and no sacred threads are given.

Although there is virtually no textual evidence concerning Jaina marital practices prior to Jinasena's time, it is very likely that there was always a certain amount of intermarriage with non-Jainas. This can be inferred not only from the lack of canonical material prohibiting such a practice, but also from the fact that even today certain Śvetāmbara Jainas, particularly those of the merchant class, do not object to marriage with Vaiṣṇavas of comparable social status.[43] But Jinasena seems to assume that spouses will be chosen only from within the Jaina fold, since he stipulates that the wedding ceremony (*vaivāhikī-kriyā*) must begin with performance of a pūjā before the siddha-image. A priest should then light the three fires, which the couple circumambulates three times. Jinasena's account concludes abruptly with the words: "Finally, let

42. kriyopanītir nāmāsya varṣe garbhāṣṭame matā/ yatrāpanītakeśasya mauñjī savratabandhanā// kṛtārhatpūjanasyāsya mauñjībandho jinālaye/ gurusākṣividhātavyo vratārpaṇapurassaram// śikhī sitāṃśukaḥ sāntarvāsā nirveṣavikriyaḥ/ vratacihnaṃ dadhat sūtraṃ tadokto brahmacāry asau// Ibid.: xxxviii, 104–106.

43. Certain stories found in the *Bṛhatkathākośa* of Hariṣeṇa (circa 940) indicate that marriage between Jainas and non-Jainas, though not prohibited, was also not looked upon with any great favor. In the Rudradattapriyābodhakathānaka (no. 54), e.g., a young Śaivite man seeks in vain to win the hand of a Jaina maiden and has to become a Jaina himself before being allowed to marry her. After the wedding ceremony he reverts to his old religion, and great strife ensues between the husband and wife.

In another story (no. 68), the son of a Buddhist merchant is warned by his father not to seek a girl from a Jaina family, "since it is impossible that they will

the kriyā be performed."[44] One detail can probably be filled in here by considering a typical Jaina wedding of today. The girl's father performs *kanyādāna,* giving the bride away, by placing her hand in that of the groom. This procedure was probably so well-known to Jinasena's contemporaries that he felt no need to mention it. In any case, he adds that the newlyweds should remain celibate for up to seven days, during which time they would do well to visit some holy place (a temple or shrine, for example). Afterwards they return home, consummate the marriage, and set up housekeeping.

Now, from the point of view of our investigation, Jinasena's silences are in a sense just as significant as his words. No Hindu wedding, at least among the upper castes, can be considered legal unless the couple takes seven steps (*saptapadī*) around the fire to the accompaniment of a Vedic chant.[45] Jinasena consciously omits this practice, of

---

give their daughter to meat-eaters" (upāsakā vayaṃ putra piśitāhāriṇas tarām/ . . . sa dadāti kathaṃ putrīm asmākam . . .// lxviii, 18–19). The young man resorts to deceit, becoming a Jaina layman endowed with vratas in order to win her hand. Soon he too returns to his former faith. Nonvegetarianism (fairly common among both the Śaivites and the Buddhists) would thus appear to have presented the most important obstacle to mixed marriage. The Vaiṣṇavas, on the other hand, have always been vegetarians; marriage of a Jaina to a member of this group would therefore not be unacceptable. Raychandbhai Mehta (see below, n. 64), the great Jaina saint, is a well-known product of such a family; his grandfather was a devout Vaiṣṇava, his mother a Sthānakavāsi Jaina.

For information on the various kinds of endogamous groups between which Jainas of the present day are willing to contract a marriage, see Sangave 1959: 150–162. Also, Upadhye (1936) has compiled a list of eighty-four exogamous groups (*gotra*) within the above mentioned endogamous ones; marriage between members of the same gotra is not allowed.

44. tato 'sya gurvanujñānād iṣṭā vaivāhikī kriyā/ vaivāhike kule kanyām ucitāṃ pariṇeṣyataḥ// siddhārcanavidhiṃ samyak nirvartya dvijasattamāḥ/ kṛtāgnitrayasaṃpūjāḥ kuryus tatsākṣitāṃ kriyām// *AP*: xxxviii, 127–128.

45. On the saptapadī, see Pandey 1969: 219. It should be noted here that this ceremony (albeit with a formula acceptable to Jainas, as mentioned in Sangave 1959: 167) eventually found a place in such later texts as the *Ācāradinakara* and *Traivarṇikācāra*; thus we can assume that a certain amount of "brahmanization" of Jaina marriage customs had occurred by the fourteenth century. Sangave has maintained that Jaina marriage was contractual rather than sacramental, and also that divorce and widow-marriage, although not favored, were certainly not unknown; indeed, both these practices are prevalent today among certain Jaina communities such as the Saitavāla and Bogāra (Sangave 1959: 173–175).

which he must certainly have been aware, thus effecting once again the kind of sham Hinduization that we have seen so often before. Through his codification of lay conduct, whether in regard to specific kriyās or to the ritual elements employed therein, he consistently managed to clothe the members of his community in a protective Hindu cloak, beneath which the beliefs and practices of Jainism could continue unabated.

As mentioned earlier, Jinasena incorporated or adapted nearly all of the Hindu saṃskāras within his own system. In fact there is only one which he omitted completely: *antyeṣṭi,* the ritual to be performed at death.[46] While the *Ādipurāṇa* does refer to the cremation of Ṛṣabha,[47] few details are given and no specific antyeṣṭi-kriyā is anywhere set forth. We should not assume, however, that this omission indicates Jaina compliance with prevailing Hindu customs pertaining to death. To the contrary, scathing attacks upon these customs appear in numerous Jaina texts, particularly the *Syādvādamañjarī* of Malliṣeṇa.[48] The object of such attacks is mainly to discredit the practice known as śrāddha, or *sapiṇḍīkaraṇa,* offering food to the spirits of the dead.

Śrāddha constitutes the final component of the antyeṣṭi-saṃskāra, and it is certainly one of the most important rituals observed in brahmanical society. The idea underlying this ceremony is that a departed soul ostensibly spends a certain amount of time in the *pitṛ-loka* (world of the fathers), a sort of heavenly way station, prior to attaining rebirth in human form. But the journey to this loka requires a special body, which the soul is not capable of producing. Therefore, it is believed, the son of the dead person must offer food in a special ceremony; this food, when eaten by brahmans, will somehow be "converted"

46. On the Hindu funeral ceremonies, see Pandey 1969: 234–274.
47. *AP*: xlvii, 343–350. See n. 38 above.
48. *SM*: k 11.

into the "subtle body" required by the spirit, thereby freeing it from its disembodied limbo and allowing it to move upwards to its new abode. The son's right to inherit, moreover, depends upon his having performed the śrāddha; only after thus fulfilling his final obligation to his parents does he become a worthy heir.[49]

It will be apparent, if Jaina doctrines pertaining to karma in general and to the mechanism of rebirth in particular are recalled, that the incorporation of śrāddha would necessarily have involved a blatant heresy; thus even Jinasena stayed clear of any attempt to bring such a practice into the Jaina community. First of all, Jaina texts are very definite about the fact that a soul normally requires but a single moment to move from one body to the next;[50] any notion of a protracted period between births, during which śrāddha would be relevant, is therefore to be rejected out of hand. Even more important is the Jaina stress upon the total individuality of the karmic process. The fruits one reaps must be those which he alone has sown; thus the idea of one person affecting the destiny of another, whether by food offerings or in any other manner, is unthinkable. Finally, Jainas have traditionally taken recourse to common sense as the best guide in evaluating the feasibility of various religious beliefs; the practice of śrāddha, clearly, does not bear up well under this sort of scrutiny. As Malliṣeṇa has said: "Who can agree that what is eaten by brahmans accrues to them [the ancestors]? For only in the brahmans do we see fattened bellies, and transference of these to the departed souls cannot be espied."[51]

49. For Hindus, only a man can perform śrāddha; if there is no son, an adopted son or the nearest male family member must carry out this duty. Thus it is that widows or daughters of Hindu families without sons cannot inherit the husband/father's property; it will go only to the one who assists the departed soul on its way to the pitṛ-loka. Jaina women, by contrast, are not barred from inheritance in this way, since among Jainas no such ritual activity is a prerequisite to receiving goods of the deceased. For a discussion of these divergent customs and their relation to classical Indian laws, see J. L. Jaini 1916a; Sangave 1959: 190–192.

50. vigrahagatau karmayogaḥ/ ekasamayā 'vigrahā/ *TS*: ii, 25, 29.

51. atha vipropabhuktaṃ tebhya upatiṣṭhata iti cet, ka ivaitat pratyetu,

For all these reasons, then, śrāddha has never been acceptable to Jainas; in those communities where, due to extreme brahmanical influence, it did appear, it was denounced as a mithyātva.[52] Given the importance of this ritual in Hindu life, and its near total absence among the Jainas, it seems unreasonable to claim that Jainas and Hindus are functionally indistinguishable. Even if our interpretation of Jinasena's work as a cleverly effected pseudo-Hinduization should prove to be unwarranted, there would still remain, as Jainas themselves have emphasized, the fundamental distinction between the two societies based upon their conflicting attitudes towards śrāddha.

Jaina Integration of Hindu Divinities

The great devotional movement (bhakti) which swept India around the fifth or sixth century has already been mentioned, in connection with the collapse of Buddhism. While numerous mythological figures became the objects of such cult worship, two stood far above all others in terms of their power to capture the popular imagination and to generate large followings. They were of course Rāma and Kṛṣṇa, the great heroes whose exploits were described in the widely told stories of the *Rāmāyaṇa* and the *Mahābhārata,* respectively, and who were raised to the status of Viṣṇu-avatāra by the epics and by the Purāṇas of the early medieval period. Had Jaina teachers ignored the tremendous fascination which these figures held for the average layperson, regardless of his religious affiliation, they would have done so at the peril of their own society's disintegration.

Thus we see in Jaina literature of the period the development of a parallel set of myths, placing Rāma and Kṛṣṇa in a Jaina context and treating their respective deeds from

---

viprāṇām eva medurodaratādarśanāt. tadvapuṣi ca teṣāṃ saṅkramaḥ śraddhātum api na śakyate . . . iti mudhaiva śrāddhādividhānam. *SM*: k 11.

52. *JY*: intro. xxiv.

the standpoint of Jaina ethics. These tales generally employed a fixed literary structure in which three types appeared: a hero (*balabhadra*), standing totally within Jaina law and leading an ideal life; a villain (*prati-nārāyaṇa*), evil personified; the hero's companion or ally (*nārāyaṇa*), representing as it were the force of righteous indignation and carrying out destruction of the villain. This device made it possible to alter the Hindu myth in such a way as to preserve the hero's pure character from the Jaina standpoint. The Jaina "*Rāmāyaṇas,*" for example, follow Vālmīki's original narrative in nearly all particulars except the killing of Rāvaṇa; whereas in the Hindu version Rāma must perform this deed (being, as an avatar, personally responsible for the destruction of evil), the Jaina texts have the murder committed by his brother Lakṣmaṇa.[53] Thus Lakṣmaṇa must go to hell for his great violation of ahiṃsā, but Rāma remains a true follower of the Jina-dharma and is shown renouncing the world and achieving mokṣa at the end of his career.

As for Kṛṣṇa, the hero of the *Mahābhārata,* his various misdeeds (both sexual and violent) were so well-known that making him into a Jaina hero was a bit too difficult to manage. Thus he was given the nārāyaṇa role, and his elder brother Balarāma was depicted as the great upholder of the Jina's teachings.[54]

53. At least eighteen Jaina "*Rāmāyaṇas*" (ten in Sanskrit, five in Prakrit, one in Apabhraṃśa, and two in Kannada) are known to exist. For a complete list, see Kulkarni 1959–1960. Compare the extent of this collection with the fact that only one such story, the Daśarathajātaka (*Jātaka*: no. 461), exists in the Buddhist tradition. See Bulche 1971: 56ff.

54. For the Jaina version of the life of Kṛṣṇa, see Punnāṭa Jinasena's *Harivaṃśapurāṇa* (A.D. 783) and Hemacandra's *TSPC*: VII. These are based on canonical accounts wherein it is prophesied that Kṛṣṇa will be reborn in hell: evaṃ khalu Kaṇhā, Bāravīe nayarīe . . . Dīvāyaṇkovanidaḍḍhāe . . . Jarākumāreṇaṃ tikkheṇaṃ . . . isuṇā vāme pāde viddhe samāṇe kālamāse kālaṃ kiccā taccāe Vāluyappabhāe puḍhavīe ujjalie narae nerayittāe uvavajjihisi. *Antakṛddaśāḥ*: §v, 9. It should be noted that Jaina authors, while condemning Kṛṣṇa to hell for his homicidal actions, were anxious to "rehabilitate" him. Perhaps with an eye to his great popularity, they suggested (following the canon) that after completing his karmic term in the nether regions (sometime during the next half-cycle), he would be reborn in Bharatakṣetra and become a Tīrthaṅkara.

In "accepting" Hindu figures as part of their own mythology, Jaina writers denied any notion that these beings were, as was often claimed, manifestations of the divine. Nevertheless, they were able to portray the heroes in a popular manner that satisfied the desire of the laity for such tales, probably helping thereby to reduce the number of Jainas who actually left the faith and allied themselves with one or another of the bhakti cults.

The Spiritual Decay of the Jaina Community

Despite the wealth accumulated during their periods of great influence, and the various efforts chronicled above to achieve "peaceful coexistence" with the Hindu majority, Jaina communities of both the north and south fell upon rather hard times in the twelfth and thirteenth centuries. Hindu opposition to the "atheistic" and anti-Vedic doctrines that were being propounded could not be kept down indefinitely; thus, as the political power of the Jainas fell to a low ebb and the wave of bhakti carried virtually everything before it, great erosions took place in Jaina society. Many people converted out of preference; others simply went along with the religious convictions of their rulers. Numerous temples were lost, subject either to takeover by militant Hindu sects (particularly in the Deccan) or to conversion into mosques by invading Muslims.[55] Serious as these developments may have been, however, the greatest threat to the continued existence of Jainism came not from some external source but from a spiritual decay within Jaina society itself.

Jainas have traditionally prided themselves on the austere life-styles of their mendicants. But with the acquisition of great riches by the community, the monks fell increas-

---

See Barnett 1907: 81–82. On the legends relating Kṛṣṇa to Nemi, the twenty-second Tīrthaṅkara, see above, Ch. I n. 75; and Kashalikar 1969.

55. For an allusion to Hindu persecution of the Jainas, see *Periyapurāṇaṃ* (tenth century): 533; and *Tiruvaḷiyātar Purāṇam* (sixteenth century): 441–479. Certain frescoes at the Mīnākṣī temple in Madura also depict such persecution, in graphic detail. See Saletore 1938: 272–281.

ingly into a temple-centered existence, living under rather luxurious conditions and devoting themselves more to the external trappings of religion than to the practices stressed by Mahāvīra. There even developed a special group of "administrator-clerics," who not only managed the temple and its associated holdings (schools, libraries, extensive areas of land) but also assumed control of the temple rituals that formed the core of lay practice. Thus they gained great power over their lay disciples, wielding the threat of excommunication against those who failed to perform the rituals (or performed them contrary to their wishes) and honoring those who did perform them. Among Digambaras, such individuals came from the ranks of the kṣullakas and were known as *bhaṭṭārakas* (venerable ones);[56] their Śvetāmbara counterparts were actual monks who carried the title of *caityavāsi* (temple-dweller) or *yati* (literally, ascetic—a rather inappropriate term for those living in such affluence as the yatis enjoyed).[57] In both sects the administrator-clerics functioned as the effective governing bodies of their communities.

It could be argued that such a situation brought with it a certain increased stability; but we must keep in mind that the solidarity of Jaina social organization had always stemmed not from the political power of the monks but from the great *moral* authority they possessed. In falling away from his proper role as a living example of the Jaina ideal (the dedicated ascetic earnestly seeking mokṣa), a monk forfeited this authority. Confronted by the spectacle of such moral stagnation among his "holy men," the Jaina layperson could have found little or no reason to assert the superiority of the Jina's path over those set forth by the Hindu schools. Thus it is probably not unreasonable to

56. For a comprehensive history of the tradition of the bhaṭṭārakas, see Johrapurkar 1958. Sangave (1959: 330–335) gives a detailed description of modern bhaṭṭārakas in South India, with particular attention to the power which they wield over their parishes.

57. On yatis, known also as *gorjis*, see Glasenapp 1925: 341.

suggest that, had these conditions continued unabated for an indefinite period, the Jaina community might well have been completely assimilated by its Hindu neighbors.

Fortunately, various individuals became aware of the gravity of the situation and strove to bring about needed reforms. As early as the ninth century the philosopher-mystic Haribhadra, disgusted by the already emerging trend towards affluence and impropriety, wrote:

> These pseudo-monks live in temples, start worshiping there like laymen, enjoy the wealth dedicated to the worship of the Jinas, take active part in erecting temples and residence halls, wear perfumed clothes of variegated colors, eat two or three times a day, and partake of food brought by nuns. They engage themselves in astrology and predict the future for the lay disciples. They take baths, adorn their bodies with all sorts of powders and oils, and waste time in sleep, in buying and selling, and in gossip. To increase their support they buy young children and make them into their own disciples, and do business in buying and selling Jaina images. They are clever in medicine, in *yantra* [mystical diagrams], in tantric practices, and in other such techniques forbidden to monks. They prevent the lay disciples from going to those monks who lead a pure life, frightening them with curses, and they fight constantly to keep their disciples from being taken by others.[58]

Jaina Reform Movements

In the year 1017, there was a movement among certain Śvetāmbara monks in the capital of Saurashtra to break the hold of the caityavāsis over local Jaina society. Although the opposition group, called *vanavāsi* (forest-dwellers), did not completely succeed in their aims, they

58. *Sambodhaprakaraṇa* of Haribhadra: k 65–76 (quoted in Premi 1956: 477–479). *Ratnamālā*, a Digambara text, goes so far as to suggest that even naked Digambara ascetics should abandon secluded places and, contrary to mendicant law, live in the temple precincts at all times: kalau kāle vane vāso varjyate munisattamaiḥ/ sthīyate ca jināgāre grāmādiṣu viśeṣataḥ// (k 22, quoted in Premi 1956: 481). It is likely that this practice began during a period of Muslim rule, when strict bans were enforced against public nudity of any kind.

did manage to establish a separate community of those adhering more closely to the traditional values. But the first truly effective rebellion against the entrenched power of the caityavāsis, as well as against the degeneration of the Śvetāmbara monkhood in general, was initiated by a devout Gujarati layman called Lonkā Śāha in 1451. A scribe by profession, he gained access to the sacred texts (at that time available in their original form only to monks) and was shocked to compare the discipline they demanded with the lax monkish behavior which he saw around him.

It is said that Lonkā Śāha considered the institution of the temple (caitya), with its great concentration of wealth and power, to be the main source of corruption and the rituals performed there as totally irrelevant to the path set forth in scripture. He became convinced, furthermore, that even worship of the Jina-image was against the rule of ahiṃsā, since erecting such an image involved digging, quarrying, and other activities harmful to minute life forms. On the basis of such ideas Lonkā Śāha declared publicly that temple worship was a mithyātva, a misdeed for any Jaina, and that such worship was not supported by the ancient texts. He also challenged the various practices of the caityavāsis; perhaps mainly because of this latter position (for many were dissatisfied with the laxity and excessive power of the administrator-monks), he began to gain followers. One of these was a very influential Jaina minister named Lakhamsi; his support helped the scribe's ideas to gain a currency much wider than they could otherwise have achieved. The result was that the entire community was shaken from its apathy and made to examine itself in the light of the scriptures.

Like the leaders of many protestant movements, Lonkā Śāha had taken a position so extreme that its complete acceptance was doomed from the start. On a purely practical level, monks whose whole career had revolved around temple rituals were not about to see those rituals abandoned; nor were laypersons who had invested great sums of money into the institution of the temple likely to stand still for the complete downgrading of actions and expenditures previously considered highly meritorious. The scriptures themselves, moreover, allowed for a certain amount of lay hiṃsā in service of the great amount of prabhāvanā generated by image erection or temple building.

Certain scholars have suggested that Lonkā Śāha was influenced by the iconoclastic ideas of the Muslims, who ruled portions of Gujarat at that time. Given that Muslim law forbids the making of images of God (even the face of the prophet Mohammed is covered in the manuscripts depicting him), whereas Jaina doctrine is not technically opposed to such a practice, this seems a reasonable conclusion. In any case, the movement founded by the scribe gained enough followers to form a viable subsect, existing separate from the Śvetāmbara mainstream, but its influence was never sufficient to radically alter the flow of that stream. The new group, known as Sthānakavāsi (dwellers in halls [as opposed to temples]), was mainly distinguished by certain practices (for example, retaining lay names and wearing face-masks [muh-patti] at all times) referred to earlier (Chapter VIII).[59] Its emphasis upon strict interpretation of scripture and adherence to a puritanical way of life, while not generally adopted by Śvetāmbaras, nevertheless exerted a beneficial effect upon the larger community by raising lay expectations as to the standards of monkish conduct and thus helping to curb the excesses into which Śvetāmbara clerics had fallen.

Digambaras too experienced an important rejuvenation as the result of a reform movement. This movement took place in Agra during the late sixteenth century and was

59. On the history of the Sthānakavāsi sect, see Glasenapp 1925: 69–72; Schubring 1962: 65–67. On the philosophy of Lonkā Śāha, see Malvania 1964. Some Digambaras of central India also seem to have come under the influence of the Sthānakavāsi movement. Known as Tāraṇapantha, i.e., the followers of one Tāraṇasvāmi (sixteenth century), this sect banned idol worship and is said to have admitted many low-caste people into its ranks. See Glasenapp 1925: 357; and Sangave 1959: 56–58.

initiated by a well-known lay poet called Banārasīdās.[60] A devout student and translator of the works of Kundakunda, Banārasīdās was deeply offended by the lax behavior of the bhaṭṭārakas and also convinced that the amount of ritual associated with temple worship was excessive. Citing the high degree of hiṃsā involved in offering flowers, fruits, and sweets in temple services, he called for the omission of such offerings from the layman's daily religious practice. According to Banārasīdās, emphasis should rather be placed upon *internal* forms of worship (meditation); this contention he supported with convincing doctrinal arguments made from the niścaya (nonconventional, that is, absolute) point of view so important in Kundakunda's philosophy.

The influence of Banārasīdās and his later followers, notably one Paṇḍita Ṭoḍarmal of Jaipur,[61] on Digambara society was profound; the crippling excesses of ritualism associated with the bhaṭṭāraka tradition were to a large extent eliminated, and the entire community was reawakened to the deep meaning of its faith. Thus Digambaras were able to enter the modern period with greatly increased vitality and with the capacity to successfully accommodate the difficult changes which that period would bring.

The Jaina Commitment to Nonviolence

Any investigation that seeks to unearth "the causes" of a complex phenomenon must eventually draw the line. In considering Jainism's survival against formidable odds, we have noted the roles played by royal patronage, by the strong involvement of the lay community, by the ability of the ācāryas to constructively compromise with Hindu influence, and by internal movements towards reform. Equal weight could have been given to the general lack of

60. On the life and works of Banārasīdās, see R. K. Jain 1966.

61. Author of the *Mokṣamārgaprakāśaka* (circa 1800), a Hindi work widely read among Digambaras in modern times. For a discussion of Ṭoḍarmal's main works, see Phoolchandra 1967: intro.

schisms within the Jaina tradition (Buddhism, by contrast, could count eighteen schools, opposed to one another on doctrinal grounds, as early as the third century B.C.), or perhaps to geographical factors. Then, of course, there are the intangibles: commitment, timing, luck, and so forth. To synthesize all of these elements in terms of some overarching dynamic or principle is perhaps tempting, but likely to generate inaccuracies that far outweigh the "benefits" of imposed coherence. Ultimately, perhaps it can only be said that the forces and events discussed, plus others mentioned but not explored, and yet others of which we are not even aware, came together in a unique and auspicious interaction to produce the phenomenon which we have labeled "the survival of Jainism in India."

For the Jainas themselves, of course, such a statement will never suffice. Every social group large and cohesive enough to constitute an identifiable community seems to cherish the idea that its behavior in the world is conditioned by certain principles to which the group firmly adheres, principles which thus "explain" whatever the facts of that group's history may be. With some such idea in mind, many Americans will, for example, construe the events of their nation's past as the natural outcome of "individualism"; Japanese may assign an equivalent role to "hierarchy" or "obligation" in their case. Jainas are also subject to this tendency, often being quick to point out that the history of their fortunes can be clearly understood as following directly from Jaina commitment to the Jina's greatest teaching, that of ahiṃsā. Although this view cannot be wholly accepted, it *is* true (as pointed out in Chapter VIII) that the ahiṃsā ideal is of paramount importance to every Jaina, and also that the Jainas as a group have traditionally been identified by Indians of all faiths with the doctrine of nonviolence. Thus it is appropriate to close this discussion on Jainism in Indian history, as well as this entire study of the Jaina experience, by considering briefly certain aspects of the relation between the Jainas, ahiṃsā, and society.

Jaina mendicants have clearly exerted great efforts to avoid *personally harming* any living thing; but their record on the issue of *condoning* violent behavior is less clear. We have seen the role of ācāryas in abetting the establishment of kingdoms; this must have taken place under circumstances in which the candidate had to engage in warfare in order to secure his throne. As has also been noted, great Jaina generals were not condemned by mendicant leaders for their violent actions; on the contrary, their high position in the state was seen as a boon to the entire religious community. Jaina literature, moreover, is by no means pacifist (in the sense that Quakers are, for example): only aggressive war is proscribed, while the subject of fighting in defense of one's country is passed over almost without comment. As for a Jaina layman's personal responsibility in time of war, it has never been confronted directly.[62] Jainas have not produced any text similar to the *Bhagavad Gītā*, in which the ethical problems of the warrior are discussed from the brahmanical standpoint. The ācāryas' silence on this issue has perhaps been due to the fact that most Jainas, not being of the kṣatriya caste, have not been called upon to engage in warfare anyway. Even so, it is a serious indictment of a tradition so closely associated with the ideal of nonviolence that it could have remained ambivalent, or at best noncommittal, on the subject of warfare.

On the positive side of the ledger, it must be said that for most Jainas the commitment to nonviolence is reflected in a real and active concern with the prevention and alleviation of suffering. Thus, the attempt by a renegade Sthānakavāsi monk called Bhīkhanji (eighteenth century) to establish a sect based on the doctrine of total nonassistance to any living being (except mendicants) was greeted by protest from nearly all members of the com-

62. Modern Jaina writers typically deal with this issue simply by quoting a single verse by Somadevasūri (tenth century): yaḥ śastravṛttiḥ samare ripuḥ syāt, yat kaṇṭako vā nijamaṇḍalasya/ astrāṇi tatraiva nṛpāḥ kṣipanti, na dīnakānīna-śubhāśayeṣu// *Yaśastilaka-campū*: II, 97. While these lines are by no means explicit, they seem to imply that killing in a defensive war is a kind of

munity.[63] It is said the Bhīkhanji could initially gather no more than twelve disciples; the sect he founded, therefore, became known as Terāpantha, which means "the path of the thirteen."

The image of the Jaina as a man of peace and goodwill is strongly imprinted on the Indian psyche; and indeed, it can be said that the Jaina community has often been a morally uplifting factor in the life of Indian society as a whole. In this connection might be mentioned Mahatma Gandhi—perhaps the greatest champion of nonviolence in our age. Gandhi claimed to have been deeply influenced, particularly in the development of his theory of ahiṃsā as a political weapon, by the revered Jaina layman Raychand-

---

virodhī-hiṃsā (see above, Ch. VI n. 32), best avoided if possible (i.e., by entering the mendicant path), but "acceptable" for laypeople. The story literature, however, makes it clear that even killing in self-defense must lead one to rebirth in hell. In the Jaina *Rāmāyaṇa*, for example, the hero Lakṣmaṇa goes to the very same hell as does the wicked Rāvaṇa, whom he "justifiably" destroyed. (Compare: adhunā narake turye saŚambūko Daśānanaḥ/ Lakṣmaṇaś cāsti, gatayaḥ karmādhīnā hi dehinām// *TSPC*: VII, x, 231.) Contrast this view with that expressed by the *Mahābhārata*, in which both Yudhiṣṭhira and Duryodhana go to heaven, the former by virtue of his righteousness and the latter through having died in battle. (svargaṃ triviṣṭapaṃ prāpya dharmarājo Yudhiṣṭhiraḥ/ Duryodhanaṃ śriyā juṣṭaṃ dadarśāsīnam āsane// *Mahābhārata*: XVIII, i, 4.) An even stronger statement of the Hindu dictum that a warrior's death brings heavenly rebirth appears in a famous line of the *Bhagavad Gītā*: hato vā prāpsyasi svargaṃ, jitvā vā bhokṣyase mahīm/ tasmād uttiṣṭha Kaunteya yuddhāya kṛtaniścayaḥ// (ii, 37).

63. Bhīkhanji's theory was that saving the life of a dog, e.g., makes one responsible for the violence committed by that dog in the future and thus should be avoided. He also claimed that "helpful" behavior almost always involved some interest in the result, hence brought an increase in karmic attachments. Bhīkhanji here exploits the doctrinal split inherent in any community that preaches the ideals of total renunciation and mokṣa, on the one hand, and the value of compassionate and charitable behavior (leading to heaven) on the other.

Pushed to a purely logical extreme, the canonical teachings might well be thought to justify the Terāpanthi interpretation. Even so, such interpretation violates the spirit of anekāntavāda and has been considered a form of ekānta by most Jainas. Since its inception, therefore, the Terāpantha sect has lived in virtual isolation from the larger Jaina community. It should be noted, however, that the Terāpantha mendicants have in recent years made important efforts to contact and influence Indian society as a whole. This tendency is most evident in the "aṇuvrata movement," a Terāpantha-based attempt to purge corruption from Indian political and economic life. For further information on this sect, see Glasenapp 1925: 354; Nathmal 1968; Tulasi 1969; Nair 1970.

bhai Mehta.[64] Among the letters exchanged by these two men there is a statement by the layman, given in answer to a pointed question by Gandhi, which deserves to be reproduced here. Raychandbhai's words seem a fitting end to this study of the Jaina religion, for they do more than simply set forth that religion's most important doctrine. In reading them we understand, as Gandhi did, that spirit of Jainism which can reach beyond the narrow confines of its community and touch the hearts of men and women everywhere.

> *Question*: If a snake is about to bite me, should I allow myself to be bitten or should I kill it, supposing that that is the only way in which I can save myself?
> *Answer*: One hesitates to advise you that you should let the snake bite you. Nevertheless, how can it be right for you, if you have realized that the body is perishable, to kill, for protecting a body which has no real value to you, a creature which clings to its own life with great attachment? For anyone who desires his spiritual welfare, the best course is to let his body perish in such circumstances. But how should a person who does not desire spiritual welfare behave? My only reply to such a question is, how can I advise such a person that he should pass through hell and similar worlds, that is, that he should kill the snake? If the person lacks the development of a noble character, one may advise him to kill the snake, but we should wish that neither you nor I will even dream of being such a person.[65]

64. "Three persons have influenced me deeply, Tolstoy, Ruskin and Raychandbhai: Tolstoy through one of his books . . . and Raychandbhai through intimate personal contact. When I began to feel doubts about Hinduism as a religion, it was Raychandbhai who helped me to resolve them." M. K. Gandhi 1958–1976: XXXII, 4.

On the life and works of Raychandbhai Mehta (1868–1901), known to his devotees as Śrīmad Rājacandra, see *SM*: J. C. Jain's intro. (in Hindi), 1–12. See pl. 32.

65. M. K. Gandhi 1958–1976: XXXII, 601–602. (The letter is dated October 20, 1894. Compare Govardhandas 1951: §530.)

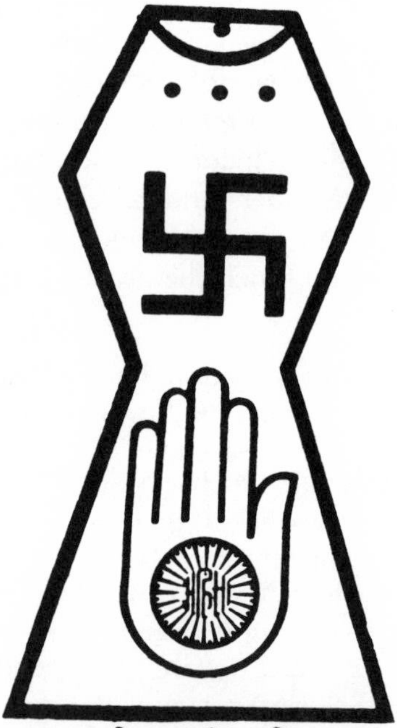

परस्परोपग्रहो जीवानाम्

PARASPAROPAGRAHO JĪVĀNĀM

33. Jaina pratīka: symbol of the Jaina faith, officially adopted during the 2,500th anniversary of Mahāvīra's nirvāṇa (1975). The palm of the hand bears the word ahiṃsā; the svastika topped by three dots and the crescent represent the four destinies, the threefold path, and the abode of the liberated souls, respectively; the slogan below the figure of loka-ākāśa calls for the mutual assistance of all beings.

Bibliography

Texts and Translations

Abhidharmakośa-bhāṣya of Vasubandhu, Sanskrit text ed. by P. Pradhan. Patna (K. P. Jayaswal Research Institute) 1967.

Abhisamayālaṅkāra of Maitreya, Sanskrit text ed. by Th. Stcherbatsky and E. Obermiller. Leningrad (Bibliotheca Buddhica) 1929.

Ācārāṅga-sūtra, ed. as *The Āyāraṃga Sutta of the Śvetāmbara Jains* by H. Jacobi. London (Pali Text Society) 1882.

———tr. by H. Jacobi in *Jaina Sūtras*, pt. 1, 1-213. Sacred Books of the East, XVL, 1895.

———ed. by Puppha Bhikkhu in *Suttāgame*, I, 1-99. Gurgaon-Delhi (Sūtrāgama-prakāśaka-samiti) 1953.

Ādipurāṇa of Jinasena, pts. 1-2, Sanskrit text with Hindi tr. Pannalal Jain. Varanasi (BJP) 1963-1965.

Aṅguttaranikāya, 5 vols., Pali text ed. by R. Morris and E. Hardy. London (Pali Text Society) 1885-1900.

Antakṛddaśāḥ (*Suttāgame*, I, 1161-1190).

———tr. as *The Antagaḍadasāo and Aṇuttarovavāiyadasāo* by L. D. Barnett. London (The Royal Asiatic Society: Oriental Translation Fund, n.s., XVII) 1907.

Anuyogadvāra-sūtra (*Suttāgame*, II, 1087-1163).

———tr. as *Aṇuogaddārāiṃ* by T. Hanaki. Vaishali (Research Institute of Prakrit, Jainology and Ahiṃsā) 1970.

Anyayogavyavacchedikā of Hemacandra, see *Syādvādamañjarī*.

Aṣṭaśatī of Akalaṅka (with Vasunandi's *Ṭīkā*). Varanasi, 1914.

Aupapātika-sūtra (*Suttāgame*, II, 1-40).

Āvassaya-sutta (*Suttāgame*, II, 1165-1172).

Bhagavad Gītā, 2 vols., Sanskrit text and tr. by F. Edgerton. Cambridge (Harvard University Press) 1946.

Bhagavatī-ārādhanā of Śivārya, Bombay (Anantakīrti Granthamālā) 1932.

Bhagavatī-sūtra, also known as *Vyākhyāprajñapti-sūtra* (*Suttāgame*, I, 384–940).

———*Pañcadaśaṃ Gośālakākhyaṃ Śatakam* (with Abhayadevasūri's *Vivaraṇa*), ed. by N. V. Vaidya. Poona (Godiji Jain Temple and Charities) 1954.

Bharateśavaibhavasaṃgraha (selections from the Kannada *Bharateśavaibhava* of Ratnākara Varṇī), ed. by T. S. Shamrao. Mysore (University of Mysore) 1966.

Bodhisattvabhūmi, Sanskrit text ed. by N. Dutt. Patna (K. P. Jayaswal Research Institute) 1966.

Bṛhatkathākośa of Hariṣeṇa, ed. by A. N. Upadhye. Bombay (Singhi Jain Series, no. 17) 1943.

Daśavaikālika-sūtra (*Suttāgame* II, 947–976).

———tr. by Kastur Chand Lalwani. Delhi (Motilal Banarsidass) 1973.

Dhavalā-ṭīkā, see *Ṣaṭkhaṇḍāgama*.

Dīghanikāya, 3 vols., Pali text ed. by T. W. Rhys Davids and J. E. Carpenter. London (Pali Text Society) 1890–1911.

Dravyasṅgraha of Nemicandra, Sanskrit text with tr. by S. C. Ghosal. Arrah (Sacred Books of the Jainas) 1917.

Dvātriṃśikā of Siddhasena, see Upadhye, A. N., 1971.

Gaṇadharavāda, Prakrit text ed. and tr. by Esther A. Solomom. Ahmedabad (Gujarat Vidyā Sabhā) 1966.

Gommaṭasāra-Jīvakāṇḍa of Nemicandra, ed. by Khubchandra Jain. Agas (Rājacandra Jaina Śāstramālā) 1959.

Gommaṭasāra-Karmakāṇḍa of Nemicandra, Marathi tr. by Nemchand V. Gandhi. Sholapur, 1939.

Harivaṃśapurāṇa of Punnāṭa Jinasena, Sanskrit text with Hindi tr. by Pannalal Jain. Varanasi (BJP) 1962.

Isibhāsiyāiṃ, ed. by Walther Schubring. Ahmedabad (Lalbhai Dalpatbhai Series) 1974.

Jaina-tarkabhāṣā of Yaśovijaya, Sanskrit text with tr. by Dayanand Bhargava. Delhi (Motilal Banarsidass) 1973.

Jambūdvīpaprajñapti-sūtra (*Suttāgame*, II, 535–672).

Jātaka, 7 vols., Pali text ed. by V. Fausboll, repr., London (Pali Text Society) 1962.

Jayadhavalā, see *Kaṣāyaprābhṛta*.

Jīvājīvābhigama-sūtra (*Suttāgame*, II, 105–264).

Jñānapīṭha-pūjāñjali, ed. by A. N. Upadhye with Phoolchandra Siddhāntaśāstrī. Varanasi (BJP) 1956.

Jñātṛdharmakathā-sūtra (*Suttāgame*, I, 941–1125).

Kalpa-sūtra (*Suttāgame*, II, app. I, 1–42).

———tr. as *Lives of the Jinas, List of the Sthaviras,* and *Rules for Yatis* by H. Jacobi in *Jaina Sūtras*, pt. 2, 217–311. Sacred Books of the East, XLV, 1895.

Karmagrantha of Devendrasūri, vols. I–II (with *Svopajña-ṭikā*). Bhavnagar (Jaina Dharmaprasāraka-sabhā) 1910–1911.

Kārtikeyānuprekṣā, ed. by A. N. Upadhye. Agas (Rājacandra Jaina Śāstramālā) 1966.

Kaṣāyaprābhṛta (*Kaṣāyapāhuḍa* of Guṇabhadra; with *Jayadhavalā-ṭīkā* of Vīrasena), 15 vols., Prakrit text with Hindi tr. by Phoolchandra Siddhāntaśāstrī and Kailashchandra Siddhāntaśāstrī. Mathura (All-India Digambara Jaina Sangha) 1942–1975.

Kaṭhopaniṣat, in *Aṣṭāviṃśatyupaniṣadaḥ*, Sanskrit text ed. by Dvarikadas Śāstrī, Varanasi (Prācya Bhāratī Prakāśana) 1965.

Laghutattvasphoṭa of Amṛtacandra, Sanskrit text with tr. by Padmanabh S. Jaini. Ahmedabad (Lalbhai Dalpatbhai Series) 1978.

Mahābandha (*Mahādhavalasiddhāntaśāstra* of Bhūtabali), 7 vols., Prakrit text with Hindi tr. by Phoolchandra Siddhāntaśāstrī. Varanasi (BJP) 1947–1958.

Mahābhārata, critically ed. by V. S. Sukthankar *et al.* Poona (Bhandarkar Oriental Research Institute) 1933–1972.

Mahāpurāṇu of Puṣpadanta, 3 pts., Apabhraṃśa text ed. by P. L. Vaidya. Bombay (Manikchandra Digambara Jaina Granthamālā) 1937–1947.

Majjhimanikāya, 3 vols., Pali text ed. by V. Trenckner and R. Chalmers. London (Pali Text Society) 1888–1902.

Māṇḍūkyopaniṣat, in *Aṣṭāviṃśtyupaniṣadaḥ*, Sanskrit text ed. Dvarikadas Śāstrī, Varanasi (Prācya Bhāratī Prakāśana) 1965.

Manusmṛti, Sanskrit text ed. by Vasudeva Lakshmana Śāstrī. Bombay (Nirnayasagara Press) 1909.

Mokṣamārgaprakāśaka of Ṭoḍarmal. Bombay (Anantakīrti Granthamālā) 1937.

Mūlācāra of Vaṭṭakera (with *Vasunandi-ṭīkā*), Sanskrit text with Hindi tr. by Manoharalal. Bombay (Anantakīrti Granthamālā) 1919.

Namaskāra-svādhyāya, Sanskrit texts with Gujarati tr. by Tattvānandavijaya Muni. Bombay (Jaina Sāhitya Vikāsa Maṇḍala) 1962.

Nandisūtram, Prakrit text with Haribhadra's *Vṛtti*, ed. by Puṇyavijaya Muni, Varanasi (Prakrit Text Series) 1966.

Nandisuttaṃ Aṇuogaddārāiṃ ca, ed. by Puṇyavijaya Muni, with D. D. Malvania and A. M. Bhojak. Bombay (Mahāvīra Jaina Vidyālaya) 1968.

Nītivākyāmṛta of Somadevasūri, ed. with Hindi tr. by Ramchandra Malaviya. Varanasi (Chowkhamba Vidyābhavan) 1972.

Nityanaimittika-pāṭhāvalī, Karanja (Kamkubai Pāṭhya-pustakamālā) 1956.

Niyamasāra of Kundakunda (with *Tātparya-vṛtti* of Padmaprabhamaladhārideva), Sanskrit and Prakrit text with Hindi tr. by Maganalal Jain. Sonagadh (Digambara Jaina Svādhyāya Mandira) 1965.

Nyāyakumudacandra of Prabhācandra, ed. by Mahendra Kumar Jain. Bombay (Manikachandra Digambara Jaina Granthamālā) 1941.

Nyāyāvatāra of Siddhasena, Sanskrit text ed. by A. N. Upadhye. Bombay (Jaina Sāhitya Vikāsa Maṇḍala) 1971.

Pañcādhyāyī of Rājamalla, 2 vols. Sanskrit text with Hindi exposition by Devakinandana Siddhāntaśāstrī. Varanasi (Varṇī Jaina Granthamālā) 1949.

Parīkṣāmukha of Māṇikyanandi (with Anantavīrya's *Prameyratnamālāṭīkā*), Sanskrit text and tr. by S. C. Ghosal. Lucknow (Ajitāśrama) 1940.

Pariśiṣṭaparva of Hemacandra, Sanskrit text ed. by H. Jacobi. Calcutta (Bibliotheca Indica, no. 96) 1932 (2d ed.).

Pāsanāhacariu of Padmakīrti, Apabhraṃśa text with Hindi tr. by P. K. Modi. Varanasi (Prakrit Text Society) 1965.

Paumacariya of Vimalasūri, ed. by H. Jacobi and Puṇyavijaya Muni, with Hindi tr. by S. M. Vora. Varanasi (Prakrit Text Society) 1962.

Periyapurāṇaṃ of Cekkilān (in Tamil), ed. by T. M. K. Pillai. Srivaikuntam, 1964.

Prajñāpanā-sūtra (*Paṇṇavaṇā-sutta*), pts. 1–2, ed. by Puṇyavijaya Muni, with D. D. Malavaniya and A. M. Bhojak). Bombay (Mahāvīra Jaina Vidyālaya) 1969.

———(*Suttāgame*, II, 235–533).

Pramāṇamīmāṃsā of Hemacandra, Sanskrit text with Hindi nn. by Sukhalalji Sanghavi. Calcutta (Singhi Jaina Series) 1939.

———text and tr. (bks. 1–2) by Satkari Mookerjee, with Nathmal Tatia. Varanasi (Tara Publications) 1970.

Prameyakamalamārtaṇḍa of Prabhācandra, ed. by Mahendra Kumar Jain. Bombay (Nirnayasagar Press) 1941.

Pravacanasāra of Kundakunda (with Amṛtacandra's *Tattvadīpikā*, Jayasena's *Tātparya-vṛtti* and Pāṇḍe Hemarāja's *Bālāvabodha-bhā-*

ṣāṭīkā), ed. with tr. of *Pravacanasāra* by A. N. Upadhye. Agas (Rājacandra Jaina Śāstramālā) 1934.
Puruṣārthasiddhyupāya, Sanskrit text and tr. by Ajit Prasada. Lucknow, 1933.

Rājapraśnīya-sūtra (*Suttāgame*, II, 41–103).
Ratnakaraṇḍaśrāvakācāra of Samantabhadra (with Prabhācandra's *Ṭīkā*), ed. with Hindi intro. by Jugal Kishor Mukhtar. Bombay (Manikachandra Digambara Jaina Granthamālā) 1925.

Śabdānuśāsana of Hemacandra, Sanskrit text with *Svopajña-ṭīkā*, ed. by Himāṃṣu Vijaya Muni. Ahmedabad, 1934.
Ṣaḍdarśanasamuccaya of Haribhadrasūri (with Guṇaratnasūri's *Vṛtti*), ed. by Mahendra Kumar Jain. Varanasi (BJP) 1969.
Saddharmapuṇḍarīka-sūtra, ed. by P. L. Vaidya. Darbhanga (Buddhist Sanskrit Texts) 1960.
Sāgāradharmāmṛta of Āśādhara, Sanskrit text with Hindi tr. by Mohanlal Jain. Jabalpur (Sarala Jaina Grantha Bhaṇḍāra) 1957.
Samādhiśataka of Pūjyapāda (with Prabhācandra's *Ṭīkā*), Sanskrit text with Marathi tr. by Raoji N. Shah. Sholapur, 1938.
Samavāya-sūtra (*Suttāgame*, I, 316–383).
Samayasāra of Kundakunda (with Amṛtacandra's *Ātmakhyāti-ṭīkā*), Prakrit and Sanskrit texts with Marathi tr. by Dhanyakumar G. Bhore. Karanja (Mahāvīra Jñānopāsanā Samiti) 1968.
———Prakrit text and tr. by A. Cakravarti. Varanasi (BJP) 1925.
Samayasārakalaśa of Amṛtacandra, Sanskrit text with Hindi tr. by Phoolchandra Siddhāntaśāstrī. Songadh, 1964.
Sambodhaprakaraṇa of Haribhadra, Prakrit text. Ahmedabad (Jaina Grantha Prakāśaka Sabhā) 1915.
Sāṃkhyakārikā of Īśvarakṛṣṇa, Sanskrit text with Hindi Intro. by Vrajamohan Caturvedi. Delhi (National Publishing House) 1969.
Sanmatitarka of Siddhasena, Prakrit text and tr. by Sukhalalji Sanghavi (with Bechardasji Doshi). Bombay, 1939.
Sarvārthasiddhi of Pūjyapāda (with *Tattvārtha-sūtra* of Umāsvāti), Sanskrit text with Hindi tr. by Phoolchandra Siddhāntaśāstrī. Varanasi (BJP) 1971.
———tr. as *Reality* by S. A. Jain. Calcutta (Vīra Śāsana Sangha) 1960.
Ṣaṭkhaṇḍāgama of Puṣpadanta and Bhūtabali (with Vīrasena's *Dhavalā-ṭīkā*), 16 vols. Prakrit and Sanskrit texts with Hindi tr. by Hiralal Jain. Amaravati (Jaina Sāhityoddhāraka Fund) 1939–1959.
Shrī Mahāvīra Jaina Vidyālaya Golden Jubilee Volume, 2 pts ed. by C. V. Shah. Bombay (Mahāvīra Jaina Vidyālaya) 1968.

Siddhiviniścaya-ṭīkā of Anantavīrya, 2 vols. Sanskrit text ed. by Mahendra Kumar Jain. Varanasi (BJP) 1959.

Śrīmad Bhāgavata, 2 pts., Sanskrit text with Hindi tr. Gorakhpur (Gītā Press) 1964.

Śrīmad Rājacandra, see Modern Works: Govardhandas, Brahmachari, 1951.

Sthānāṅga-sūtra (*Suttāgame*, I, 183–315).

Strīnirvāṇa-Kevalibhuktiprakaraṇe of Śākaṭāyana (with *Svopajña-vṛtti*), Sanskrit text ed. by Jambuvijaya Muni. Bhavanagar (Jaina Ātmānanda Sabhā) 1974.

Sūtrakṛtāṅga-sūtra (*Suttāgame*, I, 101–182).

———tr. by H. Jacobi in *Jaina Sūtras*, pt. 2, 235–435. Sacred Books of the East, XLV, 1895.

Suttāgame, 2 vols., Prakrit texts ed. by Puppha Bhikkhu. Gurgaon-Delhi (Sūtrāgama-prakāśaka-samiti) 1953. All references to Śvetāmbara canonical texts in this work are to the Suttāgame edition.

Svayambhū-stotra of Samantabhadra, see *Nityanaimittika-pāṭhāvalī*, 29–44.

Syādvādamañjarī of Malliṣeṇa (with Hemacandra's *Anyayogavyavacchedikā*), Sanskrit text with Hindi tr. by Jagdish Chandra Jain. Agas (Rājacandra Jaina Śāstramālā) 1970 (3d ed.).

———tr. as *The Flower-Spray of the Quodammodo Doctrine* by F. W. Thomas. Berlin (Akademie-Verlag) 1960.

Tattvārthasāra of Amṛtacandra, Sanskrit text with Hindi tr. by Pannalal Sāhityācārya. Varanasi (Varṇī Granthamālā, no. 21) 1970.

Tattvārtha-sūtra of Umāsvāti, Sanskrit text with tr. by J. L. Jaini. Arah, 1920.

———text with Hindi exposition following the Digambara tradition by Phoolchandra Siddhāntaśāstrī. Varanasi (Varṇī Granthamālā) 1949.

———text with Hindi exposition following the Śvetāmbara tradition by Sukhalalji Sanghvi. Varanasi (Jaina Saṃskṛti Saṃśodhana Maṇḍala) 1952 (2d ed.).

———*Svopajña-bhāṣya*: See Jacobi 1906 in Modern Works.

Tiloyopaṇṇatti of Yativṛṣabha, Prakrit text and Hindi tr. by Pandit Balacandra. Sholapur (JJG) p. 1-1943 and pt. 2-1951.

Tiruviḷayātar Purāṇam of Parañcoti Munivar (in Tamil), ed. by N. M. V. Naṭṭār. Madras, 1965.

Traivarṇikācāra of Somasena, ed. by Pannalal Soni. Bombay, 1925.

Triṣaṣṭiśalākāpuruṣacaritra of Hemacandra, ed. by Caraṇavijaya Muni. Bhavnagar (Jaina Ātmānanda Sabhā) 1933.

———tr. by Helen M. Johnson as *The Lives of Sixty-three Illustrious Persons*, 6 vols. Baroda (Oriental Institute) 1962.

Upāsakadaśāḥ (*Suttāgame*, I, 1127-1160).
———tr. by A. F. R. Hoernle as *The Uvāsagadasāo or the Religious Profession of an Uvāsaga*, 2 vols. Calcutta (Bibliotheca Indica) 1888-1890.
Upāsakādhyayana of Somadevasūri (chaps 5-7 of the *Yaśastilaka-campū*), Sanskrit text with Hindi tr. by Kailashchandra Śāstrī. Varanasi (BJP) 1964.
Uttarādhyayana-sūtra (*Suttāgame*, II, 977-1060).
———tr. by H. Jacobi in *Jaina Sūtras*, pt. 2, 1-232. Sacred Books of the East, XLV, 1895.
Uttarapurāṇa of Guṇabhadra, Sanskrit text ed. with Hindi tr. by Pannalal Jain. Varanasi (BJP) 1954.

Vaḍḍārādhane of Śivakoṭi (in Kannada), ed. by D. L. Narasimhachar. Mysore (Śāradā Mandira) 1970 (4th ed.).
Varāṅgacaritra of Jaṭāsiṃhanandi, ed. by A. N. Upadhye. Bombay (Manikachandra Digambara Jaina Granthamālā) 1938.
Viśeṣāvaśyaka-bhāṣya of Jinabhadragaṇi (with Koṭyācārya's *Vṛtti*), vol. I, ed. by Nathmal Tatia. Vaishali (Research Institute of Prakrit, Jainology and Ahiṃsā) 1972.

Yaśastilaka-campū of Somadevasūri (with Śrutadevasūri's commentary), pts. 1-2, ed. by Shivadatta Mahāmahopādhyāya. Bombay (Kāvyamālā, no. 70) 1901-1903.
Yogabindu of Haribhadra, Sanskrit text and tr. by K. K. Dixit. Ahmedabad (Lalbhai Dalpatbhai Series) 1968.
Yogaśāstra of Hemacandra, Sanskrit text with Hindi tr. by Shobhachandra Bharilla. Delhi, 1963.
Yoga-sūtras of Patañjali with *Vyāsa-bhāṣya*: See *Pātañjala-Yogadarśanam*, ed. by R. S. Bhattacharya. Varanasi (Bhāratīya Vidyā Prakāśana) 1963.

Modern Works

Alsdorf, Ludwig
1928 *Der Kumārapālapratibodha* of Somaprabha. Hamburg (Friederichsen, De Gruyter).
1973 "What were the Contents of the Dṛṣṭivāda?" in *German Scholars on India*, vol. I, 1-5. Varanasi (Chowkhambha Sanskrit Series Office).

Barnett, L. D. See *Antakṛddaśāḥ* in Texts and Translations.

Basham, A. L.
1951 *History and Doctrine of the Ājīvikas.* London (Luzac).
1958 "Jainism and Buddhism," in William Theodore de Bary, ed.,

Sources in Indian Tradition, vol. I, 38–92. New York (Columbia University Press).

Bender, Ernest.

1976 "An Early Nineteenth Century Study of the Jainas," in *Journal of the American Oriental Society*, XCVI, no. 1, 114–119.

Bhargava, Dayanand

1968 *Jaina Ethics*. Delhi (Motilal Banarsidass).

Bhatt, Bansidhar.

1972 "Vyavahāranaya and Niścayanaya in Kundakunda's Works," in *Zeitschrift der Deutschen Morgenländischen Gesellschaft*, I, no. 5, 279–291.

Bhattacharya, B. C.

1939 *Jain Iconography*. Lahore (Motilal Banarsidass).

Bhattacharya, Harisatya

1953 *Anekāntavāda*. Bhavanagar (Jaina Ātmānanda Sabhā).

1964 *The Jaina Prayer*. Calcutta (University of Calcutta).

Bloomfield, Maurice

1919 *The Life and Stories of the Jaina Savior Pārśvanātha*. Baltimore (University of Maryland Press).

Boolchand

1948 *Lord Mahāvīra*. Varanasi (Jain Cultural Research Society).

Brown, William N.

1933 *The Story of Kālaka*. Washington (Smithsonian Institution, Freer Gallery of Art, Oriental Studies, no. 1).

1934 *A Descriptive and Illustrative Catalogue of Miniature Painting of the Jaina Kalpa-sūtra*. Washington, Baltimore (The Lord Baltimore Press).

1941 *Manuscript Illustrations of the Uttarādhyayana Sūtra*. New Haven (American Oriental Society—American Oriental Series, vol. XXI).

Bruhn, Klaus

1969 *The Jina Images of Deogarh*. Leiden (E. J. Brill, Studies in South Asian Culture, vol. I).

Buhler, J. G.

1899 *Life of Hemacandra* (tr. by M. Patel of the original German *Uber des Leben des Jaina-Monches Hemacandra*: Vienna, 1936). Shantiniketan.

1903 *On the Indian Sect of the Jainas*. London (Luzac).

Bulche, Camille

1971 *Rāmakathā* (in Hindi). Prayag (Prayag Viśvavidyālaya). 1st ed. 1950.

Burgess, James
1869 *The Temples of Śatruñjaya.* Bombay (Sykes and Dwyer). Reprinted in *Jain Journal,* XI (April 1977), no. 4 (Calcutta).

Burgess, Jas
1903 "Digambara Jaina Iconography," in *Indian Antiquary,* XXXII, 459–468.

Caillat, Colette
1965 *Les Expiations dans le ritual ancien des religieux jaina.* Paris (Publications de l'Institut de Civilisation Indienne, ser. in 8 fasc. 25).
1968 "The Religious' Prāyaścittas according to the Old Jaina Ritual," in *SMJVGJV,* 1968, 88–117.
1975 *Atonements in the Ancient Ritual of the Jaina Monks.* Ahmedabad (Lalbhai Dalpatbhai Series).

Chakravarti, A.
1974 *Jaina Literature in Tamil.* Delhi (BJP).

Chopade, Tatya Keshav
1946 *Jaina āṇi Hindu* (in Marathi). Kolhapur (Vīra Granthamālā).

Deleu, Jozef
1963 (with Walther Schubring) *Studien zum Mahānisīha.* Hamburg (Gram, De Gruyter).
1969 *Nirayāvaliyāsuyakkhandha-Uvangas 8–12 van de jaina Canon.* Leiden.
1970 *Viyāhapannatti (Bhagavaī).* Tempelhof (Rijksuniversity of Gent).

Deo, Shantaram B.
1956 *History of Jaina Monachism.* Poona (Deccan College Dissertation Series, 17).

Desai, P. B.
1957 *Jainism in South India and Some Jaina Epigraphs.* Sholapur (JJG).

Devendra, Muni
1968 *Kalpa-sūtra* (Hindi tr.). Shivana (Amara Jaina Āgamaśodhasthāna).

Dhaky, M. A.
1968 "Some Early Jaina Temples in Western India," in *SMJVGJV,* 290–347. Bombay.

Dixit, Krshna K.
1976 "A new contribution to the discussion of Jaina monastic discipline," in *Sambodhi,* V, nos. 2–3, 13–48. Ahmedabad (Lalbhai Dalpatbhai Institute of Indology).

Evans-Wentz, W. Y.
1960 *The Tibetan Book of the Dead.* New York (Oxford University Press).

Fergusson, James
1891 *History of Indian and Eastern Architecture.* London (John Murray).

Fischer, Eberhard (with Jyotindra Jain)
1975 *Kunst und Religion in Indien: 2500 Jahre Jainismus.* Zurich (Rietberg Museum).

Folkert, Kendall W.
1976 "Jaina Studies: Japan, Europe, India," in *Sambodhi,* V, nos. 2–3, 138–147. Ahmedabad.

Gandhi, Mohandas K.
1958–1976 *Collected Works of Mahatma Gandhi,* 62 vols. Delhi (Government of India: Publication Division).

Gandhi, Virchand R.
1893 *Selected Speeches of Shri Virchand Raghavji Gandhi.* Reprinted in 1964. Bombay (Vallabhasūri Smārakanidhi).

Ghatge, A. M.
1934 "Narrative Literature in Jain Maharashtri," in *Annals of the Bhandarkar Oriental Research Institute,* XVI, 26–43.

Ghosh, A., ed.
1974–1976 *Jaina Art and Architecture,* 3 vols. Delhi (BJP) .

Glasenapp, Helmuth von
1925 *Der Jainismus: Eine indische Erlosungs Religion.* Berlin (Alf Hager Verlag).
1942 *The Doctrine of Karma in Jain Philosophy,* tr. from the German by G. Barry Gifford. Bombay (Bai Vijibhai Jivanlal Pannalal Charity Fund).

Gopalan, S.
1973 *Outlines of Jainism.* New York (Halstead Press).

Govardhandas, Brahmachari, ed.
1951 *Śrīmad Rājacandra* (in Gujarati). Agas (Śrimad Rājacandra Āśrama).

Guérinot, A.
1926 *La Religion djaina.* Paris (Paul Guenther).

Guseva, N. R. (Mrs.)
1971 *Jainism,* tr. from the Russian by Y. S. Redkar. Bombay (Sindhu Publications).

Hamm, Frank-Richard (with Walther Schubring)
1951 *Studien zum Mahānisīha.* Hamburg (Cram, De Gruyter).

Hanaki, Taiken
1970 *Anuogaddārāim: A Critical Study*. Vaishali (Research Institute of Prakrit, Jainology and Ahiṃsā).

Handiqui, K. K.
1949 *Yaśastilaka-campū and Indian Culture*. Sholapur (JJG).

Hoernle, A. F. Rudolf
"Ājīvika," in *Encyclopaedia of Religion and Ethics*, ed. by James Hastings (1917–1955), I, 259–269.

Jacobi, Hermann
1880 "On Mahāvīra and His Predecessors," in *Indian Antiquary*, IX, 158–163.
1884 *Jaina Sūtras*, pt. 1. Oxford (Sacred Books of the East, XXII). Reprinted in Dover Publications, New York, 1968.
1895 *Jaina Sūtras*, pt. 2. Oxford (Sacred Books of the East, XLV). Reprinted in Dover Publications, New York, 1968.
1906 *Eine Jaina-Dogmatik: Umāsvāti's Tattvārthādhigama-Sūtra*. Leipzig (*Zeitschrift der Deutschen Morgenländischen Gesellschaft*, no. 60).
1932 *Pariśiṣṭaparva of Hemacandra*. Calcutta (Bibliotheca Indica, no. 96, 2d ed.).

Jain, Balabhadra
1974 *Bhārat ke Digambara Jaina Tīrtha* (in Hindi). Bombay (Bhāratavarṣīya Digambara Jaina Tīrthakṣetra Committee).

Jain, Banarasi Das
1925 *Jaina Jātakas*. Lahore (Motilal Banarsidass).

Jain, Champat Rai
1922 *Confluence of Opposites*. London (Jaina Library).
1926 *Jaina Law*. Madras (Jaina Mission Society).
1930 *Jainism, Christianity and Science*. Allahabad (Indian Press).

Jain, Hiralal
1962 *Bhāratīya Saṃskṛti me Jaina-dharma kā yogadān* (in Hindi). Bhopal.
1974 With A. N. Upadhye, *Mahāvīra: His Times and His Philosophy of Life*. Varanasi (BJP).

Jain, Jagdish Chandra
1947 *Life in Ancient India as Depicted in the Jain Canons*. Bombay (New Book Company).

Jain, Jyoti Prasad
1964 *The Jaina Sources of the History of Ancient India*. Delhi (Munshi Ram Manohar Lal).

Jain, Kailash Chand
1963 *Jainism in Rajasthan*. Sholapur (JJG).

Jain, Kamta Prasad

1928 *Bhagawān Mahāvīra aur Mahātmā Buddha* (in Hindi). Surat.

1930 "A further note on the Śvetāmbara and Digambara sects," in *Indian Antiquary,* LIX, 151–154.

Jain, Prithvi Raj

1956 "Jamāli," in *Ācārya Vijayavallabhasūri Commemoration Volume,* 61–73. Bombay (Mahāvīra Jaina Vidyālaya).

Jain, Ravindra Kumar

1966 *Kavivara Banārasīdās* (in Hindi). Delhi (BJP).

Jain, S. A. See *Sarvārthasiddhi* in Texts and Translations.

Jaini, Jagmander Lal

1916a *Jaina Law "Bhadrabāhu Samhitā"* (text with tr.). Arrah (Central Jaina Publishing House).

1916b *Outlines of Jainism.* Cambridge.

Jaini, Padmanabh S.

1970 "Śramaṇas: Their Conflict with Brahmanical Society," in J. W. Elder, ed., *Chapters in Indian civilization,* I, 39–81. Dubuque, Iowa (Kendall Hunt).

1974 "On the Sarvajñatva (Omniscience) of Mahāvīra and the Buddha," in L. Cousins, ed., *Buddhist Studies in Honor of I. B. Horner,* 71–90. Dordrecht (Reidel).

1976a "The Jainas and the Western Scholar," in *Sambodhi,* V: *Dr. A. N. Upadhye Commemoration Volume,* 121–131. Ahmedabad.

1976b "The Jina as a Tathāgata: Amṛtacandra's critique of Buddhist doctrine," in O. H. De A. Wijesekera, ed., *Malalasekera Commemoration Volume,* 148–156. Colombo.

1977a "Jina Ṛṣabha as an avatāra of Viṣṇu," in *Bulletin of the School of Oriental and African Studies,* XL, pt. 2, 321–337. University of London.

1977b "Saṃskāra-duḥkhatā and the Jaina concept of suffering," in H. Coward and K. Sivaraman, eds., *Revelation in Indian Philosophy* (in honor of T. R. V. Murti), 153–157. Emeryville, Calif. (Dharma Publishing).

1977c "Bhavyatva and Abhavyatva: A Jain Doctrine of 'Predestination,'" in *Mahāvīra and His Teachings (2,500 Nirvāṇa Anniversary Volume),* 95–111. Bombay.

Forthcoming (a) "Disappearance of Buddhism and the Survival of Jainism: A Study in Contrast," in *Proceedings of the Seminar on the World History of Buddhism,* ed. A. K. Narayan. Madison, Wisconsin.

Forthcoming "Karma and the Problem of Rebirth in Jainism," in W. O'Flaherty, ed., *Rebirth in Classical Indian Texts* (papers presented

(b) at panel on Process of Rebirth: meetings of the Association for Asian Studies, New York, 1977.)

Jindal, K. B.
1958 *The Prefaces.* Calcutta (Sarasvati Press).

Jinendra, Varṇī
1970–1973 *Jainendra Siddhānta Kośa* (in Hindi), 4 vols. Delhi (BJP).

Johnson, Helen M. See *Triṣaṣṭiśalākāpuruṣacaritra* in Texts and Translations.

Johrapurkar, V. P.
1958 *Bhaṭṭāraka Sampradāya* (in Hindi). Sholapur (JJG).

Kailashchandra, Śāstrī
1966 *Jaina Nyāya* (in Hindi). Varanasi (BJP).
1971 *Satprarūpaṇā-sūtra* (in Hindi). Varanasi (Varṇī Granthamālā).

Kalghatgi, T. G.
1971 *Karma and Rebirth.* Ahmedabad (Lalbhai Dalpatbhai Series).

Kapadia, H. R.
1934–1935 "The Jaina Commentaries," in *Annals of the Bhandarkar Oriental Research Institute,* XVII, 292–312.
1941 *A History of the Canonical Literature of the Jainas.* Surat.

Kashalikar, M. J.
1969 "Hemacandra's Version of the Mahābhārata," in *JOI,* XIX, nos. 1–2, 234–246.

Kosambi, Dharmananda
1941 *Bhagavan Buddha* (in Marathi). Nagpur (Suvicāra Prakaśana Maṇḍala).

Kulkarni, V. M.
1959–1960 "The Origin and Development of the Rāma Story in Jaina Literature," *JOI,* IX, pt. 1, no. 2, 190–204; pt. 2, no. 3, 284–304.

Lannoy, Richard
1974 *The Speaking Tree: A Study of Indian Culture and Society.* London (Oxford University Press Paperback).

Law, B. C.
1949 *Some Jaina Canonical Sūtras.* Bombay (Bombay Branch, Royal Asiatic Society: monograph no. 2).

Leumann, E.
1934 *Ubersicht uber die Āvaśyaka-Literatur.* Hamburg (Friederichsen, DeGruyter).

Lohuizen-de Leeuw, J. E. van
1949 *The "Scythian" Period.* Leiden (E. J. Brill).

Majmudar, M. R.
1969 "Two Gujarati Documents Bearing on 'Amāri,'" in *JOI*, XIX, pts. 1–2, 286–288.

Malalasekera, G. P.
1937–1938 *Dictionary of Pāli Proper Names*, 2 vols. Reprinted in 1964. London (Luzac).

Malvania, Dalsukh, D.
1964 "Lonkāshāh aur unkī vicāradhārā" (in Hindi), in *Gurudeva Śrī Ratnamuni Smṛtigrantha*, 365–383. Agra.
1969 "Prajñāpanā and Ṣaṭkhaṇḍāgama," in *JOI*, XIX, nos. 1–2, 34–45.

Matilal, Bimal K.
1976 "A Note on the Jaina Concept of Substance," in *Sambodhi*, V, nos. 2–3, 3–12. Ahmedabad.

Mehta, Mohanlal (with K. Rishabh Chandra)
1970–1972 *Prakrit Proper Names*, 2 pts. Ahmedabad (Lalbhai Dalpatbhai Series).

Mitra, Romesh C.
1954 *The Decline of Buddhism in India.* Calcutta (Viśva-Bhārati Studies, no. 20).

Mookerjee, Satkari
1944 *The Jaina Philosophy of Non-Absolutism.* Calcutta (Bhāratī Mahāvidyālaya).

Moti Chandra (with U. P. Shah)
1975 *New Documents of Jaina Painting.* Bombay (Mahāvīra Jaina Vidyālaya).

Nahar, Puran Chand
1929 "A Note on the Śvetāmbar and Digambar Sects," in *Indian Antiquary*, LIX, 167–168.
1932 "Antiquity of the Jain Sects," in *Indian Antiquary*, LXI, 121–126.

Nair, V. G.
1970 *Jainism and Terapanthism.* Bangalore (Ādinātha Jaina Śvetāmbara Temple).

Narasimhachar, R.
1923 *Inscriptions at Śravaṇabelgola* (*Epigraphica Carnatica*, vol. II). Bangalore (Mysore Archaeological Series).

Nathmal, Muni
1968 *Acharya Bhiksu: The Man and His Philosophy.* Churu (Ādarśa Sāhitya Sangha).

Nevaskar, B.
1971 *Capitalists without Capitalism: The Jains of India and the Quakers of the West.* Westport, Conn.

Nigam, M. L.
1968 "Glimpses of Jainism through Archaeology in Uttar Pradesh," in *SMJVGJV*, 213–220.

Padmarajiah, Y. J.
1963 *Jaina Theories of Reality and Knowledge.* Bombay (Jaina Sāhitya Vikāsa Maṇḍala).

Pandey, Raj Bali
1969 *Hindu Saṃskāras.* Delhi (Motilal Banarsidass).

Phoolchandra, Siddhāntaśāstrī
1963 *Varṇa, jāti aur dharma* (in Hindi). Varanasi (BJP).
1967 *Jaipur (Khaniya) Tattvacarcā* (in Hindi), 2 vols. Jaipur (Pandit Toḍarmal Granthamālā).

Prasad, Hari K.
1968 "Jaina Bronzes in the Patna Museum," in *SMJVGJV*, 275–289.

Premi, Nathu Ram
1956 *Jaina Sāhityakā Itihāsa* (in Hindi). Bombay (Hindi Grantha Ratnākara).

Renou, Louis
1953 *Religions of Ancient India.* London.

Rice, B. Lewis
1909 *Mysore and Coorg from the Inscriptions.* London (Archibald Constable).

Rice, Edward P.
1921 *A History of Kanarese Literature.* London (Oxford University Press).

Ruegg, D. Seyfort
1969 *La Théorie du tathāgatagarbha et du gotra.* Paris.

Sahu, Nabin K.
1964 *History of Orissa,* vol. I. Cuttack (Utkal University).

Saletore, B. A.
1938 *Medieval Jainism.* Bombay (Karnatak Publishing House).

Sangave, V. A.
1959 *Jaina Community: A Social Survey.* Bombay (Popular Book Depot).

Sanghavi, Sukhalal
1963 *Samadarśī Ācārya Haribhadra* (in Hindi). Jodhpur (Rajasthan Purātana Granthamālā).

Sankalia, H. D.
1939 "Jaina Iconography," in *New Indian Antiquary,* II, no. 8, 497–520.

Satyaprakash
1972 *Kumārapāla Caulukya* (in Hindi). Delhi (Mīnākṣī Prakāśana).

Schmidt, Hanns Peter
1968 "The Origin of Ahiṃsā," in *Mélanges d'indianisme: A la mémoire de Louis Renou,* 625–655. Paris (Publications de l'Institut de Civilisation Indienne).

Schubring, Walther
1927 *Worte Mahāvīras.* Gottingen (Vandenhoeck and Ruprecht).
1962 *The Doctrine of the Jainas* (tr. from the rev. German ed. by Wolfgang Beurlen). Delhi (Motilal Banarsidass).
1966 *Drei Chedasūtras des Jaina-Kanons: Ayāradasāo, Vavahāra, Nisīha.* Hamburg (Gram, De Gruyter).
1974 *Isibhāsiyāim* (text and commentary). Ahmedabad (Lalbhai Dalpatbhai Series).

Sen, Amulya Chandra
1931 *Schools and Sects in Jaina Literature.* Calcutta (Viśva-Bhāratī Series, no. 3).

Shah, Cimanlal J.
1932 *Jainism in North India.* London (Longmans).

Shah, Nagin J.
1967 *Akalaṅka's Criticism of Dharmakīrti's Philosophy.* Ahmedabad (Lalbhai Dalpatbhai Series).
1968 "Nature of Time," in *SMJVGJV,* 63–87.

Shah, R. N.
1950 "Jain Code and Jainism," in Kamta Prasad Jain, ed., *Shrī Mahāvīra Commemoration Volume,* I, 261–271. Agra (Mahāvīra Jaina Society).

Shah, Umakant P.
1951–1952a "A Unique Jaina Image of Jīvantasvāmi," in *JOI,* I, no. 1, 71–79.
1951–1952b "Sidelights on the Life-Time Sandalwood Image of Mahāvīra," in *JOI,* I, no. 3, 358–367.
1955 *Studies in Jaina Art.* Varanasi (Jaina Cultural Research Society).
1956 "A Rare Sculpture of Mallināth," in *Ācārya Vijayavallabhasūri Commemoration Volume,* 128–129. Bombay (Mahāvīra Jaina Vidyālaya).

Sharma, Jagdish P.
1975 "Hemacandra: The Life and Scholarship of a Jaina Monk," in *Asian Profile,* III, no. 2, 195–215. Hong Kong.

1976 "Jainas as a Minority in Indian Society and History," in *Jain Journal: A Quarterly on Jainology,* X, no. 4, 137–148. Calcutta.

Sharma, S. R.
1940 *Jainism and Karnatak Culture.* Dharwar.

Sikdar, Jogendra C.
1964 *Studies in the Bhagavatīsūtra.* Mazaffarpur.
1974 "The Fabric of Life as Conceived in Jaina Biology," in *Sambodhi,* III, no. 1, 1–10. Ahmedabad.

Singh, Ram J.
1974 *The Jaina Concept of Omniscience.* Ahmedabad (Lalbhai Dalpatbhai Series).

Smith, Vincent A.
1901 *The Jain Stūpa and Other Antiquities of Mathura.* Allahabad (Government Press). Reprinted in 1969, Varanasi (Indological Book House).
1917 "The Jain Teachers of Akbar," in *Essays Presented to Sir R. G. Bhandarkar,* 265–276. Poona.
1962 *Akbar the Great Mughal,* 2d ed., rev. Delhi (S. Chand).

Solomon, Esther A. See *Gaṇadharavāda* in Texts and Translations.

Stevenson, Mrs. Sinclair
1915 *The Heart of Jainism,* Reprinted in 1970. New Delhi (Munshiram Manoharlal).

Tatia, Nathmal
1951 *Studies in Jaina Philosophy.* Varanasi (Jaina Cultural Research Society).

Thomas, F. W. See *Syādvādamañjarī* in Texts and Translations.

Tod, James
1839 *Travels in Western India.* Reprinted in 1971. Delhi (Oriental Publishers).

Trautman, Thomas T.
1971 *Kauṭilya and the Arthaśāstra.* Leiden (E. J. Brill).

Tripathi, Chandrabhal
1975 *Catalogue of the Jaina Manuscripts at Strasbourg.* Leiden (E. J. Brill).

Tripathi, R. K.
1968 "The Concept of Avaktavya in Jainism," in *Philosophy East and West,* XVIII, no. 3, 187–193.

Tukol, T. K.
1976 *Sallekhanā Is Not Suicide.* Ahmedabad (Lalbhai Dalpatbhai Series).

Tulasi, Ācārya
1969 *My Religion.* Churu (Ādarśa Sāhitya Sangha).

Upadhye, Adinath N.
1933 "Yāpanīya Saṅgha: A Jaina Sect," in *Journal of the University of Bombay,* I, no. 4, 224–231. Bombay.
1934 "Darśanasāra of Devasena: Critical Text," in *Annals of the Bhandarkar Oriental Research Institute,* XV, nos. 3–4, 198–206.
1936 "Studies in Jaina Gotras," in *Jaina Antiquary,* II, no. 3, 61–69. Arrah.
1939 "On the Authorship of a Maṅgala-Verse in Inscriptions," in *New Indian Antiquary,* II, no. 2, 111–112.
1968 "Jinasena and His Works," in *Mélanges d'indianisme: A la mémoire de Louis Renou,* 727–732. Paris (Publications de l'Institut de Civilisation Indienne).
1971 *Siddhasena's Nyāyāvatāra and Other Works* (including the *Dvātriṃśikā* and *Sammaisutta*). Bombay (Jaina Sāhitya Vikāsa Maṇḍala).
1974 "More Light on the Yāpanīya Saṅgha," in *Annals of the Bhandarkar Oriental Research Institute,* LV, 9–22.

Weber, Max
1958 *The Religion of India.* New York (Free Press).

Williams, R.
1963 *Jaina Yoga: A Survey of the Mediaeval Śrāvakācāras.* London (Oxford University Press).

Windisch, E.
1874 *Hemacandra's Yogaśāstra* (first 4 chaps. of text and tr.). (*Zeitschrift der Deutschen Morgenländischen Gesellschaft,* no. 28). Leipzig.

Winternitz, Maurice
1933 *A History of Indian Literature,* vol. II (tr. from the German by S. Ketkar and M. Kohn). Calcutta (University of Calcutta Press).

Zimmer, Heinrich
1951 *Philosophies of India,* ed. by Joseph Campbell. Princeton: Princeton University Press, Bollingen Series.

Glossary of Sanskrit and Prakrit Words

abhavya (one who is incapable of attaining mokṣa), 140
abhigraha (resolution), 219
abhiṣeka (anointing ceremony), 35n, 200, 201
abrahma-varjana (abandonment of all incontinence), 183
acakṣurdarśana (perception by means of the senses other than visual), 122, 132
ācāra (conduct), 53, 80
ācārya (head of a mendicant group; spiritual leader; monk-scholar) 1, 162–164
ādāna-nikṣepaṇa-samiti (care in the picking up and putting down of any object), 248
adattādāna-virati (not taking anything which has not been given; identical to asteya-vrata), 57
adharma-dravya (the principle of rest), 81, 97–100
adho-loka (the lower world; the home of infernal beings), 128
adhyayana (lecture), 64, 66
advaita (non-dual; cap., the monistic school of Vedānta), 135
āgama (scripture; canonical literature), 47, 78
aghātiyā (karmas that generate embodiment and particular conditions thereof), 115, 124–127, 132, 159, 255, 268, 269, 273
agni (fire), 297, 298
agurulaghutva (the quality of constancy in space-points), 58, 59
ahaṃpratyaya (self-awareness), 103
āhavanīya-agni (one of the sacred fires in the Hindu śrauta ritual), 297
ahiṃsā (nonharming), 8, 53, 86, 167, 168, 242, 249, 284n, 289, 305, 209, 312, 314
ahiṃsāvrata (refraining from harming), 170–173, 177, 187, 241–243, 281
ailaka (the highest state of a Digambara layman, wherein he retains only one piece of clothing), 18, 184, 186, 208, 219, 220, 246

ajīva (insentient), 82, 151
ajñāna (ignorance), 118
ajñānavāda (agnosticism), 53
ājñāvicaya (contemplation on the teachings of the Jina), 252
ākāśa (space), 81, 97, 98, 100
akriyāvāda (doctrine of non-action), 53
akṣatā (uncooked rice), 201
Akṣaya-tṛtīyā (the "immortal third," a Jaina holiday), 203
alaṅkāra (ornamentation), 86
ālocanā (critical self-examination), 231
aloka-ākāśa (totally empty space), 98, 127, 130n
amanaska (without mind), 110
amāri (prohibition of animal sacrifice), 284
aṃśāvatāra (minor incarnation of Viṣṇu), 32
amūḍhadṛṣṭi (freedom from delusory notions), 152
anagāra-dharma (mendicant discipline), 79
anantajñāna (infinite knowledge; a synonym for kevalajñāna), 266
anantānubandhī-kaṣāya (passions that "pursue from the limitless past," preventing the attainment of samyak-darśana), 119, 131, 143, 145, 146, 149, 157, 272
ananta-sukha (infinite bliss), 268
anarthadaṇḍavrata (refraining from the five minor types of evil activity), 179, 187
anaśana (fasting), 251
anekāntavāda (the doctrine of manifold aspects), 53, 86, 90, 94, 96, 97, 314n
anekatva (multiplicity), 91
aṅga (limb; cap., a group of twelve Jaina canonical texts), 47, 49, 51, 52
Aṅgabāhya (the subsidiary canon), 50–55
aṅgapūjā (veneration of the limbs of the lord), 202
anitya (impermanent), 91
anityavāda (noneternalism), 92
anivartin (that state from which there is no returning), 269
anivṛtti-karaṇa (the process of suppressing certain mohanīya karmas), 144, 158, 272
antarā-bhava (the state of existence between death and rebirth), 227
antarātman (the state of perceiving the self within), 148
antarāya-karma (karma that restricts the energy-quality of the soul), 123, 124, 132, 159
antar-muhūrta (a period of up to forty-eight minutes), 145n
antyeṣṭi-kriyā (funeral rites), 302
aṇu (atom; an indivisible particle of matter), 103
anubhava (retribution of a karma; intensity), 113, 144

anukampā (compassion), 150
anumatityāga-pratimā (the tenth stage in which a layman refrains from all household activities), 183, 186
anuprekṣā (reflection, twelve kinds), 248
aṇuvratas (minor vows pertaining only to laypeople), 170, 178, 187, 190, 234, 284, 314n
anuyoga (exposition; a group of postcanonical texts), 79
aparigraha (nonpossession), 86, 187
apariṇāmin (unchanging), 92
apavartanā (energy that hastens the time and decreases the intensity of karmic fruition), 139
apāyavicaya (contemplation on the means by which beings can be saved), 252
āpo-kāyika (water-bodies), 109
apramatta-virata (restraint not vitiated by carelessness, the seventh guṇasthāna), 158, 253, 272
apratyākhyānāvaraṇa (obstructors of partial renunciation), 119, 131, 157, 158, 185, 272
apūrva-karaṇa (the process by which the soul attains to an unprecedented degree of purity), 144, 158, 253, 272
arahaṃta (Prakrit for arhat), 162, 278n
ārambhajā-hiṃsā (violence occurring either accidentally or through the performance of an acceptable occupation), 171, 172
ārambhatyāga-pratimā (the eighth stage in which a layman withdraws from all professional commitments), 183, 186
arati (displeasure in regard to sense activities), 120, 131
ārati (the lamp-waving ceremony), 201
arcana (worship), 201, 220
ardha-phālaka (loincloth worn by Śvetāmbara monks), 6n
ardha-pudgala-parāvartana-kāla (the amount of time required for a soul to take in and use up half of the available karmic matter in the universe), 144
arghya (respectful offering), 201
arhaṃ (identical to arhat), 162n
arhat ("worthy of worship"; an epithet of one who has attained kevalajñāna; a synonym for kevalin), 28, 31n, 162–164, 204n, 240 258–260, 267, 268, 273, 296
arihaṃta (a variant for arahaṃta), 162n
artha (meaning of a word), 42
arūpi-ajīva (the four insentient, formless dravyas), 97
āryikā (nuns of the Digambara sect), 208, 247n
asaṃjñī (unable to reason about spiritual matters), 110
asaṃkhyāta (innumerable), 29, 99, 101, 102
asaṃyama (nonrestraint), 228

aśarīra (free from embodiment; a siddha), 164
asātā, asātāvedanīya (experience of pain), 115, 132
āśātanā (disrespect), 62
asatya (lying), 173
āścarya (extraordinary event), 23n
asi ("sword"; government), 171
āsrava (karmic influx), 82, 112, 151
āśraya (substratum), 90
aṣṭāṅga (eight limbs [of samyak-darśana]), 151
asteya (not stealing), 175, 187
asti-kāya (having extension), 98n, 101
āstikya (affirmation), 151
aśubha-karma (unwholesome karma), 82
aticāra (infractions committed by accident), 173
atiśaya-kṣetra (places where miraculous events associated with great monks have occurred), 205, 206
atithi-saṃvibhāga (sharing with [ascetic] guests), 217, 220
ātman (soul; self), 92
ātmānubhava (abiding in one's own nature), 149
aupapādika (born spontaneously), 110
avadhidarśana (the indistinct type of awareness preceding avadhijñāna), 3, 132
avadhijñāna (supermundane knowledge such as clairvoyance), 3, 110, 121–123, 132
avaktavya (inexpressible), 96
avamaudarya (eating only a very small portion of food), 251
āvaraṇīya (obscuring), 105, 121
avasarpiṇī (regressive half-cycle), 30–34, 61, 203
āvaśyaka (essential duty), 79, 189, 190, 191, 260
avidyā (ignorance), 134
avirati (nonrestraint), 157, 158, 272
aviveka (lack of discrimination), 134
āvṛta (obscured), 105
āyāga-paṭa (votive slabs), 192, 211
āyariya (Prakrit for ācārya), 162
ayoga-kevalin (the fourteenth guṇasthāna, attained by the kevalin when, in the instant before death, all his activities cease), 159, 270, 273
āyu-karma (karma that determines the span of a given lifetime), 115, 126, 132, 268, 269

bahirātman ([perceiving] the self in externals), 147
balabhadra (a Jaina literary type; the hero and companion of nārāyaṇa), 305

bandha (karmic bondage), 82, 112, 151
bandhana (energy that brings about karmic influx), 139
bhagavān (venerable), 10
bhakti (devotionalism), 135, 304, 306
bhaṅga (infractions committed intentionally), 173
bhāṣā (language), 60
bhāṣā-samiti (care in speaking), 247
bhāṣya (commentary), 82
bhaṭṭāraka (venerable ones; a class of Jaina clerics), 193n, 254n, 307, 311
bhāva (internal; states of a dravya), 38; (a synonym for paryāya), 90
bhāvanā (practice; a section of the *Ācārāṅga-sūtra*), 243n
Bhavanavāsī (those [gods] who reside in mansions), 129n
bhāva-pūjā (the internal aspect of a devotional practice), 207, 217
bhāva-samyaktva (the internal aspect of true insight), 147
bhavya (one who is capable of attaining mokṣa), 140
bhavyatva (capability of attaining mokṣa), 139–141, 259n
bhaya (fear), 120, 131
bheda (disjunction), 101
bhikṣu-pratimā (difficult austerities recommended for a mendicant), 62
bhoga (enjoyment; experience), 29, 30, 106
bhoga-antarāya (karma that restricts enjoyment), 123
bhoga-bhūmi (realm of enjoyment), 29, 221
bhogopabhoga-parimāṇavrata (restraint against practicing certain professions and partaking of certain foods), 179, 187
bhūmi (realm), 29, 30, 128
bīja (seed), 111
bījapūraka-kaṭāha (a seed-filled fruit, probably Aegle Marmelos, used for medicinal purposes), 24n
bodhi (enlightnenment), 165
bodhi-durlabha (the rarity of enlightenment), 249
bodhisattva (one who follows the career of a Buddha), 266n
boḍiya (naked), 5n
brahmacāri (celibate; one who has reached the seventh pratimā), 183, 218, 246
brahmacarya-pratimā (the seventh pratimā, in which absolute continence is observed), 183, 186
Brahman (the unitary Absolute postualted by the Vedānta school), 92
brāhmaṇa [brahman] (a member of the priestly caste), 8, 43, 57, 58, 61, 67, 74–76, 87, 275, 288, 291
brahmavrata (refraining from all illicit sexual activities), 176, 187

caitanya (consciousness), 104
caitya (temple), 234, 309

caityavāsi (temple-dweller), 307–309
cakravartin (universal monarch), 7
cakṣurdarśana (visual perception), 122, 132
caṇḍāla (untouchable; a synonym for śvapāka), 75
candana (sandalwood paste), 201
caraṇa (practice), 81
cāritra (conduct), 75, 97
cāritra-mohanīya (conduct-deluding karmas), 118, 131, 133, 157, 159, 253
caru (sweet), 201
catuḥśaraṇa (the four refuges), 77, 164, 296
caturviṃśati-stava (praise of the twenty-four Tīrthaṅkaras), 190
cātuyāma-saṃvara (Sanskrit cāturyāma-saṃvara; a synonym for cāujjāma-dhamma), 10
cāujjāma-dhamma (Sanskrit cāturyāma-dharma, the fourfold restraint ascribed to Pārśva), 15–18
chadmastha (a person in the state of bondage), 27
cheda (reduction in seniority); *-sūtra* (a law book dealing with monastic offences), 62
cūlikā (appendix; a class of Jaina canonical texts), 76

dākṣiṇa-agni (one of the sacred fires in the Hindu śrauta ritual), 297
dāna (charity; alms-giving), 106, 181, 182, 187, 190, 217, 221, 260
dāna-antarāya (a type of karma that hinders the practice of charity), 123
darśana (intuition), 23; (a system of philosophy), 81, 91, 103; (insight), 97; (perception), 104, 122, 123
darśana-mohanīya (insight-deluding karmas), 131, 145, 146, 157
darśana-pratimā (the first step on the ladder of pratimā), 161, 162, 166, 186
darśanāvaraṇīya (perception-obscuring karmas), 115, 124, 132, 159
daśa-dharma (ten forms of righteousness), 248
deśanā-labdhi (obtaining instruction in the Jaina teachings), 143
deśāvakāśika (limiting the area of one's movement), 180, 182, 187
deśa-virata (the fifth guṇasthāna where deśa-virati is attained), 272
deśa-virati (the set of restraints prescribed for a Jaina layman), 119, 158, 160
deva (heavenly beings), 82, 129; (ultimate divinity), 162
deva-brāhmaṇa (divine brahman, i.e., a Jaina brahman), 290
deva-dūṣya ("divine" cloth; a finely woven piece of cloth), 12
devāgama (the arrival of gods at a holy gathering), 83
deva-mūḍhatā (delusion pertaining to gods), 152
deva-nikāyas (the four orders of gods), 129n

devapūjā (worship of the Tīrthaṅkaras), 190–192, 199, 201, 202, 207, 217
dharma (holy law), 64, 164, 305; (elements in Buddhist doctrine), 92; (righteousness, ten forms), 248
dharmadhyāna (virtuous concentration), 252, 253, 272
dharma-dravya (the principle of motion), 81, 97–100
dharma-kathā (religious tale), 54
dharma-lābha (increase in righteousness), 208n
dharma-svākhyātatva (the absolutely true teachings of the Jinas), 249
dharma-tīrtha (holy path), 12
dhūpa (incense), 201
dhyāna (meditation), 251, 255, 257, 260n, 270
Digambara (sky-clad; name of the Jaina sect whose mendicants practice ascetic nudity), 5, 6n
dīgha-tapassī (one who engages in extended penances), 21
digvrata (restriction on the distances a person may travel), 178, 187
dīkṣā (initiation), 243, 246
dīpa (lamp), 201
divyadhvani (miraculous sound), 4, 35, 42, 260
doṣa (imperfection), 34n, 146
dravya (substance), 81, 90, 92, 97, 101, 150, 152, 266; (external), 38
dravya-mana (the physical basis of the mind), 266n
dravya-pūjā (form of worship employing external objects), 207, 217
dravya-samyaktva (the external aspect of true insight), 147
durbhikṣā (famine), 229
duṣamā (unhappy), 31
duṣamā-duṣamā (extremely unhappy), 31
dveṣa (hatred; aversion), 112, 119
dvija (twice-born), 67, 289, 290, 294, 285n, 300
dvīpa (island), 29, 32, 82
dvīpa-samudra (island-continent), 129

eka (one; unitary), 92
eka-kṣetrāvagāha (occupying the same locus), 113
ekānta (one-sided), 83, 91, 118, 314
ekāntavāda (extremism; absolutist doctrine), 53, 92
ekāntavādin (one who holds an absolutist doctrine), 86, 150
eka-phālaka (probably identical to eka-śāṭaka), 15
eka-śāṭaka (a mendicant who wears a single piece of cloth), 18
ekatva (unity), 91
ekendriya (a being with only one [namely, the tactile] sense faculty; a synonym for sthāvara beings), 109, 130, 241, 242
eṣaṇā-samiti (care in accepting alms), 248

eva (in fact; an important term in the formula of the sapta-bhaṅgi-naya), 94, 95

gaccha (a chapter of monks), 246n
gaṇa (a residence unit for monks), 246
gaṇadhara (supporters of the order, i.e., the first mendicant disciples of a Tīrthaṅkara), 4, 24n, 35–38, 42–45, 55, 63, 87, 268, 297
gandha (smell), 90
gandharva (celestial musician), 108
gaṇin (leader of the order), 62
gaṇi-piḍaga (basket of the gaṇadharas, i.e., the canon of the Jainas), 47
garbha (conception), 7
gārhapatya-agni (one of the sacred fires of the Hindu śrauta ritual), 297
gati (birth; destiny), 60, 108, 124
ghana-ambu (humid air), 127
ghana-vāta (dense air), 127
ghātiyā (karmas that have a vitiating effect upon the qualities of the soul), 115, 117, 124, 131, 133, 159, 255, 258, 270, 273
ghoratavassi (one who practices severe austerities), 45
gorjī (a term used for yati), 307n
gotra (exogamous groups), 301n
gotra-karma (karmas that determine environmental circumstances, 115, 125, 126, 132, 268
granthi (knot), 143
gumma (a chapter of monks), 246n
guṇa (quality), 58, 90, 104, 266
guṇasthāna (the fourteen stages of purification; see chart, 272–273), 141
guṇavratas (restraints that reinforce the practice of the aṇuvratas), 170, 179, 180, 187, 190
gupti (restraint), 247, 252
guru (spiritual teacher), 3, 153; (gain), 58, 162, 209
guru-mūḍhatā (false beliefs pertaining to teachers), 153
guru-upāsti (listening to and venerating teachers), 190, 207–210, 218, 221

hāsya (laughter), 120, 131
hiṃsā (injury, harming violence), 167, 170, 175, 176, 180, 282, 295, 310, 311
huṇḍāvasarpiṇī (a period of avasarpiṇī in which extraordinary events may take place), 23n

indriya (sense organ), 60
īryā-samiti (care in walking), 247
īśat-prāgbhārā-bhūmi ("slightly bent region," the name of the final abode of the liberated souls [the siddhas]), 130n, 270
iṣṭa-devatā (chosen deity), 163
Īśvara (God), 259n, 271n

Jaina (follower of a Jina, a synonym for Nigaṇṭha), 2n; (one who has samyak-darśana), 146
Jainābhāsa (false Jainas), 20
Jaina-brahman (laypeople in charge of priestly functions within certain Jaina communities), 195, 197, 199, 290, 291, 295, 297
Jaina-śāsana (teaching of the Jainas), 2n
jala (water), 201
janma (birth), 7
janma-kalyāṇa (birth; one of the five auspicious events in the career of a Tīrthaṅkara), 197
jarā (old age), 229
jāti (birth, caste), 75, 288, 295; (species within a gati), 124
jāti-karma (the variety of nāma-karma that determines one's specific destiny), 124
jāti-mantra (a litany used in celebrating the birth of a child), 296
jayamālā (garland of victory; a hymn in praise of the Jinas), 201
Jina (spiritual victor; a synonym for Tīrthaṅkara), 2
Jina-āgama (Jaina scripture), 220
Jina-bhavana (Jaina temple), 220
Jina-bimba (image of a Jina), 220
jinakalpin (a monk whose conduct is modeled upon that of Mahāvīra), 20
jīva (soul; sentient), 60, 90, 98, 99, 102–104, 151
jñāna (knowledge), 28, 91, 97, 104, 122
jñāna-cetanā (consciousness characterized as knowing itself), 148, 221
jñānāvaraṇīya (knowledge-obscuring), 115, 124, 131, 142, 159
jugupsā (disgust), 120, 131
Jyotiṣka (the stellar gods), 129n

kāla (time stages within the progressive and regressive half-cycles), 30; (time as a dravya), 97, 98, 100
kālāṇu (time-points), 100
kalpātīta (born in the highest heavenly abodes), 129, 130
kalpopapanna (born in the kalpa heavens), 129
kalyāṇaka (auspicious moments), 7
kanyādāna (ceremony of giving away the bride), 301

kāpota-leśyā (gray karmic strain), 114
karma (action) 97; (a form of matter), 102, 111–115
karma-bhūmi (realm of action), 29–31
karma-cetanā (consciousness of oneself as the doer of actions), 147
kārmaṇa-śarīra (the transmigrating body of karmic matter), 102, 125, 126
karma-phala-cetanā (consciousness of oneself as the enjoyer of the karmic fruits), 147
karma-prakṛti (the particular form into which karmic matter is differentiated, see chart, 131–133), 112
kartā (agent), 147
kaṣāya (passion), 60, 112, 113, 118, 131, 157, 159, 177, 253, 272, 273
kathā (narrative literature), 54
kavala-āhāra (food in morsels; ordinary human food), 36
kāya-kleṣa (mortifications of the body), 251
kāyotsarga (abandonment of the body, a standing or sitting posture of meditation), 190, 192, 225
keśa-loca (the practice of pulling out one's hair in five handfuls), 245
kevaladarśana (perception associated with kevalajñāna), 123, 132
kevalajñāna (knowledge isolated from karmic obstruction; infinite knowledge; omniscience; knowledge involving awareness of every existent in all its qualities and modes), 2, 4, 7, 25, 27, 28, 31n, 36, 38, 44, 46, 61, 91, 122, 123, 132, 204n, 205n, 258, 266, 273, 296
kevalin (one who has attained kevalajñāna; a synonym for arhat), 2n, 24n, 28, 31n, 44, 46, 82, 113, 120, 164, 258, 266n, 268, 269, 273, 296
krama (sequential order), 95
kriyās (actions; a Jaina term for sacred rites), 287, 293, 298, 299
krodha (anger), 119, 131
kṛṣi (farming), 172
kṛṣṇa-leśyā (black karmic stain), 114
kṣamā (forgiveness), 216
kṣamāśramaṇa (an ascetic who suffers with equanimity; title used in addressing a monk during the ritual of confession), 209
kṣaṇika (momentary), 92
kṣānti (forbearance), 260n
kṣapaṇa (destruction), 272
kṣatriya (member of a warrior caste), 6, 8, 11, 67, 75, 275, 280, 313; *-dharma* (his duties), 17n, 171
kṣaya (destruction), 145, 146, 159, 257
kṣāyika-samyak-darśana (true insight achieved by the destruction of darśana-mohanīya karmas), 146

kṣayopaśama-labdhi (attainment of purity by the destruction-cum-suppression of certain karmas), 142
kṣāyopaśamika-samyaktva (true insight achieved by the destruction-cum-suppression of darśana-mohanīya karmas; identical to vedaka-samyaktva), 146
kṣīṇa-moha (permanent dissociation from all cāritra-mohanīya karmas and from the passions which they produce, the twelfth guṇasthāna), 159, 257, 272
kṣullaka (minor; junior monk; a Jaina layman on the eleventh pratimā; one who wears three pieces of clothing), 184–186, 197, 208, 219, 220, 246, 254n
kula (family), 246n
kumāra-śramaṇa (a life-long celibate), 58
kuṇḍalinī-cakra (mystical centers of psychic energy), 254
kūṭastha-nitya (eternal and unchangeable), 92

labdhi (attainment), 142
lābha (attainment), 106
lābha-antarāya (hindrance to the attainment of something), 123
laghu (light; loss), 58
leśyā (karmic stain, the color of which indicates a soul's degree of purity), 114
lobha (greed), 119, 131
loka-ākāśa (the inhabited universe; see pl. 14), 60, 98, 100–102, 127–129, 269, 270
loka-mūḍhatā (false beliefs pertaining to everyday religious practices), 154

madhu (honey), 167
madhya-loka (middle of terrestrial world), 129
madya (alcohol), 167
māhaṇa (Prakrit for Sanskrit brāhmaṇa), 75
Mahāvīra-jayantī (birth anniversary of Mahāvīra), 203
mahāvrata (the five great vows of a mendicant), 15, 18, 160, 184, 226, 228, 243, 245–248, 253, 272, 280
māṃsa (flesh; meat), 167
mānastambha (a characteristic Jaina pillar; see pl. 23), 35n
manaḥparyayajñāna (direct awareness of thought-forms of others without the aid of mind or senses), 122, 132
mantra (holy litany), 162
manuṣya (human being), 108, 129
manuṣya-gati (human destiny), 108
maṣi (ink; writing), 172

mastakābhiṣeka (head-anointing [ceremony]), 204, 205
matijāna (mind-based knowledge), 91, 131
māyā (deceit), 119
māyāvāda (illusionism), 96
mithyādarśana (synonymous with mathyādṛṣṭi and mithyātva), 144n, 157, 272
mithyādṛṣṭi (incorrect view of reality, the first guṇasthāna), 141, 272
mithyātva (lack of insight; synonymous with mithyādarśana and mithyādṛṣṭi), 118, 134, 145, 304
mohanīya-karma (karma that prevents the true perception of reality and the purity of the soul; karma that defiles the bliss-quality of the soul), 115–118, 121, 124, 257, 258, 273
mokṣa (salvation; emancipation from the cycle of birth and death), 2, 11, 20, 31, 32, 46, 82, 97, 140, 141, 145, 146, 150, 151, 153, 155, 167, 194, 201, 204, 245, 270, 273, 305, 307, 314n
mokṣa-mārga (the path of salvation), 82, 97
muh-patti (a small piece of cloth worn over the mouth by Sthānakavāsi mendicants to protect airbodies from harm), 245, 310
mūlaguṇas (the eight basic restraints of a Jaina layman), 166, 169, 179, 187, 188, 190, 218, 295, 300
mūlasūtra (a group of texts belonging to the subsidiary canon), 64
muni (mendicant; sage), 3, 22, 261
mūrcchā (delusion), 177

nāma-Jaina (nominal Jaina), 161
nāma-karma (karma that determines destinies and body types), 115, 124–126, 132, 259, 268, 270n
namaskāra-mantra (*-pañca*) (reverent salutation to the [five] holy beings), 162, 163n, 188, 199, 201, 217, 232, 245, 254n, 255
nandyāvarta (a kind of diagram), 166n
napuṃsakaveda (sexual cravings for a hermaphrodite), 120, 131
naraka (hell; the world of infernal beings), 82
nāraki (hell beings), 108, 128
nārāyaṇa (a Jaina literary type; the hero's companion and slayer of the villain), 305
nāsti (does not exist; the second member of the sapta-bhaṅgi-naya), 95
naya (view; partial expression of truth), 83, 93, 94
nayavāda (doctrine of nayas), 97
nidāna (seeking worldly gain from the performance of good deeds and austerities), 230, 266
nidhatti (energy that renders karmas incapable of all activity save changes in fruition time and intensity), 139
Nigaṇṭha/ Sanskrit *Nirgrantha* (unattached, without possessions; ancient name for the Jaina community), 2n, 10, 18–21, 27, 217, 223, 234–236, 274n, 276, 285

nigoda (the lowest form of life), 24n, 109, 143, 168
niḥkāṃkṣita (freedom from anticipation), 152
nihnava (falsehood, heresy), 88
niḥpratīkāra (unavoidable), 229
niḥśaṅkita (freedom from doubt), 151
nikācanā (energy that renders karmas incapable of all activity), 139
nīla-leśyā (blue karmic stain), 114
nimitta-kāraṇa (external efficient cause), 99, 117, 138
niranvaya (discrete), 92
nirjarā (dissociation of karmas), 82, 113, 151
nirvāṇa (release from bondage; the final death of an enlightened human being [arhat] followed immediately by mokṣa), 3, 6n, 37, 46, 93, 155, 159, 196, 198, 299n
nirvāṇa-bhūmi (the place at which a Tīrthaṅkara attained nirvāṇa), 205, 206
nirvicikitsā (freedom from disgust), 152
niryukti (Prakrit verse commentary), 77
niścaya-naya (nonconventional view), 80, 311
nitya (eternal), 91
nityavāda (eternalism), 92
niyati (fate), 137
niyativāda (fatalism), 96
no-kaṣāya (subsidiary passions), 120, 131, 158, 177, 257, 272

oṃ (sacred sound formed by combining the first syllable of each word in the namaskāra-mantra), 42, 163

padastha-dhyāna (concentration upon holy chants), 255 256
padma-leśyā (lotus-pink karmic stain), 114
pādukā (footprint), 193
paiṇḍastha-dhyāna (concentration upon certain objects made up of the elements of matter), 254–256
pañca-kalyāṇa (the five auspicious events in the life of a Tīrthaṅkara), 196; *-mahotsava* (the celebration of these events), 197, 198, 200–202, 206, 207
pañca-mahāvrata, see also *mahāvrata*, 15
pañca-namaskāra-mantra, see also *namaskāra-mantra*, 162, 296, 297, 300
pāṇi-pātra (hand-bowl), 41
pāpa (unwholesome karmas), 151
para-dravya/ -kṣetra/ -kāla/ -bhāva (the being, location, time, or state, respectively, of other objects), 95
paramāṇu (atom), 90, 101
paramātman (the highest [the liberated] soul), 148, 256
parameṣṭhin (the supreme divinity), 163

pāramitā (perfection), 260n
parigraha (possession), 177
parigrahatyāga-pratimā (the ninth stage in which a layman abandons the cares of worldly possessions), 183, 186
parīkṣā (examination, 84
pariṇāma (modification), 90
pariṇāmin (changing), 92
pariṇāmi-nitya (eternal but constantly changing), 92
parīṣaha-jaya (victory over the afflictions), 249
parivrājaka (a non-Jaina mendicant), 56
parokṣa (indirect perception, accomplished through the senses, inference, etc.), 122n
pārthivī-dhāraṇā (visualization of certain scenes by means of the earth element), 255
parvan (Jaina holy days), 180, 217
paryāya (mode; a synonym for bhāva), 90, 150, 152, 266
paryūṣaṇa-parva (a ten-day holy period for fasting during the rainy season), 216
Pāsāvaccijja (those who follow the discipline of Pārśva), 58
pātra (bowl), 41
phaḍḍaga (a chapter of monks), 246n
phala (fruit), 201
piñchī (a peacock-feather whiskbroom), 184n, 245
pīta-leśyā (yellow karmic stain), 114
pitṛ-loka (world of the Manes), 302, 303n
poṣadha-pratimā (the fourth śrāvaka-pratimā), see also *poṣadhopavāsa*, 182, 186
poṣadhopavāsa (the third śikṣāvrata and fourth pratimā; fasting on the eighth and fourteenth days of each lunar fortnight), 180, 187, 217
posaha-sālā (fasting hall), 59
prabhāvanā (illumination), 155, 202, 207, 310
pradeśa (space-point), 98, 100, 102, 270n; (amount of karma), 113
prajñā (wisdom), 260n
prakīrṇaka (miscellaneous; a group of Jaina canonical texts), 56; (scattered stars), 129n
prakṛti (original nature of mind and matter in the Sāṃkhya doctrine), 92, 99; (types of karma), 112, 113
pralaya (demanifestation), 31
pramāda (negligence; carelessness; apathy), 120, 157, 158, 243, 253, 272
pramātṛ (the knower), 104
pramatta-virata (total restraint without overcoming pramāda; the sixth guṇasthāna), 253, 272

prāṇāyāma (yogic control of respiration), 254
praśama (ease), 149
prātihārya (miraculous phenomenon), 44n
pratikramaṇa (ritualized confession), 80, 190, 209, 216, 231
pratimā (stages of renunciation for a layman, see chart, 187), 18, 167n, 182–188, 197, 210, 237, 289, 290, 292, 299
prati-nārāyaṇa (a Jaina literary type; the villain), 305
pratyākhyāna (renunciation of certain foods; one of the six āvaśayakas), 190, 209, 216
pratyākhyānāvaraṇa/ -ṇīya (obstructors of complete renunciation), 119, 131, 157, 158, 226, 241
pratyakṣa (direct perception), 122n
pratyeka (individual; solitary), 109
pravacana-mātṛkā (the eight exercises that prepare a monk for advanced meditational states), 247
pravrajyā (renunciation), 243
prāyaścitta (repentence of transgressions), 251
prāyogya-lạbdhi (reduction of karmic matter in soul; attainment of purity due to such a reduction), 143
pṛthvī-kāyika (earthbodies), 109
pudgala (matter), 81, 97–102
pudgala-skandha (aggregate of matter), 101
pudgalavādin (follower of Buddhist school which upholds a theory of soul), 267n
pūjā (worship), 182, 190, 191, 203, 295
puṃveda (sexual cravings for a female), 120, 131
puṇya-karma (wholesome karma), 151, 152
puṇya-kṣetra (field of merit), 220
purāṇas (name of a class of sacred texts dealing with the lives of Tīrthaṅkaras), 5, 95, 204n
puruṣa (soul), 92
puruṣa-viśeṣa (special soul, i.e., the God [Īśvara] of the Yoga school), 136, 271n
Pūrva (a group of fourteen Jaina canonical texts, now extinct), 47, 49–51
puṣpa (flower), 201

rāga (desire; passion; attachment), 112, 119
rajas (principle of motion in the Sāṃkhya doctrine), 99
rajoharaṇa (a whiskbroom), 222, 245
rasa (taste), 90
rasa-parityāga (abandonment of stimulating or delicious food), 251
rati (pleasure in sense activity), 120, 131

ratnatraya (the three jewels: right faith or insight, right knowledge, right conduct), 200, 299
rātribhakta-pratimā (the sixth stage, in which one limits all sexual activity to nighttime hours), 183, 186
rātri-bhojana (eating at night), 179
raudradhyāna (meditation on the perverse pleasure of causing injury to others), 252
ṛjusūtra-naya ("straight-thread" view), 93
ṛta (Vedic concept of cosmic law), 99
rujā (illness), 229
rūpastha-dhyāna (concentration on the form of the Jina), 255, 256
rūpātīta-dhyāna (concentration on that which transcends form: the nature of the siddha), 255, 256

śabala ("disfigured"; offence), 62
sacittatyāga-pratimā (the fifth stage, in which a layman ceases to take certain vegetable life as food), 182, 186
sadā-mukta (forever free of bondage), 136
saddharma-vṛddhi (increase in righteousness), 208n
sādhāraṇa-vanaspati (souls which exist together with many others in a common plant body), 110, 168
sādhu (mendicant), 163, 164
sādhvījī (a nun of the Śvetāmbara or Sthānakavāsi sect), 247n
sakaladatti (transference of property prior to renunciation), 183n
sallekhanā (ritual death by fasting), 155, 227–233, 237–239, 268, 280, 281
sallekhanāvrata (the decision to perform sallekhanā), 181, 187, 188
samādhi-maraṇa (death while in meditation), 227, 228
samanaska (endowed with the mental capacity), 110
samavasaraṇa (holy assembly of the Jina), 35, 56, 143, 192, 196, 201, 256
samaya (moment), 45
sāmāyika (attaining equanimity; fusion with the true self), 221
sāmāyika-cāritra (avoiding all evil actions, identical to the assumption of the five mahāvratas), 17
sāmāyika-pratimā (the third stage of practicing sāmāyika), 182, 186
sāmāyika-saṃyama (a synonym for sāmāyika-cāritra), 17, 221
sāmāyikavrata (cultivation of equanimity; the second of the śikṣāvratas), 180, 182, 185, 187, 190, 191, 221–226, 253
saṃgha (order of monks, nuns, laymen, and laywomen), 27
saṃgha-pati (leader of the lay community), 198, 207
saṃghāta (aggregation), 101
samiti ([self-] regulation), 247

saṃjñī (able to think abstractly about spiritual matters), 110
saṃjvalana (smoldering; *-kaṣāya*, subtle passions which are removed as one progresses from the sixth to the twelfth guṇasthāna), 120, 131, 158, 257, 272, 273
saṃkalpajā-hiṃsā (intentional, premeditated violence), 170, 171
saṃkramaṇa (energy that contributes to the differentiation or transformation of karmas), 139
sampadā (qualifications [of an ācārya]), 62
saṃsāra (cycle of transmigration), 92, 107, 108, 136, 141, 150, 152, 153, 159, 167, 170
saṃśaya (doubt), 118
saṃskāras (sacred rites; see list, 293n), 292–295, 298, 302
saṃsthānavicaya (contemplation of the structure of the universe), 253
samudghāta (bursting forth; expansion of the soul to the limits of the loka-ākāśa), 269
saṃvara (spiritual path; the stoppage of karmic influx), 60, 82, 151
saṃvatsarī (annual ceremony of public confession), 63, 210, 216, 223
saṃvega (agitation leading to disenchantment), 149
sāṃvyavahārika-pratyakṣa (direct perception, in the conventional sense), 122n
samyak-cāritra (proper conduct), 148, 200
samyak-darśana (correct view of reality; true spiritual insight; faith in the teachings of the Jina), 62, 129, 141–152, 157, 159, 196, 200, 205, 232, 272
samyak-dṛṣṭi (the fourth guṇasthāna, in which one attains samyak-darśana), 145, 272
samyak-jñāna (correct knowledge; knowledge associated with samyak-darśana), 200
samyak-mithyātva (a state of transition in which both correct and incorrect views are present; the third guṇasthāna), 145, 272
saṃyama (restraint), 64, 190
saṅgraha-naya (synthetic view), 93
sapiṇḍīkaraṇa (a ritual connected with offering of food to the Manes), 302
sapta-bhaṅgi-naya (the sevenfold predication), 95
saptapadī (that portion of the Hindu wedding ceremony in which the couple takes seven steps around the fire), 301
śaraṇa (refuge), 164
śarīra (body), 60, 124, 125
sarvajña (an omniscient being; a synonym for kevalin), 267
sarva-virata (attainment of sarva-virati; the sixth guṇasthāna), 272
sarva-virati (total restraint of a mendicant), 158, 160, 241
śāsana-devatā (guardian spirits), 194, 254n, 295n

śāstra (scripture), 162
sāsvādana (state of "mixed taste"; the second guṇasthāna), 145, 272
sat (being), 89, 91
sātā, sātāvedanīya (experience of pleasure), 115, 125, 132
ṣaṭ-jīva-nikāya (the six kinds of living beings, namely, the five ekendriyas and the trasa), 65
satya (truth), 173; *-vrata* (the vow to abstain from lying), 174, 187, 238
savicāra (accompanied by applied thinking), 257
sayoga-kevalin (a kevalin still possessed of the activities of body, speech, and mind; the thirteenth guṇasthāna), 159, 258, 268, 273
siddha (a liberated soul; a kevalin freed from all activities whatsoever), 37, 38, 159, 162, 165, 166, 255, 256, 265, 270, 271, 274, 278n, 296
siddha-gati (the destiny of the siddha), 165
siddha-loka (the permanent abode of the siddha; a synonym for īśatprāgbhārā-bhūmi), 130, 204n
siddhānta (doctrine), 47
siddhi (yogic power), 256, 259n
śikṣāvratas (vows of spiritual discipline), 170, 180–182, 187, 190, 217, 235
śīla (conduct), 260n
śilpa (handcrafts), 172
skandha (aggregate), 101
snāpana (the ceremony of sprinkling or bathing the Jina-image), 200
snigdha-rukṣatva (moisture and dryness [of atoms]), 101
śoka (sorrow), 120, 131
sparśa (touch), 90
śraddhā (faith), 151
śrāddha (offering of food to the Manes), 154, 302, 303n, 304
śramaṇa (a non-Vedic mendicant, usually a Jaina or a Buddhist), 1, 10, 33, 136, 138, 274, 275, 278, 297, 298n
śramaṇabhūta (a novice about to become a mendicant), 184–186
śramaṇopāsaka (a disciple of the ascetics; a synonym for śrāvaka), 235–238
śrāvaka (a layman; a synonym for upāsaka and śramaṇopāsaka), 80
śrāvakācāra (book of the layman's discipline), 80, 160, 161, 177, 181, 188, 193, 254, 285
śrāvaka-pratimā (the eleven stages of the path of the layman; a synonym for upāsaka-pratimā), 161
śreṇi (ladder; a term applied to the eighth, ninth, and tenth guṇasthānas), 253, 256, 258, 272
śruta (the oral tradition of Jaina scripture), 49, 166
śrutajñāna (knowledge derived from instruction and reasoning), 121, 132

Śruta-pañcamī (the "scripture-fifth," a Jaina holiday), 204
stava (hymn of praise), 165
Sthānakavāsi (dwellers in halls; name of a Jaina sect whose members do not worship in temples), 49n, 191, 244n, 245, 247n, 263, 264, 301, 310, 313
sthāpana (ritual act of asking a monk to stop for alms), 220
sthāpanācārya (sacred objects used as a substitute for a teacher), 209n
sthāvara (immobile beings, such as plants), 75, 241
sthavira (elder), 52, 55
sthavirakalpin (a monk who lives in an ecclesiastical community), 20
sthiti (duration), 113, 144
sthtīkaraṇa (acting to promote the stability of another's faith in the Jaina path), 155
stotra (a philosophical hymn), 83
strīmukti (attainment of mokṣa in a female incarnation), 36n
strīveda (sexual cravings for a male), 120, 131
stūpa (reliquary mound), 193, 298n
śuddhi (purity), 220
śūdra (a member of the fourth caste), 67, 288, 289, 293–295
sukha (bliss), 90, 104, 125n, 149
sukhā-vedanā (feeling of happiness), 104n
śukladhyāna (pure concentration), 252–257, 269
śukla-leśyā (luminous white karmic stain), 114
sūkṣmakriyā-anivartin (the state of subtle movement), 269
śūkṣma-sāmparāya (the state of having only the subtle passions; the tenth guṇasthāna), 158, 272
suṣamā (happy), 31
suṣamā-duṣamā (more happy than unhappy), 31
suṣamā-suṣamā (extremely happy), 31
sūtra (style—aphoristic mode of presentation), 81, 82, 151; (the canonical scriptures), 42
suya-ñāṇa (scriptural knowledge), 47
svabhāva (own nature), 95, 104, 105, 148
svabhāva-pariṇāma (undefiled change), 99
svabhāva-sthita (established in one's own nature), 104
svadeha-parimāṇa (the physical dimensions of the soul identical to those of its current body), 58
svādhyāya (the study of the scriptures), 190, 251
sva-dravya/ -kṣetra/ -kāla/ -bhāva (specific being, location, time, and state, respectively of oneself), 95
śvapāka (the lowest class in Indian society), 75
svastika (well-being; the stylized wheel of life), 108, 192, 200, 211
Śvetāmbara (white [cotton]-clad; name of a Jaina sect whose mendicants wear white garments), 5, 6

Śvetapaṭa (a synonym for Śvetāmbara), 6n
syādvāda (the doctrine of qualified assertion), 54, 83, 86, 88, 90, 94, 96, 97
syāt (in some respect), 94, 95

taijasa-śarīra (heat body), 125, 126
tamas (the principle of inertia in the Sāṃkhya doctrine), 99
tanu-vāta (rarefied air), 127, 130n
tapas (austerity), 64, 80, 190, 250
Tāraṇapantha (a Jaina reform movement started by Tāraṇasvāmi), 310n
tattva (the [nine] "reals," regarded as objects of faith for a Jaina), 151
tattva-rūpavatī (the meditative practice of envisioning the body as totally pure), 256
tejo-kāyika (fire bodies), 109
Terāpantha (path of the thirteen; name of a subsect of the Sthānakavāsi), 247n, 314
ṭīkā (commentary), 85
tīrtha (ford; the path of Jaina practice; the monastic order), 35
tīrtha-kṣetra (a place where arhats have attained mokṣa), 205, 206
Tīrthaṅkara (builders of the ford; the omniscient spiritual teachers of the Jainas; a synonym for Jina), 2, 14, 18, 23n, 26, 29, 30, 33n, 34, 37, 40, 42, 59, 61, 138, 150, 155, 165n, 166, 190, 191, 193–198, 200–204, 210, 230, 254, 259, 260, 266, 268, 273, 275, 297, 305n, 306n
tīrthaṅkara-prakṛti (karmas that determine the body of a Tīrthaṅkara), 259, 260
tiryañca (animals and plants), 108, 110, 116, 124, 129, 144
titthiya (Pali for Tīrthaṅkara), 2n
trasa (mobile being; a being having two or more senses), 75, 130, 241
trasa-nāḍī (channel of the mobile beings; that portion of the loka-ākāśa in which the trasas abide), 130

ucchedavāda (doctrine of annihilation after death), 93, 96
ucchedavādin (annihilationist), 93
udaya (arising), 144, 145
uddiṣṭatyāga-pratimā (the eleventh stage, in which a layman renounces any food or lodging that has been specifically prepared for him), 184, 186
udīraṇā (energy that makes possible the premature fruition of karmas), 139
udumbara (fig), 167
udvartanā (energy that delays the time and increases the intensity of karmic fruition), 139

upabhoga (repeated enjoyment), 106
upabhoga-antarāya (hindrance to repeated enjoyment), 123
upādāna-kāraṇa (material cause), 99, 117, 138
upādhyāya (preceptor), 162, 164, 246
upagūhana (protecting a fellow Jaina), 154
upanayana (ceremony of initiation), 294, 299
Upāṅga (subsidiary to the Aṅga; a group of twelve canonical texts), 4, 56
upanīti (the ceremony of initiation for a layman), 299
upapāta (rebirth in hell or heaven), 57
upāsaka (a Jaina layman; a synonym for śrāvaka), 59, 286
upāsaka-pratimā (the eleven stages of laymanship, a synonym for śrāvaka-pratimā), 63
upaśama (suppression), 144, 145, 158, 257, 272
upaśamanā (energy that temporarily prevents karmas from coming to fruition), 139
upaśānta-moha (the eleventh guṇasthāna, in which all cāritra-mohanīya karmas are briefly rendered inoperative), 159, 257, 272
upasarga (calamity), 23n, 229
upayoga (applied consciousness), 104
ūrdhva-loka (the celestial world), 129
utpāda (origin; acquisition), 90
utsarga-samiti (care in performing the excretory functions), 248
utsarpiṇī (progressive half-cycle), 30, 31, 34, 61
uvajjhāya (Prakrit for upādhyāya), 162

vajra (diamond; adamantine), 3
vaikālika ([texts studied] beyond the prescribed hours), 64
vainayika-mithyātva (mithyātva due to indiscriminate openmindedness), 118
vairāgya (aversion leading to renunciation), 7
vaiśya (a member of the merchant caste), 67, 288, 289
vaivāhikī-kriyā (the wedding ceremony), 300
vaiyāvṛttya (respectful service), 155, 251
valaya (layer of the atmosphere), 127
vanaspati-kāya (plant beings), 109
vanavāsi (forest dweller), 308
vandana (reverent salutation), 190, 209
varṇa (caste hierarchy/ class), 74, 285, 291, 293, 295n; (color; a quality of matter), 90
varṇalābha (ritual celebrating the establishment of a new household by a married son), 299
varṇa-vyavasthā (class/ caste system), 285
varṣa (continent), 29

vāruṇī-dhāraṇā (a process of meditational "cleansing," accompanied with the water element), 256
vāsanā (trace), 111
vātsalya (disinterested affection), 155
vāyu-kāyika (air-bodies), 109
veda (sexual feelings), 60
vedaka-samyaktva (a synonym for kṣāyopaśamika-samyaktva), 146n
vedanīya-karma (karma responsible for mundane experience of pain and pleasure), 115, 125, 126, 132, 268, 269
vibhāva (defiled; impure), 104, 105
vibhu (all-pervasive), 58, 103
vicāra (shifting attention from one mode to another), 257
vidhāna (ritual), 254n
vidyā (the arts), 172
vigraha-gati (movement of a soul to its new destiny), 127
vikṛti (defiled modification), 99
vinaya (reverence to the elders), 251
vipāka (karmic retribution), 55
vipākavicaya (meditation on karmic fruition), 253
viparīta-mithātva (perverted or incorrect view), 118
Vīra-nirvāṇa (beginning of the Jaina era), 37; (death [anniversary] of Mahāvīra), 203
virodhī-hiṃsā (injury generated by standing in opposition to an enemy), 134n, 171
vīrya (energy), 91, 104–106, 123, 138, 141, 260n
vīryāntarāya (energy-obstruction), 115, 132, 142
viśuddhi (purity), 142
vītarāga (free from passion; an epithet for an arhat), 83, 113
vivakṣā (aspect emphasized by a speaker), 94
vivartavāda (the theory of illusory causation in monistic Vedānta), 92
vivikta-śayyāsana (solitary place of rest), 251
vrata (restraint), 170–173, 188, 236, 280, 287, 292, 299
vrata-pratimā (the second stage where a layman assumes the aṇuvratas), 172, 186
vṛtti (subcommentary), 82
vṛtti-parisaṃkhyāna (limiting the extent of one's begging rounds), 251
Vyantaravāsi (the peripatetic gods), 129n
vyavahāra (convention), 80n; (appropriate proceedings), 63
vyaya (loss; disappearance), 90
vyuparatakriyā-anivartin (absolute nonmotion), 270
vyutsarga (renunciation of egoistic thoughts), 251

yakṣa (demigod), 76, 108, 195
yantra (mystical diagram), 254n, 308

yathākhyāta-cāritra (conduct conforming to perfect purity), 258
yathāpravṛtta-karaṇa (the soul's ineradicable tendency towards spiritual growth), 141n, 144
yati (a spiritually advanced layman of the Śvetāmbara sect), 254n, 307
yātrā (pilgrimage), 206
yugapat (simultaneous), 95
yoga (vibration; activities), 105, 112, 269, 273; (meditation), 80, 81, 157, 159
yojana (a measure of distance equal to about eight or nine miles), 237

General Index

Abhayadeva, 16, 77, 85
Ābhidharmika, 92
absolute point of view, 53, 92, 150. *See* also view, onesided
Absolutist, 83, 86
Abu, 206
Acalabhrātā, 44, 45
Ācārāṅga-sūtra, 10, 53, 241–242, 243n
action. *See* karma
activities, 112; wholesome, 152, 159, 269; evil (five types of), 179–180; ritual, 180
affection (disinterested), 155
affirmation of existents, 151
afflictions, victory over, 249–250
agent, 147
aggregate (material), 101–102
Agnibhūti, 35, 44
agnosticism, 53
air: three types of, 127; rarefied, 130n
Airāvata, 29
air-bodies, 109; restraint against harming of, 242, 245
Ajanta caves, 281
Ajātaśatru, 276, 277
Ājīvikas, 2n; leader of, 19, 21–25, 54; non-Vedic origin of, 33; heavenly rebirth of, 57n; soul-color theory of, 114n; fatalist doctrine of, 136–139; survival of, 274n
Akalaṅka, 83–85, 87
Akampita, 44, 45
Akbar, 284n
alcohol, 53, 167
alms: presentation of, 217–221; care in accepting, 248
Ambikā, 194n
Amitagati, 80
Ammaḍa, 57
Amoghavarṣa, 281
Amṛtacandra, 80, 86
Anahilanagara, 283
Ānanda (Jaina), 55; story of, 233–240, 286
Ānanda (Buddhist), 45
Ananta, 191
Andhra, 277n
Aṅgabāhya, 51
Aṅgas, 51–56. *See* also canon (Jaina)
anger, 113, 119, 148, 149
animal, 126, 129; and plant, 108–110, 124, 144; capable of receiving religious instruction, 110n, 143; harming of, 167–169, 173
annihilationism, 53, 96
annihilationist, 93, 118
anticipation (freedom from), 152
apathy, 120. *See* also carelessness
aphorism. *See* sūtra
applied thinking, 257
Ardhamāgadhi, 42n, 47n
arhat: state attained by Mahāvīra, 28; distinction from Jina, 31n, 69, 259, 260; body of, 124n; salutation to, 162; state of, 258, 268; funeral pyre of, 298n
arts, 172
Āśādhara, 40n, 80, 195n, 228
ascetic: non-Vedic [śramaṇa], 1n, 125, 136, 138, 274, 275; soul color theory of, 114n; role in the ritual of confession, 209; temporary state attained by layman, 222, 223, 226; disciple of, 235; religious centers of, 278, 279; survival of, 293n; attitude toward the sacredness of fire, 297; stūpa-worship of, 298n

195, 197, 199, 290–291, 295; divine, 290; śrāddha ritual of, 303–304
Brahman, the Absolute, 92
Brāhmaṇas (Vedic texts), 2n
Buddha Gautama: renunciation of, 9; unknown to the Jaina canon, 10; "middle path" of, 27; chief attendant of, 45; omniscience of, 84, 267; sleeping image of, 192; his distinction from arhat, 259; as an avatar of Viṣṇu, 274
Buddhism: antiquity of, 1n; Magadhan origin of, 33; doctrinal diversity of, 88, 312; bodhisattva path of, 266n; disappearance of, 274, 285, 304; patrons of, 277
Buddhists: texts on the word titthiya, 1n; universal monarch concept of, 7; text on the Buddha's renunciation, 9; texts on Nigaṇṭhas, 10; texts on fasting, 21, 217; Pāyāsirājaññasutta of, 57; claim of omniscience for the Buddha, 84, 266–267; momentariness doctrine of, 92–93; non-substance (anātma) doctrine of, 103; intermediate existence doctrine of, 127n, 227; ignorance concept of, 134; text on Ājīvikas, 137–138; eternal bondage doctrine of [Yogācāra school], 140; meat eating practice of, 169, 300n; stūpas of, 193n; critique of Jainas, 223; nun order of, 246n; tantric influence on, 254; distinction between Buddha and arhat, 259; royal patrons of, 277, 279; cave temples of, 281; texts on lay discipline, 285n; mendicant emphasis of, 286; stūpa worship of, 298n; Rāma story of, 305n

Cakreśvarī, 194n
calamity: befalling a Tīrthaṅkara, 23n; promoting stability at the time of, 155; yakṣa worship at the time of, 195n; as one situation permitting the practice of sallekhanā, 229
Campā, 37, 56
Campāpurī, 206
Cāmuṇḍarāya, 281
Caṇḍālas. *See* Śvapākas
Candanā, 37
Candragupta Maurya, 6n, 277n
Candraprabha, 194n
canon (Jaina): sources of, 42–43; compilation and transmission of, 43–46; languages of, 47n; list of texts, 47–49; Aṅgas, 51–56; oral tradition of, 52–55; Digambara, Śvetāmbara, and Sthānakavāsi disputes on authenticity of, 49n, 51–52; written form of, 50–52, 203–204; councils of, 51–52; subsidiary, 55–56; narrative texts of, 56–62; discipline texts of, 62–64; texts on caste, 77; later commentaries on, 77; expositions of, 78–85; philosophical hymns of, 85–87
capability (for liberation), 139–140, 259. *See also* soul
carelessness, 239n; as a hindrance to the path, 120; as a cause of bondage, 157; restraint free of, 158; overcoming of, 243; restraint not free of, 253
Cārvāka, 53, 103, 134
caste system, 7; Ṛṣabha's introduction of, 32, 61; Hindu, 67, 288; Jaina reinterpretation of, 74–76, 287–291, rebirth in, 116; Jaina denial of cosmological basis of, 124; Jaina priests of, 195
cause: Ājīvika doctrine of, 137; efficient, 99, 100, 105, 117, 138; material, 99, 117, 138; of bondage, 135, 157, 159
Celanā, 276
celestial musicians, 108
celibacy:rational for, 176–177; state of, 183
Ceṭaka, 6
change, problem of, 59; caused by kāla-dravya, 100. *See also* modification
chant: of the four refuges, 164; holy, 293, 296–297
charity, 106; producing a rebirth in heaven, 116; hindrance to, 123; vow of offering alms, 181; one of the six duties of a layman, 190; commemoration of the first act of charity to a Tīrthaṅkara, 203; ritual of offering alms, 217–221;

over Mahāvīra's renunciation, 12; controversy over nudity, 13–15, 18–21; controversy on the true meaning of cāturyāma-dharma, 17; silence vow of Mahāvīra, 21; discussion on calamities befalling a Tīrthaṅkara, 23n; discussion on the eating (and other worldly activities) of a kevalin, 24n, 36, 44; account of Makkhali Gosāla, 24n; Ājīvikas identified with, 25; superhuman doctrine of a Tīrthaṅkara, 34–37; doctrinal conflicts with Śvetāmbara, 38–41; begging practice of, 40–41, 217–221; controversy over the divine sound of the Tīrthaṅkara, 42–43; language used by, 47n; canonical differences from Śvetāmbara, 49n, 50–52, 60–61; yoga texts of, 80; logic texts of, 84; doctrinal unity of Śvetāmbara, 88; controversy over time, 100; tradition of fivefold salutation, 163n; hymns of praise, 165; non-possession practiced by monks, 184; list of six lay practices, 190; Jaina-brahman class of, 195; Jina image of, 198; Jina worship of, 202-203; rejection of arhatship for a woman, 36, 39–40, 204n; holy places of, 206n; relationship of laity and monks, 208; equanimity formula of, 222; equanimity practice of, 223; monk initiation of, 244–246; monks and nuns, 246n; difficulties for a nude monk, 249; texts on meditation, 255n; arhat concept of, 268; geographical location of, 279–280; integration into Hindu society, 287; priest class of, 291; influence of Jinasena on, 300; temple-clerics of, 307; temple habitation of, 308; reforms of, 310–311

Dignāga, 85

discipline, books of, 62–64, 80–81, 160–161

disgust, 120; freedom from, 152

disjunction, 101. *See also* matter

displeasure (in sense activity), 120

disrespects, thirty-two types of, 62

dissociation (of karma), 151, 159. *See also* soul

distance (vow of limiting), 178–180

divine cloth, legends about Mahāvīra's wearing, 12–13

divine sound, 4, 196; of Mahāvīra, 35; controversy over the nature of, 39, 42–43; as a faculty of a Tīrthaṅkara, 124n, 260

divinity, devotion towards, 162; supreme, 163, 190n

doctrine: controversy between Jaina sects, 38–41; unity of Jaina, 88; affirmation of Jaina, 151; eight matrices of, 247–248

doubt, 118, 155; freedom from, 151

Dravidian, 276, 278

dreams, sixteen of Triśalā, 6–7, 197, 69(pl. 4)

dryness, as a quality of matter, 101

duration, of karma, 113, 126, 144; of insight, 145n, 268

duty (of a layman), six kinds of, 189–191, 260

Dvipalāsa, 234, 239

dynasty, Jaina, 275, 284

earth-bodies, 109, 242

ease, quality of, 149

elder, 52, 55; reverence to, 251, 260

elements, Buddhist, 92; meditation on the material, 255; non-sacredness of material, 297

embodiment, state of, 102, 107–111, 121; activities present in, 105, 159, 269; individual, 109; collective, 110; process of, 124–127; last moment of, 268–269; escape from, 269–270

emphasis (of the speaker), 94

energy: quality of the soul, 91, 104, 105–106, 111; relation with karma, 112n, 140–141; obscuring of, 117, 123; functions of, 138–139; karmic reduction by, 143, 157–158; duration of insight dependent upon, 145n; infinite, 256, 258

enjoyment, 106; realm of, 29–30, 221; hindrance to, 123

enlightenment, 165, 248; of Mahāvīra, 27–29; of the gaṇadharas, 44–46

equanimity, vow of, 180, 182, 190n, 191; meaning of (sāmāyika), 221; attainment of, 222–227; of the